Trade, Stability, Technology, and Equity in Latin America

Contributors

Edmar L. Bacha
Julio Berlinski
Mario I. Blejer
Juan Carlos de Pablo
Carlos F. Díaz Alejandro
Ricardo Ffrench-Davis
Albert Fishlow
Alejandro Foxley
Jorge M. Katz
Nathaniel H. Leff
Constantino Lluch
David Morawetz

Howard Pack
Gustav Ranis
Martha Rodríguez
Kazuo Sato
Daniel M. Schydlowsky
Jacques Silber
Moshé Syrquin
Simón Teitel
Morris Teubal
Victor E. Tokman
Larry E. Westphal
Manuel Zymelman

Trade, Stability, Technology, and Equity in Latin America

Edited by

MOSHÉ SYRQUIN

Research Center for Latin American Development Studies
Bar-Ilan University
Ramat-Gan, Israel

SIMÓN TEITEL

Economic and Social Development Department
Inter-American Development Bank
Washington, D.C.

 1982

ACADEMIC PRESS
A Subsidiary of Harcourt Brace Jovanovich, Publishers
New York   London
Paris   San Diego   San Francisco   São Paulo   Sydney   Tokyo   Toronto

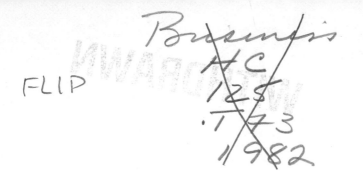

ACADEMIC PRESS, INC.
111 Fifth Avenue, New York, New York 10003

United Kingdom Edition published by
ACADEMIC PRESS, INC. (LONDON) LTD.
24/28 Oval Road, London NW1 7DX

Library of Congress Cataloging in Publication Data
Main entry under title:

Trade, stability, technology, and equity in Latin
   America.

   Includes index.
   1. Latin America--Economic conditions--Date
--Addresses, essays, lectures. 2. Technological innova-
tions--Latin America--Addresses, essays, lectures.
3. Latin America--Commerce--Addresses, essays,
lectures.   I. Syrquin, Moshe.   II. Teitel, Simon.
HC125.T73 1982   330.98'0038   82-13890
ISBN 0-12-680050-2

PRINTED IN THE UNITED STATES OF AMERICA

82 83 84 85   9 8 7 6 5 4 3 2 1

To Cecilio J. Morales

Contents

— Chapter 6 **The Vulnerability of Small Semi-industrialized Economies to Export Shocks: A Simulation Analysis Based on Peruvian Data**

Daniel M. Schydlowsky and Martha Rodríguez

Chapter 7 **Latin American External Debt: The Case of Uncertain Development**

Albert Fishlow

Part III **STABILIZATION AND GROWTH**

Chapter 8 **Macroeconomic Disequilibrium and Short-Run Economic Growth in Developing Countries**

Nathaniel H. Leff and Kazuo Sato

Chapter 13   **Technology and Economic Development: An Overview of Research Findings**

Jorge M. Katz

Chapter 14   **The Engineering Sector in a Model of Economic Development**

Morris Teubal

Chapter 15   **The Skills and Information Requirements of Industrial Technologies: On the Use of Engineers as a Proxy**

Simón Teitel

Chapter 16   **The Capital Goods Sector in LDCs: Economic and Technical Development**

Howard Pack

Part V   EQUITY

Chapter 17   Basic Needs, Distribution, and Growth: The Beginnings of a Framework

Gustav Ranis

Chapter 18   Trying to Appraise a Decade of Development: Latin America in the Sixties

Jacques Silber

Chapter 19   Growth, Underemployment, and Income Distribution

Victor E. Tokman

List of Contributors

Numbers in parentheses indicate the pages on which the authors' contributions begin.

EDMAR L. BACHA (449), Catholic University of Rio de Janeiro, Rio de Janeiro, Brazil

JULIO BERLINSKI (57), Instituto Torcuato Di Tella, 1428 Buenos Aires, Argentina

MARIO I. BLEJER[1] (43), Department of Economics, The Hebrew University, Jerusalem and Bar-Ilan University, Ramat-Gan, Israel

JUAN CARLOS DE PABLO (213), University of Buenos Aires, 1406 Buenos Aires, Argentina

CARLOS F. DÍAZ ALEJANDRO (27), Economic Growth Center, Yale University, New Haven, Connecticut 06520

RICARDO FFRENCH-DAVIS (91), CIEPLAN, Santiago 9, Chile

ALBERT FISHLOW (143), Department of Economics, Yale University, New Haven, Connecticut 06520

ALEJANDRO FOXLEY (227), CIEPLAN, Santiago 9, Chile

JORGE M. KATZ[2] (281), IDB/ECLA/UNDP Research Programme on Scientific and Technological Development in Latin America, 1022 Buenos Aires, Argentina

[1] Present address: International Monetary Fund, Washington, D.C. 20431.
[2] Present address: CEPAL, 1022 Buenos Aires, Argentina.

NATHANIEL H. LEFF (167), Graduate School of Business, Columbia University, New York, New York 10027

CONSTANTINO LLUCH (191), Development Research Department, The World Bank, Washington, D.C. 20433

DAVID MORAWETZ[3] (69), Department of Economics, Boston University, Boston, Massachusetts 02215

HOWARD PACK (349), Department of Economics, Swarthmore College, Swarthmore, Pennsylvania 19081

GUSTAV RANIS (373), Economic Growth Center, Yale University, New Haven, Connecticut 06520

MARTHA RODRÍGUEZ (125), Center for Latin American Development Studies, Boston University, Boston, Massachusetts 02215

KAZUO SATO (167), Department of Economics, State University of New York at Buffalo, Amherst, New York 14260

DANIEL M. SCHYDLOWSKY (125), Center for Latin American Development Studies, Boston University, Boston, Massachusetts 02215

JACQUES SILBER (397), Department of Economics, Bar-Ilan University, Ramat-Gan, Israel

MOSHÉ SYRQUIN (1), Research Center for Latin American Development Studies, Bar-Ilan University, Ramat-Gan, Israel

SIMÓN TEITEL (1, 333), Economic and Social Development Department, Inter-American Development Bank, Washington, D.C. 20577

MORRIS TEUBAL (317), Department of Economics, The Hebrew University, Jerusalem, Israel

VICTOR E. TOKMAN (413), PREALC, Santiago, Chile

LARRY E. WESTPHAL (255), Development Research Department, The World Bank, Washington, D.C. 20433

MANUEL ZYMELMAN (435), The World Bank, Washington, D.C. 20433

[3] Present address: 26 Tourello Avenue, East Hawthorn, Victoria 3123, Australia.

Preface

While in the past twenty years there was substantial economic and social progress in Latin America, income inequality, underemployment of resources (particularly human), and external constraints still persist. The various contributions in this book attempt to deal with specific aspects of the recent Latin American economic development process. The book offers a multifaceted, yet detailed, analysis of key issues in 21 chapters grounded around five broad topics of recent concern to specialists, both academics and policy makers: international trade, external instability, stabilization and growth, technology, and equity. The volume also includes a substantial introduction summarizing the various contributions.

Among the topics included in the first three parts of the book are: (i) testing the purchasing power parity theory of exchange rate determination and the "law of one price," (ii) extending the monetary approach to the balance of payments to incorporate terms of trade effects, (iii) the implications of opening up the Latin American economies to foreign trade, (iv) the experience with the promotion of labor-intensive exports of manufacturers, (v) the pros and cons of external debt in recent Latin American development, and (vi) results of the recent economic stabilization with opening up and structural reform in Chile. Together, the essays in these parts add up to an overall picture of the short- and long-run interactions between external factors (trade and financial flows) and the domestic economy.

The last two parts include papers reflecting a novel approach to technology in economic development and an examination of basic needs, employment, and income distribution. Among the topics discussed are: (i) technological development as a key determinant of infant-industry protection, (ii) technical and economic aspects constraining the development of a capital goods industry in the region, (iii) the basic needs approach to development, and (iv) the role of informal sectors in employment and income distribution in Latin America.

The papers in this volume represent a marriage between theory and empirical verification; they are not straitjacketed by ideological unity. They constitute a step in the direction toward a new type of development economics in which assumptions are continually revised to take into account the realities of countries undergoing a very rapid process of economic and social development.

First drafts of all chapters were presented or circulated at a meeting on Latin America's economic development problems held in Israel, between May 5 and 8, 1980, as part of the activities to celebrate the 25th Anniversary of Bar-Ilan University. On the same occasion an honorary degree was granted to Raul Prebisch.*

The comments made during the symposium were incorporated in revised versions of the papers and in the introduction. We would like to thank the session chairmen, discussants, rapporteurs, and all the participants for their contribution to the quality of the meeting.

We have also incurred a great debt to many other people and institutions for their help in organizing the symposium and in preparing this book for publication. Joseph Hodara, of Bar-Ilan University, before and during the symposium, greatly contributed to its success. Also in Bar-Ilan, we are grateful to S. Eckstein, Rector of the University, and to T. Darvish, of the Economics Department, for their help and cooperation. At the Inter-American Development Bank, we are grateful for the cooperation of I. Cainelli, who provided administrative support from Washington while the symposium was being organized, and also during the preparation of the manuscript for the book.

For financial help to organize the symposium we are grateful to the main sponsor, the Inter-American Development Bank, and, in Israel, to:

---

* A volume in honor of R. Prebisch, edited by L. E. Di Marco, *International Economics and Development—Essays in Honor of Raul Prebisch,* was published by Academic Press, New York, 1972. The introduction of the honoree made by F. Pazos for the ceremony granting the Doctor Honoris Causa, was published in *El Trimestre Económico,* **189** (January–March, 1981), 223–228. Prebisch's speech accepting the honorary degree is part of a publication edited by J. Hodara and to be published by Bar-Ilan University.

Bank Leumi, Bank Hapoalim, Bank Mizrahi, Bank Discount, Bank of Israel, the weekly *Tiempo,* and Bar-Ilan University.

A special note of gratitude goes to the late Cecilio J. Morales, of the Inter-American Development Bank, who supported the symposium when it needed the protection of an infant activity, and who, regrettably, did not live to see this volume in print.

MOSHÉ SYRQUIN
Ramat-Gan

SIMÓN TEITEL
Washington, D.C.

Introduction

Moshé Syrquin and Simón Teitel

In the past 20 years, Latin America has taken large strides toward economic and social progress. According to data from the United Nations Economic Commission for Latin America (ECLA), the region's income per capita grew from about $500 in 1960 to almost double that amount in 1980, all in 1970 dollars. This represents an approximate 3% yearly rate of growth in income per capita throughout the entire 20-year period. The importance of this performance is enhanced when one notes that during the same period the growth in population was at a staggering 2.7% yearly rate, with total population increasing from about 211 million in 1960 to some 357 million inhabitants estimated for 1980. Thus, a 150% increase in the region's population during the period in question was matched by a tripling of gross domestic product, requiring that the gross domestic product increase at a yearly rate of about 5.8%. This process of economic growth was accompanied by a tremendous expansion of the external sector. Exports and imports grew about 10 times in nominal value, and more importantly, the proportion of exports of manufactures in total exports increased from about 3.4% on average in 1960 to about 19% in 1978.

This impressive economic record was paralleled by substantial social

1

progress. The first and major achievement—to the extent to which it succeeded in the region—was the absorbing into productive employment of most of the expansion in the labor force resulting from the growth in population. In addition, social development indicators also point to a substantial performance. Latin American's life expectancy increased, measured as an unweighted average, from about 55 years in 1960–1965 to about 63 years in 1975–1980. General schooling grew from covering about 41% of the population of school age as an unweighted average in 1960 to about 57% of the population in 1980. Infant mortality, which was about 111 per thousand population in 1960–1965, decreased to about 74 per thousand in 1975–1980, and the share of the population with access to potable water increased from about 33% in 1960 (also unweighted average) to about 62% in 1977.

Although, as just noted, economic and social progress has been substantial, inequality as well as unemployment of resources (particularly human) still persist, and given the region's generous natural and human resource endowment, this seems to be really unwarranted.

The various chapters in this book attempt to deal with specific aspects of the recent Latin American economic development process. The book is divided into five parts, each containing several chapters. These parts are: International Trade, External Instability, Stabilization and Growth, Technology, and Equity.

Part I deals with the opportunities and problems posed by international trade, which has long been a concern of Latin American development analysts. The chapters in this part and in Part II, External Instability, consider the international economy both in terms of the opportunities that it provides and the potential hindrance it may represent to the domestic economy. The limitations imposed by the external sector are no longer regarded, as they were some 30 years ago, as a serious obstacle to the region's development.

The increased preoccupation with trade flows is one aspect of the strengthening of the interdependence with the world economy. An additional aspect, which has only emerged in the last decade, is the dramatic opening of the capital market. The opportunities provided by large capital inflows as well as their potential detrimental effects are discussed in Part II, External Instability.

Part I, International Trade, includes chapters by C. F. Díaz Alejandro, M. I. Blejer, J. Berlinski, and D. Morawetz.

In Chapter 1, Díaz Alejandro focuses on the long-run behavior of the real exchange rate in Argentina. He first summarizes the information available on real exchange rates since 1913 and then tries to provide an explanation for departures of the real exchange rate from purchasing power parity (PPP).

Relative to the 1913–1919 period, the real exchange rate showed a sustained increase through the end of the Second World War. As Díaz Alejandro points out, the real peso depreciation during the 1930s helped Argentina weather the Great Depression rather successfully. The first major reversal occurred during the first Perónist government, right after the war. By 1950–1955, real exchange rates had fallen below the levels attained in the 1920s. Since 1955, the trend has been upward, with some reversals.

The overall picture is one of a long-term increase in the real exchange rate, accompanied by significant variability over shorter periods of time, particularly in the last 30 years.

Díaz Alejandro tries to explain the year-to-year variability in real exchange rates and the departures from PPP in terms of three main factors: (i) variations in the external terms of trade; (ii) differences in productivity growth between tradables and home goods; and (iii) the protectionist bias of domestic commercial policies, as reflected in the relative movements of external and internal terms of trade and his interpretation of policy history.

The results of regression analysis show a significant link between the real exchange rate and terms-of-trade variables, both contemporary and lagged. The productivity effect, measured by a trend variable, yielded a persistent tendency toward real depreciation of the peso, which reflects, according to Díaz Alejandro, the technological lag in rural production and the excesses of the import-substituting industrialization policy prevalent during much of the period. Finally, the bias in the commercial policies also shows a significant effect toward retarding the depreciation as the degree of protectionism increases.

Díaz Alejandro concludes his chapter with a cautionary note on the applicability of the "law of one price" to Argentina and other semiindustrialized economies. This has, of course, a bearing on the chance for success of adjustment policies together with opening of the economies that depend on the convergence of rates of interest in world and domestic markets, a point that comes up later in Part III, Stabilization and Growth.

Díaz Alejandro's results indicate the limitations of a pure monetary approach over long periods of time. Abstracting completely from the operation of real markets in the short run is even more questionable.

In Chapter 2, Blejer extends the monetary approach to the balance of payments to incorporate real effects. Specifically, he relaxes the usual assumption of constant relative prices within the tradable sector and considers the effects on the balance of payments of exogenous changes in the terms of trade of a small open economy with a fixed exchange rate. A simple model is presented in which an exogenous increase in the price of the export commodity increases the level of real activity and creates an imbalance in the money market leading to an inflow of capital and the accumulation of foreign-exchange reserves. In the empirical part of the chapter, the model is estimated for Guatemala, and the effects of changes in the price of coffee on real output and on the balance of payments between 1949 and 1977 are analyzed.

Guatemala appears to be a very good case on which to test the model. It comes as close as can be found in Latin America to being fully integrated, on the monetary side, with the world economy (U.S.), and as Blejer shows in his results, the domestic rate of price variation follows quite closely the rate of foreign (U.S.) inflation.

The results as a whole are in accordance with the hypotheses of the monetary approach, but more importantly, they reveal significant terms-of-trade effects on real output and money demand and, hence, on the balance of payments. Though there is not much new in the determination of a terms-of-trade effect on income (after all it was one of the cornerstones of the Prebisch–Singer approach), the novelty of the results lies in the careful quantification of the terms-of-trade effect within the framework of a general model and in its incorporation into the monetary approach.

Starting from different perspectives, both Díaz Alejandro and Blejer show the importance of disaggregating the tradable sector to explain departures of real exchange rates from PPP and to gain additional insights into the context of the monetary approach to the balance of payments.

The next two chapters, by Berlinski and Morawetz, respectively, address themselves to specific aspects of attempts at trade liberalization.

Opening up to international trade includes the opportunity to obtain information on efficiency prices. To the extent that barriers to trade exist in the form of tariffs and quotas, the effectiveness of the signaling function of prices in the domestic economy is reduced. In Chapter 3, Berlinski seeks to examine some of the implications of opening the Argentine economy to these efficiency signals.

The chapter first presents estimates of nominal and effective rates of protection in 1977 for a group of selected industries based on direct price comparisons. The most striking feature of these estimates is not their average level but their very wide dispersion, which undoubtedly obscures the link between the resulting price structure and the comparative advantage of the sectors involved. The chapter then attempts to assess the effects of a tariff reform aimed at eliminating most of the artificially created distortions in the price structure by reducing the average level of protection and, more important, its high dispersion. For this purpose, in a general equilibrium framework, effective rates of protection are cut to some predetermined level and the implied changes in nominal rates are worked out. The calculated variations in nominal tariffs are an approximation to the expected change in relative prices that firms would face in making their output decisions.

A comparison of the results obtained by this simulation with the change in relative prices that followed the tariff reform in Argentina during 1979 yields large differences. To explain this lack of convergence between external prices and the internal price structure, Berlinski presents a partial equilibrium analysis, wherein the delays in the response of the domestic sector are due to the absence of competition and to lags in the exchange rate behind domestic costs. An extreme case is used in which a monopolist, who was formerly an exporter, becomes an importer of close foreign substitutes, thwarting the expected changes in relative prices.

The chapter clearly indicates the potential adverse effects upon comparative advantage, not only of trade barriers, but also of high dispersion in their values as a result of the differential effect over time of domestic price distortions, lack of competition, and artificial rates of exchange.

In the symposium discussion that followed the presentation of Berlinski's paper,[1] it was suggested that it would be useful to distinguish analytically between two often contradictory aspects of recent policies in Southern Cone countries. The first refers to the short-run measures aimed at domestic stabilization, and the lagging exchange rate may be one of them. The second is the avowed objective of rationalizing resource allocation, over a longer period of time, through policies such as reducing the level and spread of tariffs. Because these two aspects of policies sometimes work in opposite directions, the question becomes one of the appropriate mix of instruments and their optimal sequencing over time. This question appears in various guises in several of the chapters and was often raised during the symposium discussions. We return to it in Part III, Stabilization and Growth.

Part I concludes with an examination of the potential for employment creation through the expansion of Latin America's manufactured exports. The rapid expansion, in recent years, of manufactured exports from several East Asian countries (Hong Kong, Korea, Singapore, and Taiwan) has led to significant increases in employment. By contrast, the rate of employment growth in those Latin American manufacturing industries that export has been much less impressive. In Chapter 4, Morawetz

[1] Symposium on Latin America's economic development problems held in Israel in May, 1980. (See Preface.)

hypothesizes that, in order for the typical firm in Latin America to be able to enter the world market, labor productivity has first to rise substantially— often by as much as 50–100%. Therefore the initial surge in exports cannot be expected to effect employment very much. It is only when a sustained export drive exceeds a certain threshold level that the impact on employment begins to be felt.

Between 1970 and 1974–1975, Colombia's clothing exports grew at a rapid rate from an almost negligible base. This was accompanied by significant rises in productivity, but, well before it could make itself felt in employment, the export drive came to a halt, with sales to the United States and Europe declining sharply after 1975.

Morawetz divides the causes of the rise and fall of Colombia's clothing exports into price and nonprice factors. The single most important factor accounting for the increase in exports after 1970 was the continuous rise in the effective exchange rate since 1967 after a quarter century of erratic behavior. According to Morawetz, it took two to three years for the 1967 reforms to influence fully the entrepreneur's behavior that resulted in the export drive. After 1973, there was an unexpected policy reversal and, again, after about two years of almost continuous decline in the effective exchange rate, exports to the United States and Europe showed a marked decline.

Harder to quantify but no less important in explaining the slow development of Colombia's garment exports are the nonprice factors. These include inadequate quality control and unpunctuality of deliveries caused by management deficiencies, administrative delays, and cultural factors.

The chapter effectively brings out the difficulties that exist in the creation of an export mentality. The main findings of Morawetz's study about the obstacles to a sustained export drive and the resulting low employment creation may also be typical of other industries and other Latin American countries.

In addition to their potential contribution to increased productivity and employment, manufactured exports could also fulfill roles as potential buffers at times of instability in the earnings from primary commodities, as will be argued in Chapter 6, and constitute a potential source of much needed foreign-exchange earnings for the financing of future Latin American development.

Part II, External Instability, includes chapters by R. Ffrench-Davis, D. M. Schydlowsky and M. Rodríguez, and A. Fishlow. They examine various aspects of the difficulties posed by the resurgence of potential and actual instability in trade flows and capital markets.

The trade optimism partly reflected in the chapters in Part I was largely the result of the rapid expansion of world trade during the period

1965–1973, which also registered both favorable prices for many of the exports from the region and attractive financial conditions. The increases in petroleum prices since 1973, the world recession that followed, the reappearance of trade barriers, and the growing uncertainty in capital markets all created many more difficulties for exporting countries than were characteristic of the earlier period, when it appeared that exports might indeed serve as an engine of growth.

In the beginning of Chapter 5, Ffrench-Davis looks at the sources of external instability for 16 Latin American countries during the period 1951–1979, distinguishing between trade and capital flows. The figures clearly indicate a decrease in instability during the sixties for most of the countries, and for the region as a whole, followed by a significant rise in the 1970s, which surpassed even the original high levels of the 1950s. He concludes that, in general, the instability of export values was the combined result of both price and quantity variability and that the main source of price instability was the large weight in exports of primary products and raw materials and the heavy concentration in a few—often one—products. At the end of the 1970s, the concentration still remained high, in spite of the significant diversification achieved during the period.

During the seventies, the financial relations of Latin America with the international markets changed considerably. A rapid increase in capital inflows was observed, particularly in the form of loans from commercial banks. The main effects of the larger capital inflows were to dampen the adverse effects of trade instability, but at the same time, they added new sources of uncertainty, such as variable interest rates, and a heavy dependence on a continued supply of loans to service the debt in the short and medium run to avoid liquidity crises. These aspects will be discussed at length in Chapter 7 by Fishlow.

In the second half of Chapter 5, Ffrench-Davis discusses the transmission of external instability to the domestic economy. He observes that during the fifties the main response to external shocks in Latin America was through changes in import restrictions. During this period, the real exchange rate usually fell when the availability of foreign exchange improved or went through abrupt devaluations when a shortage developed. The compensating mechanism of reserve adjustment played only a secondary role during the 1950s and early 1960s.

The greater predictability of the exchange rate since the mid-sixties has led to a stabler import policy and has probably stimulated the development of nontraditional exports, which might—as will be argued by Schydlowsky and Rodríguez in Chapter 6—have helped to reduce the vulnerability of these countries to any existing instability.

The large inflows of private financial capital have introduced two unintended additional elements of instability into the domestic market: first, the appreciation of exchange rates, in spite of large trade deficits, which had a negative impact on nontraditional exports; second, a fast accumulation of reserves that imposes a heavy burden on monetary policy.

Schydlowsky and Rodríguez also deal with instability in their chapter and, specifically, try to assess the vulnerability to export shocks of small semiindustrialized economies. Their analysis refers primarily to countries that only recently have begun to shift from import substitution policies to a more balanced trade orientation. The system of incentives in such countries had not been conducive to the development of nontraditional manufactured exports and this, according to Schydlowsky and Rodríguez, increased their vulnerability to shortfalls of export receipts from primary commodities.

The main theme of the chapter is that, in the absence of nontraditional exports, adjustments to external shocks come primarily through a lowering of the level of economic activity. When manufactured exports are present, the possibility of market substitution from traditional to manufactured exports limits the deflation necessary to bring the balance of payments back into equilibrium.

To measure the effect of market substitution as an automatic compensatory mechanism, the authors present a set of interindustry models that capture the response to export shortfalls arising from either quantity or price variations, and, in each case, with and without manufactured exports.

For each model, the authors derive the multipliers for income, trade balance, and fiscal receipts with respect to a fall in traditional exports (through either price or quantity or a combination of both). These are calculated for Peru in the late 1970s. At the beginning of 1979, Peru reversed a 10-year-long policy of aggressive import substitution, which had discouraged nontraditional exports.

The principal result of the empirical implementation of the model is that, in the presence of nontraditional exports, the income fall following an export shock is considerably buffered. Qualitatively similar results were also found for the trade balance and fiscal multipliers, though quantitatively they are less important than in the case of the income multiplier.

The authors conclude that their results "warrant the inclusion of nontraditional export promotion policy in the arsenal of economic stabilization tools."

During the symposium discussion about the papers by Ffrench-Davis and Schydlowsky and Rodríguez, their suggestion, that the longer the list of exports the better off the country is, was contrasted with the proposition that trade is more beneficial the higher up the country is on the list of comparative advantages. This static formulation of comparative advantage abstracts precisely from the uncertainty and instability that are the main reasons calling for diversification. In addition, it may be efficient to develop manufactured exports because of dynamic considerations. One of them, the infant-industry argument, will be analyzed in part IV, Chapter 12, which emphasizes the importance of protecting infant industries to attain technological capacitation, but in a selective way rather than by indiscriminate protection.

Another, more important tool for stabilization that avoids reduction of income is the incurring of an external debt, and Chapter 7 by Fishlow is devoted to this topic.

The first part of this chapter describes recent changes in the size and composition of the Latin American foreign debt. As compared with a nominal doubling during the 1960s, the Latin American debt increased more than sevenfold in the 1970s. At the same time, the composition shifted from predominantly official finance in the 1960s to a progressively larger role of private flows, especially from commercial banks.

An accommodating Euro-currency market discovered Latin America in the late 1960s, offering attractive borrowing terms to countries seeking capital to finance higher growth rates. With the Brazilian debt-led growth model primarily in mind, Fishlow describes the early 1970s as a time when "current account deficits were not a constraint to expansion but rather a planned means for mobilizing external savings."

After 1973, borrowing became "less an option than a necessity to sustain the higher costs of imports essential to economic growth." Many countries, particularly the poorest, adjusted to the increase in oil prices by reducing income. A few (e.g., Brazil and Mexico) were able to follow a debt-financed gradual adjustment.

During the early 1960s, capital inflows were predominantly official. When public assistance started to decline, private financial markets more than substituted. This change did not prejudice the growth of the public sector, as the principal recipients of loans remained state enterprises, official banks, and other public institutions.

Fishlow identifies three adverse effects associated with increased borrowing from private sources. These are: (i) higher interest costs as private loans did not incorporate the substantial grant element of the official lending; (ii) shorter maturity structures; and (iii) flexible instead of fixed interest charges, which nullified the inflationary transfer implicit in fixed rates.

In the next section of his chapter, Fishlow examines the real cost of the debt and illustrates it for the actual capital inflows received by Brazil in the 1970s. The major conclusion is that "debt was a bargain in the 1970s." Yet there is a generalized concern about the magnitude of the debt, which Fishlow explains by the short-term necessity to service the debt to avoid liquidity crises and a medium-term transformation problem, namely, the need to divert increased productive capacity to export.

To be successful, a model of debt finance requires a continuing supply of credit. Fishlow illustrates this dynamic aspect of the debt with a simple simulation model, which also projects the merchandise balance. The most important determinant of *terminal* debt level turns out to be, not surprisingly, the growth of exports. In the short run, however, the capital account dominates, as exports are unlikely to satisfy immediate foreign-exchange needs. A continuing adequate export performance is nevertheless still needed as a sign of the credit worthiness that assures a continued supply of private loans.

In the last section, Fishlow turns from the projections of regional aggregates to the specific case of Brazil, to elucidate the oil-importer adjustment dilemma. Brazil's development strategy before the oil crisis was one of "debt-led growth." After 1973, it turned into a model of "growth-led debt"—foreign loans became necessary to "offset the current account deficits associated with successful efforts to sustain high rates of growth." Higher oil prices led to debt increases and these added new vulnerability. By early 1981, each percentage point in interest rates meant about $500 million in net costs.

The Brazilian experience highlights the dominant role of a continuing supply of capital in alleviating a liquidity crisis. It also reveals the links between economic policies and credit worthiness, particularly when the need for additional finance becomes strongest.

Part III of this book, Stabilization and Growth, consists of chapters by N. H. Leff and K. Sato, C. Lluch, J. C. de Pablo, and A. Foxley. The central themes in this part are the persistence of inflation and its costs and the stabilization programs and their costs. An additional topic of current interest—the role of financial and trade openings in stabilization programs—also figures prominently in some of the chapters.

The first two chapters (by Leff and Sato and Lluch) suggest, on empirical and analytical grounds, that the economic system in semiindustrialized countries is inherently unstable, often rendering conventional stabilization policies counterproductive. The two concluding chapters are more specific. De Pablo forcefully cautions against being "soft on inflation," illustrating his argument with the Argentine experience. In sharp contrast, Foxley, in the last chapter, emphasizes the costs incurred since 1974 as a result of the Chilean policy of stabilization and induced structural change.

In Chapter 8, Leff and Sato present a model of the adjustment process in situations of macroeconomic disequilibrium, modified to incorporate some specific features of developing countries. Interest rate changes are replaced by credit creation as a determinant of investment. This variable, the authors argue, does not greatly depend on domestic savings but is determined by the monetary authority often in response to government deficits. Investment and saving functions are also assumed to be responsive to the rate of inflation.

The model is summarized in an *IS*-type reduced form equation relating income growth to the rate of inflation. It is then estimated for four Latin American countries (Argentina, Brazil, Chile, and Costa Rica) and two other economies (Israel and Taiwan) for the period 1950–1973. The parameter estimates suggest that the macroeconomic adjustment processes tend to be destabilizing. The comparative responses of saving and investment to changes in income growth or the inflation rate are such that any initial gap between saving and investment would tend to increase. Once out of equilibrium, strong pressures exist for its persistence. A similar conclusion is also reached by Lluch from a different perspective (see the following discussion).

To close the model, the equilibrium condition in the monetary sector is introduced. Though no empirical results are presented, the section suggests that monetary factors can serve as stabilizing elements but also that they lead to a trade-off between inflation and real growth in the short run.

In practice, the adjustment mechanism for achieving internal stability usually involves reducing the growth of domestic credit. This has a direct impact on investment and, more generally, on real output through the dependence of the rate of capacity utilization on the supply of working capital.

Because of the high economic and political costs of this type of stabilization, other mechanisms have been tried, including a heavy reliance on foreign capital (as noted in the previous discussion of the chapter by Fishlow). When these other possibilities are not feasible, however, a developing country may be forced to rely on credit restrictions as an instrument for achieving internal balance.

In the symposium discussion it was noted that a different response of saving to the inflation rate could be expected from the private and the public sectors (a point mentioned in the chapter but not followed up). Similarly, the crucial credit variable refers to total domestic credit. This is an effective constraint for the private sector, which has to conform itself with whatever credit is available, but not the government, which can simply print money. In addition to the destabilizing mechanism noted in the chapter, further destabilization may be due to wage–price linkages, which are either of a formal type through indexation or informal. A general drawback of indexation is that by removing some of the short-term costs of inflation, the will to fight against it is reduced.

In Chapter 9, Lluch is also concerned with the role of credit in stabilization. The purpose of his chapter is to provide a simple analytical framework for examining the impact of changes in bank credit on output and the price level. This attempt was largely motivated by the observation that, in recent stabilization programs in Latin America, the recessional impact had been much larger than expected.

Lluch points out that unlike the case of more advanced economies, where quantities frequently adjust faster than prices, in less advanced economies "in the short run, the quantities of goods transacted are given by past decisions, whereas labor incomes follow from current decisions by firms about how much output is profitable to bring to market in the next period." This view highlights the importance of distinguishing between contractual and residual incomes and of disaggregating over time instead of assuming continuous processes with simultaneous adjustments. He suggests that the analysis should be conducted in terms of periods that can reflect the distributional impact of inflation when adjustments are not simultaneous. In particular, the timing conventions should allow the share of profits to vary with inflation.

One important feature of the assumptions about the timing of transactions is that current labor payments, which are determined on the basis of planned output and investment, are part of bank credit to firms.

The equilibrium condition in the output market links the principal endogenous variables: employment, the real wage, the rate of interest, and the price level. The relation is useful for suggesting the type of data necessary to implement the model empirically. Conventional income accounting cannot readily incorporate the proposed disaggregation over time.

Lluch next examines the working of the labor market and derives one of the basic features of the model. For a given expectation of inflation, an increase in the nominal rate of interest leads to a decline in the current demand for labor because of the increase in financial costs.

Equilibrium in the output and labor markets can be summarized in a schedule in the interest rate–price level plane, representing all equilibrium pairs such that both markets clear. With the assumptions of the model, it is likely that this schedule will have a "perverse" positive slope.

Even after closing the model by adding an equilibrium schedule in the market for credit, the resulting overall equilibrium cannot be assumed to be stable.

In the next chapter, de Pablo draws some lessons about the influence of inflation on growth, based on the recent Argentine experience. His chapter focuses on the behavior of the government, given the existence of inflation, and on the corresponding response of the private sector.

In the first section, which surveys the costs of inflation, de Pablo mentions the traditional argument about the tax on cash balances and two additional sources of real costs related to the uncertainty introduced by imperfect foresight. One is due to "pure" forecasting errors, and the other to unexpected inflation-induced changes in economic policies. The discriminatory nature of measures associated with repressed inflation and the distortion in relative prices that they entail induce a socially wasteful (but privately potentially very lucrative) rent-seeking behavior on the part of the private sector.

De Pablo then turns to the impact of inflation on growth and argues that it goes beyond a once-and-for-all permanent reduction of the level of income resulting in a lower rate of growth. The "stop–go" characteristic of the inflation-induced policies probably reduces the savings ratio of the economy and surely, de Pablo claims, diminishes the social productivity of investment. At the same time, the rent-seeking behavior absorbs resources, particularly scarce human capital.

Given the significant costs of inflation in general and of repressed inflation in particular, great incentives exist for its elimination. The last section of the chapter argues that, in moving away from repressed inflation, a gradual approach has to be followed, first transforming the repressed inflation into open inflation. The pattern of relative prices has to change before aiming for price stability.

In the last chapter of Part III, Foxley analyzes the economic policies for stabilization applied in Chile after 1973 and their impact on the structure of the economy.

Judging by the behavior of most macro indicators, these policies appear to have been successful: inflation came down from the extremely high levels of 1974; the fiscal deficit was almost eliminated; though the trade balance remains in deficit, capital inflows have more than offset the deficits and sizable reserves have been accumulated; and growth after 1976 recuperated from the earlier recession.

Still at the macro level, there are some clouds: investment rates declined; unemployment went up and would have been even higher but for the make-work programs; and real wages in 1979 were below the 1970 levels, even after a partial recovery since 1976.

To better elucidate the workings of the stabilization policies, Foxley traces in detail short-run policy changes and the evolution of the economy over four distinct phases. In the initial phase, the objectives are to restore a preeminent role for market mechanisms and private property and to institute reforms for long-term structural changes. After a severe contraction in demand, the emphasis shifts to curbing inflationary expectations, and then, aided by the large reserves accumulated in the wake of the financial opening, there is the transition to the final phase of global monetarism. In this stage, the economy is open to international trade, and presumably, international inflation will now regulate the rate of domestic price increases. A slow downward trend is observed in inflation, unemployment, and interest rates, accompanied by a slow expansion in industrial production.

The macroeconomic indicators are the more visible but perhaps, according to Foxley, the less important part of the process of change in Chile during this period. Deep structural changes with significant long-term implications have been an integral part of the transition to a free market economy. Foxley refers specifically to three aspects of these structural transformations. The first one is a drastic privatization of the economy. It includes a reduction in the economic presence of the government, both as employer and as a producer, and is evident in the large transfer of state enterprises to the private sector (at very advantageous terms), in the rapid expansion of private financial institutions, and in the return of some of the lands previously expropriated.

A second transformation of long-term significance is the shift from a closed to an open economy. The result is a significant export expansion and greater specialization in production. In industry, production efficiency had to increase to meet the import challenge. The adjustment was facilitated, according to Foxley, by the fall in wages relative to the exchange rate and industrial prices and by the access to foreign loans.

The final aspect analyzed refers to the change in the composition of production and in the distribution patterns of income and wealth. Although these effects are slow to take form, some tendencies are already evident. During this brief period, there was a reorientation of production from industry and infrastructure to primary production, commerce, finance, and personal services. At the same time, a higher degree of asset and income concentration was observed, as was the emergence of powerful conglomerates or "economic groups" with ample economic and political influence.

One important aspect of the trade and financial openings was the liberalization of capital inflows. When accompanied, as in Argentina and Chile, by a preannounced schedule of devaluations (usually expected to fall short of the inflation differential) for the following 6 to 12 months, it offered a substantial subsidy to borrowers. Sanguine observers have characterized this liberalization as "liberalized plunder."

During the symposium discussion following the paper's presentation, the still unfulfilled need to design practical alternatives to high-cost stabilization was repeatedly brought up. Particularly revealing was the remark that structuralists had been unable to follow their criticism of the International Monetary Fund (IMF) approach with suggestions for a viable alternative option. The famous polemic between monetarists and structuralists, according to Prebisch, led to "absolutely nothing that could guide the IMF nor the developing countries."

The original monetarism – structuralism controversy has now been superseded in the region by a less doctrinaire examination of the costs and benefits of alternative approaches. It was also pointed out as ironic that the more extreme monetarist programs carried out in the Southern Cone countries have also incorporated, as an integral part of their strategy, major structural reforms.

Parts IV and V of this book contain essays on technology and equity. Part IV consists of chapters by L. E. Westphal, J. M. Katz, M. Teubal, S. Teitel, and H. Pack.

In his chapter, Westphal returns to the often-discussed question of infant-industry protection and, on the basis of (i) World Bank research on trade and industrial policies, (ii) results of microeconomic studies on technical change carried out by the IDB/ECLA/UNDP[2] Programme of Studies on Scientific and Technological Development in Latin America, and (iii) his own familiarity with Korean development policies, makes several points. First, protection of infant industries is warranted so that they can acquire technological mastery of the production processes involved; second, the process of acquiring this technical competence is a long and costly one, and the levels of protection required could be very high—of the order of 100% or more; third, this flies in the face of policy prescriptions emerging from comparative trade policy research that generally advocate uniform low levels of protection, of the order of 10 to 15% and, for selected industries, if warranted, no more than about 20 to 25% protection; and last, because of the high levels of protection required, i.e., the heavy costs involved, and assuming that the benefits will eventually justify the protection, the infant industries selected for protection should be few at any given time.

Westphal's arguments are cogent and well presented; the reader may, however, be left wanting more of an explanation about: (i) how to select the industries to be promoted, (ii) why the acquisition of technological competence requires such high levels of protection, and (iii) the related

---

[2] IDB: Inter-American Development Bank; ECLA: Economic Commission for Latin America; UNDP: United Nations Development Program.

question of what is involved in acquiring "technical competency or mastery"? Some answers, though partial ones, are to be found in the other chapters in Part IV.

In his chapter, Katz ponders the results achieved in the IDB/ECLA/UNDP Programme of Studies on Scientific and Technological Development, carried out under his direction. Over a number of years, this program has produced a number of monographs about technical adaptation and technical change, initially in process-centered industries: cement, petrochemicals, steel, cigarettes, etc. Similarly oriented studies are now being undertaken in the metalworking sector. The studies generally involve field work in industrial plants in various Latin American countries and include writing technical evolution histories of the firms and industries under investigation.

The studies in the program have detected very interesting cases of technological adaptation, modification, and creation of indigenous technologies, including their export. It is, however, very hard to summarize the results in the confines of the framework adopted by Katz for the chapter in this volume. Katz argues that technologies used in developing countries are different from those used in the industrialized countries. There are two reasons for this: first, the specificity or idiosyncratic nature of technology adaptation—valid for all countries—and second, the peculiar conditions and endowments of developing countries, particularly the effects of small market size upon the size of production runs, and the continuity of the process. He places great emphasis on the technical evolution sequences followed by the firms with which he and his associates worked. For example, he states that product design generally comes first, then so-called process engineering. This view is based on his experience with metalworking firms devoted to the manufacture of electrical appliances. It is also somewhat confirmed by the experience of studying a machine-tool manufacturer. This view seems to be at variance with that presented by Pack in his chapter about capital goods. Katz also includes, as the latest stage in the sequence, the activities of industrial engineering departments. However, this seems to be a reflection of the lack of competition prevailing for long periods of time in the industries he studied rather than any sequence based on the nature of the technical activities or of the processes of learning by doing.

Teubal's aim in Chapter 14 is to formulate a three-sector model with the following characteristics: (i) a primary export sector, with exponentially growing demand but a terminal horizon, (ii) an engineering sector, which provides inputs (machinery) for the primary exports sector and develops, after a certain time, the ability to create techniques to produce other manufacturing goods, and (iii) the manufacturing sector producing consumer goods whose appearance is conditioned by the development of the engineering sector.

Although this model has some interesting features, it is still too early to say to what extent it captures some of the various development aspects that seem to concern Teubal. Obviously much more research into the properties of such models and their relevant assumptions is required. It may be important to define, in a more disaggregated fashion, the skills required in the engineering or machinery sector. Teitel (Chapter 15, to be discussed next) would argue that no such thing as an engineering sector exists and that various types of engineering skills constitute the crucial variables. Also, as was noted in the symposium discussion, there is need to justify the development sequence selected, which differs from the one that seems to have prevailed in Latin America, i.e., first consumer goods and then capital goods, or the Soviet type of planning model, i.e., first heavy industries (steel and other intermediate inputs and machinery) and, later, consumer goods.

In Chapter 15, Teitel attempts to characterize the different manufacturing industries according to the engineering specialties they employ; he also tries to characterize the technological development level of different countries on the basis of several indicators.

According to Teitel, the interpretation, modification, and creation of technical information demand specific skills. Engineers are engaged in a variety of research- and production-oriented activities that deal with technical information interpretation, modification, and creation. They may be engaged in product and process design, maintenance and plant repair, production planning and control, process trouble shooting, etc.

The manufacturing industries differ substantially in their utilization of engineers. Although the data are not always strictly comparable and further analysis is required, they point to a preliminary conclusion of some interest: engineers are employed to perform different tasks in different industries; these tasks may be more research oriented in some industries and production oriented in others.

In trying to answer the question of what type of engineers do the various industries utilize, the following features of the classification of U.S. manufacturing industries by engineering skills emerge: (i) A majority of the industries employ only a few of the engineering specialties. (ii) Only one engineering specialty is employed in all of the industries in substantial proportions: industrial engineering. This seems to be the only type of engineering skill of "universal" applicability. (iii) Industries like clothing, leather and leather products, and printing and publishing have little or no engineering-specific requirements and employ only industrial engineers. (iv) "Process-centered" industries are characterized by the use of chemical engineers. (v) There is a "metal-based" group of industries that is characterized by the high proportion of mechanical and metallurgical engineers. (vi) Similarly, the electrical machinery industry is characterized by the high proportion of electrical and electronic engineers. (vii) Important industry-specific engineering specialties are limited in U.S. manufacturing to motor vehicles (presumably automotive engineers) and petroleum and coal products (presumably petroleum or mining engineers).

This chapter also attempts to characterize the level of technological development of various countries, using for this purpose data on engineering manpower as well as various other indicators. An attempt was also made to determine an overall rank of the various indicators for a group of countries for which the data were available, with the result that the overall rank was quite closely correlated with that obtained by using the proportion of engineers in the manufacturing labor force as a single indicator.

In Chapter 16, Pack examines the very difficult issue of the development of capital goods industries in LDCs. He aims to make several points: (i) the development of capital goods industries requires the continuous efforts of technical change to improve the products in competition with the producers in DCs. (ii) LDCs do not conduct product research because they do not have the necessary skills. This puts them at a disadvantage with the producers in DCs; a disadvantage for which they hardly compensate with lower costs for the skilled labor employed in producing the capital goods. (iii) Thus the prognosis for future development of healthy capital goods industries in LDCs is a dubious one at best.

Although the chapter is extensively supported by reference to various studies, it includes only secondary evidence, and this probably accounts for its pessimistic conclusions. Thus, Pack recommends that LDCs concentrate, for example, on the production of bearings and fasteners, which constitutes quite a limited view of the capital goods production capabilities of semiindustrialized countries in Latin America. He also argues that evidence shows that, although exports of capital goods from LDCs go to other LDCs, there is little or no evidence of any adaptation, by which he generally means more labor-intensive operation, to suit the market conditions in those countries. But, as emerges from Katz's paper in this volume and from metalworking industries studies in the IDB/ECLA/UNDP Programme referred to previously, the machine tools or the special-purpose agricultural machinery exported from Brazil or Argentina indeed show changes and even innovations in their design to take into account material, labor, climate, and other conditions prevailing in such countries.

Although Pack makes a great deal of the difference between process innovations and product innovations, the difference, as it exists, does not seem to be that sharp or pronounced. Product innovations or redesign efforts imply changes in materials, machines, techniques of production, etc., which, in turn, lead to concomitant process changes. Similarly, process improvements many times imply changes in product design necessitated by changes in tolerances, materials, etc.

He is also critical of the lack of subcontracting arrangements in the capital goods industry in developing countries—a point also noted by Katz in his chapter and attributed to the limitations on specialization imposed by the restricted market size.

A debatable premise in the author's approach is that externalities do not constitute a good justification for developing capital goods industries because they are not easily measurable. However, the main point of Westphal's chapter in this volume is that the infant-industry argument is mostly about the acquisition of technical competence. If the development of capital goods industries has special interest, it is because of the apparent connection between the production of capital goods and the application of engineering skills. This process is enhanced through learning by doing as production takes place, and the acquired knowledge is diffused to the rest of the economy by means of improved products and technical practices.

Part V, Equity, consists of chapters by G. Ranis, J. Silber, V. E. Tokman, M. Zymelman, and E. L. Bacha.

In Chapter 17, Ranis's aim is to provide an accounting and analytical framework for the production and distribution of goods and services satisfying basic needs. The basic-needs approach assumes that poverty cannot be eliminated in a short enough period of time by relying solely on the improvement in the distribution of money income. The chapter distinguishes among the money income earned by the household, the nonmonetized services it provides, the transfer of goods and services provided to the household by the government, and the goods and services produced communally. The needs to be satisfied include those considered basic, including food, education, and health. Shelter is not included, although it is also often considered as a basic need. Many of the basic needs are public goods or services, and this poses the problem of the most efficient organization for their production, i.e., whether they should be carried out by the central government, private suppliers, or the community. The ultimate objective is to optimize "full life," that is, longevity, the duration of our presence on earth, and the quality of the years lived, i.e., hopefully, life free of morbidity, pollution, etc. The author recognizes that quality is an elusive concept, e.g., should aesthetic pleasures be included? And leisure? Furthermore, if, as certain authors have argued, consumption of certain goods, e.g., enjoying classical music, requires learning, how is that to be included in the posited framework?

The author pinpoints the crucial role played in the framework by the "meta-production function," that is, the connection between the inputs of factors and the achievement of the "full life" standards. There are many problems in its application, including the existence of feedback between the attainment of certain objectives (e.g., health) and the capacity to produce basic-needs and nonbasic-needs goods and services. While recognizing the inherent limitation of the basic-needs approach, the author makes a contribution by pointing to the nature of the problems involved in its application.

Some of the results of a decade of economic growth for several Latin American countries are assessed in Chapter 18 by Silber. He contrasts indicators such as gross domestic product per capita with life expectancy and the equivalent length-of-life value. Recent concern with the adequacy of development indicators has led to various attempts to compute indexes that overcome some of the shortcomings of the income per capita measures. These new indexes generally try to include some measure of the quality of life and the extent of inequality in the distribution of income. The index proposed by Silber is an attempt to introduce equity considerations in the distribution, not of income, but of life expectancies, i.e., to make the distribution of expected life years intertemporally more egalitarian by attaching weights to the various age groups. Two different approaches are used for this purpose, one based on keeping the index invariant to proportional increases in the number of years lived and the other on keeping it invariant to equal additions in the number of years lived.

The data show that those Latin American countries included did generally worse in terms of improvement in the expected life of their citizens than in terms of increments in GDP per capita. Generally, also, differences in terms of GDP per capita tend to be amplified compared with differences in life expectancy where discrepancies remain narrower. When life expectancy is regressed vis-à-vis GDP per capita, Panama, Costa Rica, El Salvador in both 1960 and 1970 and Barbados, Argentina, and the Dominican Republic in 1960 fared better than expected on the basis of income per capita. Among the countries that did worse than expected were Guatemala, Chile, and Mexico in 1960 as well as 1970 and Venezuela in 1960. When the comparisons are repeated with the expected length-of-life index instead of straight life expectancy, i.e., by taking into account inequality in the life expectancy of the various groups, the results are magnified if the index used attaches higher weights to young age groups. This implies that the level of development of some Latin American countries is lower than implied by their GDP per capita levels. In terms of change in the decade, Silber finds that the progress made generally depends on the type of indicator used.

It was suggested by several participants in the symposium discussion that the "new" development economics should include empirical case studies and hypothesis testing as well as model building. Tokman's Chapter 19 belongs to the second of these categories. Kuznets hypothesized that, given a two-sector model and migration from agriculture to industry in the process of growth, inequality of income would initially rise and then fall at a certain level of income per capita. Recent Latin American data seem to disprove, not the general point of the hypothesis, but the specific results associated with its initial formulation. To explain the discrepancy, Tokman postulates a third sector, the informal or less-organized part of the urban sector, and, using various statistical fits with convenient assumptions, shows that, in fact, having a buffer sector that initially receives the farm migrants contributes to a delay in reaching the plateau at which inequality, on average, declines and also contributes to a maintaining of higher inequality during a longer period.

The author assumes that income inequality within the informal sector is lower than in the formal urban sector. He further assumes that inequality in the agricultural sector is lower than in the urban sector in spite of the distinctive pattern of high land concentration in Latin American agriculture. The nature and magnitude of these assumptions is crucial for the decomposition of the measure of inequality used—the variance of the logarithm of income—into its between-groups and within-groups components and also for the results of the various statistical exercises.

Although the author uses various sources and both time series as well as cross-sectional data, the reliability of the data in this field has been seriously questioned. Problems also exist with the assumptions used to deal with the underreporting of income, which are crucial for both the data on agriculture labor as well as with regard to the income of the informal urban sector. So although it is apparent that disguised unemployment, peddling, "papa–mama" shops, home subcontracting, etc., play a certain role in providing occupation and income to a portion of migrants from the countryside not readily absorbed in the industrial sector, it is not clear that some of these activities do not represent a permanent or long-term feature of the economy, which, however, poses a problem if correct factual accounting of its income is desired. Furthermore, it is also not clear if the distribution of income is more egalitarian within this sector than in the rest of the industry sector; in fact, the opposite may be true. A similar observation could probably be made with respect to the small-farm subsector in agriculture.

An attempt is made by Zymelman in Chapter 20 to relate income per capita to the sectorial composition of the economy and the productivity of labor—a well-established empirical fact through the work of Kuznets, Chenery and Syrquin, and the United Nations—as well as to the occupational distribution within sectors and thus to the educational requirements of various industries. Focusing on Latin America, the author compares, on average, the sectorial and occupational structures of the region with those of the OECD countries and purports to show that to attain the income level of the OECD countries (about four times that of Latin America for the year for which the data is provided) there would be a far greater impact as a result of the inherent changes in the occupational structure that follow changes in the sectorial composition of output than of the latter changes per se. That is, although the shift in employment, for example, from agriculture to industry leads to a substantial increase in average productivity, an even greater change results from the evolution of the occupational distribution in terms of skilled workers within the same sectors. Because, as Zymelman argues, the changes in skills are coupled with higher levels of average output per worker, the implication is clearly that a concomitant educational effort is required on the part of the Latin American countries, assuming, of course, that technical change will be skill-neutral in the process.

Given the differences in the demographic composition of these countries and in the degree of enrollment in primary, secondary, and higher education, the financial requirements in terms of proportion of GNP or of income per capita allotted to education are staggering. But, the effort is clearly required as part of the growth process, and acceleration of the same will imply the need to increase substantially the proportion of GNP allotted to education and of the rate of investment in this sector.

In Chapter 21, the final one, Bacha is also concerned with the testing of a hypothesis that has had singular importance to the development of a major phase of the economic development literature in the last 25 years. Bacha finds that Lewis's hypothesis about unlimited supply of labor from agriculture determining a fixed constant wage for industry is contradicted by the recent Brazilian experience. The author argues that there is duality within agriculture. He considers the family farming unit as being outside the realm of modern farming techniques and thus not influenced by changes in productivity in the modern sector of agriculture. Movements in real wages in agriculture in Brazil are explained by two factors: (i) institutional, i.e., the setting up and enforcing of a rural minimum wage, and

(ii) the increase in money wages owing to the increase in world prices and the improvement in the terms of trade for agriculture. Thus, if it were not for institutional reasons, there would have been no changes, as between the period of the early 1960s and 1977. And although there is a money increase in wages (deflated by the GDP deflator) since agricultural prices increased, the real wage, using agricultural product as the *numéraire,* remained practically constant.

The symmetry with Tokman's treatment of the urban sector is worthwhile noting. To explain the data, he resorts to subdividing the urban sector into two; Bacha does the same with the rural sector.

With reference to the urban wage, Bacha indeed finds the constancy of the Lewis hypothesis justified, but mainly owing to political reasons (military dictatorship making union power inoperative), not to the working of the labor market. Although his econometric tests are not fully satisfactory, it is clear that variables such as the agricultural–industrial terms of trade and the rate of growth of labor productivity in these two sectors have a bearing on the wage ratio. However, both are mitigated by institutional factors; namely, the power of organized labor to bargain for higher wages. This is, at times, complemented by the government through minimum wage legislation and, at others, working from the opposite direction, by the repression of unions. Bacha argues that institutional measures in the countryside, such as agrarian reform, would have a similar effect in raising the wages of small agriculture.

Thus, the rigid formulation of the unlimited labor supply model as determining, by rural unemployment, the level of urban wages need not be taken in a fatalistic manner as inherent in the economic system.

MOSHÉ SYRQUIN
Research Center for Latin American
  Development Studies
Bar-Ilan University
Ramat-Gan, Israel

SIMÓN TEITEL
Economic and Social Development
  Department Inter-American
  Development Bank
Washington, D.C. 20577

Part I

International Trade

Chapter 1

Exchange Rates and Terms of Trade in the Argentine Republic, 1913–1976

Carlos F. Díaz Alejandro

This chapter will present estimates of the Argentine real exchange rate since 1913. Departures from purchasing power parity (PPP) will be partly explained by fluctuations in the external terms of trade (TOT) and other variables. Much of twentieth-century Argentine economic history will be reflected in tables showing real exchange rates and terms of trade. Because data required for these exercises have not been available in one place, they were put together by the author. Some appear in the text and the rest in a lengthy statistical report [see Díaz Alejandro (1982)].

I. REAL EXCHANGE RATES SINCE 1913

Table 1 presents estimates of the real exchange rate with respect to the U.S. dollar. A similar table with respect to the British pound sterling appears in Díaz Alejandro (1982). During most of this century, Argentine in-

27

TABLE 1

Dollar Exchange Rates at 1929 Prices[a,b]

	Using cost of living		Using wholesale prices	
Period	Imports	Exports	Imports	Exports
1913–14		1.81	—	
1915–19		1.70	—	
1920–24		2.54	—	
1925–29		2.43	2.38[c]	
1930–33		3.23	2.70	
1934–36	3.34	2.97	2.82	2.51
1937–39	3.14	2.87	2.61	2.40
1940–45	3.60	3.25	2.40	2.16
1946–49	2.85	2.47	2.11	1.83
1950–55	1.99	1.80	1.55	1.40
1956–58	3.52	3.67	2.45	2.55
1959–61	3.92	4.01	2.63	2.69
1962–63	3.78	3.76	2.53	2.52
1964–66	3.04	2.96	2.01	1.96
1967–69	3.53	3.47	2.61	2.57
1970–72	3.47	3.39	2.39	2.33
1973–75	2.47	2.62	1.89	2.01
1976	3.02	3.82	2.08	2.64

[a] Pesos per U.S. $1.
[b] *Source*: Díaz Alejandro (1982, Table S-8).
[c] Refers to 1926–1929 only. The dollar exchange rate in 1929 averaged 2.391 pesos.

ternational economic links were characterized by marked triangularity, as in the Canadian case. Surpluses were registered in trading with Britain, whereas trade with the United States yielded deficits. Before the Second World War, financial links were dominated, although in a declining fashion, by Britain. Other countries, particularly in Europe, were important in Argentine foreign economic relations, but the weight of Britain plus the United States was paramount.

Since 1933, *de facto* or *de jure* multiple exchange rates have been the norm; Table 1 presents the average buying (export) and selling (import) rates. Export rates have tended to be lower than those applicable to imports, but this has not always been the case (see Table 2).

The years grouped together in Table 1 can be regarded as roughly homogeneous from the viewpoint of economic policy and circumstances. Thus, 1940–1945 cover the years of the Second World War; 1946–1949

TABLE 2

Export Exchange Rate as a Percentage of Import Exchange Rate[a]

Year	Percentage	Year	Percentage
1934	88.3	1956	118.2
1935	89.2	1957	94.9
1936	89.3	1958	101.3
1937	94.2	1959	106.4
1938	93.6	1960	100.0
1939	87.6	1961	99.6
1940	87.9	1962	99.6
1941	89.6	1963	99.6
1942	91.2	1964	99.0
1943	92.6	1965	98.0
1944	91.6	1966	95.0
1945	88.2	1967	95.0
1946	86.4	1968	99.9
1947	85.7	1969	100.0
1948	85.9	1970	96.8
1949	90.4	1971	99.7
1950	92.2	1972	96.8
1951	80.7	1973	96.9
1952	89.9	1974	102.3
1953	89.3	1975	121.5
1954	91.3	1976	126.6
1955	103.6		

[a] *Source*: Data from Díaz Alejandro (1982, Table S-1).

and 1950–1955 cover the first Perónist era; and 1973–1975 cover the second such era.

Real exchange rates have been computed using both cost-of-living and wholesale price indexes. Some important differences exist between these estimates. Table 3 shows how the cost of living has evolved relative to wholesale prices within each of the relevant countries. In both the United Kingdom and the United States, the two indexes have evolved in roughly similar ways. Cost-of-living increases in Argentina tended to lag behind those of wholesale prices during 1926–1949; since then (the more inflationary period), they have moved more or less in step. Estimates using cost of living are a priori preferable to those using wholesale prices, whose indexes are dominated by traded goods; Argentine cost-of-living estimates also go further back than those for wholesale prices.

Table 1 indicates real peso depreciation during the 1920s relative to the 1913–1919 period and further depreciation during the 1930s. Following the real exchange rates calculated using cost-of-living indexes, one notes that even the rates applicable to exports underwent depreciation during the 1930s relative to the 1920s. Real depreciations during the 1930s helped Argentina weather the Great Depression fairly successfully.

Somewhat surprisingly, the depreciation trend continued during the Second World War. Part of the explanation lies with a steadier cost-of-liv-

TABLE 3

Cost-of-Living and Wholesale Price Indexes Compared Nationally[a,b]

Period	Argentina	United Kingdom	United States
1926–29	98	98	99
1930–34	91	118	110
1935–39	82	109	97
1940–44	64	97	94
1945–49	63	98	88
1950–54	66	103	85
1955–59	60	116	86
1960–64	61	120	91
1965–69	68	127	95
1970–72	69	131	100
1973–76	67	130	89

[a] Cost of living/wholesale prices; 1929 = 100.

[b] *Sources*: The Argentine average annual cost of living covers the Federal Capital; data were obtained from Direccion Nacional de Estadistica y Censos, *Costo del Nivel de Vida en la Capital Federal*, Buenos Aires, February 1963, *Statistical Bulletin* of the Banco Central de la Republica Argentina, and more recent publications of the Instituto Nacional de Estadistica y Censos. United States data were obtained from the U.S. Department of Commerce, *Statistical Abstract of the United States*, recent issues. United Kingdom data were obtained from *The British Economy, Key Statistics 1900–1970*; indexes refer to "Consumers' expenditure average value index." For recent years, *International Financial Statistics* was used as the source.

ing index in nonbelligerent and food-abundant Argentina than in the United Kingdom and even compared with the U.S. performance. This may be seen in Table 4, which covers years when Argentine price level movements were not far off those in the United Kingdom and the United States; since 1948–1950, Argentine inflation has been clearly ahead of those of the other two countries. Table 4 also shows that wholesale prices signal mild "autonomous" Argentine inflation starting in the 1930s and accelerating during 1940–1944 relative to the United States.

The first Perónist era was characterized by a clear trend toward appreciation. By 1950–1955, real exchange rates were below those for the 1920s and are the lowest average rates registered in Table 1. Since 1955, exchange rates depreciated again; the 1964–1966 period (the Illia administration) and the second Perónist era stand out for their relative appreciations.

Comparing the fairly normal 1967–1969 years with 1925–1929, one sees significant depreciations for both dollar and pound rates when cost-of-living indexes are used as deflators. Less clear results obtain for series deflated by wholesale prices.

Substantial instability in real exchange rates is shown even by the averaged periods of Table 1. Yearly figures presented in Díaz Alejandro (1982, Tables S-8, and S-9) naturally show even greater variation. There were particularly abrupt changes between 1955 and 1956; 1958 and 1959; 1966 and 1967; and (in an opposite direction) between 1972 and 1973.

TABLE 4

Cost-of-Living and Wholesale Price Indexes Compared Internationally[a,b]

	Cost of living		Wholesale price	
Period	Argentina/ United Kingdom	Argentina/ United States	Argentina/ United Kingdom	Argentina/ United States
1914	136	130	—	—
1915–19	114	137	—	—
1920–24	99	113	—	—
1925–29	99	99	99[c]	101[c]
1930–34	94	103	122	125
1935–39	97	110	127	129
1940–44	77	108	119	161
1945–47	95	125	155	184
1948–50	138	177	192	222

[a] 1929 = 100.
[b] *Sources*: Same as Table 3.
[c] Refers to 1926–1929 only.

The real exchange rate is one of the key prices influencing an open economy. Another inportant relative price is given by the terms of trade, defined as export dollar prices divided by import dollar prices. Argentine TOT are presented in Table 5. The 1920s show deterioration relative to

TABLE 5

Argentine External Terms of Trade^{a,b}

Period	TOT	Period	TOT
1913–14	111.8	1950–55	102.2
1915–19	97.1	1956–58	79.5
1920–24	70.3	1959–61	90.4
1925–29	91.9	1962–63	96.0
1930–33	81.5	1964–66	99.2
1934–36	93.6	1967–69	95.8
1937–39	110.6	1970–72	97.8
1940–45	102.3	1973–75	111.0
1946–49	134.6	1976	84.3

^{a} 1929 = 100.

^{b} *Sources*: Pre-1928 data obtained from Banco Central de la Republica Argentina, *La Evolucion del Balance de Pagos de la Republica Argentina*, Buenos Aires, 1952. Post-1928 data from CEPAL, Naciones Unidas, *America Latina: Relacion de Precios del Intercambio*, Santiago de Chile, 1976 and later issues.

1913–1919, and this broad trend reaches a trough in the early 1930s. An upward trend is visible after 1930–1933, culminating in 1946–1949, which registers the best terms of trade for the years covered in Table 5. A new declining trend reaches its low point in 1956–1958, a trough similar to that of 1930–1933. Mild recovery characteristics the 1960s, with a peak during the second Perónist era (1973–1975) similar to the levels of 1937–1939. For the period as a whole, no significant trend is apparent.

Tables 1 and 5 indicate some negative correlation between real exchange rates and TOT. But, before going into this relationship, a fuller discussion of variables influencing departures of the real exchange rate from PPP is needed.

II. DEPARTURES FROM PPP

Consider an economy whose TOT are exogenously given and whose exchange rate fluctuates freely. Standard models[1] would predict that the following variables would influence its real exchange rate (or would lead to departures from PPP):

(a)   TOT; an improvement would lead to appreciation.

[1] One example is presented in Rodriguez and Sjaastad (1979).

(b)   Domestic commercial policy; higher import and export taxes or restrictions would lead to appreciation.

(c)   Biased domestic productivity changes; higher-than-average productivity improvements in exportable or importable production would lead to appreciation.

(d)   Capital flows; a capital inflow would lead to appreciation.

(e)   Stage in the business cycle; recessions would typically lead to appreciation.

Application of these notions to Argentina present a number of difficulties. During the period under study, the nominal exchange rate was seldom freely floating, and it is doubtful that prices adjusted quickly enough to yield yearly equilibrium real exchange rates in spite of official manipulation of nominal rates. The small-country assumption, although fairly realistic for the Argentina of the 1970s, is debatable for at least some export products until the 1950s. Data problems are also present, particularly for capital flows covering the whole of 1913–1976; the difficulties would be greater if one attempted to measure stocks of financial assets and liabilities.

In spite of these problems, an attempt has been made to measure the effect of variables (a)–(c) on the Argentine real exchange rate, on the assumption that they may be regarded as independent variables. Terms of trade and a simple trend are fairly easily quantified; the commercial policy variable presents complications.

Letting $p*$ be the external terms of trade, one can define the *internal* terms of trade as[2]

$$p \equiv p*\text{CP}, \tag{1}$$

where CP summarizes the net bias of domestic commercial policy between importables and exportables. For example, a CP lower than one could arise from export or import taxes, quantitative restrictions on exports and imports, or multiple exchange rates lower for exports than for imports. Taking $p*$ as exogenously given, one can obtain an index of the protectionist bias of commercial policy:[3]

$$\text{CP} \equiv P/p*. \tag{2}$$

[2] One could simply work with p, rather than breaking it down into its $p*$ and CP components. This procedure is followed by Rodríguez and Sjaastad (1979). Note, however, that a change in $p*$ will have income effects for the home country that are different from those arising from a change in CP. Thus it is important to establish whether a change in p comes from a change in $p*$ or a change in CP.

[3] A similar index was presented in Naciones Unidas (1959, Part I, page 21 and Table 19).

Since 1935, Argentine wholesale price indexes have included the sub-category of rural goods, which made up the bulk of exports during most of the period under study. They have also included the subcategory of imports; these, however, may not accurately reflect local prices for all *importable* goods because Argentine imports of manufactured goods became increasingly concentrated on raw materials and intermediate and capital goods, which were noncompeting with domestically produced manufacturers. A third subcategory refers to all nationally produced nonrural goods, which includes import-competing goods. Unfortunately, it also includes a number of commodities that could be more accurately defined as nontraded or quasi-nontraded. These indexes are presented in Díaz Alejandro (1982, Table S-10).

Tables 6 and 8 present estimates of CP as the ratio of internal to external terms of trade, using three possible definitions for domestic terms of trade. Both tables use rural wholesale prices as proxies for the domestic prices for exportable goods. Table 7, covering 1913–1927, estimates CP directly using data on average import and export taxes (no significant quantitative restrictions existed in that period).

TABLE 6

Indexes of Protection Using Wholesale Prices[a,b]

Period	Using national nonrural index	Using all nonrural index[c]	Using import index
1928–29	—	142	129
1930–33	—	118	107
1934–36	—	105	103
1937–39	100	100	100
1940–45	75	65	47
1946–49	74	66	52
1950–55	77	73	66
1956–58	114	105	82
1959–61	110	103	75
1962–63	111	103	80
1964–66	102	94	82
1967–69	102	94	72
1970–72	116	106	79
1973–75	93	84	49
1976	111	95	36

[a] 1937–1939 = 100. Definition of index of protection (CP) is explained in the text.

[b] *Sources*: Data from Díaz Alejandro (1982, Table S-10) and sources listed in Table 3. For 1928–1935, wholesale prices were obtained from the *Anuario Geografico Argentino, 1942/43*.

[c] The all nonrural index includes both imports and national nonrural goods.

TABLE 7

Index of Protection, 1913–1927[a,b]

Year	Using import and export taxes	Dummy[c]
1913	100.46	0
1914	101.79	0
1915	104.02	0
1916	104.99	0
1917	106.34	0
1918	106.64	0
1919	106.81	0
1920	105.46	0
1921	105.06	0
1922	104.27	0
1923	103.78	0
1924	102.29	0
1925	100.19	0
1926	101.54	0
1927	101.88	0

[a] 1929 = 100.

[b] *Sources*: Import and export tax data obtained from *Memoria de la Contaduria General de la Nacion* and from *Anuario de Comercio Exterior*, 1943.

[c] For an explanation of the use of the dummy variable, see the discussion in the text.

Although the broad movements of the CP indexes calculated in Tables 6–8 are roughly in line with knowledge about the various economic policies adopted during 1913–1976, divergences between indexes using import and national nonrural goods are large. The dummy variable presented in Tables 7 and 8 is a bold attempt to capture information from both policy history and the indexes calculated for CP. The dummy rises as policy becomes more protectionist; it takes a value of zero before 1930; of one during the 1930s; of three during both Perónist eras (carrying into 1976); and of two the rest of the years. The application of the dummy to Second World War years requires an ad hoc interpretation; world circumstances during those years, including increases in effective transport costs, resulted in domestic price movements similar from those generated by more protectionist policies.

Table 9 presents ordinary least squares regressions with annual data, where logarithms of real dollar exchange rate indexes, deflated using cost-of-living indexes, are the dependent variables. Logarithms of both contemporary and lagged TOTs are included as independent variables; the results shown represent the best obtained after some experimenting with various Almon lag specifications. The expression [TOT] refers to the sum of all terms-of-trade coefficients. A simple time trend is included to capture any systematic relative productivity changes; CP refers to the dummy for commercial policy. Error terms showed marked serial correlation in earlier regressions; the ρ numbers in Table 9 represent the correction for the estimated serial correlation. All regressions are based on 59 annual observations; t statistics are given in parentheses under the respective coefficients.

Both TOT and CP have the signs expected a priori. Note, however, that the introduction of the CP variable reduces the significance of the TOT variables. (Lagged CP variables yielded poor results.) The trend variable yields a persistent tendency toward real depreciation, a result not so surprising in light of what is known about the technological lag in rural Pampean production and the excesses in import-substituting industrializa-

TABLE 8

Indexes of Protection, 1928–1976[a]

Year	Using rural/imported	Using rural/all nonrural	Dummy[b]
1928	96.23	96.23	0
1929	100.00	100.00	0
1930	86.98	86.98	1
1931	85.69	85.69	1
1932	74.04	74.04	1
1933	78.45	78.45	1
1934	70.45	70.45	1
1935	81.31	73.46	1
1936	82.10	73.16	1
1937	76.98	69.56	1
1938	76.62	68.47	1
1939	73.83	68.78	1
1940	56.36	57.44	2
1941	39.88	44.81	2
1942	31.07	40.35	2
1943	26.79	38.27	2
1944	26.42	39.86	2
1945	32.15	48.67	2
1946	36.72	49.63	3
1947	41.14	46.43	3
1948	38.96	43.24	3
1949	41.47	43.54	3
1950	42.64	42.64	3
1951	42.62	46.44	3
1952	49.75	51.60	3
1953	50.36	50.16	3

TABLE 8 (*cont.*)

Year	Using rural/imported	Using rural/all nonrural	Dummy[b]
1954	58.98	55.90	3
1955	55.75	53.55	3
1956	54.18	69.88	2
1957	63.74	73.54	2
1958	68.26	74.21	2
1959	57.58	77.16	2
1960	55.28	70.87	2
1961	56.91	64.61	2
1962	62.93	74.37	2
1963	58.80	67.20	2
1964	65.74	68.26	2
1965	60.21	62.35	2
1966	61.28	63.51	2
1967	53.39	62.35	2
1968	57.00	65.65	2
1969	54.34	65.80	2
1970	58.47	72.79	2
1971	64.63	72.88	2
1972	55.51	74.29	2
1973	40.80	57.74	3
1974	37.67	58.47	3
1975	32.18	57.15	3
1976	27.52	65.57	3

[a] *Sources*: As in Table 6.
[b] For an explanation of the use of the dummy variable, see the discussion in the text.

tion during much of the period under study. Pound regressions were also run with similar results.

There is a positive correlation between the CP and TOT variables. Under the small-country assumption, such a link would be regarded as a historical accident (e.g., for many years during the Perónist eras there were both exceptionally favorable TOTs and strict protectionism). If one abandons the small-country assumption, then one can argue that protectionism led to both overvalued exchange rates and favorable TOTs. In spite of its ad hoc character, the former explanation appears more satisfactory for Argentine experience than the latter one.

Omitted variables for capital movements and cyclical phases may explain some of the serial correlation that persists even after the correction by the ρ variable indicated in Table 9. A glance at the 1930s error terms of these regressions, for example, shows actual values exceeding fitted ones for most years, i.e., larger than expected real depreciations. This is

TABLE 9

Indexes of Real Exchange Rates as Dependent Variables[a]

	Dollar exchange rate	
Variable	(a)	(b)
Constant	−10.58	−24.52
	(1.15)	(2.19)
Trend	0.010	0.017
	(2.04)	(2.92)
TOT_t	−0.23	−0.14
	(1.59)	(0.97)
TOT_{t-1}	−0.22	−0.15
	(2.37)	(1.53)
TOT_{t-2}	−0.19	−0.13
	(1.94)	(1.37)
TOT_{t-3}	−0.14	−0.11
	(1.45)	(1.10)
TOT_{t-4}	−0.08	−0.06
	(1.18)	(0.92)
[TOT]	[−0.85]	[−0.58]
	(2.32)	(1.54)
CP	—	−0.15
		(2.09)
$\bar{R}^2$	0.63	0.65
DW	2.01	1.90
ρ	0.8	0.8
F statistic	34.1	28.2

[a] Using cost of living; 1918–1976. Numbers in parentheses are the corresponding t statistics.

consistent with what is known about the sharp decline in capital inflows during the 1930s.[4]

Given the variety of exchange rate regimes that existed in Argentina

[4] Similar regressions were estimated for exchange rates deflated by wholesale prices covering 1927–1976. The results were inferior to those shown in Table 9; generally, TOT and trend variables performed worse and the CP variable performed slightly better. When the same variables and regression of Table 9 are run for 1927–1976, roughly similar results are obtained, although with some loss of significance.

during 1913–1976 as well as the data imperfections, the link established between the real exchange rate of contemporary and lagged terms of trade appears quite robust. Note that the same lag structure was imposed for the whole period, even though different degrees of stickiness in nominal exchange rate (and prices) existed during 1913–1976, depending on policy attitudes.[5]

III. THE LAW OF ONE PRICE

From evidence presented so far, it is clear that annual data do not closely fit the simplest version of the law of one price, stated as follows:

$$\hat{P} = \hat{E} + \hat{P}^*, \tag{3}$$

where the $\hat{P}$s represent the annual percentage changes in price levels in Argentina and "the rest of the world," respectively, and $\hat{E}$ refers to the annual change in the average nominal exchange rate.

Attempts were made to fit Eq. (3) to data presented in Díaz Alejandro (1982), including Argentine and U.S. cost of living and wholesale prices. The results were poor; the best fit was the following:

$$\hat{P}_t = 13.97 + 1.18\,\hat{E}_t + 6.10\,\hat{P}^*_{t-1} \tag{4}$$
$$(1.20) \quad (2.36) \quad (2.01)$$

where $\bar{R}^2 = 0.15$ and DW $= 0.77$.

In this regression, $\hat{P}$ refers to the percentage changes in the Argentine wholesale price index, $\hat{P}^*$ to changes in the U.S. cost-of-living index (lagged one year), and $\hat{E}$ to the percentage change in the average peso per dollar rate. The period covered was 1927–1976. Other lags and combinations of dollar and Argentine price indexes were used, but they all yielded lower $\bar{R}^2$s. In Eq. (4), the coefficient for $\hat{E}$ makes more sense than the extravagant coefficient obtained for $\hat{P}^*$.

Since 1973, many observers have noted that inflation in the dollar prices of the basket of tradable goods relevant to countries such as Argentina is not accurately reflected by U.S. cost-of-living and wholesale price indexes. Table 10 compares the long-term evolution of the average dollar unit values for Argentine imports and exports, obtained from Díaz Alejandro (1982, Table S-6), relative to the U.S. cost of living and wholesale prices since 1913. From 1915–1919 until 1935–1939, tradable dollar unit values rose less (or fell more) than either the U.S. cost of living or whole-

---

[5] Links between the real exchange rate and terms of trade have been found for other Latin American countries [Díaz Alejandro (1979, pp. 14–17)].

TABLE 10

Comparison of Dollar Price Indexes[a,b]

Period	Argentine import unit values/U.S. cost of living	Argentine import unit values/U.S. wholesale prices
1913–14	134[c]	108
1915–19	188	129
1920–24	131	119
1925–29	112	110
1930–34	71	78
1935–39	50	48
1940–44	57	54
1945–49	77	67
1950–54	90	77
1955–59	84	73
1960–64	66	60
1965–69	62	59
1970–72	61	61
1973–76	87	77

[a] 1929 = 100.
[b] *Source*: Díaz Alejandro (1982, Table S-6).
[c] Refers to 1914 only.

sale prices. The opposite trend is visible between 1935–1939 and 1950–1954. Between 1950–1954 and 1973–1976, tradable dollar unit values on the whole rose less than other dollar price indexes, a fact also noted for other semiindustrialized economies. "Imported inflation" during 1973–1976 would be underestimated if one relied simply on estimates based on U.S. price indexes. Note, however, that the tradable dollar unit values were also used in regressions such as Eq. (4) without yielding better results than those shown.

ACKNOWLEDGMENTS

A good share of this chapter was prepared while visiting the Centro de Estudios Macroeconomicos de Argentina (CEMA) in Buenos Aires. I am grateful for the Centro's hospitality and for helpful comments received from Guillermo Calvo, Pedro Pou, Carlos Alfredo Rodríguez, and Mario Vicens. Mr. Vicens in Buenos Aires and Ms. Cynthia Lee Arfken in New Haven provided splendid research assistance without which this chapter could not have been written. I am also grateful for comments received during a seminar held at the Instituto Torcuato Di Tella in Buenos Aires.

REFERENCES

Díaz Alejandro, C. F. (1979). "Some Historical Vicissitudes of Open Economics in Latin American," pp. 14–17, New Haven (processed).

Díaz Alejandro, C. F. (1982). "Statistical Report," unpublished, available from the author.

Naciones Unidas (1959). Analisis y Proyecciones del Desarrollo Economico, V, *El Desarrollo Economico de la Argentina.*

Rodriguez, C. A. and Sjaastad, L. A. (1979). "El Atraso Cambiario en Argentina: Mito o Realidad?" *CEMA, Documentos de Trabajo,* (2) (June) (processed).

Economic Growth Center
Yale University
New Haven, Connecticut

Chapter 2

The Terms of Trade, Real Output, and the Balance of Payments in a Primary Exporting Country: A Model and Some Estimates for Guatemala

Mario I. Blejer

Following the well-known and often-quoted contributions of Johnson (1972) and Mundell (1971), a large number of theoretical and empirical studies have been devoted to emphasizing the role of the money market in the determination of the balance of payments.[1] Much effort has been directed to extending the basic monetary model and to applying the central ideas associated with this approach to the analysis of specific policy questions.[2] The purpose of this chapter is to consider an issue that has not

[1] See, for example, the volume edited by Frenkel and Johnson (1976) and the one from the International Monetary Fund (1977).

[2] The effects of devaluation within the monetary framework were analyzed by Dornbusch (1973) and the consequences of alternative commercial policies were studied by Mussa (1976) and by Blejer and Hillman (1978). Frenkel (1978) analyzed exchange-rate determination in a floating regime and the working of the model under a crawling-peg system was studied by Blejer and Leiderman (1981).

43

received much attention in the context of the monetary model but that may have considerable importance in the determination of short-run balance-of-payments fluctuations. The question to be addressed concerns the effects of exogenous changes in the terms of trade in a small, open economy exporting a primary commodity and operating under a fixed-exchange-rate system.

Most of the studies within the monetary-approach framework, whether or not they consider the existence of nontradable commodities, have assumed the constancy of relative prices in the tradable-goods sector and have therefore not been concerned with the possible effects of changes in the terms of trade. A notable exception is Rodriguez (1976), who presents a theoretical formulation in which changes in the relative price of importables and exportables are expected to have different short-run effects on the balance of payments. The mechanism by which these are brought about is a combination of the real-cash-balances effect and the effect of changes in the terms of trade on the level of current real income. Although Rodriguez does not test this hypothesis, Levy (1980) uses a similar framework to study the effects of the relative increase in the price of oil on Turkey's domestic rate of inflation and balance of payments.

The basic characteristics of the model presented here are similar to those of the Rodriguez analytical framework. Each of the building blocks of the analyst, however, is subjected to empirical verification and, from the results obtained, it is possible to quantify the importance of the terms-of-trade effect.

The basic model is presented in Section I, where the estimating equations are discussed. In Section II, we consider the case of Guatemala and present some of the country's export characteristics and its terms of trade. The hypothesis about the exogeneity of the domestic rate of inflation is also subjected to empirical verification in that section. Section III presents the results of estimating the complete model and the main conclusions of the study are discussed there.

I. THE MODEL

The model is a version of the monetary approach to the balance of payments. We consider the case of a small, open economy, defined as one for which the price of its tradables, both importables and exportables, is exogenously determined. The main feature of this version is that it accounts for the effects of changes in the terms of trade on the level of real activity and, through them, on the demand for real balances and the balance of payments.

Three equations describe the monetary sector:

$$M_s \equiv a(R + D), \tag{1}$$

$$M_d = Pm_d, \tag{2}$$

$$m_d = f(y, C), \qquad f_1 > 0; f_2 < 0, \tag{3}$$

where M_s is the nominal supply of domestic money; a the money multiplier; R the foreign-exchange reserves held by the central bank; D the domestic-credit component of the monetary base; M_d the demand for nominal cash balances; P the domestic price level; and m_d the real demand for money, assumed to be a function of real income y and the alternative cost of holding money C.

Assuming for simplicity that the money market clears in each period so that the nominal stock of money is equalized *ex post* with the demand for nominal balances, we require the existence of the flow equilibrium

$$M_s^* = M_d^*, \tag{4}$$

where the asterisk indicates the percentage rate of change of the variable (i.e., $X^* = d \log X$). Differentiating Eqs. (1) and (2) logarithmically, the flow-equilibrium condition can be rewritten as

$$a^* + (1 - \gamma)R^* + \gamma D^* = P^* + m_d^*, \tag{5}$$

where $\gamma = D/(R + D)$ is a factor of proportionality and P^* the domestic rate of inflation.

Assuming a semilogarithmic specification for money demand m_d^*, the rate of growth of the demand for real cash balances can be written as

$$m_d^* = \eta_y y^* - \eta_c \, dC, \tag{6}$$

where η_y is the income elasticity and η_c the cost semielasticity.

Solving now for R^*, which is the rate of change of the international reserves held by the central bank, we obtain the expression for the money account of the balance of payments:

$$(1 - \gamma)R^* = P^* + m_d^*(y^*, dC) - a^* - \gamma D^*, \tag{7}$$

which indicates that the balance of payments is negatively related to the rate of change of domestic credit and the money mulitplier and to changes in the alternative costs of holding money and that it is positively related to the rate of price increase and the rate of growth of real output.[3]

---

[3] The effect of prices on the balance of payments can be rationalized in terms of money-market equilibrium. In the absence of changes in the domestic-credit component of the money supply, any increase in the nominal demand for money (caused either by an increase in the real demand or by a rise in prices) must be equilibrated through the accumulation of foreign-exchange reserves.

In the present formulation, it is assumed that all commodities are tradables and the rate of domestic inflation for the small economy operating under a fixed-exchange-rate regime is therefore exogenous.[4] The level of real activity, and, therefore, the determination of the growth rate of real output, is assumed to be exogenous with respect to monetary variables[5] but affected by changes in the country's terms of trade. The postulated relationship is

$$y_t = g(\lambda)(\mathrm{RP}_t; A_t), \qquad g_1 > 0; \quad g_2 > 0 \qquad (8)$$

where $g(\lambda)$ is a polynomial lag function, RP the terms of trade measured by the relative price of exportables in terms of importables , and A_t a vector of other variables, including the supply of factors and technology, which are assumed to change exogenously.

The positive relationship between the terms of trade and the level of real output can be rationalized in terms of a simple model of an open economy producing a single commodity X_1, which is both domesticially consumed and exported. Imports X_2 consist only of final consumer goods.[6] Assuming that X_1 is produced by labor L and a set of fixed factors (the supply of which changes exogenously over time), the cyclical fluctuations of real domestic output round its trend will be determined by the changes in employment. Postulating an elastic supply of labor with respect to real wages in terms of a domestic consumption basket (which includes X_1 and X_2) and a labor-demand function derived from the value of the marginal productivity of labor in the X_1 sector, we obtain

$$L_s = f(W/P), \qquad f' > 0, \qquad (9)$$

$$L_d = g(W/P_1), \qquad g' < 0, \qquad (10)$$

where W is the nominal wage rate; P the domestic consumer price index, which is a weighted average of P_1 and P_2,

$$P = \beta_1 P_1 + \beta_2 P_2, \qquad (11)$$

where P_1 and P_2 are the prices of X_1 and X_2, respectively, and β_1 and β_2 their share in consumption. From (9)–(11), we observe that a deterioration in the terms of trade (an increase in P_2 relative to P_1) tends to reduce

---

[4] The assumption is that the domestic rate of inflation is determined by the rate of inflation in the rest of the world or in the main trading partners. Empirical support for this claim in the Guatemalan case will be presented in the next section. This assumption has been used in many studies of the monetary approach [see Frankel and Johnson (1976, Section II)]. For a model including nontradable goods and endogenous inflation, see Blejer (1977).

[5] We thus assume a version of the natural-rate hypothesis.

[6] For an empirical test of the terms-of-trade effect on real output in industrialized economies, see Leiderman (1980).

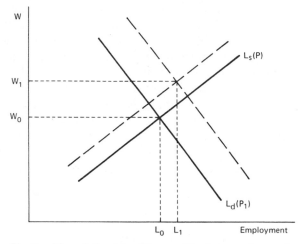

Fig. 1. The relationship of terms of trade to employment.

employment and therefore domestic output, and the opposite happens for a rise in P_1 with respect to P_2. This is illustrated in Fig. 1. Starting from an initial position at W_0 and L_0, consider an increase in P_1, the price of the exportable, while P_2 remains unchanged. In that case, the rise in the labor-demand schedule (the displacement of L_d to the right) will not be fully offset by the contraction of labor supply at the given nominal wage. The resulting equilibrium at W_1 and L_1 implies a higher real wage in terms of the initial consumption basket and a lower real wage in terms of the domestic commodity. This, of course, leads to a rise in the level of employment.[7] Within the same framework, we can observe that an increase in the price of imports tends to reduce output by shifting L_s without affecting L_d.

In Eq. (8), we postulated a lagged mechanism of adjustment of domestic output to changes in relative prices. This lagged effect may result from rigidities in the process of price and wage determination or in the adjustments of labor demand and supply. Such rigidities may arise mainly in the presence of long-term labor contracts or when the relative price change is not expected to last.

The complete model can be now summarized by Eq. (6)–(8), from which we observe that a once-and-for-all improvement in the terms of trade will raise the level of income, thus accelerating the economy's rate

[7] We ignore here the alteration in consumption patterns that may follow the changes in the terms of trade. Clearly, the increase in employment will be greater the smaller the fraction of exportables in the domestic consumption basket, which is a suitable assumption for countries exporting primary commodities.

of growth during the transitional period. To satisfy the increase in the demand for real cash balances resulting from the higher level of income, an inflow of foreign-exchange reserves will be induced (provided that the rate of domestic-credit expansion remains unchanged). After all adjustments have taken place, the level of income will remain higher but the rate of growth will revert to its original trend and so will the balance of payments. Assuming an initially balanced balance of payments, a once-and-for-all improvement in the terms of trade will result in a once-and-for-all payments surplus with the consequent accumulation of foreign reserves. After the period of adjustment, the balance of payments reverts to its initial equilibrium position. An illustration of the process is provided in Fig.

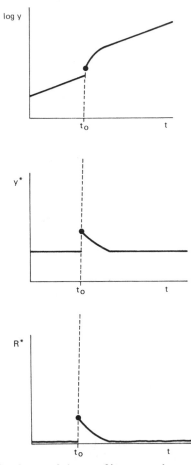

Fig. 2. The relationship of rates of change of income and monetary reserves over time.

2, where the terms of trade improve at time t_0 and remain constant thereafter.

II. THE CASE OF GUATEMALA: SOME GENERAL CONSIDERATIONS

We apply the model described in the preceding section to the experience of Guatemala during the period of 1948–1977. Guatemala is a suitable case to test the predictions of the present extended version of the monetary approach to the balance of payments for a number of reasons. In the first place, it has maintained a pegged exchange rate vis-à-vis the dollar during the entire period analyzed here (the quetzal is at par with the U.S. dollar) and the country certainly fits well the small-open-economy assumption. In addition, Guatemala relies heavily on the exports of primary commodities, particularly coffee, and therefore the terms-of-trade effect is relatively well defined and can be expected to have significant effects throughout the economy. The country's development in terms of real-output growth and balance-of-payments performance has been relatively stable, although year-to-year fluctuations have been important.[8]

The share of coffee in total exports has changed considerably during the 30 years covered here. It reached a peak of more than 70% in the 1950s and fell to about 30% in the 1970s. Given the importance of coffee in Guatemala's economy, we have defined the terms of trade here as the relative price of coffee in terms of the price of imports.[9] The terms of trade so defined are reported in Table 1, together with the share of coffee in Guatemala's exports.[10] As can be seen, the terms of trade have fluctuated considerably. A sharp deterioration is observed in the 1960s and 1970s with some recovery in the last two years considered. The real effects of these variations will be considered in the next section.

An important assumption made in the presentation of the model is the exogeneity of the inflation rate with respect to domestic monetary variables. Equations (6)–(8) describe a complete system only if this assumption is upheld; therefore its validity should be tested for the case considered. To do so, a Granger causality test is performed. Granger's

[8] For a discussion of the economic structure of Guatemala, see Piedra Santa (1977); the role of the coffee industry is discussed in Chapter VII. See also Hernandez Cisneros (1978).

[9] In preliminary estimations, the terms of trade were weighted by the share of coffee in total exports. Because the results were not significantly affected by the correction, we used the simple price ratio (in logarithmic terms) as the more appropriate measure.

[10] All data in this study are annual and, except for real output, are obtained from the International Monetary Fund (various issues). The series on real output were obtained from United Nations (1978).

Mario I. Blejer

TABLE 1

The Terms of Trade and the Share of Coffee in Total Exports: Guatemala, 1949–1977[a]

Year	Terms of trade[b]	Coffee as percent of total exports	Year	Terms of trade[b]	Coffee as percent of total exports
1949	0.158	59.2	1964	0.349	43.9
1950	0.549	66.9	1965	0.414	48.8
1951	0.649	69.4	1966	0.341	43.7
1952	0.660	75.6	1967	0.251	34.1
1953	0.686	68.4	1968	0.124	32.2
1954	0.757	70.7	1969	0.084	31.6
1955	0.786	70.5	1970	0.373	34.5
1956	0.907	74.5	1971	0.257	34.1
1957	0.774	71.0	1972	0.264	31.5
1958	0.566	72.8	1973	0.240	32.9
1959	0.415	71.4	1974	0.116	30.1
1960	0.428	67.4	1975	−0.142	25.9
1961	0.300	61.4	1976	0.343	31.2
1962	0.242	57.9	1977	0.944	44.5
1963	0.203	51.3			

[a] *Source*: International Monetary Fund (various issues).
[b] Defined as the price of coffee P_c relative to import prices P_m: $RP = \log (P_c/P_m)$.

procedure allows us to test the causal patterns in a bivariate system [see Granger, (1969)]. A version of this test for the problem at hand can be carried out by means of the regressions

$$P_t^* = K_0 + \sum_{i=1}^{n} g_i P_{t-i}^* + \mu_t, \tag{12}$$

$$P_t^* = K_0' + \sum_{i=1}^{n} g_i' P_{t-i}^* + \sum_{i=i}^{m} h_i X_{t-i} + \mu_t' \tag{13}$$

where K is a constant, P^* the rate of domestic inflation, X the growth rate of any exogenous variable, and μ the residual term. Equation (12) is an autoregressive representation of the rate of inflation, and Eq. (13) adds a set of lagged values of the exogenous variable whose causal effect on P^* is being tested. The Granger test of causality asserts that if the information added in Eq. (13) does not improve the forecast of P^* over that made on the basis of its own lagged values, changes in inflation are statistically independent of X, i.e., there is no causal pattern from X to P^*. To implement the test, Eq. (12) and (13) can be estimated by least squares and an F test conducted on the null hypothesis that the parameters $h_i = 0$, ($i = 1, \ldots, m$).

TABLE 2

The Effects of Domestic and Foreign Variables on Inflation, Guatemala, 1948–1977:
F *Statistics for the Granger Causality Test*[a]

P^* regressed on[b]	R^2	$F(16, 4)$
P^*_{t-i}	0.697	
P^*_{t-i} and D^*_{t-i}	0.768	1.22
P^*_{t-i} and $M1^*_{t-i}$	0.746	0.77
P^*_{t-i} and $M2^*_{t-i}$	0.732	0.52
P^*_{t-i} and EXC_{t-i}	0.771	1.29
P^*_{t-i} and π^{US}_{t-i}	0.858	4.53#

[a] The table is based on the estimation of Eqs. (12) and (13). The reported F statistics are appropriate for testing the null hypothesis that there is no causality from x to P^* (or that $h_1 = h_2 = h_3 = h_4 = 0$). Rejection of the null hypothesis at the 0.05 significance level is indicated by #.

[b] The lags are $i = 1, 2, 3, 4$.

Here we have carried out this test for five variables.[11] Four of them are domestic monetary variables: D^* is the growth rate of domestic credit; $M1^*$ the rate of growth of M1 (currency plus demand deposits); $M2^*$ the rate of growth of M2 (M1 plus time deposits); and $EXC = (\gamma D^* + a^* - y^*)$, which is a measure of the growth rate of the excess money supply. The additional variable π^{US}, the rate of inflation in the United States (Guatemala's major trading partner), is exogenous to the country. The results of the Granger test are reported in Table 2. The F statistics are used to test the hypothesis that, in an autoregressive representation of inflation, the coefficients of the additional right-hand-side variables are zero. The results that emerge from our test are very favorable to the market-integrated hypothesis, which, in a small, open economy, implies exogeneity of the domestic rate of inflation. The hypothesis that there is no causality from changes in the domestic monetary variables to the rate of the inflation cannot be rejected for any of these variables. In the case of foreign inflation, however, we can easily reject the no-causality hypothesis.

Thus, it is tempting to conclude from these results that there is evidence of causality running from foreign to domestic inflation, whereas the alternative hypothesis, namely that domestic inflation is caused by domestic monetary imbalance, is not upheld by our results. In the next section, we shall therefore proceed on the assumption of an exogenous rate

[11] The length of the lag structure [n and m in Eq. (12) and (13)] cannot be established a priori. In our tests we used alternative lengths of lag and obtained similar results. The results reported in Table 2 correspond to $n = m = 4$.

of domestic inflation, which implies that domestic monetary disequilibrium will be solved only through balance-of-payments adjustments.

III. EMPIRICAL RESULTS

The complete model estimated for Guatemala is based on Eq. (6)–(8). However, the empirical forms estimated are slight variants of these equations. The system, as implemented in this case, is

$$\log y_t = \alpha_0 + \alpha_1 t + \alpha_2 RP_t + \alpha_3 \log y_{t-1}, \tag{14}$$

$$\log m_d = \beta_0 + \beta_1 \log y_t + \beta_2 C, \tag{15}$$

$$(1 - \gamma)R^* = \delta_0 + \sum_{i=0} \lambda_i \theta_{t-1}^*, \tag{16}$$

where $RP_t = \log(P_c/P_m)t$ and $\theta_t^* = P^* + m_d^* - a^* - \gamma D^*$. Equation (14) is the empirical, log-linear version of (8). The real-output effect of the terms of trade is directly measured by α_2,[12] and a time trend t measures the exogenous growth of resources and technology. The lagged adjustment discussed in connection with (6), as well as the persistence of effects from year to year, are captured by y_{t-1}.

The real demand for money [Eq. (15)] is estimated using a semilogarithmic specification. The money definition used is $M2$, although similar results are obtained using $M1$. The cost variable C used here is a measure of expected inflation calculated on as the fitted values of a regression of the form[13,14]

$$P_t^* = f(P_{t-1}^*, P_{t-2}^*, P_{m,t-1}^* P_{m,t-2}^*). \tag{17}$$

Equation (16) is a distributed-lag representation of Eq. (7). It postulates that the balance of payments, measured by the rate of change of foreign-exchange reserves, is determined so as to equilibrate the money market; reserves will therefore change by the difference between the growth rate of the demand for nominal balances ($P^* + m_d^*$) and the rate of expan-

---

[12] Note that the implied long-run elasticity is equal to $\alpha_2/(1 - \alpha_3)$.

[13] We have experimented with a number of alternative formulations for expected inflation. For simplicity, the results discussed here are those that correspond to what has been called the "partially" rational expectations process [see Sargent (1973)].

[14] An alternative variable tried was U.S. treasury bills, which seemed to be a good approximation of the alternative cost of holding money, particularly under the assumption of free capital movements. However, the American interest rate did not produce significant results; the reported results are therefore based on the expected rate of inflation.

sion of the domestic sources of the money supply ($a^* + \gamma D^*$). Unlike Eq. (7), which postulates immediate equilibrium (requiring a unitary coefficient of θ_t), Eq. (16) allows for a lagged process of adjustment, requiring only that $\Sigma_{i=0} \lambda_i = 1$. The length of the adjustment is, of course, left to be determined empirically.

The set of equations (14)–(16) is a fully recursive system. This simplifies the problem of estimation because in this case ordinary least squares is a best linear unbiased method of estimation. The results of estimating Eq. (14) and (15) are

$$\log y_t = 1.882 + 0.017t + 0.037\text{RP}_t + 0.700y_{t-1} \qquad (18)$$
$$\quad\quad\ (5.87)\quad\ (7.22)\quad\quad (2.79)\quad\quad\ (13.95)$$

$R^2 = 0.998$ and $h = -0.76$, and

$$\log m_2 = -8.708 + 1.606\ \log \hat{y}_t - 0.632C \qquad (19)$$
$$\quad\quad\ (23.42)\quad\ (30.78)\quad\quad\quad\ (1.71)$$

$R^2 = 0.993$, DW $= 1.90$, and $\rho = 0.389$, where the numbers under the coefficients are t values. The estimation of Eq. (15) use the Cochrane–Orcutt technique to account for first-order serial correlation; ρ is the final value of the autocorrelation coefficient; h Durbin's statistic for the test of serial correlation in autoregressive models; and $\hat{y}_t$ the fitted value of y_t in (18).

All the estimated coefficients have the right sign and are significant; the equations are free of first-order serial correlation. The results indicate a significant and important effect of the terms of trade in real activity. The long-run elasticity of y with respect to RP is 0.12, which indicates that a 10% deterioration in the terms of trade will induce a reduction of more than 1% in real output.

The results of estimating Eq. (16) are reported in Table 3.[15] As a whole, the results are satisfactory for the hypotheses of the monetary approach to the balance of payments. They indicate a strong effect of monetary disequilibrium on the rate of change of foreign-exchange reserves. When alternative lengths of lag are tried, the results appear to indicate that the monetary imbalance works itself out through the balance of payments within 2 years. The coefficient of θ_t^* is lower than the predicted value of unity when only the contemporaneous value is included but the sum of coefficients is not significantly different from unity when θ_t^* and θ_{t-1}^*

---

[15] To estimate Eq. (16), the fitted values from (19) are first differentiated in order to obtain m_d^*.

Mario I. Blejer

TABLE 3

Foreign Exchange Reserves and Monetary Variables: Guatemala 1951–1977[a,b]

Variable	A	B	C
Constant	0.011	−0.010	−0.058
	(0.51)	(0.45)	(0.22)
θ_t^*	0.759	0.780	0.845
	(4.41)	(4.65)	(4.45)
θ_{t-1}^*		0.353	0.342
		(2.10)	(1.92)
θ_{t-2}^*			−0.167
			(0.87)
R^2	0.459	0.545	0.552
DW	1.956	1.835	1.626
SER	0.092	‚0.088	0.091

[a] Numbers in parentheses are t values.

[b] $(1 - \gamma)R^* = \delta_0 + \sum_{i=0} \lambda_i \theta_{t-i}^* + \mu$ and $\theta^* = P^* + \hat{m}_d^* - a^* - \gamma D^*$.

are considered. The inclusion of an additional lag does not prove to be significant and the standard error of the estimate is increased.[16]

The results obtained stress the importance of monetary variables in balance-of-payments determination. Domestic-credit expansion over and above the desired rate of money accumulation by the public results in losses of foreign-exchange reserves which will persist as long as the credit expansion is not consistent with the money demand.

The overall terms-of-trade effect on the balance of payments can now be calculated. In this model the balance of payments is affected by the terms of trade via their effect on real output and the money demand. From the estimated coefficients, we obtain a long-run elasticity of $(1 - \gamma)R^*$

[16] Because Eq. (16) implies the restriction of equal coefficients for p^*, m_d^*, a^*, and γD^* an additional test of the monetary-approach hypotheses can be obtained by estimating Eq. (7) unrestricted. The results are

$$(1 - \gamma)R^* = 0.010 + 1.338 P^* + 0.683 \hat{m}_d^* - 1.295 a^* - 0.636 \gamma D^*$$
$$(0.24) \quad (3.61) \quad (1.82) \quad (2.38) \quad (3.03)$$

for $R^2 = 0.560$, DW $= 2.208$, and SER $= 0.089$. All the variables are significant and have the correct sign. Except for γD^*, the hypothesis that the coefficients are equal to unity cannot be rejected. It is apparent, therefore, that, although the effects of the different variables are in line with the predictions of the monetary approach, their time pattern needs additional investigation, which was not pursued here.

with respect to RP of 1.92. A 10% deterioration in the terms of trade will therefore reduce output and money demand, resulting, for a reserve ratio of 0.6, in a reduction of about 3.2% in the level of international reserves.

The model and the statistical procedure used here are relatively simple; the results obtained are, however, quite conclusive regarding the importance of terms-of-trade fluctuations on both real activity and the balance of payments. At the theoretical level, they emphasize the fact that much additional insight can be gained by further disaggregation in the context of the monetary approach to the balance of payments. Empirically, they quantify and tend to support the preoccupation of primary exporting countries with the terms of trade.

ACKNOWLEDGMENTS

The author is thankful to H. Cardona for her help and to S. Freond for editorial suggestions.

REFERENCES

Blejer, M. I. (1977). "The Short-Run Dynamics of Prices and the Balance of Payments." *American Economic Review* **67** (June), 419–428.

Blejer, M. I., and Hillman, A. L. (1978). *On the Dynamic Non-Equivalence of Tariffs and Quotas in the Monetary Model of the Balance of Payments.* Foerder Institute Working Paper No. 14–78. Tel Aviv: Tel Aviv University.

Blejer, M. I., and Leiderman, L. (1981). "A Monetary Approach to the Crawling Peg System: Theory and Evidence." *Journal of Political Economy* **89** (February), 132–151.

Dornbusch, R. (1973). "Devaluation, Money, and Nontraded Goods." *American Economic Review* **63** (December), 871–880.

Frenkel, J. A. (1978). "A Monetary Approach to the Exchange Rate: Doctrinal Aspects and Empirical Evidence." In *The Economics of the Exchange Rate: Selected Studies* (J. A. Frenkel and H. G. Johnson, eds.), pp. 1–26. Reading, Massachusetts: Addison-Wesley.

Frenkel, J. A., and Johnson, H. G. (eds.) (1976). *The Monetary Approach to the Balance of Payments.* London: Allen and Unwin; Toronto: University of Toronto Press.

Granger, C. W. J. (1969). "Investigating Causal Relations by Econometric Models and Cross-Spectral Methods." *Econometrica* **37** (July), 424–438.

Hernandez Cisneros, M. E. (1978). "Un Modelo Contable y de Control para la Industria del Café." Unpublished M. A. thesis, San Carlos University, Guatemala.

International Monetary Fund (1977). *The Monetary Approach to the Balance of Payments.* Washington, D.C.

International Monetary Fund (various issues). *International Financial Statistics.* Washington, D. C.

Johnson, H. G. (1972). "The Monetary Approach to Balance-of-Payments Theory." In *Further Essays in Monetary Economics.* London: Allen and Unwin.

Leiderman, L. (1980). "Output–Inflation Tradeoffs and the Terms of Trade." *Review of Economics and Statistics* (May)

Levy, V. (1980). *Oil Prices, Relative Prices, and Balance-of-Payments Adjustment: The Turkish Experience,* Discussion Paper No. 808. Jerusalem: Falk Institute.

Mundell, R. A. (1971). *Monetary Theory.* Pacific Palisades, California: Goodyear Publ.

Mussa, M. (1976). "Tariffs and the Balance of Payments: A Monetary Approach." In *The Monetary Approach to the Balance of Payments* (J. A. Frenkel and H. G. Johnson, eds.). London: Allen and Unwin and Toronto: University of Toronto Press.

Piedra Santa, R. (1977). *Introducción a los Problemas Económicos de Guatemala.* Guatemala City: Ediciones Superiores.

Rodriguez, C. A. (1976). "The Terms of Trade and the Balance of Payments in the Short Run." *American Economic Review* **66** (September), 710–715.

Sargent. T. J. (1973). "Rational Expectations, the Real Rate of Interest, and the Natural Rate of Unemployment." *Brookings Papers on Economic Activity* (2), 429–472.

United Nations. ECLA (1978). *Series Históricas del Crecimiento de América Latina.* Santiago de Chile.

MARIO I. BLEJER*
Department of Economics
The Hebrew University and Bar-Ilan University,Israel

* Present address: International Monetary Fund, Washington, D. C.

Chapter 3

Dismantling Foreign Trade Restrictions: Some Evidence and Issues on the Argentine Case

Julio Berlinski

I. INTRODUCTION

The purpose of this chapter is to discuss some evidence and issues related to Argentine foreign trade restrictions. It also includes an exercise in the effect of protection cuts on prices.

First, estimates of nominal and effective rates are presented for a group of selected industries by calculating implicit tariffs. Next, an exercise in tariff dismantling, focusing on the production effect is presented. This is done by cutting high effective rates to predetermined levels and then working back to the equivalent nominal rates. Finally, the comparison of expected (estimated) and actual (1979) change in relative prices with a simple model of micro behavior is presented in the last section.

Some of the assumptions made are broad, but bringing up the subject may open possibilities for further research beyond the scope of this chapter.

57

II. NOMINAL AND EFFECTIVE PROTECTION[1]

A key element in the estimation of nominal rates was the adjustment for water in tariffs. This is especially relevant in the case of Argentina, given the importance of nontariff instruments used to control imports. For a select group of products and activities, "implicit" tariffs[2] were first estimated.

The weighted nominal rate of 40 selected activities[3] was 37%. However, variability was high (see Table 1): 41% for intermediate products and 26% for machinery. Table 2 shows that 70% of the sectors were concentrated in the range of rates up to 50%, and with the inclusion of the next range (51–75%), 90% of the cases were covered.

Regarding nominal protection on exports, given the absence of estimates on the subsidy equivalent of tax and credit incentives, only the rebate called *reembolso* was measured. The average rate (see Table 1) was 14%, but whereas the rate for machinery was 23%, intermediate products showed only 2%, indicating a strong association of the size of the *reembolso* to the degree of fabrication. The more disaggregated rates (Table 2)

TABLE 1

Nominal and Effective Protection for Selected Activities (1977)[a]

Categories	Nominal protection		Effective protection to domestic sales	
	Domestic sales (%)	Rebates (reembolsos) to exports (%)	Balassa (%)	Corden (%)
Nondurable consumer goods	45.6	19.0	44.2	43.8
Durable consumer goods	29.1	16.7	17.1	17.0
Intermediate products	41.0	1.6	56.8	55.2
Machinery	26.3	22.6	7.4	7.3
Transport equipment	33.5	23.8	10.0	9.9
Average	37.1	13.9	39.1	38.3

[a] *Source*: Berlinski (1978).

[1] The rates are conventional partial equilibrium estimates at private prices. No adjustment for overvaluation of the exchange rate was made.

[2] To this end, a survey of 141 plants was made that measured, for principal products, the FOB plant price and the comparable CIF price of potential imports.

[3] The selected activities correspond to the main production chains, excluding those related to traditional agriculture. Sectors included were five-digit I.S.I.C. Rev. 2 breakdowns of the following groups: textiles, clothing, pulp and paper, rubber products, chemical products, nonmetallic minerals, basic metals, metal products, machinery, and transport equipment.

TABLE 2

Frequency Distribution of Protective Rates for Selected Activities (1977)[a]

Rates of protection (%)	Nominal protection (number of sectors)		Input protection[b] (number of sectors)	Effective protection to domestic sales (number of sectors)
	Domestic sales	Rebates (reembolsos) to exports		
Less than 0	1	5		11
Between 0 and 25	14	34	16	7
Between 26 and 50	13		10	4
Between 51 and 75	8		13	2
Between 76 and 100	2		1	8
Greater than 100	2			8
Total	40	39[c]	40	40

[a] *Source*: Berlinski (1978).

[b] Corresponds to tradable inputs.

[c] Includes only sectors that did export in 1976.

showed a high concentration of rates up to 25% (87% of sectors), whereas in the same bracket only 35% of the activities relating protection to domestic sales were found. (The Spearman rank correlation coefficient of nominal protection to both destinations showed low statistical significance).[4]

Finally, Table 1 also presents the estimates of effective protection rates on domestic sales.[5] The similarity between the average nominal rate (37%) and the effective rates (39% and 38%) is not observed at more disaggregated levels. Thus, although in machinery nominal rates are higher than effective rates, the opposite is true in intermediate products; the former shows an effective rate of 7% and in the latter it amounts to 57% (55%). Also, the degree of dispersion of effective rates is higher than the one observed for nominal rates. At the five-digit level (Table 2), 45% of sectors show effective rates lower than 25% with another 40% corresponding to rates higher than 76%. The principle cause of the higher dispersion of effective rates relative to nominal rates should be found in the effect of input protection. Here the average rate on tradable inputs was 37%, with 29% for intermediate products and 54% corresponding to machinery. The

[4] Estimation of additional incentives (tax and credit subsidies) may change this conclusion.

[5] Regarding nontraded inputs, two alternative criteria were followed: see Corden (1971) and Balassa (1972).

Spearman rank correlation between rebates on exports and rates on input protection was statistically significant (0.73), showing the attempt to remove the impact of high input costs.

III. AN EXERCISE IN TARIFF DISMANTLING

The evidence presented in Section II regarding the high dispersion of effective rates seems to be hardly justified on normative grounds. It is known that in the presence of trade restrictions without discrepancies between private and social prices the optimal trade policy would be to set effective protection at uniform rates [see Bertrand (1972)]. Taking into account dynamic elements would probably not drastically alter the pattern of static efficiency. In the absence of relevant information about the aforementioned facts, we shall assume that the estimated effective rates represent a fair approximation to the comparative advantage of the sectors involved.

In order to simulate the long-run change in relative prices, the so-called concertina method was followed [see Corden (1974)], which consists in cutting effective rates to some predetermined level and then, if necessary, moving it further downward. This was done under the assumption that any tariff reform should be aimed, at least, at reducing extreme (high) rates. It should also be mentioned that the main problem with such an approach is its concern with only production effects, discounting the possible consumption effects.

For the transformation of effective into nominal rates, an input–output framework was used, similar to the one suggested by Balassa and Schydlowsky (1974). In the procedure that was followed, explicit consideration of nontraded sectors in the Balassa tradition[6] was made, and goods were split according to the extent of import competition. This is important in the Argentine history of tariffs, where rates on noncompetitive imports were set at lower levels than those corresponding to import-competing products. In this way, given the target for effective rates and the predetermined rates on imported current inputs, an interindustry consistent set of nominal protective rates may be obtained as

$$T_\mathrm{p} = [(I - A)^{-1}]' \, (\hat{V}Z + \hat{M}T_\mathrm{m}) \tag{1}$$

where: T_p is the vector of nominal protection rates, A the input–output matrix at world prices, $\hat{V}$ the diagonal matrix of value-added coefficients

---

[6] In this case, the effective protection rate of nontradables is assumed to be zero.

at world prices, Z the vector of effective protection objectives, $\hat{M}$ the diagonal matrix of imported coefficients at world prices, and T_m the vector of rates on imported inputs.

Because the available interindustry table for Argentina corresponds to 1963 (Banco Central de la Republica Argentina, 1973), Eq. (1) was first applied to a complete set of protection data for 1969 [see Berlinski and Schydlowsky (1982)] in order to check for the bias that may arise (given the high level of aggregation) from using an outdated table at domestic prices. The estimated nominal rates compared with those obtained by detailed calculation showed a high Spearman rank correlation coefficient (0.92), justifying the continuation of this exercise.

If it is further assumed that the interindustry table remains unchanged after protection levels are modified, then (1) may be rewritten in terms of increments of protection as

$$\Delta T_p = [(I - A)^{-1}]' \, (\hat{V} \, \Delta Z + \hat{M} \, \Delta T_m) \tag{2}$$

Because the data used is outdated, the purpose of this exercise is to emphasize the interindustry nature of tariff reform and to show some directional changes to be expected in relative prices if protection changes are enforced. The data on effective rates used came from the study referred to in Section II; this is another limitation because that information is not comprehensive for the sectors of the available input–output table.

Equation (2) was computed following the criteria outlined earlier of cutting high rates down to some chosen level. In the case of effective rates, the cut was to the weighted average. Regarding imported inputs, it was assumed that, in the long run, nontariff instruments were going to be removed, so the legal rate (10%)[7] was used as the norm. Table 3 presents the assumed changes in effective rates and imported inputs, and the predicted changes in nominal protection. These are also shown in relation to agriculture.[8] The results of the exercise do show that the sectors where more change in nominal protection should be expected were basically the same as those where effective rates were cut: textiles, clothing, paper, basic metals, and electrical machinery and appliances.[9] In the next section this pattern of long-run changes in relative prices will be contrasted with the actual developments during 1979.

---

[7] See Ministerio de Economia, Resolución 1634/78.

[8] This sector produces traditional exports of a wage–good nature. Here domestic prices are determined by international prices and the exchange rate.

[9] The picture does not basically change if the assumption regarding tariffs on imported inputs becomes pessimistic by stating $\Delta T_m = 0$.

TABLE 3

Changes in Effective Rates (Concertina Method[a]) and Corresponding Changes in Nominal Rates[b]

Sector	ΔZ (%)	ΔT_m (%)	ΔT_p (%)	$\dfrac{(1 + \Delta T_{pj})}{(1 + \Delta T_{pi})}$
Agriculture, forestry, fishing	0	0	-1.4	1.000
Mining and quarrying	0	0	-2.1	0.993
Food, beverages, and tobacco	0	0	-1.4	1.000
Textiles	-45	-8	-17.3	0.838
Clothing and footwear	-92	0	-31.6	0.694
Wood and furniture	0	0	-1.5	0.998
Paper and printing	-35	-6	-17.7	0.834
Leather and fur	0	0	-1.2	1.002
Rubber	0	-5	-2.4	0.989
Chemical products	0	-14	-3.0	0.984
Petroleum refining	0	0	-0.9	1.005
Nonmetallic minerals	0	-3	-1.3	1.000
Basic metals and products	-25	-11	-15.0	0.861
Machinery (nonelectrical)	0	-35	-5.2	0.962
Electrical machinery and appliances	-38	-16	-20.8	0.803
Transport material	0	-26	-3.8	0.975
Miscellaneous industries	0	0	-1.1	1.002
Electricity, gas, and water	0	0	-0.6	1.008
Construction	0	0	-1.8	0.996
Commerce, restaurants, and hotels	0	0	-0.4	1.009
Transport and communications	0	0	-1.3	1.001
Housing	0	0	-0.3	1.011
Personal and financial services	0	0	-0.5	1.009

[a] See Corden (1974). Notation: ΔZ, the changes in effective rates; ΔT_m, the changes in tariffs on imported inputs; and ΔT_p the changes in nominal protection.

[b] *Source*: See Eq. (2).

IV. ON THE CHANGE IN RELATIVE PRICES

If it is assumed that commodity arbitrage [see Isard (1977) and Richardson (1978)] may be perceived at the level of aggregation of Table 3, a short-cut in evaluating the opening of the economy during 1979 would be to look at the behavior of relative prices. This is so because one of the important benefits of tariff dismantling is the increased welfare of consumers reflected in lower prices. In this way we would be comparing the expected change in relative prices with the actual short-run behavior, looking for convergence. We are aware that the level of aggregation may be too high to assume that imported goods and domestic substitutes sell at

TABLE 4

Tariff Reform Framework (Average Levels and Changes)[a]

Category	Starting level t_0 (January 1979) (%)	Changes in the cost of imports (%) $[(1 + t_0)/(1 + t_n)] - 1$	
		1979–84	1979–80
1. Consumer goods (excludes those under 2)	75	29.5	2.7
2. Food, beverages, and tobacco	45	27.4	2.8
3. Intermediate goods	46	20.7	2.8
4. Raw materials and basic products (excludes those under 5)	39	18.5	3.0
5. Raw materials and basic products of agricultural origin	25	11.6	1.6
6. Goods not produced	10	—	—
7. Capital goods	48	20.0	20.0

[a] *Source:* Based on Ministerio de Economia, Resoluciónes 1634/78 and 493/79.

the same price, in which case it may still remain as a provocative hypothesis for further research. But in the meantime, it will serve for the purpose of discussing some of the issues involved.

During 1979, changes in the costs of imports owing only to tariff modifications were no higher than 3% (Resolución 1634/78), except in the case of capital goods, which, by Resolución 493/79, implied a 20% decrease (see Table 4). There were other exceptions. For example, some important special regimes were renegotiated: cars (Law 21932), engines (Decree 3317/1979) and tractors (Decree 3318/1979). Also, the decrease in tariffs may have been higher for selected products where Resolución 6/79 was applied, according to which, tariffs were reduced on certain goods whenever price increases exceeded a predetermined norm. On the other hand, during this year, the nominal exchange rate increase was 62%, compared with a rise in wholesale domestic prices of 130%.[10] So, after allowing for any reasonable rate of foreign inflation, the exchange rate seems to have been the most important general instrument used during 1979 to increase import competition.

Table 4 also gives information about the time schedule of tariff reductions. For the whole period (1979–1984), it implies a decrease in the cost of imports, discounting other instruments, of around 30% for consumer goods and lower rates (20% or less) for intermediate and capital goods. Regarding changes over time, the 1979–1980 decrease shows, except in

[10] The increase in agriculture prices was 120%.

the case of capital goods, that tariff reductions were planned at increasing rates.

In Table 3, it was shown that cutting high effective protection rates to the average would imply a change in relative prices for the sectors involved. The stronger long-run expected changes (vis-à-vis agriculture) corresponded to textiles, clothing, paper, basic metals, and electrical machinery and appliances. On the other hand, actual price increases during 1979 show[11] that relative prices did not move in the expected direction. Apart from the problems involved in such a comparison (available data, level of aggregation), there may be several explanations for this lack of convergence: (a) Water in tariffs still exists; (b) Nontariff protection (quantitative restrictions, official prices, special regimes, etc.) was not completely removed; (c) There is a lag involved in import competition; (d) There is incomplete substitutability in consumption [see Norman (1975) and, for a more comprehensive view, see Ardnt (1979)]; (e) This is the outcome of the behavior of firms in the adjustment period. These reasons may not be independent, but for the present purpose, we shall try to develop hypothesis (e) a bit more.

Figure 1 presents the elements of a model that is only a crude simplification of actual behavior. It describes a profit-maximizing firm (at time zero) selling $0V_1$ in the domestic market, where it acts as a monopolist,[12] and exporting V_1V_2 at marginal cost.[13] The reward for domestic sales is higher than rebates on exports and water in tariffs exists.[14]

Let us assume further that during period one no change in tariffs and rebates took place but the nominal exchange rate lagged behind domestic costs. This lowers incentives on exports and at the same time reduces the real cost of competitive imports. At some point the firm will stop exporting and the cost of imported close subsitutes will fall below domestic prices, for example, to $[P_e^1 R^1(1 + t)]$. In this case the firm will face the option of acting as an importer or letting somebody else compete, thus losing the monopolistic position.

With knowledge of the market[15] and the tastes of the consumers, the

[11] Instituto Nacional de Estadistica y Censos, "Precios mayoristas," December 1979–December 1978 increase in prices: agriculture 120%; textiles 126%; clothings 133%; paper 167%; basic metals 134%; electrical machinery and appliances 138%.

[12] In this way, equilibrium of the firm and the industry are simultaneously determined.

[13] Some underutilization of capacity may still exist.

[14] Two similar models have been used in the past to explain Argentine manufacturing exports: Mallon and Sourrouille, (1975), and De Pablo (1977). For a necessary condition for water in tariffs under monopoly, see Fischelson and Hillman (1979).

[15] There is evidence that independent importers tend to use the distribution channels of domestic producers of close substitutes.

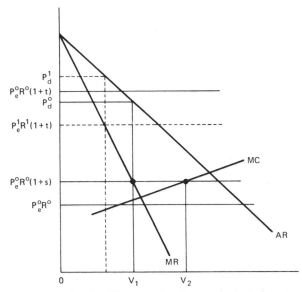

Fig. 1. The Elements of a simplified model, where: P_e is the international price (valuation FOB = CIF), R the exchange rate, s the rebates on exports (%), P_d the domestic price, AR the average revenue, MR the marginal revenue, MC the marginal cost, t the tariffs (%), 0 the base period, and 1 the next period.

producer seems the best qualified to become an importer and, by so doing, to stretch out the adjustment period while looking for areas of specialization. In this case, the producer's maximizing behavior will evolve from that of a monopolist practicing market discrimination (in period zero) to a monopolist with several sources of output.

Maximizing profits in period one implies making marginal revenue equal to marginal cost from each source. In the case described in Fig. 1, the producer will be in a suboptimal situation to prevent competition. If competitive imports are supplied at constant cost, P_d^1 will correspond to the domestic price when the market would be supplied only by imports, but that price could not prevail in the absence of nontariff protection. On the other hand, the supply mix will be determined by plant flexibility because marginal cost of producing may be sensitive to changes in the level of output.[16]

[16] The rate at which production may be discontinued will also involve other costs, such as severance payments. Here, the older the firm and the more labor intensive, the more expensive would be that shift.

From Fig. 1 it may also be seen that any shift in the demand curve (average revenue), owing to the entry of competing importers, will not change the main conclusions if newcomers would profit under the price umbrella set by the producer.

At this point there would seem to be decreasing returns for further elaboration. The elements of the simple model presented may be compatible with the lack of convergence between long-run expected and actual (1979) relative prices, but to what extent is this polar case a fair representation of market organization in the sectors involved? Before orienting further research to answer that question, it would be worthwhile to take a closer look at some of the alternative hypotheses outlined earlier. Among them, the case of nontariff instruments of protection seems to have priority.

V. SUMMARY AND CONCLUSIONS

First, an overview of a recent study made by the author was presented. For 40 selected activities, the average rate of effective protection was 39%, with extreme values of -35 and 428%. The frequency distribution showed that 45% of the selected sectors had rates up to 25%, whereas another group of similar size showed rates higher than 76%. In this way, the dispersion of effective rates was higher than the one for nominal rates. On the other hand, rebates on exports were strongly associated to the degree of fabrication, but they were not symmetric with the nominal protection of domestic sales. Finally, the discriminatory effect of input protection in the Argentine system was stressed.

Next, the long-run relative price change associated with tariff reform were evaluated. The criteria presented in Table 3, consisted of a simulation of a cut of high effective rates to average levels (concertina method) and then an estimation, through an input–output transformation of the implied change in nominal rates. Although the data used are outdated, the purpose of this exercise was to emphasize the interindustry nature of tariff reform and to show directional changes in relative prices. The highest expected changes corresponded to textiles, clothing, paper, basic metals, and electrical machinery and appliances.

In the absence of water in tariffs and of quantitative restrictions, we could have expected, if competitive conditions prevailed, that commodity arbitrage would have resulted in some change in relative prices during 1979. In that year, opening the economy relied more on a lagged exchange rate behind domestic costs than on a stronger change in tariffs. But, although some special regimes were renegotiated (cars, engines, tractors), higher reductions in tariffs for capital goods took place and also some selected products were subject to stronger tariff declines in trying to keep their price increases in line.

In conclusion, the elements of a model that may contribute to the explanation of the lack of convergence between expected long-run change in relative prices and the actual short-run behavior were constructed. This model described a producer under imperfect competition, where a lag in the exchange rate behind domestic costs induces the producer to become an importer of a close foreign sustitute, providing enough room for delays in expected changes in relative prices.

ACKNOWLEDGMENT

I am grateful to A. L. Hillman of Bar-Ilan University for a helpful discussion of water in the tariff.

REFERENCES

Ardnt, H. W. (1979). "The Modus Operandi of Protection." *Economic Record* (June).
Banco Central de la Republica Argentina (1973). "Transacciones intersectoriales de la economía argentina año 1963." Febrero.
Balassa, B. (1972). *The Structure of Protection in Developing Countries,* p. 16. Baltimore, Maryland: Johns Hopkins Press.
Balassa, B., and Schydlowsky, D. (1974). "Indicators of Protection and of Other Incentive Measures." In *The Role of the Computer in Economic and Social Research in Latin America,* (N. D. Ruggles, ed.). N.B.E.R.
Berlinski, J. (1978). "La protección arancelaria de actividades seleccionadas de la industria manufacturera Argentina." Ministerio de Economía.
Berlinski, J., and Schydlowsky, D. M. (1982). "Argentina" in Balassa, B. *et al., Development Strategies in Semi-Industrial Economies,* Baltimore, Maryland: Johns Hopkins Press.
Bertrand, T. J. (1972). "Decision Rules for Effective Protection in Less Developed Economies." *American Economic Review* **62** (September), 743–746.
Corden, M. (1971). *The Theory of Protection,* Chapter 7. London and New York: Oxford Univ. Press.
Corden, W. M., (1974). *Trade Policy and Economic Welfare,* p. 369. London and New York: Oxford Univ. Press.
DePablo, J. C., (1977). "Beyond Import Substitution: The Case of Argentina." *World Development* (January/February).
Fischelson, G., and Hillman, A. L. (1979). "Domestic monopoly and redundant tariff protection." *Journal of International Economics* **9** (February), 47–56.
Isard, P. (1977). "How far can we push the law of one price." *American Economic Review* **67** (December), 942.

Mallon, R., and Sourrouille, J. V., (1975). *Economic Policy Making in a Conflict Society: The Argentine Case*. Cambridge, Massachusetts: Harvard University Press.

Norman, N. R., (1975). "On the Relationship between Prices of Home Produced and Foreign Commodities." *Oxford Economic Papers* **27** (November), 426–439.

Richardson, J. D. (1978). "Some Empirical Evidence on Commodity Arbitrage and the Law of One Price." *Journal of International Economics* **8** (May), 341–352.

Instituto Torcuato Di Tella
Buenos Aires, Argentina

Chapter 4

Manufactured Exports, Labor Productivity, and Employment in Latin America: A Hypothesis Based on the Clothing Industry in Colombia*

David Morawetz

I. INTRODUCTION

Latin America's exports of manufactured goods increased more rapidly during the 1970s than was expected a decade or two before, when export pessimism was widespread; nevertheless, on a per capita basis, they remain well below manufactured exports from East Asia (Table 1). Furthermore, whereas the growth of exports of manufactures from Hong Kong, Korea, Singapore, and Taiwan appears to have been instrumental in mopping up much of the employment and underemployment in those countries,[1] the growth rates of employment in manufacturing industries

---

* This chapter is based on Morawetz (1981), which was financed by the World Bank.

[1] On the relationship between manufactured exports and increased employment in East Asia, see, e.g., Watanabe (1972), Cole and Westphal (1975), and Liang and Liang (1975–1976).

69

David Morawetz

TABLE 1

Population, GNP per Capita, and Exports of Clothing and All Manufactured Goods for Selected East Asian and Latin American Countries, 1976[a]

Country	Population (millions)	GNP per capita ($)	Exports of all manufactured goods ($ millions)	Exports of clothing ($ millions)[b]
East Asian countries				
Korea	36	700	6675	1846
Taiwan	16	1050	6921	1322
Hong Kong	4	2230	6480	2907
Total	56	909[c]	20,076	6075
Latin American Countries				
Brazil	110	1300	2332	99
Mexico	62	1060	2327[d]	174[d,e]
Argentina	26	1580	972	38
Colombia	24	650	659[f]	40
Venezuela	12	2540	115[e]	—
Chile	10	1050	109[g]	—
Total	244	1256[c]	6514	351

[a] *Sources*: Columns 2 and 3, World Bank 1978; column 4, Chenery and Keesing 1978, Table 8); column 5, United Nations (1977); Keesing (1978, Table 10).
[b] Dashes indicate a negligible amount.
[c] Weighted average.
[d] Estimated including border zone, with help of U.S. as well as Mexican data.
[e] 1975.
[f] Plesch (1979, Table B.10) gives this figure as 384.
[g] 1974.

that export in Latin America have been rather less impressive. A study that I recently completed on Colombian and East Asian exports of clothing may help to shed some light on the reasons for the difference.

Two of the main questions tackled in the study were:

1. Why is it that to date Colombia has been so much less successful at exporting garments than the East Asian countries? (Hong Kong, Korea, and Taiwan exported $2.9 billion, $2.0 billion, and $1.3 billion of apparel, respectively, in 1977, whereas Colombia exported less than $50 million.)

2. More generally, what can be learned from Colombia's experience with exporting clothing concerning the reasons that Latin American nations in general have been less successful at exporting most types of man-

ufactured goods than Hong Kong, Korea, and Taiwan? Do the East Asians have cheaper labor? Do they work harder? Do they have a transport cost advantage? Do they receive massive government subsidies? Are they better at selling the goods? Or what?

In an attempt to elucidate the answers to these questions, the managers of 30 Colombian firms that export or have exported clothing were interviewed, as were Colombian government and private sector officials, and executives of 14 U.S. corporations that import or have imported clothing from the firms in the sample. A detailed report on the findings of the project was presented elsewhere (Morawetz, 1981). This chapter presents a brief summary of some of the main conclusions in the report and expands on one aspect of the study not discussed there: namely, the relationship between increased exports of clothing and increased employment.

The next section summarizes the information on the level of protection, the export performance, and the level and growth of labor productivity. Section III surveys the causes of the rise and fall of Colombia's exports of clothing. The findings are generalized to other industries and other Latin American countries in Part IV, followed by a brief concluding section.

II. PROTECTION, EXPORTS, AND LABOR PRODUCTIVITY

Even after Colombian government policies tilted toward export promotion in 1967, Colombian garment makers were protected against foreign competition for sales in the domestic market. Imports of almost all types of apparel were prohibited until 1973 and have been subject to licensing since then.

A rough quantitative estimate of the extent to which the Colombian trade incentive system has favored domestic sales over exports can be obtained by comparing the effective rates of protection that have been granted to import substitutes with those granted on exports (Table 2).

The average nominal tariff on imports of apparel was 90–95% during 1974–1979, and effective protection calculated from nominal tariffs averaged 119–124% during this period (Table 2). Although there was undoubtedly some water in these tariffs (Table 3), the domestic market was fragmented enough that many of its segments contained only a handful of competing producers (fashion clothing for upper-income middle-aged women; jeans for consumers in the Bucaramanga area; men's woolen sports shirts; and so forth). Thus, domestic prices were well above world

TABLE 2

Effective Protection for Import Substitutes and Exports of Clothing, 1967–1979[a]

Item	1967	1968	1969	1970	1971	1972	1973	1974	1975	1976	1977	1978[b]	1979[b]
Average tariff on clothing (%)[c]	207.45	207.45	207.45	207.45	207.45	207.45	182.90	94.89	94.89	92.30	91.17	91.17	91.17
Average tariff on fabric (%)[d]	69.11	69.11	69.11	69.11	69.11	69.11	69.12	65.31	66.18	65.18	63.75	63.75	63.75
Value of fabric per value of clothing (estimated) (%)	50	50	50	50	50	50	50	50	50	50	50	50	50
Prior deposit for imports of clothing (%)	132.19	130.00	130.00	130.00	130.00	130.00	23.92	—	—	—	—	—	—
Prior deposit for imports of fabric (%)	126.10	126.43	122.96	121.82	121.82	121.82	22.50	—	—	—	—	—	—
Effective protection for import substitutes (%)	346	346	346	346	346	346	297	124	124	119	119	119	119
Effective protection for exports (%)													
Limited company not using Vallejo Plan	−40.80	−38.14	−37.68	−36.96	−36.58	−36.16	−35.04	−26.22	−50.70	−48.40	−36.10	−26.04	−26.04/−31.16
Public company not using Vallejo Plan	−23.36	−20.70	−20.24	−19.52	−19.14	−18.72	−17.60	−17.52	−47.32	−45.02	−34.76	−25.78	−25.78/−31.36
Limited company using Vallejo Plan	28.32	30.98	31.44	32.16	32.54	32.96	33.41	19.56	7.74	8.38	13.84	18.86	18.86/16.30
Public company using Vallejo Plan	45.76	48.42	48.88	49.60	49.98	50.40	50.86	25.80	9.42	10.08	14.50	19.00	19.00/16.20

[a] *Sources*: Tariffs: Banco de la República, *Revista*, various issues; prior deposits: Resolutions of the Junta Monetaria Nos. 2 of 1965, 6 and 9 of 1967, 61 of 1969 (Jan. and Oct.), 40 of 1971, and 9 of 1973; and Decree No. 1121 of 1973.

[b] Projected. Where there are two figures, the second is applicable for exports to the United States only.

[c] Most clothing items were on the list of prohibited imports during 1967–1973, and were on the prior licensing list thereafter.

[d] Most items of fabric were on the prior licensing list until 1973 and on the free list in 1974. From 1975 onwards, some were free and others, especially synthetic fabrics, have been subject to licensing.

Price Differentials and Effective Protection for Domestic Sale and for Export of Jeans and Blouses and Shirts, 1978[a]

Item	Jeans	Blouses and shirts
Excess of domestic price over export price[b]		
Finished garment (%)	50	100
Fabric (%)	70	100
Fabric costs per total costs (%)	50	50
Effective protection		
For domestic sale (%)	30	100
For export not using Vallejo Plan (%)	−32	−62
For export using Vallejo Plan (%)	38	38

[a] *Source*: Interviews with firms (see text discussion).

[b] The export price excludes the value of the CAT and PROEXPO credit because these are taken into account directly in the calculation of effective protection for export sales.

levels (50% for classic blue jeans, 100% for many shirts) and Colombian firms selling only in the domestic market were not forced to be as efficient as East Asian enterprises to stay in business.

During the interviews, I was fortunate enough to come across a number of Colombian managers who were aware that a U.S. company (usually an importer–manufacturer or a licensor of an internationally used trademark or brand name) was producing a garment identical to the one that they themselves were fabricating and who were willing and able to provide data on the precise number of minutes required to cut, make, and trim that garment both in the United States and Colombia. I was able also to obtain estimates of average labor productivity in the manufacturing of specific garments in Colombia, East Asia, and the United States from a firm of international consultants that has specialized in the apparel business for several decades and that knows all three geographic areas well. The average figures for Colombia and the United States that were provided by the consulting firm are roughly consistent with the data provided by the Colombian managers; if anything, the consultant's estimates of labor productivity in Columbia are a little higher than those derived from the interviews.

The set of information that is available on labor productivity in the garment industry in Colombia, East Asia, and the United States from both the interviews and the consulting firm is summarized in Table 4.[2] For the present purposes, two main features emerge from the table. First, on average, labor productivity appears to be 30–50% higher in East Asia than in Colombia, whereas productivity in the United States may be up to 50% higher again. That is, if a given number of workers produces 100 shirts or pairs of jeans per hour in Colombia, the same number of workers produces 130–150 garments per hour in East Asia and 200 or more per hour in the United States. Second, the two Colombian firms that were able to give reliable before-and-after figures for productivity report that, after they received technical assistance from U.S. firms, their labor productivity increased by 110% (firm No. 2 in jeans) and 67% (firm No. 1 in suit coats), respectively. Although none of the other sample firms provided before-and-after productivity data at this level of detail, most of the larg-

TABLE 4

Labor Productivity in the Clothing Industry in Columbia, East Asia, and the United States, 1978[a]

Type of garment and location of producer	Number of garments produced per machine operator in an 8-hr day	Index (U.S. = 100)[b]
Classic jeans (five pockets)		
Colombian average	19–24	43–55
East Asian average	28–30	64–68
U.S. good average firm	44	100
U.S. theoretically best possible	53	120
Colombian firm no. 1		
Actual output	9	24
Best possible output is no raw material holdups, etc.	16	45
U.S. firm producing identical garment	37	100
Colombian firm no. 2		
Output in 1975 before help from U.S. firm	10	31
Actual output	21	66
U.S. firm producing identical garment	32	100
Colombian firm no. 3		
Output that "would be good"	16–19	36–43
Colombian firm no. 4	12	27
Colombian firm no. 5	14	32

[2] The full table in Morawetz (1981) includes also information on men's casual slacks and men's suits. The discussion in the text applies to these categories as well.

TABLE 4 (*cont.*)

Type of garment and location of producer	Number of garments produced per machine operator in an 8-hr day	Index (U.S. = 100)[b]
Men's dress shirts (single pocket, banded collar, about $9 at Sears or $11 at dept. store, branded)		
Colombian average (a guess)	~16	~57
East Asian average	23	82
U.S. good average firm	28	100
U.S. theoretically best possible	37	132
Colombian average	<24	<67
Breakeven point with U.S. wages	24	67
U.S. and East Asian average	~36	100
Colombian firm no. 1	6–7	21–25
Colombian firm no. 2	5–6	18–21
Men's tailored suit coats (grade X)		
Colombian average	3	38
East Asian average	5	63
U.S. good average firm	8	100
Colombian firm no. 1		
Output before help from U.S. firm	3	43
Actual output	5	71
Colombian firm no. 2		
Producing identical garment	3	43
U.S. firm producing identical garment	7	100

[a] *Sources*: The first sets of figures under jeans, shirts, and suit coats are from an international apparel consultant in New York (15–20% should be subtracted from these figures if style changes, downtime of machines, and the like are to be taken into account). The second set of figures under shirts is from a U.S. shirt manufacturer. All other data are from interviews with Colombian firms.

[b] Where U.S. figures for identical garments are available, they are used as the base for this index. In all other cases, the base is the output of a good average U.S. firm as indicated in the table.

est exporters reported that they, too, had had to increase labor productivity substantially before they were able to begin exporting to the United States or Europe.

It is because labor productivity often has to rise substantially before domestic firms can enter the world market that the *first* surge of exports in any particular industry may well do little for total employment in the industry. This effect appears to be quite straightforward; nevertheless, to the best of my knowledge, it has yet to be mentioned in the literature on the employment-generating effects of labor-intensive manufactured exports. In a word: before Colombian clothing firms could begin to compete in the international apparel market, they had to increase their rates of labor productivity substantially, often by as much as 50–100%. This, in turn, meant that the first surge of exports tended to be produced with the existing labor force. It was only after the volume of exports exceeded 50–100% of preexport production levels that new workers had to be hired. Colombia's exports of clothing never exceeded 25% of the total volume of production in the 1970s; indeed, the proportion was 15% or less during most of the period. At the level of the individual enterprise, half of the 30 Colombian firms that were interviewed were exporting less than 30% of their total value of output during the mid to late 1970s. *This means that, with the exception of a small number of exceptionally fast growing exporters, most companies needed to hire few, if any, extra workers to cope with increased production for export. The real increase in demand for workers would have occurred only if exports had grown much faster than they did.*

III. CAUSES OF THE RISE AND FALL OF COLOMBIA'S CLOTHING EXPORTS

Before 1970, Colombia's clothing exports were negligible. Between 1970 and 1974–1975, exports to all markets grew rapidly, but after 1975, sales to the United States and Europe declined sharply.[3] The reasons for these trends can be divided into price and nonprice factors.

A. Price Factors

The most important single reason why Colombia's exports of clothing to the United States and Europe began to grow rapidly after 1970 is that the government's exchange rate and export incentive policies had begun to make them profitable (Table 5). Before 1967, Colombian governments tended to tackle balance-of-payment problems by carrying out a jump devaluation, waiting until inflation had eroded away its benefits, and then jump devaluing again. As a result, between 1953 and 1967, there were never more than two consecutive years in which the real effective exchange rate moved in the same direction.[4] This made exporting a risky

[3] For details, see Morawetz (1981).
[4] The real effective exchange rate is the nominal or official exchange rate adjusted for export incentives and for domestic and foreign price increases. As used in this study, it measures the relative profitability of exporting as opposed to selling goods domestically.

business indeed, because a businessman could never be sure what his real returns would be from one year to the next.

From 1967 onward, there was a dramatic and well-publicized change. As a result of the introduction of a crawling peg exchange rate and other export incentive measures, for the first time in over a quarter of a century the real effective exchange rate rose continuously, or at least did not fall significantly, for six consecutive years. Not surprisingly, it took two or three years until this new policy began to bear fruit. It took time until entrepreneurs began to believe that exporting goods other than coffee and petroleum might be feasible and profitable and that this profitability might be maintained; time until plant and equipment could be adapted and workers retrained to meet the stringent requirements of export markets; and time until buyers could be found, orders received, goods produced, and an export momentum built up.

Then, in 1973, this time without any official pronouncement—on the contrary, government statements continued and continue to stress the importance of exports for the country's future—the new post-1967 policy was reversed. For the next six years, the real effective exchange rate underwent an almost continuous decline. Once again, it took two or three years until entrepreneurs perceived what was happening, believed that it was likely to continue, adjusted their plans, and either cut back their exports or switched them to easier neighboring markets. By late 1978, depending on the particular index chosen, the real effective exchange rate was either equal to or 15% *below* the level at which it had stood in the balance of payments crisis year of 1967. The improvement in the profitability of exporting relative to selling domestically that had been achieved during 1967–1973 had been totally reversed.

The second main price-related factor restraining the growth of clothing exports is the level of protection afforded both to outputs and to inputs. The protection afforded *outputs* has made selling domestically more profitable in general than selling to the difficult, if potentially lucrative, markets in the United States and Europe. Thus, a producer who saturates the domestic market in a particular item is likely to prefer to diversify into other goods for domestic sale or, at best, to export to the small, not-well-known, high-price markets in Venezuela and the Caribbean, rather than trying to export to the United States and Europe. (Venezuela's free port, the Margarita Islands, was the destination of half of Colombia's clothing exports in 1978, and Panama and the Caribbean took a further 20%). On the *input* side, local textile producers received 64–69% nominal protection against imports throughout 1967–1979, this despite the fact that they were exporting tens of millions of dollars worth of textiles annually during much of this time. Furthermore, most synthetic textiles were subject to

TABLE 5

Nominal, Real, Effective, and Real Effective Exchange Rates for Clothing Exports, 1967–1978[a]

Item	1967	1968	1969	1970	1971	1972	1973	1974	1975	1976	1977	1978
Nominal exchange rate												
Pesos per dollar	14.88	16.48	17.53	18.68	20.26	22.14	23.98	26.66	31.58	35.21	37.20	39.06[b]
Index	100.0	110.8	117.8	125.5	136.2	148.8	161.2	179.2	212.2	236.6	250.0	262.5
Wholesale clothing prices												
Colombia	100.0	104.3	111.5	119.0	131.9	145.6	181.7	249.2	285.8	334.0	405.4[c]	492.7
United States	100.0	103.6	107.4	110.8	112.9	114.8	119.0	129.5	133.4	139.9	147.3	152.4[b]
General consumer prices												
Colombia[d]	100.0	105.9	116.6	124.5	135.8	153.8	185.1	229.6	281.7	338.6	448.7	530.4
United States	100.0	104.2	109.8	116.3	121.3	125.3	133.2	147.7	161.3	170.6	181.8	195.5
Real exchange rate, deflating												
With wholesale clothing prices	100.0	110.0	113.5	116.9	116.5	117.3	105.6	93.1	99.1	99.1	90.8	81.2
With general consumer prices	100.0	109.0	111.0	117.3	121.6	121.2	116.0	115.3	121.5	119.3	101.3	96.7
Effective exchange rate												
Limited companies												
Not using Vallejo Plan	100.0	112.0	119.4	127.7	138.7	151.8	165.2	187.6	200.3	224.7	249.3	273.3
Using Vallejo Plan	100.0	111.7	117.6	125.2	136.3	150.2	155.7	161.3	183.8	204.6	219.4	234.5
Public companies												
Not using Vallejo Plan	100.0	112.0	119.3	127.5	138.5	151.6	164.9	183.4	189.0	212.0	233.0	254.2
Using Vallejo Plan	100.0	111.7	117.6	125.2	136.3	150.1	156.0	156.3	175.2	195.1	208.4	222.4

Real effective exchange rate, deflating with wholesale clothing prices

Limited companies												
Not using Vallejo Plan	100.0	111.3	115.0	118.8	118.7	119.7	108.1	97.5	93.4	94.1	90.5	84.5
Using Vallejo Plan	100.0	110.9	113.3	116.5	116.7	118.4	101.9	83.8	85.8	85.7	79.7	72.5
Public companies												
Not using Vallejo Plan	100.0	111.2	114.9	118.7	118.5	119.5	108.0	95.3	88.2	88.8	84.6	78.6
Using Vallejo Plan	100.0	110.9	113.3	116.5	116.7	118.4	102.2	81.2	81.8	81.7	75.7	68.8

Real effective exchange rate, deflating with general consumer prices

Limited companies												
Not using Vallego Plan	100.0	110.2	112.4	119.2	123.9	123.7	118.9	120.8	114.6	113.2	100.9	100.7
Using Vallejo Plan	100.0	109.8	110.7	116.9	121.8	122.4	112.1	103.8	105.2	103.1	88.9	86.4
Public companies												
Not using Vallejo Plan	100.0	110.1	112.3	119.1	123.7	123.5	118.7	118.0	108.2	106.8	94.3	93.7
Using Vallejo Plan	100.0	109.9	110.8	116.9	121.8	122.3	112.3	100.6	100.3	98.3	84.4	82.0

[a] For the definitions of the different exchange rates, see text. Figures are based on 1967 = 100 index. *Sources:* Nominal exchange rate: averages of quarterly data presented in International Monetary Fund, *International Financial Statistics*, 1967–1978; Wholesale clothing price indexes: Branco de la República, *Revista*, various issues; U.S. Department of Commerce, *Business Statistics 1977*, p. 50 and *Survey of Current Business*, Dec. 1978, p. S-9; consumer price indexes: International Monetary Fund, *International Financial Statistics*, 1967–1978; Export incentives: See Morawetz (1980, Tables 2.1 and 2.2).

[b] Projected.

[c] A typographical error in the published data has been corrected.

[d] Index for blue-collar workers.

prior licensing throughout almost the entire period. As a result of this tar-
iff-licensing combination, Colombian textile producers were able to sell
their fabrics domestically at prices that were 50–100% above world
levels. Because the value of the fabric is often about 50% of the value of a
garment, this made it difficult indeed for Colombian clothing producers to
compete in the low-price U.S. and European markets.

The Colombian clothing exporters interviewed for this study generally
blamed cheap labor, heavy government subsidization, or cheap transport
costs for the superior performance of Hong Kong, Korea, and Taiwan.
On all three counts, they were wrong.

Because of rapidly rising East Asian standards of living, garment industry wages in Hong Kong are not 50–100% above those in Colombia,
whereas wages in Korea and Taiwan are at least not significantly below
Colombia's. Government export subsidies are nonexistent in Hong Kong;
in Korea and Taiwan, they seem to be no greater than in Colombia. In
transport, if, as is common, Colombians, use air whereas East Asians ship
by sea, it is the Colombians who have a significant advantage: they can
land goods in New York for the same transport costs as East Asians but at
a saving of four weeks in in-transit time. The fact that transport and com-
munication services tend to operate more frequently and more reliably in
East Asia partly, but only partly, offsets this advantage.

B. Nonprice Factors

Nonprice factors, too, have played an important role in explaining Colombia's inability to increase garment exports at a more rapid rate and,
hence, its failure to increase substantially employment in the garment industry. Colombian quality control has not always been up to U.S. and European standards. Goods have not always been delivered on time; because the four selling seasons for apparel in the United States and Europe
last only 12 weeks each, a delay of only a week or two can be crucial. The
Vallejo Plan drawback scheme, under which exporters may import raw
materials that are to be embodied in finished products and reexported, involves an administrative delay of 2 weeks or so. Once materials have arrived, additional delays from 4 to 6 weeks are encountered in clearing
goods through customs; bribery in customs and theft in the ports are problems as well. These inadequacies, difficulties, and delays tend to offset
the one big advantage that Colombian firms have over their East Asian
rivals—the ability to quote short lead times, or, in the case of exports carried out under the U.S. 807 off-shore assembly scheme, short cycle times.

Furthermore, these problems tend to compound themselves. Because only a narrow range of fabrics of world quality is available from local textile producers—indigo denim and corduroy are the main items—the available range of garments made of domestic fabrics is limited. By contrast, the standard buyers' refrain is that in Hong Kong (or Korea, or Taiwan) you can get any garment that you want, made of any material (cotton, wool, synthetics, leather, fur) at a reasonable price, of acceptable quality, and delivered on time. In addition, because Colombia has not done well in the export business by world standards, not one U.S. or European garment importer or retailer maintains a full-time buying office in the country, and relatively few buyers come to visit. In East Asia, by contrast, there are tens of buying offices in each of the main exporting countries, and hundreds of itinerant buyers pass through each year.

One nonprice factor that has *not* been a major cause of Colombia's disappointing export performance is U.S. quotas on imports of apparel. During 1975–1976 and 1978–1979, in 70% of the 60 apparel categories that are listed in the United States–Colombia bilateral agreements, less than 10% of the allotted quota was utilized. Only in two categories was 85% or more of the quota utilized.

IV. GENERALIZING TO OTHER INDUSTRIES AND OTHER LATIN AMERICAN COUNTRIES

It may be useful to examine the extent to which the conclusions and policy implications derived from this study can be generalized to other Colombian manufacturing industries. In the absence of similarly detailed studies of other industries, the following discussion is necessarily somewhat tentative.

Clothing is similar to other industries in which developing countries have achieved export success in that average wages are low, the share of wages in value added is high, and economies of scale are unimportant (Helleiner, 1976). Garments tend to be differentiated from each other more than some other developing-country manufactured exports, but the marketing problems that arise from this differentiation are generally taken care of by the developed-country buyers. This all-important role of the buyers is by no means limited to the clothing industry; rather, it is common in many types of developing-country manufactured exports (Hone, 1974; Morawetz, 1981).

The most important problems that have restricted Colombia's clothing exports seem likely to have affected other Colombian industrial export and potential-export industries as well: a combination of high protection for domestic sale of final goods and declining real effective exchange rates that has caused a decline in the relative and absolute profitability of exporting as opposed to selling domestically;[5] lack of access to inputs at world prices because of high protection granted to domestic input producers and because of problems with the Vallejo Plan, the ports, and customs; and low labor productivity, inadequate quality control, and unpunctuality of deliveries resulting from management deficiencies and cultural factors. Clothing is also typical of other Colombian industries in the disproportionate importance of a small number of firms in total foreign sales; the apparent inability of most small firms to export whether alone, through intermediaries, or through consortia; the failure of the Free Zones to stimulate exports (with the partial exception of manufactured metal products); and the inability of local exporters to capture a significant share of total marketing profits.[6]

One difference between clothing and other industries is that seasons are more important and fashions change more frequently in garments, which means that short lead times and punctuality in delivering are more important in apparel than in most industries. Nevertheless, no exporter of manufactured goods is likely to keep clients for long if the deliveries are continually late or if lead times are weeks longer than those of competitors. For example, one U.S. manufacturer closed down an electronics assembly plant that it had established in Haiti in favor of one in Mexico because, even though Mexican wages were more than double those in Haiti, the cycle time was two weeks shorter in Mexico (Keesing, 1978a).

It might be thought that quality control is more important in apparel than in other industries, yet for many manufactured products this is surely not the case. The damage that results when trousers shrink, colors run, or zippers break can hardly be compared with the consequences that would ensue if a lathe's cutting edge or an automobile's wheel nuts were defective. Indeed, there must be few manufactured goods in which quality control is not of primary importance. It might seem, too, that it is more important for exporters of garments to have access to a wide range of imported inputs than it is for producers of other goods, yet some 90% of all manufactured exports from developing nations originate in countries that guarantee their producers this kind of access.

Finally, perhaps the most important difference between apparel and other sectors for the present discussion is that clothing is currently one of the few industries in which developing-country exports are subject to quota restrictions. The distribution of quotas among exporting nations tends to be based on historical performance; thus, Colombia's garment

---

[5] The real effective exchange rate deflated by general consumer prices shows a similar trend over time to that deflated by wholesale clothing prices.

[6] For the references supporting these statements, see Morawetz (1981).

quotas are only a fraction the size of those of Hong Kong, Korea, and Taiwan. This means that even if all obstacles to increased exports were removed tomorrow, Colombia could still look forward to only modest rates of increase in its exports of apparel to the United States and Europe.[7] This difference will not necessarily continue in the future; it seems at least possible that the increasingly protectionist developed countries will impose quantitative restrictions sooner or later on imports of other manufactured goods as well. These quotas, too, are likely to be distributed on the basis of past export performance, which serves to underline the urgency of the need for policy reform in Columbia if exporting manufactured goods is to continue to be a central focus of the national development strategy.

In summary, clothing shares several important characteristics with other industries in which developing countries have achieved export success to date; and the key problems that have impeded Colombia's clothing exports in the past seem likely to have retarded the exports of other Colombian manufactured goods too. Thus, the findings of this study may well be of some relevance, not only to clothing, but also to other Colombian export and potential-export industries.

Finally, to what extent are the conclusions and policy implications of this study likely to be relevant to Latin American countries other than Colombia? In most relevant respects, Colombia is about as close to an "average" Latin American country as can be found. It ranks fourth after Brazil, Mexico, and Argentina in size of population, and fifth after these three and Venezuela in size of gross national product (GNP). It is neither among the most- nor the least-industrialized Latin American nations; in terms of GNP per capita, it is poorer than many countries but it is by no means the poorest; the growth rate of its GNP per capita has been close to, if slightly below, the Latin American average for two and a half decades; and its distribution of wealth and income is typically skewed (World Bank, 1977; Morawetz, 1977).

In total value of clothing exports, Colombia ranks third with Argentina behind Mexico and Brazil; in total value of exports of all manufactured goods, it ranks fourth behind Brazil, Mexico, and Argentina. In clothing exports per head of population, Colombia ($2) is surpassed only by Mexico ($3); whereas in per capita exports of all manufactured goods, Colombia ($27) is surpassed by Mexico ($38) and Argentina ($37), but ranks

[7] The possible increases would be modest, but they would by no means be zero. To begin, clothing exports could increase severalfold before all the existing quota is utilized. After that, the successful East Asian strategy of upgrading items within quota categories (and hence increasing the value of exports while the volume is held constant) could be followed.

ahead of Brazil ($21), Chile ($11), Venezuela ($10), and most, if not all, other Latin American countries. By Latin American standards, therefore, Colombia has been at least moderately successful as an exporter of clothing and other manufactured goods; certainly, its inability to compete with Hong Kong, Taiwan, and Korea has not been unusual (Tables 1 and 6).

Colombia has been typical in the timing and nature of its policy changes: several other Latin American countries shifted from import substitution to export promotion strategies during the mid to late 1960s. It has also been about average for Latin America in its degree of political and policy continuity: some less democratic countries have had more stable economic policies, but other nations (Chile, Peru, Argentina, Bolivia) have been much more unstable.

Many of the problems that have hampered Colombia's exports of clothing and other manufactured goods seem likely to have been similarly

TABLE 6

Per Capita Exports of Clothing and All Manufactured Goods for Selected East Asian and Latin American Countries, 1976[a]

| | Per capita exports ($) | |
Country	All manufactured goods	Clothing[b]
East Asian countries		
Hong Kong	1620	727
Taiwan	433	83
Korea	185	51
Average[c]	359	108
Latin American countries		
Mexico	38[d]	3[d,e]
Argentina	37	2
Colombia	27	2
Brazil	21	1
Chile	11[f]	—
Venezuela	10[e]	—
Average[c]	25	1

[a] *Sources*: Column 2, Chenery and Keesing (1978, Table 8); column 3, United Nations (1977); Keesing (1978, Table 10).
[b] Dashes indicate a negligible amount.
[c] Weighted average.
[d] Estimated including border zone, with the help of U.S. as well as Mexican data.
[e] 1975.
[f] 1974.

important in other Latin American countries as well. In the face of sharply fluctuating world prices for natural-resource-based exports and moderate-to-runaway domestic rates of inflation, few countries have managed to maintain constant real effective exchange rates (and hence constant real returns to exporting) for any length of time. In most countries export subsidies were simply grafted onto the existing import substitution structure; because protection against imports remains high, the incentive to sell domestically is still greater than that to export (Balassa, 1978). Many countries still hamper their firms' access to imported inputs when domestically produced substitutes are available (Balassa, 1978); and the port, customs, transport, and communications problems of Colombia are by no means unique.[8] Colombia's low level of labor productivity in garment production is typical for Latin America—if anything, Colombian productivity is 5% above the Latin American average.[9] Some of the cultural characteristics thay may help to cause Colombia's relatively inadequate productivity, quality control, and punctuality performance (for instance, the relatively relaxed attitude toward time) are shared with much of Latin America.[10]

Colombia differs from much of Latin America in being ideally located to sell to the U.S. east coast market; but Central America and the Caribbean islands share this locational advantage, whereas Mexico has still easier access to the U.S. market. The Colombian drug trade has distorted the nation's economy somewhat; but the main effect has been to cause a domestic boom that exacerbates rather than causes the differential in profitability between selling goods domestically and exporting them. It seems unlikely that growers, processors, and smugglers of drugs would themselves be producing and exporting manufactured goods if the drug trade were shut off. Illegal sectors of economic activity are hardly unknown elsewhere in Latin America.

In summary, Colombia is in many respects as "average" a Latin American country as one could find; its manufactured export performance has been quite good by Latin American standards; and many of the problems that have impeded its exports of clothing and other manufactured products seem likely to have retarded the manufactured exports of other Latin American countries, too. Thus, the findings of this study may be of relevance, not only to Colombia, but also to some other Latin American nations.

[8] In Haiti, it can take from one day to two months for imported goods to clear customs, depending on who the importer is (Thoumi, 1979).

[9] Data were supplied by a New York consulting firm specializing in the garment industry worldwide.

[10] In Bolivia, difficulties in standardizing quality control, among other things, have hampered exports of handicraft garments (Inter-American Development Banks, 1979).

V. CONCLUSION

The experience of Colombia's clothing industry indicates that, after having been sheltered by protection against competing imports, firms generally have to increase labor productivity substantially before they can begin to compete in the difficult world markets. This, in turn, implies that until exports reach 50–100% or so of the value of preexport production, they may induce little, if any, extra hiring of labor. Because few Colombian garment-making firms have exported volumes as great as these, this may explain why the increase in Colombia's clothing exports has led to relatively little increase in the demand for labor in the nation's apparel industry. Because clothing may not be too untypical of other industries in which manufactured goods are exported and because Colombia is, in many ways, not untypical of Latin America, this hypothesis may help to explain why exports of labor-intensive manufactured goods from Latin America have created less additional employment to date than might have been expected on the basis of simple extrapolation from the East Asian experience.

REFERENCES

Balassa, B. (1978). "Export Incentives and Export Performance in Developing Countries: A Comparative Analysis," *Weltwirtschaftliches Archiv* **114,** No. 1, 24–61.
Chenery, H., and Keesing, D. (1978). "The Changing Role and Composition of LDC Exports," mimeo, Washington, D.C.: World Bank.
Cole, D., and Westphal, L. (1975). "The Contribution of Exports to Employment in Korea," In *Trade and Employment in Korea* (W. Hong and A. Krueger, eds), Seoul: Korea Development Institute.
Helleiner, G. K. (1976). "Industry Characteristics and the Competitiveness of Manufacturers from Less Developed Countries," *Weltwirtschaftliches Archiv* **112,** No. 3, 507–524.
Hone, A. (1974). "Multinational Corporations and Multinational Buying Groups: Their Impact on the Growth of Asia's Exports of Manufactures—Myths and Realities," *World Development* **2,** No. 2 (February), 145–149.
Inter-American Development Bank (IDB) (1979). "Bolivian Handicrafts: A Pastime is Converted into a Vital National Industry," *IDB News* **6,** No. 8 (October), 3–4.
Keesing, D. (1978a). "Developing Countries' Exports of Textiles and Clothing: Perspectives and Policy Choices," mimeo, Washington, D.C.: World Bank (first draft).
Keesing, D. (1978b). "Program on 'Production Sharing,' Flagstaff, Arizona, July 14, 1978," mimeo, Washington, D.C.: World Bank.
Liang, K. S., and Liang, C. I. (1975–1976). "Exports and Employment in Taiwan," *Conference on Population and Economic Development in Taiwan,* Taipei: Academia Sinica.
Morawetz, D. (1977). *Twenty-five Years of Economic Development,* Baltimore, Maryland: Johns Hopkins Press.
Morawetz, D. (1981). *Why the Emperor's New Clothes Are Not Made in Colombia.* London and New York: Oxford Univ. Press.

Plesch, P. A. (1979). "Statistical Trends in Developing Countries' Exports and Imports of Manufactures," mimeo, Washington, D.C.: World Bank.

Thoumi, F. (1979). "Socio-political Obstacles to Economic Development in Haiti, with Special Analysis of the Export Assembly Manufacturers," mimeo, Washington, D.C.: Inter-American Development Bank.

Watanabe, S. (1972). "Exports and Employment: The Case of the Republic of Korea," *International Labour Review* **106,** No. 6 (December), 495–526.

World Bank (1978). "Atlas." Washington, D.C.: World Bank.

United Nations (1977). *Yearbook of International Trade Statistics.*

DAVID MORAWETZ*
Deparment of Economics
Boston University
Boston, Massachusetts

* Present address: 26 Tourello Avenue, E. Hawthorn, Victoria, Australia.

Part II

External Instability

Chapter 5

Old and New Forms of External Instability in Latin America: Sources, Mechanisms of Transmission, and Policies

Ricardo Ffrench-Davis

I. INTRODUCTION

Instability has been a common feature of less developed countries' (LDCs') economies. The phenomenon is due partly to domestic sources, either of climatic or social origin, or is policy induced. However, a significant source of instability originates in the world economy.

The most documented source of instability has been that of export proceeds, given that exports have usually been concentrated, predominantly, in one or two raw materials with highly unstable prices. As is well known, this phenomenon has been characteristic not only of the smaller and poorer LDCs but also of Latin American countries (LACs), despite their relatively larger size and higher economic development. In fact, during the fifties and sixties, for several LACs, one basic commodity generated over 50% of exports.

91

Since the mid-sixties, several changes have been taking place in the mostly semiindustrialized LACs. First, in many countries the primary export activities have been nationalized; thus the LDCs improve their share of the surplus or economic rent of their natural resources, but they also get the full burden of price instability. Second, exports have become more diversified; this tends to reduce the instability of the quantum and unit values of exports but also adds new commodities to the export basket. These commodities tend to be demanded in the domestic market more intensively than the main export. In other words, the share of exportables in domestic output increases and their weight in domestic demand tends to rise even faster. Third, several countries have liberalized their imports and have eliminated nontariff restrictions and tariff redundancies; this trend tends to promote exports, but it also facilitates the transmission of external stability or instability to the domestic economy. Fourth, capital flows have increased steeply for the region as a whole: as long as they remained "large," they softened the intensity of domestic adjustments in the face of changes of the barter terms of trade (in response to increases in oil prices or to fluctuations of the remainder tradables). However, under feasible assumptions, they have added three streams of instability: (a) to monetary management and the composition of base money, when capital flows are left completely free or are misregulated, (b) to exchange-rate policy, when this policy responds to transitory changes in reserves derived from the ups and downs of capital flows, and (c) to overall balance of payments, when the supply of foreign funds suffers abrupt shifts because of changes in the "confidence" of lenders in specific debtor countries, in interest rates, or in the general availability of funds in international capital markets.

The issue of external instability has not been the first priority of economic research. However, the literature on business cycles, on dynamic adjustment in response to alternative exchange-rate and fiscal and monetary policies, on the firm under uncertainty, and on the economics of limited information is especially relevant for the understanding of instability originated externally. Of course, external and domestic instability must have analytical and empirical frameworks with a lot in common.

Section II of this chapter concentrates on the study of the sources of external instability that seem to be most relevant for Latin American countries; Section III discusses the mechanisms of transmission of instability and some of its effects on the process of adjustment of the domestic economy, in the face of changes in the international setting; and Section IV focuses on some issues related to the design and scope of domestic policies geared toward reducing the effects of external instability. Several representative pieces of theoretical and empirical research are surveyed during the discussion; the corresponding selective view of the state of the art shows that many questions still remain open for future research.

The main point of the chapter is that external instability is a relevant issue for LDCs and for semiindustrialized countries. The policy–recipe of accumulating international reserves in "good" years and disbursing them in "bad" years and/or letting futures markets operate is extremely incomplete and tends to ignore the actual problems faced by economic authorities. Criteria for decisions of when and how much to accumulate are still weak or simplistic, with limited empirical basis. Questions related to the effects of reserve policy-cum-external instability on producers, consumers, government, and money markets are still open, and so on. In what follows we intend to bring to light some of the more crucial issues.

II. SOURCES OF EXTERNAL INSTABILITY

There are three aggregate channels communicating the domestic economy with the external world: exports, imports, and capital movements. The most conventional approach assumes that the small developing country faces a given international market. However, even if it were not influenced by the behavior of the LDC, the external market would not be static; it changes constantly and in that process suffers some instability and generates uncertainty. But even "small" countries may influence specific segments of those international markets with which they relate, as well as the policies of "large" countries (Keesing, 1979, pp. 60–61). In brief, integrating with the international economy may bring trade gains and stability, but it may also bring instability and both the allocative and distributive costs associated with it.

Research has focused primarily on exports of basic commodities, but exports of services (principally tourism) and imports have also been sources of instability, and since 1973, oil has been an example of external negative shocks for the large majority of LACs. The diversification of exports has brought manufactured goods into the picture; the recurrence of quantitative restrictions, countervailing tariffs, and "voluntary" export restraints (VERs) imposed by importing developed countries represent a source of instability for certain lines of exports of interest to LDCs. Finally, aside from trade flows, capital movements have been gaining an increasing weight in the balance of payments of the region, fostered by the growth of international financial markets; these financial flows have an influence on domestic stability, with both positive and negative implications.

A. Instability of Trade Flows

There are several empirical works on instability, focused mainly on exports of commodities. Research concentrates on variables such as the origin of instability (whether it is price or quantity changes, demand or supply shifts), the effects on producers income, the role of commodity and geographical concentration, the domestic consumption of exportables, and the effect of the size and per capita income of the exporting country (see, for instance, Massell, 1970). Practically all research has operated with indexes of instability of export receipts and prices in current dollars[1] and has estimated regression equations for cross-country data. Data refer usually to samples of LDCs, but some studies compare LDCs with developed countries, and most cover different periods encompassed within 1946 and 1972.

The results diverge from one author to another, but some points emerge rather conclusively. First, export instability (XS) is notoriously larger in LDCs than in developed countries. The mean XD is larger in LDCs by between one-third (MacBean, 1966, for 1946–1958) and more than double (Erb and Schiavo-Campo, 1969, for 1954–1966; IMF–IBRD, 1969, for 1950–1965). Second, XS tends to be positively correlated with commodity concentration and negatively correlated with size of the country (Massell, 1970)[2]. Concentration is a very distinctive feature; 55 countries depend for more than half of their export earnings on one agricultural product; the average instability of these main products was 16% in 1967–1972 as compared with an average of 12% for total national agricultural exports (Lancieri, 1979).

Third, instability is determined *by changes in both prices and volumes;* on average, both tend to reinforce each other, with rates of change in receipts being larger than in prices or volumes separately (Glesakos, 1973);[3] instability of *quantities* appears to be more important than that of *prices* (Glesakos, 1973; Murray, 1978). Fourth, XS—in earnings, prices,

---

[1] In some cases, export values have been deflated by an index of import prices (MacBean, 1966); in many cases instability has been defined as a coefficient of trend-adjusted export receipts. This is an implicit imperfect form of clearing the data of world inflation.

[2] Yotopoulos and Nugent (1976, p. 339) partially dispute this conclusion. Conversely, Helleiner (1971, p. 84) indicates that, as shown by Massell (1970), *if other relevant variables are controlled,* concentration emerges significantly correlated with export instability. One very relevant variable is the particular relation between central countries and their former colonies. Additionally, Tuong and Yeats (1976) demonstrate the influence of alternative degrees of aggregation on the indexes of concentration.

[3] Murray (1978), with data for 1952–1971, arrives at a partially different result. For a sample of 25 LDCs, he finds that for 15 countries the covariance of the logs of price and quantity is negative.

and quantum—turns out to be smaller in the sixties as compared with the fifties (Kenen and Voivodas, 1972, Table 2); the fall in price instability is relatively larger for developed countries (Murray, 1978, Table 1). The remaining results are less conclusive, providing divergent answers, depending on the period, countries, and variables included.

Here we will take a brief look at annual data on total exports of goods for 16 LACs (the 11 LAFTA countries and the 5 CACM countries), for the period 1951–1979; in the last year, they cover 93% of all Latin American exports. We broke the data into sub-periods in order to test the evolution of instability. First, we were faced with the usual problem of how to measure instability. Two indicators are used here: the average percentage annual variation

$$PV = (100/n) \sum [(X_t - X_{t-1})/X_{t-1}]$$

and S, the standard deviation of the residuals from a trend divided by the mean of the variable. The trend is obtained from an ordinary least squares estimate of the linear relation between the log of the dependent variable (prices or quantities or value) and time; this is very crude, but it is common in the literature on stability.

As is well known, there is not a unique, ideal index.[4] The two indicators chosen here have relevant, different implications. The PV takes the previous year as a reference for measuring change; thus, it measures the intensity on a year-to-year basis, without considering autoregressive properties (or duration and cumulative features of disturbances). Conversely, S measures deviations from the trend; thus it is corrected by a trend component, and it does not take into account (directly) the actual level in the previous year. The PV measures instability as seen by economic authorities, as if they had accommodated their policy decision to the actual outcome of the previous year, regardless of its position with respect to "normal" or trend values. The mean S is the opposite, being a good measure of instability as seen by authorities concerned exclusively with deviations from the trend, assuming that the trend is predictable.

In Table 1, data on the PV of prices, quantum, and value of exports for the 16 countries selected are presented for each of the subperiods into which we separated the data. Three comments on the methodology are necessary. First, world inflation became an increasingly relevant feature throughout the period: in the first two decades, world prices rose by roughly one-fifth, whereas during the seventies, international prices

[4] Brief discussions on the subject appear in Massell (1970, Section 1), Kenen and Voivodas (1972, Section 1), and Yotopoulos and Nugent (1976, pp. 330–331). A high correlation between alternative indexes is commonly asserted; see especially the latter reference.

TABLE 1

Instability of Value, Quantum, and Prices of Exports: 1951–1979[a]

Country	1951–1960			1961–1970			1971–1979		
	Prices	Quantum	Value	Prices	Quantum	Value	Prices	Quantum	Value
LAFTA									
Argentina	7.3	15.8	17.9	5.2	9.8	8.7	8.8	17.2	18.0
Brazil	8.7	11.0	10.6	5.7	9.4	8.6	9.3	5.9	10.4
Chile	10.8	8.1	12.6	7.3	4.4	5.8	16.1	11.5	27.1
Mexico	4.6	5.7	8.1	3.7	5.8	5.7	7.8	10.4	10.6
Paraguay	10.7	12.1	10.3	4.4	8.4	9.2	10.4	5.2	13.9
Uruguay	11.1	25.0	22.9	6.7	13.6	10.9	11.5	13.9	13.2
Andean Pact									
Bolivia	8.6	9.0	16.3	9.3	7.7	12.4	16.7	10.1	18.2
Colombia	9.6	9.5	15.5	7.1	5.0	8.6	19.9	13.1	12.1
Ecuador	8.4	9.8	15.3	6.7	10.9	8.8	22.3	16.3	25.1
Peru	7.0	6.8	9.6	5.8	6.4	8.9	15.3	13.2	17.7
Venezuela	6.7	7.9	9.2	5.1	2.8	5.1	22.9	7.7	23.6

CACM									
Costa Rica	10.1	15.1	10.4	2.6	7.1	7.9	11.6	5.5	11.7
El Salvador	9.9	7.4	8.4	4.1	5.9	6.0	13.9	6.4	13.3
Guatemala	8.4	5.4	7.4	3.3	10.4	10.1	10.6	4.8	13.4
Honduras	8.2	13.3	17.3	4.9	8.0	10.6	8.6	7.7	11.6
Nicaragua	11.1	16.2	10.6	3.0	8.1	9.3	13.4	8.4	16.4
Latin America									
Consolidated average	5.4	4.0	6.5	2.9	1.7	3.2	9.9	5.0	12.2
Simple average of 16 countries	8.8	11.1	12.7	5.3	7.7	8.5	13.7	9.8	16.0

[a] Data are given as average annual percentage variation.

Sources: ECLA (1977; mimeo, September 1980). Prices were deflated by the index of U.S. dollar unit values of manufactured exports of developed countries to LDCs (IPMX); see IBRD (1979, p. 32). Quantum figures were deflated by the average annual rate of growth of each country's quantum. Export receipts (values) were deflated by both the latter and the IPMX. For Latin America, the first row represents the PV of the respective figure for all Latin America (for lack of disaggregated information, it includes the 16 countries, plus the Dominican Republic, Haiti, and Panama); the second row represents an unweighted average of the PVs of each country.

approximately tripled. Consequently, we have deflated figures in current dollars (prices and export receipts) by an index of international inflation. Second, the quantum normally changes from year to year because there is a positive trend in export capacity. These changes can be predicted to some degree, but a country-by-country study would be required. Here we performed a very simple adjustment of the raw data, by measuring the annual PV as $[Q_t - Q_{t-1}(1 + r)]/Q_{t-1}(1 + r)$, where r is the cumulative rate of growth of quantum between 1950–1952 and 1977–1979. This method still leads to an overestimate of the actual instability of Q. Third, because the evolution of instability is not linear, the subperiodization of the data might be crucial. In broad terms, observation of the annual data indicates that changes coincide approximately with the calendar decades 1951– 1960, 1961–1970, and 1971–1979, which are the subperiods that were used in Tables 1–4, but alternative breakdowns (not shown in the tables), which will be discussed later, were also used.

The clearest conclusion derived from Table 1 is that, in fact, price and value instability fell in the sixties, as compared with the fifties, for the large majority of LACs and for the region as a whole; but in the seventies, price and value instability increased for each country, as compared with the previous decade, and for most countries (in all three variables) in comparison with the fifties. Thus, a problem that appeared to recede significantly one decade ago, surged up again with intensified force.

If the subperiodization is changed, the pattern described is confirmed. The results are very sensitive, however, to the disaggregation of the seventies. The years 1970–1972 were a transition toward higher price instability, which reached peak values in 1973–1979: the simple average PV for the 16 countries was 7.6% in the former period and 14.9% in the latter.

Instability of export earnings (PVV) is a combined result of changes in prices (PVP) and quantities (PVQ). Fluctuations of the latter also diminished in the sixties and increased in the seventies; however, changes in quantities along the subperiods were smoother than in prices and proceeds. The result has been an increased weight of price fluctuations: in the first decade, in only 5 countries was PVP larger than PVQ; then in the second decade it was in only 4 countries, increasing to 13 out of the 16 countries in 1971–1979. Finally, for the same period, PVP and PVQ reinforced each other in 13 countries and for the region as a whole.[5]

Data in Table 1 indicate that conclusions derived from prior research, which were strongly influenced by the market behavior in the sixties, might have underestimated the strength of price instability. However, our

---

[5] It must be recalled that the data are biased toward a negative relation between prices and quantum because the estimate of the index of unit prices is derived from the division of the indexes of value and quantum.

results could be influenced by the particular index of instability used and by the method used to operate on the raw data. In Table 2, data for the whole period 1951–1979 are presented, according to three alternative statistical procedures: (a) the same as in Table 1; (b) the same PV based on the raw data; and (c) the mean standard deviation from the trend of real prices, quantum, and value.

The second set of results provides a pattern similar to the first one: although, as expected, figures undeflated by inflation and output trends show indexes of instability somewhat larger than Table 1 suggests, the pattern along the period (not reported in the tables) is also similar in the three methodologies. The figures in the fourth, seventh, and last columns provide an overestimate of "instability." Fitting a unique linear (semilog) trend for the whole period 1951–1979 imposes a heavy burden on the estimate, generating large statistical residuals. That is clearly observed in the case of Venezuela, where output and real prices of oil changed drastically since 1973. By simply allowing the trend to change from one decade to another, the residuals fall and the mean S moves clearly closer to the figures estimated according to the methodology of Table 1.[6]

The main source of price instability is the heavy presence of raw materials. Indeed, they explain most fluctuations of the export price index. The basic data are presented in Table 3. The fourth and fifth columns show the percentage share in total exports for the initial and final five-year periods. In 1951–1955, one commodity represented over 50% of total exports for 9 countries, with an (unweighted) average of 54% for the region. By the end of the period covered by the data, exports had diversified considerably, with only 3 countries having one commodity sharing over 50% of national exports. Interestingly, in the case of 8 countries, there was a shift in the product holding the higher share: meat, coffee, and oil, in two cases each, gained the first place. Notwithstanding the diversification achieved, concentration remained high: only one commodity covered 36% of export receipts for the average LAC (in 1974–1978). The price variability (PV) of the main export is described in the last four columns; there the same pattern of price instability as in Table 1 can be observed, with a fall in 1961–1970 and a large increase in 1971–1978.

Average annual price variations hide fluctuations within the year. For instance, average monthly variations in the price of coffee were 9.5% in 1977 and 6.9% in 1978. In the case of copper, average monthly variations were 8.9% in 1973 and 11.1% in 1974; the higher price exceeded by 270%

[6] The figures are not shown in order to save space. Two examples indicate the change brought about by breaking the trend estimates: (a) the means S for Venezuela are 18%, 5%, and 19% for prices, quantum, and value, respectively; for Latin America, the respective figures are 7%, 4%, and 8%.

TABLE 2

Instability of Prices, Quantum, and Value: Alternative Methodologies: 1951–1979[a]

Country	Prices			Quantum			Value			
	PV nominal[c]	PV real[b]	Mean S from trend[e]	Gross PV[c]	Net PV[b]	Mean S from trend[e]	PV nominal[c]	PV real[d]	Net PV real[b]	Mean S from trend[e]
LAFTA										
Argentina	9.3	7.0	13.6	14.3	14.2	19.4	16.7	13.8	14.7	14.1
Brazil	9.6	7.8	15.1	10.7	8.9	13.4	14.3	10.3	9.8	24.0
Chile	13.4	11.2	19.8	8.7	7.9	11.8	19.6	15.6	14.7	21.1
Mexico	7.6	5.3	7.2	8.2	7.2	13.7	13.4	9.3	8.1	15.6
Paraguay	10.9	8.4	14.6	9.7	8.7	6.6	14.5	11.6	11.0	16.8
Uruguay	11.3	9.7	14.5	17.9	17.6	23.7	17.3	15.6	15.7	23.2
Andean Pact										
Bolivia	15.4	11.3	15.8	9.1	8.9	17.1	19.5	15.9	15.5	24.4
Colombia	12.0	11.9	18.5	9.5	9.1	11.8	14.2	11.4	12.0	18.8
Ecuador	13.6	12.1	18.7	13.3	12.2	17.1	19.7	16.2	16.1	29.8
Peru	11.2	9.2	13.6	9.6	8.6	22.9	15.7	12.3	11.9	26.3
Venezuela	13.4	11.2	32.6	6.3	6.1	22.7	14.7	12.3	12.3	20.7

CACM									
Costa Rica	9.3	8.0	13.1	10.9	9.4	15.1	14.0	11.0	13.7
El Salvador	10.5	9.2	17.0	7.6	6.6	12.5	13.4	9.6	13.2
Guatemala	8.6	7.3	12.6	9.5	6.9	9.2	13.4	11.2	14.5
Honduras	7.3	7.2	8.9	10.1	9.7	15.1	13.9	13.0	17.2
Nicaragua	9.9	9.0	10.7	13.1	11.0	17.7	14.8	13.1	16.9
Latin America									
Consolidated average	7.9	5.9	10.6	5.0	3.5	4.9	11.2	7.6	10.9
Simple average of 16 countries	10.8	9.1	15.4	10.5	9.6	15.6	15.6	12.6	19.4

[a] Data are given as average annual percentages for the period 1951–1979.

[b] These columns are estimated as in Table 1, but cover the whole period 1951–1979.

[c] These columns are built with the raw data.

[d] Based on nominal receipts deflated by IPMX (IBRD, 1979, p. 32).

[e] These correspond to the standard deviation of the annual residual from a linear trend divided by the average of the dependent variable: monetary figures were deflated by IPMX.

Sources: Same as Table 1.

TABLE 3

Main Export: Changing Shares and Prices[a]

Country	Main export		Share in exports of main product (%)[b]		Annual variation of price of main export (%)[c]			
	1951–1955	1974–1978	1951–1955	1974–1978	1951–1960	1961–1970	1971–1978	1951–1978
Argentina	Wheat	Wheat	18.3	11.6	3.5	4.4	19.7	8.5
Bolivia	Tin	Tin	71.4	45.6	7.7	8.8	15.8	10.3
Brazil	Coffee	Coffee	64.6	15.8	14.1	10.2	34.8	18.6
Colombia	Coffee	Coffee	81.8	57.9	14.1	7.9	27.3	15.7
Costa Rica	Bananas	Coffee	46.4	31.4	5.6	7.8	32.6	12.4
Chile	Copper	Copper	60.1	57.1	14.2	17.8	21.5	17.6
Ecuador	Bananas	Oil	44.1	46.5	5.6	5.0	31.5	10.2
El Salvador	Coffee	Coffee	87.0	47.9	13.4	9.4	32.6	17.5
Guatemala	Coffee	Coffee	71.1	34.7[a]	13.4	9.4	32.6	17.5
Honduras	Bananas	Coffee	58.8	27.7	5.6	7.8	32.6	12.4
Mexico	Cotton	Oil	27.5	21.7	4.9	4.1	31.5	11.1
Nicaragua	Coffee	Cotton	38.4	25.6	13.4	6.8	20.3	13.3
Paraguay	Timber	Beef	23.9	12.6	15.5[e]	12.3	21.3	12.8
Peru	Cotton	Copper	29.1	20.5	4.9	11.0	21.5	13.4
Uruguay	Wool	Beef	52.5	20.6	16.2	12.6	21.3	16.0
Venezuela	Oil	Oil	94.2	95.0	7.7	3.9	31.5	13.1

[a] *Sources*: IMF, *International Financial Statistics*, Yearbook 1979 and May 1980, and IBRD (1979).

[b] Data include only exports of goods.

[c] When the main export is not the same in 1951–1955 and in 1974–1978, the procedure adopted is the following: (a) for 1951–1960, the PV (during the decade) of the main export in 1951–1955; (b) for 1961–1970, the simple average of the PVs of the two products; (c) for 1971–1978, the main export 1971–1978; and (d) for 1951–1978, the simple average of the PVs of the two products in the full period.

[d] Average 1973–1977.

[e] Average 1958–1960.

the lower price of the biannual period, demonstrating the cumulative behavior of variations.[7]

Import prices also show some variablity. However, Table 4 indicates that export prices fluctuated more than import prices. This is true, on average, for each of the three subperiods considered. Raw materials are the main explanation behind the difference in behavior: the 17 basic commodities (excluding oil) cover 43% of all exports of LACs, whereas they include only 5% of the imports (ECLA, 1976, Table 5). The evolution of the PV of import prices also shows the pattern of reduced instability in the sixties and then a sizable increase during the seventies; but changes among subperiods are softer than in the case of export prices.

The influence of commodity concentration on overall instability is reflected, to some degree, in the gap between the two estimates of the average figures for LACs: one is the simple unweighted average of the PVs of the 16 countries; the other is the PV of the price index of the region as a whole. The latter, obviously implying a largely more diversified basket of export goods, has a lower PV, equal to between two-thirds and one-half of the simple average (Table 1, last two rows).

Most LACs have been diversifying their exports. This is a phenomenon shared by several LDCs, and one that is not confined to manufactures but extends also to various basic commodities, processing activities, and services (Keesing, 1979). The outcome depends both on domestic and foreign variables. First, particularly with respect to manufactured exports, the increases in industrialization achieved by some countries have made more effective the new—more outwardlooking—trade policies being implemented since the mid-sixties by several LDCs.[8] Second, during the sixties and the first half of the seventies, there was an important liberalization of governmental restrictions on trade in developed countries. There are, however, two qualifications to be made with respect to the latter. As is well known, liberalization was more intensive in commodities produced and/or marketed by transnational corporations or traded only among industrialized countries. On the other hand, more recently, there has been an upsurge of protectionism in these countries; it has been called the "new protectionism" because of its emphasis on nontariff restrictions (Mendive, 1978; Perry, 1980).

Diversification tends to reduce the instability of export unit prices and

[7] This change overestimates the average behavior of the price of copper, but in 1979–1980, a similar gap between higher and lower prices occurred.

[8] The growth of manufactured exports is highly concentrated in a few countries. Hong-Kong, Singapore, South Korea, and Taiwan cover about half of all manufactured exports by LDCs and, with Brazil, Mexico, and Yugoslavia, they accounted for three-fourths of such exports by the mid-seventies (Keesing, 1979, Table 19).

TABLE 4

Price Instability: Exports, Imports, and Terms of Trade^a

Country	Export prices				Import prices				Terms of trade			
	1951–1960	1961–1970	1971–1979	1951–1979	1951–1960	1961–1970	1971–1979	1951–1979	1951–1960	1961–1970	1971–1979	1951–1979
LAFTA												
Argentina	7.3	5.2	8.8	7.0	5.5	3.3	6.5	5.0	8.7	5.3	11.5	8.4
Brazil	8.7	5.7	9.3	7.8	5.7	3.3	6.6	5.2	8.8	6.0	10.5	8.3
Chile	10.8	7.3	16.1	11.2	5.5	4.1	4.0	4.6	12.1	7.8	13.2	11.0
Mexico	4.6	3.7	7.8	5.3	4.7	4.2	4.7	4.5	7.0	3.5	5.8	5.4
Paraguay	10.7	4.4	10.4	8.4	4.4^b	3.6	12.9	6.8	10.4^b	3.8	12.0	8.6
Uruguay	11.1	6.7	11.5	9.7	9.4	3.4	11.0	7.8	20.2	7.1	14.0	13.8
Andean Pact												
Bolivia	8.6	9.3	16.7	11.3	6.4	3.7	3.3	4.5	11.8	9.8	14.8	12.1
Colombia	9.6	7.1	19.9	11.9	4.1	2.6	4.1	3.6	8.2	7.4	20.4	11.7
Ecuador	8.4	6.7	22.3	12.1	2.1	4.0	4.4	3.5	6.9	8.4	23.4	12.5
Peru	7.0	5.8	15.3	9.2	2.7	4.7	3.3	3.6	8.5	7.1	13.7	9.6
Venezuela	6.7	5.1	22.9	11.2	3.2	3.8	3.3	3.4	5.6	5.5	23.8	11.2

CACM

Costa Rica	10.1	2.6	11.6	8.0	3.8	3.1	5.8	4.2	9.9	3.9	13.7	9.0
El Salvador	9.9	4.1	13.9	9.2	2.3	2.9	5.0	3.4	10.0	5.7	13.8	9.7
Guatemala	8.4	3.3	10.6	7.3	5.1	4.2	4.3	4.6	6.2	4.3	10.2	6.8
Honduras	8.2	4.9	8.6	7.2	5.3	3.1	4.5	4.3	6.5	5.8	4.1	5.5
Nicaragua	11.1	3.0	13.4	9.0	6.9	3.5	3.5	4.7	15.2	3.5	13.4	10.6
Total Latin America	5.4	2.9	9.9	5.9	2.6	2.3	4.8	3.2	4.8	2.3	7.2	4.7
Simple average of 16 countries	8.8	5.3	13.7	9.1	4.8	3.6	5.5	4.6	9.8	5.9	13.6	9.6

[a] Data are given as average annual percentage variation.

[b] Average 1958–1960.

Sources: ECLA (1977; mimeo, September 1980). Figures in nominal terms were deflated by the IPMX (IBRD, 1979, p. 32); figures for 1979 are provisional. The figure for total Latin America is the PV of the respective deflated index for our 16 countries plus the Dominican Republic, Haiti, and Panama.

105

proceeds: fluctuations of different commodities compensate each other partially. Thus, the deconcentration of exports of raw materials experienced by several LACs probably worked in the direction of reducing average price and quantum instability. Moreover, manufacturing prices are, on average, more stable than those of basic commodities (UNCTAD, 1979), and these products increased their share of exports. However, in the seventies, price levels and relative prices were much more unstable than in the two previous decades. As a consequence, despite the sizable diversification of LACs' exports, as shown by Table 1, average price instability became larger in the seventies.

Cyclical changes in developed areas and the spread of the "new protectionism" have increased the instability of both prices and quantum of manufactured exports. For instance in 1975, the unit price of these exports by LDCs fell in absolute terms (Keesing, 1979, Table 24). The increased use of nontariff protectionist devices has also brought enlarged instability for some categories of commodities. These devices exert the opposite effect in the developed economies because these countries apply the nontariff mechanisms in order to compensate with changes in import restrictions those changes occurring in their domestic demand or in their ability to compete with foreign producers. These practices have become widespread with respect to textiles, clothing, footwear, and some processed agricultural products, which are precisely the categories in which exports of LDCs have been substituting domestic output in developed economies (Helleiner, 1979; Perry, 1980).

In LDCs, and particularly in several LACs, the policy trend has been the reverse. In fact, quantitative restrictions and other nontariff mechanisms have been gradually removed, with the influence being strongest upon competitive imports.[9] Together with the lowering of tariffs and the nature of the diversification of exports, they have left the domestic economy more susceptible to changes in foreign prices. If the external framework were stable, liberalization would contribute to the overall stabilization of domestic markets. However, in the seventies, the external framework has exhibited various forms of instability, thus contributing to the destabilization of some segments of the domestic economy. This instability is of a microeconomic nature because it works directly over specific commodity markets rather than through the overall balance of payments or fiscal budget. Because more outward-looking trade policies have been adopted, using different approaches, throughout LACs, the incidence of external instability differs from one country to another, being stronger in countries such as Argentina, Chile, and Uruguay, that have moved closer to free trade policies, as compared with countries with "moderate" policies.

B. Instability and Capital Flows

During the seventies there was a notable change in the financial relations of Latin American economies with international markets. The overall volume of inflows increased rapidly throughout the seventies. The rise concentrated in loans rather than in direct foreign investment, thus showing a pattern notably different to that of the fifties (see Table 5); a growing share of the loans originated in private financial institutions instead of official sources, as had been the case in the two previous decades (Díaz Alejandro, 1980). This fact explains why the maturation period of the loans became shorter: because private banking operates on shorter terms.[10] A final relevant feature is that inflows exceeded the also growing deficit in current accounts of the region (ECLA, 1979b), thus allowing an increase in international reserves. The basic data on capital movements for Latin America appear in Table 5.

TABLE 5

Composition of Capital Movements in Latin America: 1951–1978[a]

Period	Net direct foreign investment	Medium- and long-term loans	Short-term credit	Other	Changes in reserves (− increase)	Total net inflows
1951–60	636.8	278.4	156.0	0.1	220.2	1291.5
1961–70	547.5	1264.6	406.9	−128.7	−397.6	1692.7
1971–73	859.8	3544.8	966.2	−663.7	−1877.8	2829.3
1974–78	1086.9	6277.8	560.2	−1105.3	−1419.9	5399.7
1951–78	709.2	2051.9	404.6	−314.4	−518.1	2333.2

[a] Data are given as annual averages in millions of U.S. dollars.

Sources: ECLA (1979b and mimeo, September 1980). Includes LAFTA and CACM countries plus the Dominican Republic, Haiti, and Panama. Flows in current dollars have been deflated by the IPMX (IBRD, 1979, p. 32).

Of course, the aggregate figures disguise large differences among countries and fluctuations from year to year. Are fluctuations equilibrators or disequilibrators of the domestic economy? Also, an extremely relevant variable was not included in Table 5; that is, the cost of foreign loans. Nominal interest rates fluctuated widely during the past decade; if

---

[9] The evolution of trade policies in several LDCs, including two LACs, is traced in a NBER project that was led by J. Bhagwati and A. Krueger; see Bhagwati (1978), especially Chapters I and II.

[10] This is not observed in Table 5 because of the aggregation of the data. Column three includes loans with terms of one year or more.

consideration is taken of the inflationary process prevailing in the world economy in recent years, an additional characteristic emerges: apart from large fluctuations, real interest rates were negative in several instances. This obviously encouraged indebtedness by those with access to international capital markets.

The presence of negative real interest rates should be viewed as a transitory situation, reflecting world market deviations from long-run "equilibrium." Also, from the point of view of the national economies, capital inflows may imply nonequilibrating movements.

In basic textbooklike competitive small economies, flows are equilibrating. The adjustment process, for instance, in response to an opening to capital inflows, is assumed to be smooth, with the process stopping when the domestic interest rate becomes equal to the international interest rate. However, actually, there are many sources of departure from the basic textbook case. First, international markets are not stable. As has already been noted, nominal and real interest rates fluctuate. Consequently, the larger the debt position and the deficit in current account of a country, the larger the wealth and allocative effects that changes in real interest rates may exert. (More on this in Section III.) Second, the "product" of financial markets is not "homogeneous." There is a risk premium charged by lenders that differs among debtors and changes with time. The supply of funds faced by a given country may actually be horizontal and imply a low-risk surcharge, but it may also become abruptly vertical. The specific form depends on "confidence," which is determined by economic and political factors, in markets characterized by limited and lagged information: Latin America offers cases close to both extremes. Third, capital flows may be influenced by many different causes. (a) There are flows that compensate for transitory changes in the current account or flows that press for an increased disequilibrium in the current account, as discussed in Section III. (b) Accumulations of international reserves may react to a desire by economic authorities to achieve a certain stock target, duly coordinated with its effects on monetary markets. (c) Accumulations of reserves by the Central Bank may respond to an inflow of capital to the private or decentralized sector that is larger and/or at a faster pace than the domestic economy is capable of absorbing without negative effects on the goods markets.

In brief, capital flows may contribute to soften the effects of unexpected changes in trade, but they can also introduce external instability into the domestic economy, either because of changes in the availability of funds or interest rates in international markets or because of changes in the evaluation done by lenders of the "confidence" deserved by specific debtor countries. The subject is becoming increasingly relevant, although empirical and policy-oriented research on the subject is rather scarce.[11]

III. THE TRANSMISSION OF INSTABILITY

The main effects of external instability ES occur when it finds channels by which it is transmitted to the national economy. However, ES can cause some costs even if it is stopped at the border. Even in the case in which instability is predictable, there is need for foreign-exchange reserves, which implies foregoing some capital returns. But it is the uncertainty tied to external instability that brings potentially higher costs. In this case, the demand for reserves is increased further, and stopping instability at the border implies at least an administrative cost incurred in the design and implementation of the corresponding economic policies.

Notwithstanding that in the real world there are countless devices by which governments try to stop instability at the countries' borders,[12] it will tend to propagate to the domestic economy. In this section we shall concentrate on the mechanisms of transmission of ES, discussing briefly some of their probable effects. In the discussion we shall be heavily influenced by those features that characterized some LACs throughout the past three decades.

Instability has been transmitted to the domestic economy via the balance of payments, the fiscal budget, and the money market at the aggregate level. At the microeconomic level, it has spread via actual and expected changes in relative prices and in market availability of tradables and funds to given producers and consumers.

A. The Outcome of Mainstream Research

Empirical and theoretical researches on the issue of ES are of a very heterogeneous nature. Until recently, both shared a relatively low priority

[11] With a group of Latin American researchers, CIEPLAN, with the support of the Ford Foundation, developed a research project that involved an investigation of those features of international capital markets that are more relevant for the region, and case studies of the international financial relations of five LACs; see Ffrench-Davis (1981).

[12] On the average, developed countries are more effective in their efforts to stop ES at their frontiers. This very fact increases the instability prevailing in the remaining segments of the world market. Also, transnational corporations may aim to "residualize" those markets over which they lose control after nationalization steps taken by LDCs, pushing the output of these countries to the status of "suppliers of last resort" (Helleiner, 1979, pp. 75–76).

for policy-oriented work directly relevant for LDCs. However, in the last few years, progress has been fostered by the discussion developed around the UNCTAD proposal for an Integrated Program for Basic Commodities, including the Financial Common Fund (Avramovic, 1978).

Most available empirical research, rather than focusing on the effects of alternative mechanisms of transmission and of alternative policies to deal with those effects upon the domestic economy, look instead directly for quantitative links between export instability and some economic variables such as rates of growth of GNP and aggregate investment behavior. Available results are heterogeneous. For instance, Yotopoulos and Nugent (1976) conclude that investment ratios are stimulated by export instability (via an assumed positive effect on savings, on the basis on the permanent income hypothesis); on the other hand, Kenen and Viovodas (1972) find a statistically significant inverse relation. With respect to the link with economic growth, the more publicized empirical results tend to be statistically insignificant or show a positive relation. The argument supporting the positive relation—XS appears fostering growth, thus it was initially an unexpected result—has been, again, that it originated in encouraged savings that bring a subsequent increase in investment.

The empirical results correspond to cross-country regressions, with growth rates of GNP or investment ratios as a variable depending on XS and other variables are assumed to be independent. In the case of Yotopoulas and Nugent, they introduce an additional variable, which is domestic income instability or, alternatively, per capita GNP; and a broader set of variables is considered in the cases of MacBean and of Kenen and Voivodas. A unique functional relationship is assumed for all countries in the respective sample between a given level of XS and the growth rates or investment ratios, as it was recalled critically by Maizels (1968a).[13] Of course, the dependent variables are affected by many other variables, some of which may differ significantly among countries; that includes the savings and investment behavior of the public sector, the adjustment capacity of the domestic market, and the economic policies for coping with external instability (Helleiner, 1972, p. 85; Lim, 1976). For instance, the effects of a given XS on the domestic economy would be quite different if producers were small farmers as compared with the subsidiary of a trans-

---

[13] With basically the same function of MacBean, but using a different sample of countries, Maizels (1968b) obtains very different results. The rationale for using different sets of countries, depending on the hypothesis being tested, is discussed in Lim (1976). Lancieri (1978), with a large sample of 101 developed and developing countries, finds, for 1961–1972, a close negative Spearman rank correlation between export instability and gross domestic product (GDP) growth rates.

national enterprise, which reaps the economic rent and internalizes its transitory changes in response to world price fluctuations.

Three recent empirical works use more comprehensive approaches. Lim (1976, 1980) derives the functions to be estimated from more careful analysis of the hypothesis to be tested. He finds (Lim, 1980) that in 1968–1973 instability had a positive effect on savings ratios (GNS/GNP) in a sample of 52 LDCs.[14] However, if the estimates are limited to the 18 western hemisphere countries (that include 14 of our LACs sample), the relation becomes negative, though not statistically significant. Lim (1976), building on previous research by Voivodas (1974), introduced, apart from XS, the changes of foreign capital inflows and of exports. Results continue to be very sensitive to the particular period chosen and to the specification of the functions regressed. Nonetheless, XS (with a negative regression coefficient) and changes in flows of funds appear as statistically significant variables in explaining the growth rate of GDP for the period 1956–1968 (though not for the longer period 1956–1973), in the "improved" specification derived by Lim.[15]

Adams *et al.* (1979) also introduce the discussion of the role of domestic policies and the channels of transmission of instability.[16] A simulation model is applied to Brazilian data, simulating the incidence of coffee, output and prices on GDP, inflation, and other variables. As the authors state, the model measures rather static effects on the demand side. More properly, it is not instability but one change in output or price of coffee that is at stake.

The previously mentioned efforts improve the relevancy for LDCs of this area of empirical research but are only encouraging first steps. Theoretical and empirical researches, of course, have influenced each other. But the issue of ES, predominantly related to prices of basic commodities, has had a rather independent path in a "pure" theoretical front. The literature concentrates on microeconomic effects of price instability. The initial conventional approach considered consumers and producers *separately,* linear stable downward-sloping demand and upward-sloping

---

[14] It may be that the particular periods chosen gives a positive bias to the estimators. In fact, the period 1968–1973 exhibits an upward swing of relative prices of primary exports; hence, what is being measured is not exactly fluctuations *around* the trend.

[15] If capital flows F are compensatory of XS, then changes in F and X (and their respective variances) would tend to be correlated, introducing some multicollinearity. This phenomenon might have been more significant in the longer period tested, 1956–1973: XS and fund flows (see Table 5 for LACs) were, in general, larger in 1969–1973 than in 1956–1968. However, this might not have been the case for the specific sample used by Lim.

[16] See also Adams and Behrman (1981), published since this chapter was written. An institutional and qualitative analysis of the role of instability of copper in Chile appears in Ffrench-Davis and Tironi (1974).

supply curves, additive disturbances, and the standard economic surplus analysis. It was easily concluded that, in that framework, instability was welfare increasing for consumers and for producers. However, Massell (1969), in a closed model, showed that, integrating both faces, instability would be detrimental to consumers and producers taken together (given actual compensation). The extension of the analysis to an open economy continues to show that for both sides (now the two countries or the world), given actual international and domestic compensation, stabilization is welfare increasing. But for each particular country or economic agent, the origin of instability (domestic or foreign, supply or demand) is an important determinant of the welfare effects of price stabilization on consumers, producers, and countries as a whole.

The standard conclusion reached within this analytical framework is that if instability originates mostly from supply shifts, exporters will gain with price stabilization and importers will loose (Hueth and Schmitz, 1972). No explicit incorporation was made of the heterogeneity of suppliers, of private stockholding behavior, and of the institutional framework within which real-world markets function (Cuddy, 1980).

Another category of crucial assumptions relates to the prices considered for output and the consumption decisions. The standard assumption in the models developed has been that those decisions are guided by actual market prices; thus, if economic agents face adjustment problems, it is taken for granted that, although prices change constantly, they are able to keep well informed with respect to prices in the future and they process them "rationally".

In fact, however, information is limited and imperfect, and this is enhanced by instability; price instability in itself is usually a source of price uncertainty, rather than of pure variability. Hence, external instability will tend to introduce an additional source of uncertainty into the domestic market. Then, the effects of external disturbances will depend on how price expectations are built and how the behavior of consumers and producers is modified by uncertainty.

There is a growing literature on the firm under uncertainty. Its point of departure is that many decisions on production, stocking, and investment must be taken without knowledge of the actual selling price of output. Consequently, adjustments to the changing price relations of output and inputs can be made only at some cost, in terms of collecting and processing information, with room for miscalculations.

The recognition that supply depends on expected rather than on actual prices leads to larger net potential welfare gains from stabilization (Turnovsky, 1978). Beyond that conclusion, its implications are less conclusive. The former general conclusions of the sort of modeling used in this area—that producers benefit with instability if disturbances originate in demand[17]—is modified under adaptive expectations, unless demand fluctuations are highly autocorrelated (Turnovsky, 1978, p. 130). However, the former results hold with rational expectations.

In brief, under uncertainty, stabilization appears even more convenient for the world as a whole, but the distribution of benefits and costs among countries and between domestic and foreign producers and consumers depends now on the formation of expectations, the nature of disturbances, and the elasticities of supply and demand (Turnovsky, 1978).

Last, but not least, practically all theoretical and empirical research has been based on the assumption of full stabilization and no administrative costs.[18] Actually, proposed and implemented stabilization schemes are usually partial, in the sense that they do not cover all countries or all commodities or do not imply a unique price as the target of stabilization, but a band of prices.

On the other hand, any stabilization scheme, even if very profitable, will imply some operating costs. As will be discussed in Section IV, (a) limited, costly, and imperfect knowledge on what price or income to stabilize, (b) the administrative costs involved, and (c) the "opportunity" cost of the attention devoted by economic authorities (Simon, 1978) lead to the relevant issue of "optimal" stabilization, as opposed to the less relevant dilemma confronting full laissez faire with complete stabilization.

The outcome of conventional research, although it is not conclusive, does not seem to support strongly the apparent priority given by LDCs to stabilization of prices and income of basic commodities. In fact, LDCs have allotted more attention to *ES* than it appears to deserve according to most of that research. However, this paradox is due to (a) the crucial role that these countries assign to variables often omitted and (b) the crucial departures between the actual working of international and domestic LDCs markets and the behavior assumed by the more standard models and empirical research on this issue (Cuddy, 1979). We shall turn to this subject now.

---

[17] It must be recalled that this conclusion depends on the assumption of additive disturbances. If they are multiplicative, producers tend to "gain from having either demand and/or supply disturbances stabilized if demand is elastic and supply inelastic" (Turnovsky, 1978, p. 127), irrespective of the source of fluctuations.

[18] A recent movement toward the real world is related to theoretical analysis of the influence of trade restrictions on the effects of instability. The scarce literature on the subject focuses mainly on the comparative effects of tariffs and domestic buffer stocks; see Sarris and Taylor (1978).

B.   Macroeconomic Effects: Balance of Payments, Fiscal Budget, and Monetary Channels

The most direct impact of *ES* is on the balance of payments. Changes in export and import prices, in access to external markets, in international interest rates, and in the supply of foreign funds, affect different components of the foreign sector accounts. But, *ES* may also directly affect the fiscal budget and the money market. What happens after the initial impact depends strongly on the sort of domestic policies implemented and on the nature of the external shock.

First, let us consider some issues related to balance-of-payments policy. The impact of *ES* will bring a departure from the assumed "equilibrium" of the sector and this must be compensated for somehow. In practice, compensation has come from a mixture of policies, which have been changing through the last few decades.[19] In the fifties, the response to external shocks was mainly via changes in import restrictions; import deposits and quantitative restrictions (QRs) were preferred instruments. Because in several LACs imports of consumer goods had been reduced drastically by import substitution policies, QRs fell principally on capital and intermediate goods. That fact may contribute to explaining the significant role that foreign-exchange shortages seem to have played in capital formation (Díaz Alejandro, 1976). The influence on the exchange rate *ER* was more passive. In periods in which *ES* improved the availability of foreign exchange (for instance, above "normal" export prices), it contributed to the longer freezing of nominal *ER*s whose purchasing power was being eroded by the rather high rates of inflation prevailing in South America. During the fifties and early sixties, the compensating mechanism of foreign-reserve adjustments played a secondary role. Then *ES* was transmitted from the balance of payments to the domestic economy mainly by changing restrictions on imports, and passive falls in real *ER*s and subsequent abrupt devaluations were often partially compensated for by relaxed QRs or other nontariff obstacles to imports.

In the mid-sixties, *ER* started playing a growingly active role, with several South American countries adopting crawling-peg policies (ECLA, 1975; Williamson, 1981). In the past ten years or so, *ER* instability and unpredictability has tended to fall as compared with the previous period. The outcome has been twofold: first, it probably contributed to the re-

---

[19] Recent accounts of different segments of economic policies dealing with the external sector in Latin America appear in Bhagwati (1978), ECLA (1975), Grunwald (1978), Ffrench-Davis and Tironi (1980), and Williamson (1981).

moval of most QRs and to stabler import policies; second, data (though weakly) seem to support the hypothesis that reduced real *ER* instability fosters nontraditional exports (Coes, 1981; Díaz Alejandro, 1976), and apparently the positive effect is stronger on manufactured goods.

The somewhat greater stability of foreign trade rules has been associated, as mentioned, with stabler real *ER*s in several countries. But in most countries there was also a change in the behavior of international reserves, which is partly a companion of the new exchange-rate policy. As a whole, LACs increased the stock of reserves held as a share of imports. Gross reserves, after a fall in the fifties and sixties, rose from 37% of yearly imports to 59% between 1951–1952 and 1978–1979. This new situation helped to compensate for or soften the impact of external shocks.

A new feature in the seventies was the relaxation of the restrictions on capital movements and a fast increase in the inflows of private funds. This was tied to the specific trends in domestic economic policies in some countries of the region, but it was supported by the growth of the international capital markets and the excess supply of funds that seems to have prevailed in those markets during the second half of the seventies (Díaz Alejandro, 1980).

Lately, a large inflow of private financial capital has been introducing two forms of instability (or at least short-run adjustments) into the domestic market. First, it has been pressing for an appreciation of *ER*, notwithstanding large current account deficits and/or likely negative effects on nontraditional exports.[20] The domestic economies have been accommodating increased amounts of foreign financial resources. A relevant question in this respect is whether or not the increased access to capital markets is stable and whether it will continue to be so open through the next decade. A negative answer would open a large potential source of instability for those LACs that are becoming increasingly dependent on net inflows of foreign capital. The effective use of these funds implies a larger deficit in current accounts and a higher share of foreign importables in domestic expenditure. Consequently, a forced fall in inflows, originated abroad, may cause a costly process of adjustment. A somewhat related issue refers to the instability of the cost of foreign loans, which has been an actual feature of international capital markets in the seventies. Complete

[20] The clearest cases are those of Argentina and Chile since 1979; see papers by Martirena-Mantel and Ffrench-Davis in Williamson (1981). An interesting out-of-the-region case corresponding to a liberalization of capital movements and of *ER* occurred in Israel in 1977, with a drastic market appreciation of *ER*; see Bruno and Sussman (1981).

opening of the domestic economy to capital movements imposes exposure to changes in external interest rates, bringing into the analysis an almost new area of research (Arellano, 1980).

Also, increased capital flows have brought a heavy burden on monetary policy; although a sizable fraction of funds has been absorbed via import liberalization, reserves have been accumulating at a fast pace, with the corresponding impact on money supply. Apart from the adjustment via *ER* policy, changes in money supply have apparently been larger than those desired by government authorities. Two channels of sterilization have been the restriction of both domestic credit and public expenditures. The combined effects are far from neutral in some of the LACs that have been increasing their external financial openness. First, foreign funds—at least initially—tend to accrue to only some segments of the domestic economy, whereas those supporting the credit squeeze may be other segments; in fact, in the Chilean economy, segmentation seems to have persisted for over five years, with a large interest spread between domestic and foreign funds (Zahler, 1980). Second, the compensatory reduction of public expenditures tends to restrict investment and social services, transmitting instability to the markets associated to them. (As is well known, fluctuations in public investment have been an important source of economic cycles and of structural unemployment in LACs.)

Finally, *ES* also reaches the fiscal budget by other channels. Fluctuations in export prices have an impact on tax proceeds; the incidence has been increased with the nationalization of the production of exportable basic commodities, which has taken place throughout LACs in the last decade; oil, iron, copper, and sugar, to a lesser extent, provide significant examples. Countries, and particularly the public sector, have captured a higher share of the economic rent, but also its instability (Helleiner, 1979, pp. 75–76). Thus the spending behavior of the public sector, vis-à-vis export instability, becomes more crucial (Ffrench-Davis and Tironi, 1974). The structuralist approach to inflation argued that *ES* brought instability into public expenditure. Periods of high external prices increased expenditure; however, when prices fell, expenditure was reduced but with a lag and/or only partially, thus producing a fiscal deficit (Prebisch, 1963; Sunkel, 1957). An analog of this combination of political pressures and downward-limited expenditure flexibility is present in the ratchet effect of fluctuations of external prices on the domestic price level (Bruno and Sussman, 1981); the relevance of this effect appears to have a positive correlation with the degree of industrialization. One particular channel by which the ratchet effect is put into motion is the impact that transitory high export prices may have on wages in the export sector, which behaves as a leading sector for wage setting in the rest of the economy.

C. Less Conventional Effects on Producers

The previous section started with a discussion of the transmission of *ES* via (active or passive) macropolicies. It ended with a reference to one particular channel of transmission, the domestic price of exportables.

In a fully open market economy, *ES* easily reaches domestic economic agents producing (and those using or consuming) the commodities subject to instability. Here we shall discuss briefly four points related to the framework faced by producers in a "free" market economy. The first point refers to futures markets; the other three relate to international income distribution, domestic income distribution, and the general efficiency of investment.

It is argued by orthodox theorists that instability would not be harmful to producers because futures markets would develop to contribute to the stabilization of the actual price of their output. It may be useful to raise two points in relation to the actual working of commodities markets. First, futures markets may contribute to the stabilization of the price received by producers within the term covered by futures contracts and serve to guide investment decisions. Nonetheless, there is some evidence that futures prices are bad predictors of spot prices, except for near-term expirations or in points of time that are seasonally abundant in information (Smith, 1978, p. 170)[21]. This may be a partial explanation of the very short maturity of most futures contracts. Second, day-to-day fluctuations are large: apparently they "walk randomly" in the short run, in the sense that the direction of change in a given day appears to be independent of the signs of changes in the previous days (Smith, 1978, p. 165). This may be interpreted as a sign of unpredictability and market disequilibrium, as it is reported to be in this last reference.

The random walk may be consistent with the more predictable direction of prices in the long run, in particular in commodities whose changes in installed capacity imply long maturing periods: after several years of one-sided deviations from the price trend, a price change in the opposite direction can be expected, with increasing probability. Low predictability arises when the exact time and strength of the change are estimated. But, when the change does occur, it tends to take only a brief period to achieve a new plateau, with its respective random walk.

Even if short-run fluctuations were to have little influence on the allocation of resources, they can have a larger influence on income distribu-

---

[21] Recent work by Kawai (1981) suggests that the addition of futures stabilizes spot prices if the spot consumer demand disturbance is the dominant random element, but not if the inventory demand disturbance is predominant. This suggests that even theoretically, futures markets are not necessarily stabilizing.

tion. Avramovic (1978) showed that the average price received by countries exporting a given basic commodity has a positive correlation with their level of income or development. Once crucial explanatory variable seems to be the capacity of exporters to choose the timing of their sales (staying capacity). Of course, the short-timed price fluctuations already mentioned render the timing of selling important, but they also make relevant the lower capacity of LDCs to develop independent marketing channels and to improve their participation in the less than fully efficient and competitive international markets (Cuddy, 1980; Helleiner, 1979).

The prior issue—implying heterogeneity among producer countries—brings us to the topic of domestic income distribution. Because the search for information implies some fixed cost, instability imposes a proportionally higher informational cost to smaller domestic producers. Together with their more restricted access to capital markets, this gives them a limited staying power and scarcer knowledge with respect to better selling opportunities within the national economy. In brief, price instability, in a real world featuring structurally heterogeneous producers and limited imperfect information, gives way to price differentials that have distributive effects across and within countries.

Finally, the investment process is also affected by price uncertainty. First, it tends to lead to overinvestment and underinvestment (Smith, 1978, p. 175). Firms' expectations seem to be influenced heavily by the near past and present prices (Arrow, 1974), which makes them slow to prepare for increased output capacity when the price upswing starts. However, this may be rationalized as a consequence of capital market imperfections: if prices have been low and profits are below normal, it may become more uncomfortable for the management to propose to the board new large indivisible investments (as in mining) and it may become more difficult to obtain sizable long-term loans from the capital market. Second, the transmission of instability into the domestic market might be a deterrent to efforts geared to introduce cost-reducing technological change. Third, an unstable environment is prone to foster a speculative, or "rentier," rather than an "industrious" attitude (Tironi, 1980) and to increase the weight of short-term dealings in the domestic capital market.

IV. POLICIES FOR STABILITY: SOME ISSUES FOR RESEARCH

The sort of policies that are optimal for a given country depends on the nature of effects that instability generates on the domestic economy. We have seen in previous sections that important effects are of a macroeconomic nature; effects on the exchange rate, the fiscal budget and monetary management, and the foreign-exchange availability appear to have been policy relevant. But the microeconomic impact at the level of the producer may also exert secondary macroeconomic effects on inflation, employment, and investment.

Many efforts have been directed to achieving stability at the international level. However, even if negotiations reach a successful end, instability is going to remain because the coverage is restricted to only some sources of external instability and for these specific sources the target is only partial stabilization. It is quite obvious that autarky is not the answer to *ES*. International economic relations contribute to the domestic growth of LDCs and may compensate instability originated domestically. Because the relevant option is neither autarky nor full integration with the world economy, the definition of stabilization, how it must be done, and to what extent, remain a target of domestic economic policies.

One of the issues that has deserved more attention is that of exchange-rate policy. Within the field of managed *ER*, changes in the domestic economy and in trade relations pose problems to determine what is a real *ER*, what target must be pursued, and what is the optimal path for its implementation. One issue is the detection of the need for permanent changes in the real rate;[22] for instance, in response to autonomous changes in the terms of trade or in foreign capital supply. But the crucial related issue is what to do with respect to transitory changes. The general line seems to be to stop their transmission to *ER*. However, there are two aspects that recommend some flexibility of real *ER*. One is that *ER* policy usually is not sufficient by itself to avoid the transmission of instability; there is also need of other policies, such as fiscal, credit-monetary, and foreign debt policies, each implying some cost in terms of implementing capacity by the government. The other refers to the implications of uncertainty or limited knowledge; it is impossible to distinguish fully and correctly between normal and transitory components of the balance of payments. Thus, in order to minimize mistakes, it is convenient to accept some instability in the short run; this can help to avoid forced adjustments in the long run if errors accumulate. What is the optimal mix of policies; where is the optimum cutting point for stabilization; what are the components of trade that must be "normalized" as an input for policy purposes?

The policy mix is relevant in various senses. It is standard to discuss the assignment problem in terms of all or nothing, but given uncertainty, market segmentations, limited futures markets, distributive implications,

---

[22] One approach in fashion in orthodox quarters is the return to a fixed nominal exchange rate. The monetary approach to the balance of payments, within which that proposal has found its new home, tends to ignore the issues covered by this chapter. Numerous arguments for crawling-peg policies as opposed to frozen *ER*s appear in Williamson (1981).

and other simultaneous imperfections, the relevant question becomes that of how to mix different policies. The impact of instability and the process of transition toward (a probably modified) equilibrium disequilibrate several markets. In the case of a price fluctuation of the main export of a given country, the external impact disequilibrates the balance of payments, eventually the fiscal budget and the monetary market, and the domestic market of the given commodity. Thus, stopping or reducing the transmission of instability requires acting with more than one policy simultaneously.

Recently, throughout Latin America, one recurrent feature has been the enlarged size of foreign private capital movements and the associated abrupt changes in foreign reserves and base money supply. This problem is related to the questions of what is the actual capacity to absorb foreign funds efficiently and how stable is its supply. Both the availability of funds and the real interest rate have been changing considerably since 1973. What is the optimal degree of opening to capital flows; what are the implications of alternative policies toward the transmission of changes in the cost of foreign funds (Arellano, 1980)? It is extremely doubtful that these questions can be solved optimally by the market. What price or direct mechanisms can operate better in the case of small- and medium-sized semi-industrialized countries, in the alternative, more feasible scenarios provided by international capital markets during the eighties?

One faces, with respect to the problems just posed, questions such as the definition of "normal" prices for "strategic" export and import commodities and for financial flows, and the mechanisms better suited for regulating the destabilized markets. Mechanisms that work directly on prices or on quantities represent two options that may complement each other. For instance, if the supply of funds is unstable, in the sense described in Section II, some sort of quantitative regulations may become convenient; and in fact, several countries (developed and developing) do have quantitative-equivalent restrictions. But, price mechanisms may be required also as a distributive device for the resulting domestic/foreign price differentials and as an improved market signal (pure quantitative restrictions tend to segment the market and to lead to implicit price differentials in the domestic market).

ACKNOWLEDGMENTS

Research for this chapter was supported in part by the International Development Research Center of Canada. I acknowledge the research assistance of J. Scherman and the comments of J. P. Arellano, J. Behrman, R. Cortázar, and G. Helleiner and of participants at the International Symposium on "Latin America: Trade, Development and Equity," Bar-Ilan University.

REFERENCES

Adams, G., and Klein, S. (eds.) (1978). *Stabilizing World Commodity Markets.* Massachusetts: Lexington Books.

Adams, G., and Behrman, J. (1981). *Commodity Exports and Development.* Massachusetts: Lexington Books.

Adams, G., Behrman, J., and Roldan, R. (1979). "Measuring the Impact of Primary Commodity Fluctuations on Economic Development: Coffee and Brazil." *American Economic Review* (May).

Arellano, J. P. (1980). "Estabilidad y Grado Óptimo de Apertura,"mimeo. CIEPLAN (October).

Arrow, K. (1974). "Limited Knowledge and Economic Analysis." *American Economic Review* (March).

Avramovic, D. (1978). "Common Fund: why and of what kind?", *Journal of World Trade Law* (September–October).

Bhagwati, J. (1978). *Foreign Trade Regimes and Economic Development: Anatomy and Consequences of Exchange Control Regimes.* Massachusetts: NBER-Ballinger.

Bruno, M., and Sussman, Z. (1981). "Floating Versus Crawling: Israel 1977–79 in Hindsight." In Williamson (1981).

Coes, D. (1981). "The Crawling-Peg and Exchange Rate Uncertainty." In Williamson (1981).

Cuddy, J. (1979). "The Case For an Integrated Programme for Commodities." *Resources Policy* (March).

Cuddy, J. (1980). "Theory and Practice of NIEO Negotiations on Commodities." *Conference on Relevance of Economic Theory for North-South Negotiations,* Refsnes Gods (July).

Díaz-Alejandro, C. (1976). *Foreign Trade Regimes and Economic Development: Colombia.* New York: NBER.

Díaz-Alejandro, C. (1980). "International Finance: Issues of Especial Interest for Developing Countries." In Ffrench-Davis and Tironi (1982).

Dornbusch, R. (1980). *Open Economy Macroeconomics.* New York: Basic Books.

ECLA (1975). "Políticas de Comercio Exterior en América Latina: origen, Objetivos y Perspectivas." E/CEPAL/L. 117 (April).

ECLA (1976). "Temas del Nuevo Orden Económico Internacional." *Cuadernos de la CEPAL* (12).

ECLA (1977). "América Latina: Relación de Precios del Intercambio, 1928–76." E/CEPAL/1040 (August).

ECLA (1979a). "Anuario Estadístico de América Latina: 1978" (June).

ECLA (1979b). "El balance de pagos de América Latina: 1950–77", *Cuadernos Estadísticos de la CEPAL,* September.

Erb, G., and Schiavo-Campo, S. (1969). "Export instability, level of development and economic size of LDCs", *Bulletin of the Oxford Institute of Economics and Statistics,* 31, November.

Ffrench-Davis, R. (1968). "Export quotas and allocative efficiency under market instability", *American Journal of Agriculture Economics,* August.

Ffrench-Davis, R. (ed.) (1981). *External Financial Relations and National Development,* in preparation.

Ffrench-Davis, R., and Tironi, E. (eds.) (1974). *El cobre en el desarrollo nacional,* Ediciones Nueva Universidad: abridged versions appear in A. Seidman, ed., *Natural resources and national welfare,* Praeger Publishers, New York.

Ffrench-Davis, R., and Tironi, E. (eds.) (1982). *Latinamerica and the New International Economic Order*. London: Macmillan.

Glesakos, C. (1973). "Export Instability and Economic Growth: A Statistical Verification." *Economic Development and Cultural Change* (July).

Grunwald, J. (ed.) (1978). *Latin America and World Economy: A Changing International Order*. Beverly Hills, California: Sage Publications.

Helleiner, G. (1972). *International Trade and Economic Development. Modern Economics*. Middlesex, England: Penguin.

Helleiner, G. (1978). "World Market Imperfections and the Developing Countries: An Assessment of the Data." *Overseas Development Council* Occasional Paper N°11.

Helleiner, G. (1979). "Structural Aspects of Third World Trade: Some Trends and Some Prospects." *Journal of Development Studies* (April).

Hueth, D., and Schmitz, A. (1972). "International Trade in Intermediate and Final Goods: Some Welfare Implications of Destabilized Prices." *Quarterly Journal of Economics* (August).

IBRD (1979). "Commodity Trade and Price Trends." Report (166), 1979 Edition (August).

IMF-IBRD (1969). "The Problem of Stabilization of Prices of Primary Products." Washington, D.C.

Kawai, M. (1981). *Price Volatility of Storable Commodities under Rational Expectations in Spot and Futures Markets*. Baltimore, Maryland: John Hopkins Press.

Keesing, D. (1979). "World Trade and Output of Manufactures: Structural Trends and Developing Countries Exports." *World Bank Staff Working Paper (316)* (January).

Kenen, P., and Voivodas, C. (1972). "Export Instability and Economic Growth." *Kyklos* Fasc. 4.

Lancieri, E. (1978). "Export Instability and Economic Development: A Reappraisal." *Banca Nazionale del Lavoro Quarterly Review* (June). Vol. XXXI, No. 125, 135–152.

Lancieri, E. (1979). "Instability and Agricultural Exports: World Markets, Developing and Developed Countries." *Banca Nazionale del Lavoro Quarterly Review* (September). Vol. XXXII, No. 130, 287–310.

Lim, D. (1976). "Export Instability and Economic Growth: A Return to Fundamentals." *Oxford Bulletin of Economics and Statistics* (November).

Lim, D. (1980). "Income Distribution, Export Instability and Savings Behaviour." *Economic Development and Cultural Change* (January).

MacBean, A. (1966). *Export Instability and Economic Development* London: Allen and Unwin.

Maizels, A. (1968a). *Exports and Economic Growth of Developing Countries,* London and New York: Cambridge University Press.

Maizels, A. (1968b). Review of MacBean (1966), *American Economic Review* (June).

Massell, B. (1970). "Export Instability and Economic Structure." *American Economic Review* (September).

Mendive, P. (1978). "Proteccionismo y Desarrollo: Nuevos Obstáculos de los Centros al Comercio Internacional." *Revista de la CEPAL* (6).

Moran, C. (1979). "Internacional Trade Under Uncertainty." *Working Paper* (28) CEPAL (October).

Murray D. (1978). "Export Earnings Instability: Price, Quantity, Supply, Demand?" *Economic Development and Cultural Change* (October).

Perry, G. (1980). "World Markets for Manufactures and Industrialization in Developing Countries." In Ffrench-Davis and Tironi (1982).

Prebisch, R. (1963). *Hacia una dinámica del desarrollo latinoamericano*. México-B. Aires, Fondo de Cultura Económica.

Sarris, A., and Taylor, L. (1978). "Buffer Stock Analysis for Agricultural Products: Theoretical Murk or Empirical Verification." In Adams and Klein (1978).

Simon, H. (1978). "Rationality as Process and as Product of Thought." *American Economic Review* (May).

Smith, G. (1978). "Commodity Instability and Market Failure: A Survey of Issues." In Adams and Klein (1978).

Sunkel, O. (1958). "La Inflación Chilena: un Enfoque Heterodoxo." *El Trimestre Económico* (100) (October–December).

Tironi, E. (1980). "National Policies Towards Commodity Exports." In Ffrench-Davis and Tironi, (1982).

Tuong, H., and Yeats, A. (1976). "A Note on the Measurement of Trade Concentration." *Oxford Bulletin of Economics and Statistics* (November).

Turnovsky, S. (1978). "The Distribution of Welfare Gains from Price Stabilization: A Survey of Some Theoretical Issues." In Adams and Klein (1978).

Unctad (1979). *Handbook of International Trade and Development Statistics*, Annual Supplement.

Voivodas, C. S. (1974). "The Effect of Foreign Exchange Instability on Growth." *Review of Economics and Statistics* (August). Vol. LVI, 410–412.

Williamson, J. (ed.) (1981). *Exchange-rate rules: The Theory, Performance and Prospects of the Crawling-peg*. London: Macmillan.

Yotopoulos, P., and Nugent, J. (1976). *Economics of Development*. New York: Harper.

Zahler, R. (1980). "Repercusiones monetarias y reales de la apertura financiera al exterior: el caso chileno, 1975–78." *CEPAL Review* (10) (April).

CIEPLAN
Santiago, Chile

Chapter 6

The Vulnerability of Small Semi-industrialized Economies to Export Shocks: A Simulation Analysis Based on Peruvian Data

Daniel M. Schydlowsky and Martha Rodríguez

I. THE SMALL SEMI-INDUSTRIALIZED ECONOMY AND ITS BALANCE-OF-PAYMENTS ADJUSTMENT MECHANISM

A. Structure of the Small Semi-industrialized Economy

The small semi-industrialized economy in Latin America today is typically a graduate of an import-substituting industrialization policy. It therefore exports primary goods and imports raw materials and intermediate goods, which it processes domestically behind high tariff barriers or behind quantitative restrictions. Imports are mostly noncompetitive with domestic production. Industrial exports may or may not exist, depending on the nature of the international trade policy. Industrial costs are typically well above world market prices, resulting from

125

TABLE 1

Typical Exchange-Rate System of a Semi-industrialized Country[a]

Product	Market	Financial rate	Trade taxation (%)	Total rate
Primary export	Domestic	10	—	10
	export	10	—	10
Financial	—	10	—	10
Raw material	Domestic	10	20	12
	export	10	—	10
Semimanufactures I	Domestic	10	35	13.5
	export	10	—	10
Semimanufactures II	Domestic	10	50	15
	export	10	—	10
Finished products	Domestic	10	80	18
	export	10	—	10

[a] Data are given in pesos per dollar.

backward integration of the industrial structure behind the high import restrictions. Although for domestic sales the high input costs are compensated by either higher tariffs or quotas on the finished product, thus yielding positive effective protection for sales on the domestic market, symmetric protection is rarely supplied for industrial exports. In the absence of vigorous export promotion, negative effective protection on export sales ensues, and industrial production for export markets becomes unprofitable.[1]

The impact of the trade policy on the structure of trade can be visualized easily by interpreting the composite of exchange rate and trade taxation measures as an implicit multiple-exchange-rate system. A typical structure of such an exchange-rate system is shown in Table 1. There it can be seen that the "total exchange rate" is the result of compounding the financial rate with the trade taxation. The escalation of the tariff produces successively higher rates for raw materials, different kinds of manufactures, and finished products. Production costs at higher stages of transformation are affected by the total exchange rates of lower stages; however, the cascading in the rates produces profit-

[1] The documentation of antiexport bias is voluminous; see, for instance, Little *et al.* (1970) and Balassa (1971, 1982).

ability of sales on the domestic market despite the excess of the cost exchange rates over the financial rate.

When, however, export sales are at issue, the level of the cost exchange rate becomes crucial to the possibility for competing in world markets. In the case of Table 1, the cost exchange rate for the average product is of the order of 35 to 50% above the financial rate as far as material inputs are concerned. Labor costs, however, will also be affected by the tariff system insofar as the supply of labor depends on the real wage and consumption goods are affected by the tariff on finished goods. Thus, in this example, the cost exchange rate for wages will be an average of 18 for finished products and 10 for food, yielding a "wage exchange rate" of perhaps 13. Finally, the total exchange rate for capital goods must be taken into account, too. Thus, the average cost exchange rate for all inputs is likely to be of the order of 13 or so. If no export support is provided under such circumstances, the export rate will be 10 and exports are unlikely to be profitable. On the other hand, if export promotion measures are in place and the export exchange rate is sufficiently high, a number of activities will find sales in the foreign market attractive, depending on the interaction between the industry's specific cost exchange rate and the export rate available.

It is worth noting that this structure of the implicit multiple-exchange-rate system tends to cause misleading evaluations of the efficiency of industrial production in semi-industrialized countries. Thus, for example, if one takes domestic costs of production and divides them by the "exchange rate" to obtain the dollar equivalent for comparison with world (import) prices, one will generate an overstatement of excess costs. This "inefficiency illusion" arises because the exchange rate used is naturally the financial rate, whereas the domestic producer's cost is based on the total rate affecting these inputs on the average. Because this cost exchange rate is invariably above the financial rate, the distortion caused by using the latter for the cost comparison may be quite considerable. In the example used previously, the producer's cost rate was 13; transforming this cost to dollars with an exchange rate of 10 would produce an overstatement of 30%. Unfortunately, the actual cost exchange rate for individual producers are not usually available, and thus the simple comparison of domestic costs with world prices using the financial exchange rate is the common one and leads both policy makers and industrialists to the conviction that industry in the semi-industrialized economy is much more inefficient that in fact it is.[2]

[2] See Schydlowsky (1972) for an early discussion of this problem and Berlinski and Schydlowsky (1977) for a careful quantification for Argentina.

B. The Adjustment Process

How the small semi-industrialized economy adjusts to an external shock, say, a reduction in the volume of its exports of traditional goods or a reduction in the price of such goods, depends crucially on whether it does or does not export manufactures as well. If no manufactures are exported, the loss of export income will cause a reduction in the level of domestic economic activity through the foreign trade multiplier. The induced fall in domestic demand may cause a reduction in the relative price of nonexport goods and thereby may induce a shift in the composition of domestic final demand toward such nonexport goods, thus moderating the deflation somewhat.

However, the scope for change in relative prices in semi-industrialized economies is severely limited for several reasons:

(i)   most industrial and service production occurs under constant or declining costs,

(ii)   most industrial goods and services have significant import components, the prices of which do not fall with a reduction in domestic demand, and

(iii)   wages in these economies are typically rigid downward as a result of either minimum wage legislation or unionization, or both.

Thus, in the absence of industrial exports, the shortfall of export earnings will work its way through the economy almost entirely through the foreign trade multiplier and the balance of payments will be brought back into equilibrium through a lowering of the level of activity.

If industrial exports do exist, the adjustment mechanism is different. Under these circumstances, when traditional export revenues fall and the domestic market shrinks, an increased amount of industrial production becomes available for export. Thus, market substitution takes place in the area of nontraditional exports and a reduction in domestic demand results in an increase in foreign-exchange earnings on account of nontraditionals. Evidently, this market substitution limits the deflation necessary to bring the balance of payments back into equilibrium. Moreover, the increased exports of nontraditionals are feasible by virtue of the smallness of the semi-industrialized economy in the world market, which allows it to face an infinitely elastic demand for its nontraditional export products.

C. Implications of the Adjustment Process

An adjustment mechanism that relies fundamentally on deflation of economic activity is a very costly one. It implies that whenever exports turn down, unemployment of labor and of installed capacity will ensue and, moreover, balance-of-payments-induced cycles of domestic activity will be the rule. Under such circumstances, a counter-cyclical policy based on off-setting fluctuations in domestic demand is not feasible because it will automatically induce balance-of-payment deficits, which are not finance-able in the long run unless reserves are built up during the boom years to be run down during the slack. The existence of nontraditional exports provides an indispensable cushion under such circumstances, for it allows the excess supply resulting from domestic demand deflation consequent to shortfalls in traditional exports to spill into the foreign market, earn foreign exchange, and maintain income levels in industrial and, to some extent, service production. Thus, when nontraditional exports are present, the multiplier effect of a reduction in traditional export earnings is contained principally within the traditional export sector because of the offset occurring in industrial exports thanks to market substitution. It follows therefore that instituting an export promotion policy for nontraditionals is an important policy tool for reducing the vulnerability of small semi-industrialized economies to external shocks affecting their traditional exports.

It is important to note that the counter-cyclical role of nontraditional exports previously noted is additional to any averaging effect that a more diversified structure of exports may provide. Thus nontraditional exports in fact do double duty:

(i)   by their mere existence they reduce the average shortfall of export revenue below what it would otherwise be and

(ii)   by their market-switching capacity they automatically expand in volume when the traditional export revenue falls.

This chapter is concerned with the second of these effects; however, the relative quantitative importance of either of the effects will naturally vary by country and circumstance.

II.   MULTISECTORAL MODELS OF ADJUSTMENT TO EXPORT SHORTFALLS

This section is intended to set out the structure of models capable of describing the response of semi-industrialized economies to export short-falls. At the same time, the specification for the simulation of the following section will be exposited.

A. Types of Shock and Types of Adjustment

Export shortfalls can come in two polar forms:

(i) the quantity sold can decrease but the price stays unchanged and
(ii) the price can fall but the quantity sold stays constant.

The first case is typical of a cartelized situation or one in which multinational companies ration selling opportunities among their subsidiaries, or it can result from a supply shortfall caused, for example, by bad weather or a natural calamity. The second case is more typical of the price-taking small country that sells as much as its installed capacity will allow at the going price. The most usual case, however, is a combination of the two polar ones: the price falls and the quantity produced and exported falls in consequence.

Which of the two polar situations occurs or in what mix they occur together makes a considerable difference. If the quantity falls, so does the demand for all inputs into export production and the deflationary impact is spread to suppliers of material inputs as well as to receivers of factor incomes. If the price falls at a fixed quantity, there is no reduction in the demand for physical inputs into export production, only the income of the residual income recipient, usually profit and rent receivers, will fall. Hence, in this case, the deflationary impact is transmitted from the export sectors to the rest of the economy only through a fall in final demand. Evidently in both cases, tax revenue will also be affected but again in different ways: in the quantity case, both indirect and direct tax revenue from export production will fall; in the price case, only profit tax revenue will decrease.

The price–quantity distinction thus requires two different models. Moreover we also need to distinguish the case where nontraditional exports are competitive in the world market from the case where they are not. Thus four models in all are needed. Finally, a hybrid category in which price and quantity adjustments both occur, in accordance with some prespecified elasticity, also will have two variants according to the absence or presence of nontraditional exports.

B. Quantity-Shock Models

Consider first the case where no nontraditional exports can exist because there is an implicit export tax on them.[3]

---

[3] The equations for this case are based on Schydlowsky (1978).

We can write the balance equations for the economy as

$$Q + CM = AQ + F + X + G, \tag{1}$$

where Q is the gross value of production, a vector; CM the competitive imports, a vector; A the input–output requirements for the kinds of things produced domestically, a matrix; F the domestic final demand, a vector; X the exports, a vector; and G the government final demand, a vector.

Final demand, in turn, depends on factor incomes (after taxes) by sector v', and the manner f in which such income is spent, where both v' and f are vectors. Hence,

$$F = fv'Q. \tag{2}$$

Note further that the elements of f do not sum to 1 whenever there is final demand for complementary imports.

Because only traditional exports exist, the export vector will have only a few nonzero elements:

$$X = \begin{bmatrix} X_T \\ 0 \\ 0 \end{bmatrix}, \tag{3}$$

where the suscript stands for traditional.

Competitive imports will exist whenever the total demand for a sector's product exceeds the installed capacity to produce it:

$$CM = \text{pos}[AQ + F + X + G - Q_{max}]. \tag{4}$$

Evidently there will be no competitive imports in the traditional export sector and there will also be none in the service sector, for services cannot be traded. Thus, in both these types of sectors, installed capacity must always be adequate to satisfy domestic demand. This requirement can be satisfied in computation by making Q_{max} very large for the respective sectors.

Replacing (2) and (4) in (1) yields an expression for the level of output as a function of traditional exports.

$$Q = [I - A - fv']^{-1} [X + G - \text{pos}(AQ + fv'Q + X + G - Q_{max})]. \tag{5}$$

Note that the multiplier in this case includes not only the direct and indirect material requirements but also the final demand loop. Furthermore, competitive imports are endogenized and determined simultaneously with the output level.

Although Eq. (5) does not have an explicit analytical solution, it can be solved through numerical approximation by means of an iterative gradient algorithm.

Determining the impact of an exogeneous reduction in the quantity exported is now quite straightforward. It involves merely solving Eq. (5) for two different values of X, while G and $Q_{\max}$ are held constant. The output impact will be equal to the augmented input–output inverse whenever no competitive imports exist, otherwise the output impact is less. In general, the income effect of an export change can be written as

$$\lambda_{Q_T} = dY/d1'X_T = v'\,\Delta Q/1'\,\Delta X_T, \tag{6}$$

where $1'$ is a row vector of ones, Y stands for income, and the T index of the multiplier indicates that only tradtional exports exist. In turn, the balance-of-payments impact will be,

$$\beta_{Q_T} = dBOP/d1'X_T = (1'\,\Delta X - 1'\,\Delta M)/1'\,\Delta X_T, \tag{7}$$

where $\Delta M = \Delta CM + m'\,\Delta Q + f_m v'\,\Delta Q$ and m is the complementary import coefficient vector for intermediate inputs and f_m the complementary import coefficient for final demand. Finally, the fiscal effect of an export shortfall will be

$$\phi_{Q_T} = d_{\text{Fisc}}/d1'X_T = (t'\,\Delta Q + t_c'\,\Delta CM + t_\pi'\,\Delta\Pi)/1'\,\Delta X_T, \tag{8}$$

where t is the indirect tax coefficient (indirect taxes and import duties on noncompetitive imports), t_c the tariff rate on competitive imports, and t_π the tax rate on profits (wages are assumed not to pay taxes).

Turn now to the case where nontraditional exports can occur thanks to an appropriate export promotion policy. Now output in the traditional sectors and in services are demand determined as before but output in the nontraditional export sectors will be supply determined at $Q_{\text{NT}}^{\max}$ because any excess supply will now be exported. Our model must therefore be disaggregated and separately specify the equations governing traditional, nontraditional, and service sectors.

For the traditional sector, we have

$$Q_T - A_{T,T}Q_T - A_{T,NT}Q_{\text{NT}}^{\max} - A_{T,S}Q_S - f_T(v_T'Q_T + v_{\text{NT}}'Q_{\text{NT}}^{\max} + v_S'Q_S) \\ - G_T - X_T = 0. \tag{9}$$

For the nontraditional sectors, we have

$$Q_{\text{NT}}^{\max} - A_{\text{NT},T}Q_T - A_{\text{NT},NT}Q_{\text{NT}}^{\max} - A_{\text{NT},S}Q_S \\ - f_{\text{NT}}(v_T'Q_T + v_{\text{NT}}'Q_{\text{NT}}^{\max} + v_S'Q_S) - G_{\text{NT}} - XM_{\text{NT}} = 0, \tag{10}$$

where XM_{NT} represents the excess demand for these types of goods. A positive element indicates that exports occur, negative elements, that competitive imports come in. For services we have

$$Q_S - A_{S,T}Q_T - A_{S,NT}Q_{\text{NT}}^{\max} - A_{S,S}Q_S \\ - f_S(v_T'Q_T + v_{\text{NT}}'Q_{\text{NT}} + v_S'Q_S) - G_S = 0. \tag{11}$$

This is a system of three sets of equations in three sets of unknowns, Q_T, Q_S, and XM_{NT}; its solution merely requires some matrix manipulation, which will not be reproduced here.

Quantifying the impact of an exogenous reduction of the quantity exported is again quite direct. However, the precise expressions differ somewhat from Eq. (6)–(8) because in this case the output level of nontraditionals does not change, whereas exports of these kinds of commodities exist and their sale on the world market requires fiscal support from the treasury. The income effect of a change in traditional exports can therefore be written as

$$\lambda_{Q_{NT}} = v' \, \Delta Q / 1' \, \Delta X_T = (v_T' \, \Delta Q_T + v_S' \, \Delta Q_S) / 1' \, \Delta X_T, \tag{12}$$

where the NT index of the multiplier indicates the existence of nontraditional exports.

In turn, the balance-of-payments impact will be

$$\beta_{Q_{NT}} = (1' \, \Delta X_T + 1' \, \Delta X_{NT} - 1' \, \Delta M) / 1' \, \Delta X_T. \tag{13}$$

where all exports are defined at FOB prices, all imports at CIF prices, and ΔM is defined as in Eq. (7).

Finally, the fiscal effect of an export shortfall will be

$$\phi_{Q_{NT}} = (t' \, \Delta Q + t_c' \, \Delta CM - t_s' \, \Delta X_{NT} + t_{II}' \, \Delta\Pi) / 1' \, \Delta X_T, \tag{14}$$

where the symbols are as in Eq. (8) and t_s' represents the subsidy rates on nontraditional exports.

C. Price-Shock Models

Consider again first the case where nontraditional exports are not feasible. The balance equation for the economy continues to be as shown in Eq. (1):

$$Q + CM = AQ + F + X + G.$$

The shortfall in export prices will affect factor incomes; therefore, in this case, we need to disaggregate the final demand vector into its components: wages (W), profits (Π), and depreciations (d).

$$F = f[W_1 + \Pi_1(1 - t_\pi) + d'Q], \tag{15}$$

where the subscript 1 indicates that we are in a price-shock model and d' is a vector of depreciation allowances.

The total real expenditures of wage earners will be equal to their nominal wages w plus any gain they have from the reduction in the price of the export goods they purchase. Thus,

$$W_1 = w'Q - P'fW_1 = (1 + P'f)^{-1}w'Q \qquad (16)$$

where P is a vector of output-price increases in the economy (negative for a price reduction).

Real expenditures from profits are a bit more complicated. Profitability goes down because export revenue has fallen. Moreover, the price of domestic sales to intermediate use and to final use has fallen, together with the export price, thus causing further loss of revenue. One sector's loss of revenue on account of intermediate sales, however, is another sector's gain. Thus in the aggregate, the changes in profitability due to the price fall on the intermediate sales cancel out. Losses to entrepreneurs from sales for final use to themselves also cancel out. Thus the only loss to aggregate profits from domestic operations accrues on domestic sales for final use to wage earners:

$$\Pi_1 = \pi'Q + P'X + P'fW_1. \qquad (17)$$

Inserting Eq. (16) into (17), we obtain

$$\Pi_1 = \pi'Q + P'X + P'f(1 + P'f)^{-1}w'Q. \qquad (18)$$

Replacing (18) and (16) in (15) and the latter in (1) and (4) yields expressions for output and competitive imports as follows:

$$Q = \{I - A - f[(1 + P'f(1 - t_\pi))(1 + P'f)^{-1}w' \\ + \pi'(1 - t_\pi) + d']\}^{-1}[X + f(1 - t_\pi)P'X + G - CM], \qquad (19)$$

$$CM = \{AQ + f[(1 + P'f(1 - t_\pi))(1 + P'f)^{-1}w' + \pi'(1 - t_\pi) + d']Q \\ + f(1 - t_\pi) P'X + X + G - Q_{max}\}. \qquad (20)$$

Again, the summary statistics on income, balance of payments, and fiscal effects can easily be written.

When nontraditional exports can exist, it is necessary to operate again with a system of simultaneous equations for traditional, nontraditional, and service sectors. It differs from the system in Eqs. (9)–(11) only in the disaggregation of the final demand vector into its factor-income components:

$$F = \begin{bmatrix} f_T \\ f_{NT} \\ f_S \end{bmatrix} [W_1 + \Pi_1 + D_1] \qquad (21)$$

where

$$W_1 = (1 + P'f)^{-1}w'Q = (1 + P'f)^{-1}[w'_T Q_T + w'_{NT} Q_{NT} \\ + w'_S Q_S], \qquad (22)$$

$$\Pi_1 = (1 - t_\pi) [\pi'_\mathrm{T} Q_\mathrm{T} + \pi'_\mathrm{NT} Q_\mathrm{NT} + \pi'_\mathrm{S} Q_\mathrm{S} + P'fW_1 + P'X_\mathrm{T}], \qquad (23)$$

$$D_1 = d'_\mathrm{T} Q_\mathrm{T} + d'_\mathrm{NT} Q_\mathrm{NT} + d'_\mathrm{S} Q_\mathrm{S}. \qquad (24)$$

The summary expressions for the impact of changes in exports on income, balance of payments, and fiscal situations are unchanged from previous expressions.

D. Mixed Models

Consider now the situation where the quantity of traditionals exported is a function of the price obtainable on the world market in accordance with some supply elasticity. Under such circumstances, any specified change in price would be paired with a specific change in quantity. Correspondingly, the effect on the economy would be the combined effect of the price and quantity changes. The simulation of the effects of a combined price–quantity shock can be most easily undertaken by dividing the total effect into its price and quantity components and then applying the appropriate pure model to each of them. Such a division can be undertaken as follows.

Call the proportionate change in export revenue for each sector

$$\dot{Z}_i = (P_0^i X_0^i - P_1^i X_1^i)/P_0^i X_0^i$$

where Z_i is the total value of exports, P_t^i the export price in period t for sector i, X_t^i the export quantity in period t for sector i, and the overdot denotes proportional change. Now decompose (for sector i):

$$\frac{P_0 X_0 - P_1 X_1}{P_0 X_0} = \frac{P_0 X_0 - P_0 X_1 + P_0 X_1 - P_1 X_1}{P_0 X_0}$$

$$= \frac{P_0(X_0 - X_1) + (P_0 - P_1) X_1}{P_0 X_0} = \frac{X_0 - X_1}{X_0} + \frac{(P_0 - P_1)X_1}{P_0 X_0}.$$

Then,

$$\dot{Z}_i = \dot{x}_i + \dot{p}_i(1 - \dot{x}_i). \qquad (25)$$

Moreover, by definition,

$$\dot{x}_i = e_i \dot{p}_i \qquad (26)$$

where e_i is the export supply elasticity for sector i. Hence,

$$\dot{Z}_i = e_i \dot{p}_i(1 - \dot{p}_i) + \dot{p}_i. \qquad (27)$$

Therefore, in order to determine for any given elasticity what part of the percentage fall in revenue is due to the price effect and what part is due to fall in the quantity, it is necessary to solve the following equation for $\dot{p}_i$:

$$e_i \dot{p}_i^2 - (1 + e_i)\dot{p}_i + \dot{Z}_i = 0. \tag{28}$$

With this division undertaken, the income, BOP, and tax effects are then built up by applying (25) to the multipliers developed in the previous two sections. Thus, for instance, in the absence of nontraditional exports, the income effect of a change in export revenue will (for sector i)

$$\lambda_{M_\tau} = dy/dZ = \{\dot{x}\lambda_{Q_\tau} + (1 - \dot{x})\dot{p}\lambda_{P_\tau}\}/\dot{Z} \tag{29}$$

where the index M indicates that we are in a mixed model.

III. SIMULATION RESULTS FOR PERU

A. The Setting and the Data

Peru in the late 1970s is a good case on which to try out the models developed in the previous section.[4] Since 1969, Peru has followed a very aggressive import substitution policy, using increasingly severe import licensing to restrict purchases abroad to only those things that could not possibly be produced at home. The result was exclusive dependence for export revenue on primary production and the discouragement of nontraditional exports. It was only at the beginning of 1979, after it was abundantly clear that the previous ten years of policy had led to an extraordinary disaster, that Peruvian foreign-trade policy took a turn and that export promotion of nontraditionals was aggressively undertaken. The result has been the doubling of nontraditional exports in one year as well as a very considerable increase in the range of products exported.

Although Peru's economic debacle of 1975, which included a 10% per capita drop in GNP over the next years, was not primarily due to terms-of-trade effects, the loss in purchasing power of Peru's exports certainly helped make matters worse. Moreover, the limitations of Peruvian industrial production to the domestic market certainly was an important element in the depth of the depression that occurred, for it has been abundantly demonstrated that during 1979 Peruvian industry had the capability of selling abroad if the incentive structure was right. Moreover, it has also been demonstrated that the installed capacity to sell in volume was there. Hence, a counter-cyclical policy through mar-

---

[4] For a close look at ten years of recent Peruvian economic history, see Schydlowsky and Wicht (1979).

ket substitution for nontraditional exports was clearly a feasible policy option for Peru in 1975.

A 40-sector input–output table is available for Peru for 1969 and has been used for the simulation exercise. However, in 1969, Peru still imported a fair amount of competitive imports. These were subsequently eliminated by policy. Thus, to approximate the situation in the late 1970s, the 1969 input–output table has been updated by distributing the competitive imports to using sectors, treating them as noncompetitive imports. In the absence of new empirical data on the structure of current noncompetitive imports, this procedure is an adequate approximation.

Productive capacities were taken in the simulation as equal to the observed levels of output in 1969. This does not correspond to reality, for, even in 1969, installed capacity in nontraditional and service sectors was significantly above the realized values, and this capacity has since grown considerably. However, incorporating a large capacity figure in our simulations would introduce an extraneous element into the comparisons. We wish to isolate the effect of market substitution as an anticyclical automatic compensatory mechanism. If the real capacity levels are used in the simulation, a change of policy toward promoting nontraditionals will show up in the simulation calculation as an absorption of that capacity and the generation of vast amounts of nontraditional exports. These would result, not only from the substitution of markets, but also from the utilization of previously idle capacity. Although such results would be correct reflections of reality as regards the effects of a change in policy toward nontraditional exports, they obviously do not correctly measure the potential for market substitution. When capacity utilization is held constant, however, it is possible to isolate the market substitution effect.

B. Results and Their Implications

Table 2 shows the various multipliers obtained in Peru using a 10% reduction[5] in either the quantity or the price of Peru's basket of traditional exports; the mixed case involving supply elasticities is shown in Table 4 and will be discussed later.

Consider first the impacts on income. Without nontraditional exports, income will fall by more than twice as much as exports, whether quantities or prices vary. In the presence of nontraditional exports, the income fall is buffered the most. The buffering is particularly strong in the case of quantity variations, where the corresponding multiplier falls from 2.3 to

---

[5] Note that increases may not be symmetrical in their effects because of a limitation on domestic productive capacity [cf. Eq. (4)].

TABLE 2

Simulation Results

Multiplier[a]	Quantity variation	Price variation
Income		
Without NTX	2.263	2.499
With NTX	0.987	1.311
Wage bill		
Without NTX	1.010	0.272
With NTX	0.401	−0.312
Profit and depreciation bill		
Without NTX	1.253	2.227
With NTX	0.586	1.623
BOP and fiscal		
Without NTX	0.541	0.592
With NTX	0.423	0.486

[a] NTX = nontraditional exports.

0.99. In the case of price variation, the multiplier falls from 2.5 to 1.3. There is no question, then, that market substitution in the nontraditional exports sector reduces very substantially the vulnerability of the small semi-industrialized economy to export shocks.

Of interest as well is the relative situation between quantity and price variations. Whether or not nontraditional exports exist, the economy appears to be more sensitive to price than to quantity variations. This is rather unexpected because one would think that with the impact of price variations contained initially to profits, as compared with the impact of quantity variations that affect all material inputs as well as the labor requirements, quantity variations would have a higher overall impact. It appears that the contrary occurs as a result of the relative incidence of the various leakages. It must be remembered that, in all these models, the leakages from the income stream are imports, indirect taxes, and profit taxes. Under quantity variation, there are immediate leakages into imports and indirect taxes; under price variation, such leakages do not exist. On the other hand, under quantity variation, the impact change of profits is smaller than under price variation, hence the leakage into profit taxes will be proportionately smaller as well. Whether the total impact leakage is greater from quantity variation or price variation therefore depends on the relative size of the import coefficient, the indirect tax coefficient, and the profit tax rate.

Table 3 gives the income multipliers at different profit tax rates. No-

TABLE 3

Sensitivity of Income Multipliers to Profit Taxation

Quantity variation[a]		Profit tax rate (%)	Price variation[a]	
Without NTX	With NTX		Without NTX	With NTX
1.65	0.83	35	1.26	0.76
2.04	0.93	20	2.03	1.12
2.20	0.97	15	2.36	1.25
2.26	0.99	13	2.50	1.31

[a] NTX = nontraditional exports.

tice that, as the profit tax rate rises, the multiplier for price variation falls with regard to quantity variation. This is quite consistent with expectation because, as the profit tax rate rises, the leakage through this fiscal instrument becomes greater relative to the other leakages and it is this leakage that is particularly effective in the price variation case.

It is also interesting to note that the stabilizing impact of nontraditional exports is relatively greater under quantity variation than under price variation. This makes sense once again if we recall that the initial impact under quantity variation on the demand for intermediate goods is considerable. Thus, under quantity variation, there is an immediate reduction in demand for inputs and therefore a greater freeing of nontraditional export capacity. Under price variation, this does not occur, for the initial impact is exclusively through final demand.

The effect of nontraditionals on the functional income distribution can also be seen from Table 2. In the quantity variation case, the buffering favors wages slightly at the expense of profits; this probably results from the particular configuration of Peruvian numbers. However, the price variation case is more substantive, for in this case the existence of nontraditionals implies an improvement in the real wage bill when prices fall. It would appear, then, that in this case the real income gain from the price fall outweighs the nominal income loss from lower activity (and the reverse when prices rise).

The balance-of-payments and fiscal multipliers are shown together because they are identical in value. This results from the construction of the models in which there is only a single domestic leakage (taxes) and only a single foreign leakage (imports). It is remarkable that the amount of buffering that nontraditional exports can provide the balance-of-payments and fiscal situations is considerably less than it provides to the income

TABLE 4

Simulation Results: Mixed Case

Multiplier[a]	Price variation	Mixed case			Quantity variation
		$e = 0.2$	$e = 0.6$	$e = 1.0$	
Income					
Without NTX	2.499	2.459	2.408	2.378	2.263
With NTX	1.311	1.256	1.187	1.145	0.987
Wage bill					
Without NTX	0.272	0.397	0.556	0.651	1.010
With NTX	−0.312	−0.191	−0.038	0.054	0.401
Profit and depreciation bill					
Without NTX	2.227	2.062	1.853	1.727	1.253
With NTX	1.623	1.445	1.218	1.082	0.586
Balance of payments and fiscal					
Without NTX	0.592	0.583	0.572	0.566	0.541
With NTX	0.486	0.475	0.462	0.454	0.423

[a] NTX = nontraditional exports.

level. Whereas for the latter, the buffering is about 50%, for the balance-of-payments and fiscal multipliers, it is merely 20%. Moreover, there is no major difference visible between quantity and price adjustments in this case.

We now turn to the results from the mixed adjustment model shown in Table 4. Evidently, the mixed multipliers will lie between the values for the polar cases and will be closer to the quantity case the higher the supply elasticity is. Correspondingly, the buffering available from nontraditional exports is also a mix of the pure quantity and price buffering. This mixing leads to particularly interesting results for the wage bill; with an export elasticity of 0.745, the wage bill is completely insulated from fluctuations in export revenue.

IV. POLICY CONCLUSIONS

Stabilization of domestic economic conditions in the face of fluctuations of prices or quantities of traditional exports has been a main policy goal pursued by national authorities for some time. Most of the emphasis in this connection has been devoted to the stabilization of the prices themselves or to the accumulation of adequate foreign-exchange reserves to serve as a buffer in bad times. In this chapter we endeavored to show the role that can be played by nontraditional exports in buffering fluctuations originating in the traditional export sector. Simulation results for Peru show that 50% or more of the income fluctuations resulting from changes in export earnings can be offset through the automatic mechanism of market substitution if nontraditional exports exist. Moreover, the balance of payments and fiscal impacts of flucutations are also reduced by approximately 20%. Such results warrant the inclusion of nontraditional export promotion policy in the arsenal of economic stabilization tools.

Policy measures to promote nontraditional exports are well known from other contexts. They consist essentially of alternative means for bringing the export-exchange rate into line with cost-exchange rates either by refunding taxation of inputs (traditional drawback and generalized drawback), by providing compensating subsidies on output, by adopting a compensated devaluation in which exchange-rate and trade-tax systems are modified in offsetting fashion, or, yet again, in combinations involving the preceding. Moreover, internal fiscal and credit measures can be used in complementary fashion. The literature on these measures is extensive and need not be reproduced here. What should be underlined is that the allocational arguments, employment-generating arguments, and capacity utilization arguments that are traditionally given for promoting nontraditional exports are reinforced by the finding that the existence of such a policy installs an automatic stabilization mechanism that can buffer the small semiindustrialized economy against the fluctuations originating in its primary export sector.

REFERENCES

Balassa, B., and Associates (1971). *The Structure of Protection in Developing Countries.* Baltimore, Maryland: Johns Hopkins Press.

Balassa, B., and Associates (1982). *Incentives for Industrialization in Semi-Industrialized Countries.* Baltimore, Maryland: Johns Hopkins Press.

Berlinski, J., and Schydlowsky, D. M. (1977). "Incentives for Industrialization in Argentina." Boston University/CLADS, Occasional Paper #1, October.

Little, I. M. D., Scitovsky, T., and Scott, M. (1970). *Industry and Trade in Some Developing Countries: A Comparative Study.* London and New York: Oxford University Press.

Schydlowsky, D. M. (1972). "Latin American Trade Policies in the 1970's: A Prospective Appraisal", *The Quarterly Journal of Economics* **86** (May).

Schydlowsky, D. M. (1978). "Competitive Imports in Input–Output Analysis: An Endogenous Treatment", mimeo. Boston, Massachusetts: Boston University.

Schydlowsky, D. M., & Wicht, J. J. (1979). *Anatomía de un Fracaso Económico: Perú 1968–1978*, 4th ed. Lima: Universidad del Pacífico.

Center for Latin American Development Studies
Boston University
Boston, Massachusetts

Chapter 7

Latin American External Debt: The Case of Uncertain Development

Albert Fishlow

I. INTRODUCTION

Until recently in the analysis of postwar Latin American development, capital flows appeared only as a minor element. When external capital was considered, it took on significance as much for its dominant form—direct investment by transnational corporations—as for its role in the balance of payments. In fact, external finance proved negligible for Latin America for much of the period. As an ECLA study on indebtedness noted in the early 1960s, "Lastly, the contribution of autonomous capital movements as a whole to the capacity to import, and consequently to balancing the Latin American countries' external payments, seems very modest if account is taken of the region's huge service payments abroad." [See Economic Commission for Latin America (1965).]

Circumstances have changed profoundly in the past ten years, especially since 1973. Unprecedented increases in the external indebtedness

143

of developing countries have been registered. Latin American countries have been especially prominent. Debt and its management will play a different role in the decades ahead than they did for much of the postwar period. From a modest supplement to direct investment, loan finance has been transformed into a fundamental determinant of development strategy in many countries.

This chapter addresses three central aspects of the present Latin American situation.[1] Section II traces the changes in the magnitude and composition of the debt. Section III examines the real cost of the loans contracted. Section IV focuses on the implications of past indebtedness for future policy choices and considers the Brazilian case in special detail. The basic conclusion of this chapter is that a development model structured upon significant external debt involves a delicate balance. All that is certain is the obligation to repay: returns and even real costs are unknown. Coping with such uncertainty imposes important constraints on future decisions. There is a narrow margin between success and failure.

II.   THE COMPOSITION AND MAGNITUDE OF THE DEBT

Table 1 presents information on current and past levels of Latin American debt and its composition. Two trends dominate. One is the explosion of debt in the 1970s. The other is the progressively larger role of private financial flows, especially from commercial banks.

During the past decade, Latin American debt increased more than sevenfold compared with a doubling in the 1960s. Deflated for inflation and with income growth subtracted, the differences are even more dramatic: a mere real rise of 8% in the 1960s, 117% in the 1970s. Reliance on external loan financing has demonstrably increased, but foreign direct investment expanded much more slowly. From 1956 and 1965, direct investment exceeded loans; from 1976 to 1980, direct investment amounted to only 20% of total borrowing. Debt has become the predominant form of capital transfer.

The new access to capital markets evolved in two phases. In the first, beginning in the late 1960s and lasting until 1973, the Euro-currency market discovered Latin America. Demand and supply factors in the industrial countries and selected larger developing countries both contributed. Low costs for bank credit in the early 1970s, owing to industrial country recession and lowered loan volume, conferred attractive borrowing terms on Latin American countries in search of capital to finance higher growth

[1] A partially overlapping treatment of the Latin American debt problem, with more attention to the contribution of international economic policy, can be found in Fishlow (1981).

TABLE 1

Latin American Medium- and Long-Term Debt[a]

Source of loan	1960	1967	1970	1973	1976	1978	1980
Public or publicly							
guaranteed	5.5	10.7	15.3	24.8	53.1	82.7	114.6
Official	—	5.9	8.0	11.0	17.4	22.7	28.5
Private	—	4.8	7.2	13.8	35.7	60.1	86.1
Financial markets	—	2.2	3.7	10.0	30.3	51.5	80.3
Banks	—	—	2.6	8.4	27.9	44.8	—
Nonguaranteed	2.9	4.6	5.9	13.2	22.8	33.2	38.8
Banks	—	—	—	—	17.1	24.9	29.1
Total disbursed	8.4	15.3	21.2	38.0	75.9	115.9	153.4

[a] Table excludes Venezuela and Trinidad and Tobago, which were consistent oil exporters during the period. Values are given in billions of dollars. Dashed entries indicate data that were not available.

Sources: For public and publicly guaranteed external debt, 1960—Inter-American Development Bank (1979); 1967–1978—World Bank (1979); 1980—World Bank (1981). For total disbursed debt, 1960–1970—balance-of-payments-based estimates of cumulative capital inflows, reported in an earlier working paper ("Debt, Growth and Hemispheric Relations"), adjusted upward by 1.05. This factor is the relationship between the earlier 1973 estimate and the new direct 1973 estimate; 1973–1978—National Foreign Assessment Center (1979) to which the public debt of Ecuador has been added and with Argentine debt estimated independently from Bank of International Settlements and national sources; 1980—International Monetary Fund (1982). The nonguaranteed debt was computed as the total minus public and publicly guaranteed. For nonguaranteed bank debt, the proportion of bank loans to nonguaranteed debt is for Brazil, 1977/1978—World Bank (1979).

rates. Domestic savings were not as easily channeled, and internal interest rates were greater than international charges despite large spreads. These, as much as 4% over the London Inter-Bank offer rate (LIBOR) in the late 1960s, translated into substantial bank profits for lending to countries whose buoyant exports and improved economic prospects conferred newly discovered creditworthiness. As the volume of lending increased, bank competition and syndication led to dramatic and rapid declines in spread and longer maturities. In the early 1970s, current account deficits were not a constraint to expansion but rather a planned means for mobilizing external savings. Brazil followed such a strategy of debt-led growth in designing its "economic miracle."

After 1973, borrowing was of another kind, less an option than a necessity to sustain the higher cost of imports essential to economic growth. Quadrupling of oil prices increased the direct cost of Latin American oil imports by more than $3 billion between 1973 and 1974 and affected even countries like Peru and Mexico, which only later emerged as exporters. Prices of some principal Latin American exports, on the other hand, turned downward in 1975 under the impact of recession in the United States and Europe.

Borrowing was not the only option in the face of the sudden increase in oil prices. One alternative, difficult in the short term, was to use less oil. Individual countries could also compensate by cutting back on imports of other products, helped along by the adverse terms of trade effect on real income. They could also export more. Oil importers could thus self-finance their higher oil bills by adjusting other trade accounts. As time went on, more Latin American countries took such measures. But in 1974 and 1975, industrial country recession made exports less certain, and reduced growth rates were not a popular choice after recent favorable experience. Debt-financed gradual adjustment was an attractive alternative.

In opting for such a strategy, and maintaining their already high levels of capital formation, a few countries in the region—Mexico, Peru, and Brazil—accounted for almost 80% of the regional doubling of the debt between 1973 and 1974 and simultaneously helped solve the global recycling problem. Oil consumers could not all avoid deficits. Some countries had to borrow or the petro-dollar surpluses would not be effectively recycled. *Ex post,* the surpluses of the oil producers would always equal other deficits; the question was at what world income level. Willing debtors translated into larger global demand.

Not all developing countries had the luxury of seeking to sustain economic growth in this more hostile external environment. Many, particularly the poorest, had to follow the more painful path of immediate income adjustment despite larger official resources mobilized in their behalf. Because of their previous access to private financial markets, the larger Latin American borrowers could continue to rely on debt. Loan terms did not move adversely to discourage them. Indeed, after an initial rise under the impulse of new demand and the Herstatt failure in 1974, spreads narrowed again on Euro-currency lending to developing countries, falling by 1979 to less than 1%.

This story of greatly increased Latin American external indebtedness is therefore also a story of progressively larger participation of private lenders. During the early 1960s, Latin America was still heavily dependent on official finance. New U.S. bilateral programs under the Alliance for Progress transferred large amounts of public resources. When public assistance soon fell out of fashion, private financial markets more than substituted. During both phases of rapid debt increase, the role of private sources—and especially commercial banks—was ascendent.

Table 1 also traces this changing composition of the debt. Official capital made up a third of disbursed debt as late as 1970; its current proportion is about 20%. In terms of net flows, official participation is now on the order of 10%; the official share of gross lending is about the same.[2] Two-thirds of the region's debt now is owed to banks, twice the 1970 proportion.

Private finance did not bring with it the dire consequences that some had anticipated. The new loans did not prejudice the growth of the public sector in Latin America. Quite the contrary. Government, state enterprises or firms with public participation, and official banks remained the principal recipient of loans. Public guarantee was an important attraction to commercial banks, providing an improved access to capital for the state sector and underwriting its expansion. This was a far cry from the 1950s when Latin American governments pleaded, largely in vain, for official capital to finance public projects. Smaller national firms dependent on domestic credit are more likely losers. But even in this case, national laws discouraging multinational enterprises from utilizing local credit and raising relative costs still more, have partially redressed the balance. Such legislation not only responds to nationalist sentiment but also encourages continuing new infusions of foreign exchange by multinationals. Non-guaranteed loans for subsidiaries have been obtained with relative ease, and such debt financing has been preferred by the firms to larger equity commitments in a period of uncertainty.

Private capital has been available quickly to borrowers. Agreements can be concluded in a matter of weeks and months, not years. Project evaluation is rudimentary even though the majority of loans remains specific in application. Even this requirement is bypassed in the case of direct loans to governments or loans to banks to be reloaned to their clients.

Private lenders have also been less exigent than the World Bank and the regional development banks in monitoring performance, at the project level as well as for the economy as a whole. Each bank views its exposure partially and apolitically, at least until a crisis emerges. Countries gain a freer hand and benefit from the intense competition that now characterizes the international financial market. Bilateral aid and even multilateral loans have frequently possessed greater ideological content and imposed greater constraints.

Such an interpretation does not square with a dependency view of the adverse implications of greater bank finance. One commentator speaks of such financial dependence as "potentially the most limiting type of exter-

---

[2] The net flow ratio of official capital for 1978 for Latin America is calculated at 0.14 for publicly guaranteed debt. [see World Bank (1979)]. Additional nonguaranteed private net inflow of perhaps another $5 billion reduces the ratio to 0.11. The gross flows yield a similar ratio.

nal vulnerability." Others contend that "most recipient regimes have been authoritarian and/or highly repressive. Bank loans, open-door regimes, and repressive policies have frequently coincided. . . . The technocratic posturing and apolitical rhetoric of bank officials is merely a mask for far-reaching political actions" [Aronson (1979)].

Dependency analysts are quite right in stressing a linkage between openness of economies and external indebtedness. An export orientation both attracts lenders and is a necessary condition for servicing loans. But they go beyond that connection to a more dubious normative judgment that openness is inevitably bad. Such analysts are right again in recognizing implicitly the asymmetry of bank interests: they are much more active in unabashedly pressing for orthodox and conservative policies, economic and political, during crises than prosperity. But they fail to credit the willingness of private banks, compared with governments, to lend to a variety of regimes, and they see economic crises as only of external origin and not rooted even partially in policies that flaunt market forces. Finally, a dependency view interprets the authoritarian solution that may emerge from the crisis to have its exclusive basis in international capitalist imposition rather than related to populist mismanagement.

This is not to argue that borrowing from private sources imposes no burden. Three adverse financial impacts have been felt. One is higher interest costs than for official finance; the second is shorter maturities than for public loans; the third is flexible, not fixed, interest charges.

The higher interest cost of free market borrowing is clear. Official loans contain an intended and explicit grant element because of concessional interest rates and long grace periods. Even when multilateral banks have raised rates to compensate for the higher cost of their borrowed resources, their charges have been much lower than those prevailing in the Euro-currency market. For Latin America, the grant element in official loans has been substantial: 39% of loan value in the late 1960s and 22% as late as 1979.[3] Beyond this intended grant component, uncompensated inflation afforded another unintended subsidy. Fixed nominal interest rates benefited debtors. Previously contracted loans turned out to be available at negative real rates. By contrast, private Euro-currency loans soon evolved into variable rate instruments adjusted on a semiannual basis by the LIBOR. As the latter progressively incorporated expected inflation, the transfer to debtors from inflation was nullified.

The shorter maturity structure of private debt is a second unfavorable characteristic. Official loans to Latin American countries had an average term of about 20 years in the 1960s, declining to about 15 years in the later

[3] See Inter-American Development Bank (1979) p. 89, for the grant element formula applied to the terms of official loans provided on p. 90 in that reference.

1970s. Private loans have been of far shorter maturity. Even in the best of worlds—as in 1973 when the Brazilian government could set a minimum term of 10 years in the flush of a debt-led "economic miracle"—the average length of private debt remained much lower. In the debt adjustment phase, when pressing capital needs made the countries once again the more ardent suitors, maturities sometimes shortened to as few as 5 years, settling now closer to 8 once again. Brazil's well-documented experience is illustrative of the fluctuation. Average maturity declined from 5.6 years in 1970 to 4.7 in 1972 as Euro-market borrowing accelerated. It rose again to 5.6 in 1974 because the term of private debt lengthened. In 1977, the average reached a new low of 4.3 years as considerable borrowing occurred under less favorable terms [see Batista (1980)].

Short maturities limit gains from inflation. They levy high continuing service charges against export earnings and increase the vulnerability of debtors to fluctuations in exchange receipts. The constant need to refinance outstanding loans allows a narrow margin for error.

At the same time, private capital markets have themselves become more variable. International lending rates have become less predictable and increasingly dependent upon the internal monetary policies pursued by the industrial countries. The 1980 roller coaster is a good example. Current interest rates apply to past as well as present borrowing. Consequently, a one-percentage-point change in nominal interest rates can provoke a swing in the regional balance of payments of almost $1 billion. Oil price increases actually tilt the trade balance for the region as a whole favorably and, excluding Venezuela, cancel out.

These characteristics of private capital markets combine to reduce the benefit to developing-country borrowers. Higher interest costs, shorter maturity, and greater uncertainty expose debtors to a greater short-term risk and at the same time lower the long-term net gain. A strategy of indebtedness under private auspices is therefore distinct from reliance on official lending. The next section will elaborate on this theme, by contrasting the long-term returns on investment of loans with the liquidity problem posed in the short term.

III. THE RATE OF RETURN TO EXTERNAL BORROWING

One of the principal arguments offered in favor of the debt option preferred by many Latin American countries in the past decade is that money was cheap, the consequence of efficient financial intermediation and unanticipated inflation. This impression of low, even negative, real interest rates depends very much on the deflator chosen. Table 2 sets out the pre-

TABLE 2

Euro-Dollar Real Interest Rates[a]

Year	Euro-dollar deposit rate	U.S. GNP deflator (annual increase)	Export price deflator (annual increase)	Brazil spreads	All developing country spreads
1969	9.8	5.0	4.5	4.0	
1970	8.5	5.4	10.9	3.0	
1971	6.6	5.1	−3.9	2.0	
1972	5.5	4.1	8.2	1.25	
1973	9.2	5.8	37.7	0.7	
1974	11.0	9.7	35.6	1.2	1.1
1975	7.0	9.6	1.0	1.7	1.7
1976	5.6	5.2	14.0	1.9	1.7
1977	6.0	5.9	24.6	2.0	1.6
1978	8.7	7.4	−8.5	1.6	1.2
1979	12.0	8.8	10.8	1.0	0.9
1980[b]	14.3	9.0	15.4	1.50	

[a] Values are expressed as percentages. *Sources*: For Euro-dollar rate, IMF (1980a); for U.S. GNP Deflator, 1969–1978—U.S. Bureau of the Census, *Statistical Abstract*, 1979, 1980—IMF (1980b); for western hemisphere export unit value (excluding petroleum)—IMF (1980a); for Brazil spreads— Batista (1980), and *World Financial Markets* (1980); for all developing country spreads—World Bank (1980).

[b] Estimated.

vailing Euro-dollar deposit rate (fractionally different from the offer rate), the variable spread (for Brazil specifically, and all developing countries), the U.S. GNP deflator, and a Latin American export price deflator. With the exception of 1975, the real rate calculated with the GNP deflator has been consistently positive. In the early 1970s, prior to the oil crisis, it averaged around 1.5%. The real rate fell in the mid-1970s as increased nominal charges failed to keep pace with raging inflation and rose again subsequently as the OPEC surplus diminished and its investment in other assets increased. In 1980, the average real rate approximated 5%.

The pattern of real rates measured in constant export terms is quite different. Because prices of exports (and imports) rose much more rapidly during this period than the GNP deflator, the export-deflated rate is very much lower, being especially negative in 1974 and 1974. Because prices of exports are more variable, real rates fluctuate widely.

Neither of these deflators is adequate to measure the real cost of the debt because neither *numéraire* captures accurately the value of the for-

TABLE 3

Cost of Brazilian Capital Inflows, 1970–1979[a]

Real interest rate 1981–1995	U.S. GNP deflator	Trade price deflator
−1	1.9	−3.0
1	2.5	−2.4
3	3.1	−1.9
5	3.7	−1.3

[a] Values are expressed as percentages. *Source:* U.S. GNP deflator and import/export prices—IMF (1980a).

eign exchange acquired and repaid. A related problem is that private debt is contracted and repaid at different times. Whatever the past pattern of interest rates, real costs actually incurred cannot be calculated without reference to future interest rates and the path of amortization.

I have, therefore, incorporated a different deflation procedure and explicit allowance for the future in calculating an internal cost implicit in the actual capital inflows received by Brazil in the 1970s.[4] Because detailed information on inflows and amortization, actual and projected, is not available for the region as a whole, the estimate is country specific. The importance of Brazil in Latin American and world debt is so large and the similarity in country borrowing costs so great that the results are of wider interest.

Table 3 presents eight different estimates for the cost of Brazilian borrowing during the decade of the 1970s, assuming two different nominal interest rates for the repayment period 1981–1995, 9 and 13%, and two different rates of future inflation, 8 and 10%. Three conclusions can be drawn.

One is that the choice of deflator makes a difference of about 5 per-

[4] The inflows are the gross medium- and long-term loans received between 1970 and 1979; the outflows are amortization and interest payments accruing from those loans until 1995 (when a small residual amortization remains due). For the period 1970–1979, these outflows are estimated by subtracting service on the old debt obtained from the amortization schedules on debt outstanding at year end 1969, and corresponding interest payments adjusted for current rates, from current service payments. Future amortization is given for the debt outstanding as of December 1979; interest payments are estimated under different rate assumptions. The inflows are corrected to constant dollars by an import price index and the outflows by an export price index. Thus the initial capital inflows are measured in terms of real imports and the subsequent repayments in terms of real exports. All data are from the *Bolletim,* Banco Central do Brasil.

centage points in determining the cost. The trade deflator, eroding the value of dollars much more than the GNP deflator, indicates a negative real cost for foreign debt contracted during the period. This presumes that export prices will not rise more rapidly than the GNP deflator in the future. Were they to continue to do so, the cost differential would widen further. Conversely, if the export index increased less rapidly, the divergence would narrow.

In the second instance, the cost calculation is sensitive to the future real interest rate. Each percentage point increase in those rates raises the cost on past debt by about a smaller, 0.3 percentage point. The impact is attenuated because the actual costs incurred in the 1970s remain unchanged. The rate of return is a weighted average of such past experience and the future. From Table 3 it appears that the real rate implicit in the 1970s was a little less than 3% for the GNP deflator and about −4% for the trade deflator.

The third conclusion is the most basic. Regardless of deflator and future real interest rates, debt was a bargain in the 1970s. Average real rates even as high as 3% compare favorably with historic norms. And there is good reason to prefer a trade deflator. However weighted, it will yield much lower costs. Real returns in Brazil—to applications in infrastructure, alternative energy sources, and directly productive investment— have been demonstrably greater. The large share of capital in Brazilian income and a relatively low capital–output ratio implies real rates that are considerably higher.[5]

Properly speaking, therefore, there is no debt problem. The debt in the long run could adequately repay itself. Negative costs, of course, make such a formulation even more evident. Yet, there is generalized concern about the magnitude of the debt, and not least, about the Brazilian debt.

That worry is well-founded. It derives from the twofold requirement that the debt be continuously serviced in the short term and paid in foreign exchange. The problem therefore centers around the short-term elasticity of capital supply and the medium-term prospects for exports. The larger the service obligations, owing to short maturities and high nominal interest rates, the more susceptible are countries to a liquidity crisis and the ensuing adjustment costs.

---

[5] The marginal rate of return can be expressed as $r = (O/K)\beta$, where β is the share of capital and O/K the output–capital ratio. The share of capital in Brazilian value added is about 0.4, and the present marginal capital–output ratio, 3.5. Letting the latter approximate the average, which in the "miracle" years was lower, the estimated real rate is 11%. What counts is the order of magnitude, which, given the Brazilian growth rate, capital share, and investment ratio, must substantially exceed the cost of debt.

In sum, long-term positive returns on borrowed resources do not guarantee the foreign exchange when needed in the short term. The time profiles of benefits and costs are likely to diverge, requiring continued financing until returns are realized over a longer horizon. If additional external loans are not available, short-term obligations may not be met, or only at the expense of other imports and consequently of economic growth. Exports are unlikely to satisfy immediate foreign-exchange needs even with rapid growth. But they are also an essential element to avoiding a debt trap. The short-term liquidity problem has its counterpart in a medium-term transformation problem: the capacity to divert increased productive capacity to export. Debt can only be repaid, or its rate of growth slowed, through a growing merchandise surplus.

An adequate supply of new loans and liberal access to markets are not assured in the present difficult international economic environment. In addition, nominal rates of interest in 1980 and 1981 are at peak levels and show little sign of consistent decline. They are likely to lag behind reductions in inflation. Oil-poor countries have the gloomy prospect of deteriorating terms of trade as future oil prices outstrip export prices. Together these factors could cause a real debt problem: the costs of the new loans in the 1980s necessary to meet the short-term liquidity requirements of the debt of the 1970s could very well begin to outstrip real returns. A fundamental limitation of a model of debt finance is that it requires a *continuing* supply of credit on favorable terms for its advantages to be realized. Debt in the 1970s could turn out to be more expensive than it seemed.

We expand upon this theme in the next section, examining in quantitative terms the near- and medium-term foreign-exchange requirements of Latin American debtor countries, with special emphasis on the case of Brazil.

IV. PROJECTIONS OF LATIN AMERICAN FINANCING NEEDS

The dynamic of the debt is best understood quantitatively by embedding its required continuing service within a structure that also projects the merchandise balance. The simplest model for so doing is one that relates import requirements to product growth. Despite its abstraction from real-economy complexity, such an approach—because of its orientation to the future—is more informative than reliance upon static debt service ratios or similar measures. It also is more accurate than regression-derived estimates of current account deficits that ignore the mounting role of debt, rather than of the merchandise account, in perpetuating those deficits.[6]

The basic reduced form model used here is:[7] $\Delta D = M_0(1 + \alpha g)^t - X_0(1 + r)^t + iD$, where D is the debt, M the imports, α the elasticity of imports to income, g the rate of growth of gross product, X the exports, r the rate of growth of exports; and i the interest rate. Implicit in such a formulation is the assumption that new financing is available in the quantity required and that domestic consumption can be determined by tax and other direct policies. The model is designed to spell out the implications of parametric change upon borrowing requirements. In their net form, they are as just specified. In gross terms, $L = aD + \Delta D$, where L is gross loans, and a the reciprocal of the average maturity of the debt. The faster amortization occurs, the greater the volume of loan activity for a given increase in the debt.

From the first equation, it is clear that a debt maximum is reached only if $\alpha g < r$, that is, a merchandise surplus must eventually emerge. Trade thus determines the long-run dynamics of the debt. In the short term, the higher the interest rate and initial level of debt, the longer it will take until such a turning point is reached. Once the maximum is attained, the debt will subsequently steadily diminish.

Table 4 sets out a series of debt simulations for Latin American non-oil-exporting countries, conditioned upon different assumptions regarding these key determinants of foreign-exchange requirements. These projections are less estimates of what will happen than tendencies inherent in the particular situations they describe. They have been designed to permit a direct comparison of the importance of each of the factors that have significant influence upon the evolution of the debt: export growth, product growth, import elasticity, and financial market conditions.

It is not surprising under the assumed circumstances that export growth is the single most important determinant of terminal level debt and the state of the current account deficit. The 1-percentage-point reduction in real export growth portrayed in part B of Table 4 leads to a terminal

---

[6] A recent article by Cleveland and Brittain (1977) estimates the current account deficit as a percentage of income by regressing it against real income per capita, OECD real income relative to trend, the change in the value of oil imports, and a measure of excess money supply. By ignoring debt service, they eliminate one growing source of the problem. This helps to explain their sanguine conclusion that "LDCs' current deficits and foreign borrowing needs will decline in real terms from now on. . . . If so, worries about the LDC debt problem should soon fade" (pp. 746, 748).

[7] The original model is available from the author on request. The initial conditions are largely estimated from the macroeconomic and balance-of-payments statistics of the Inter-American Development Bank (1979). Debt characteristics come from the sources used in the tables.

debt that is almost twice as large as the base projection. Instead of eventually reaching a significant merchandise trade surplus, that account is barely balanced by the end of the decade, while large factor payments abroad continue to produce a deficit on current account. What is represented here as a change in the rate of growth of export volume applies equally to the influence of price. A declining trend in the terms of trade at a rate of 1% a year would produce an identical debt effect, but with greater resource cost.

The import side of the merchandise account enters through the variation in the product growth rate in part C of Table 4. The effect of more rapid product growth is dampened here by an aggregate import elasticity that is slightly less than unity; petroleum imports are assumed to increase less than proportionally to product so that even with increasing relative prices, their importance declines. An import elasticity greater than one would magnify the influence of product growth on trade account. That is exactly what happens during a debt-led phase. Accelerating rates of product growth require a higher elasticity. Greater import content is associated with an investment boom as bottlenecks and technological lags limit competitive domestic supply. If this relationship between the import elasticity and the growth rate were introduced, the adverse balance of payments implications of above-average growth rates in part C could easily rival those of reduced export growth. Thus, if the import elasticity for nonpetroleum products were to increase from 1 to 1.1 as the product growth rate rose from 6.0 to 6.6%, import growth would rise from 5.9 to 7%. That would just about replicate the debt consequences of part B.

Such a magnified effect of product growth is implicit in policies calling for alleviation of debt service pressures through recession. If the impact on import demand is more than proportional, helped along by price changes that make imports relatively more expensive, an economic slowdown can improve the balance of payments more than the average elasticities indicate. Equally effective, of course, and potentially less costly is a reduced import elasticity that averts or limits the decline in aggregate growth. That difference in approach is central to the continuing controversy between monetarists and structuralists in Latin America.

Harder financial terms affect interest payments as well as the time profile of amortization. The negative impact from higher interest rate charges is buffered to some extent by the higher earnings from extensive reserves that many countries now hold. It is also eased by the fact that interest on past official debt is fixed. Part of the continuing increase in net interest costs relative to the base projection is caused by the progressive importance of private debt. Although the positive merchandise balance still produces a current account surplus by the end of the decade, the higher

TABLE 4

Debt Projections: Latin America[a]

Year	Official debt	Private debt	Gross loans	Amorti-zation	Net interest[b]	Debt service	Current account deficit/GDP	Current account deficit	Debt service/Exports[c]	Net debt[d]/GDP	National savings/GNP
1980	30.2	124.6	47.9	22.7	14.1	36.8	21.7	0.044	0.41	0.24	0.20
A. Base projection (10% inflation; 6.0% real GDP growth; 8% real export growth; easy financial terms: 2% real private rate; −3% real official rate; 0.8 loans private, 0.2 official; 8-year private maturity)											
1983	51.9	161.5	50.1	30.6	18.8	49.4	22.8	0.029	0.33	0.21	0.23
1986	76.2	184.7	55.0	42.3	22.1	64.4	17.5	0.014	0.25	0.15	0.24
1990	88.3	137.2	15.6	44.0	16.7	60.7	(20.6)[e]	(0.009)[e]	0.12	0.04	0.26
B. Lower export growth (7% real export growth)											
1983	53.6	168.0	55.2	31.0	19.3	50.3	27.5	0.035	0.34	0.22	0.22
1986	86.5	219.9	75.6	45.4	25.8	71.2	35.0	0.028	0.30	0.19	0.23
1990	140.9	299.3	97.1	62.5	34.8	97.3	42.5	0.019	0.21	0.14	0.24

C. *Higher product growth (6.6% real GDP growth)*

Year											
1983	52.0	162.2	50.8	30.6	18.8	49.4	23.4	0.030	0.33	0.21	0.26
1986	78.9	194.6	61.8	43.0	22.9	65.9	23.3	0.018	0.26	0.16	0.27
1990	107.6	199.5	48.8	50.4	22.8	73.2	5.2	0.002	0.14	0.07	0.28

D. *Harder financial terms (3% private real interest rate; 1% official real interest rate; 0.9 loans private; 0.1 official; 6-year private maturity)*

Year											
1983	38.8	180.0	58.3	26.1	21.5	57.6	25.5	0.033	0.38	0.22	0.23
1986	52.6	229.0	80.8	61.6	28.6	90.2	28.6	0.023	0.35	0.17	0.23
1990	68.3	216.8	54.4	71.3	28.2	99.5	(9.1)[e]	(0.004)	0.20	0.07	0.26

E. *Lower export growth, higher product growth, harder financial terms*

Year											
1983	39.8	188.2	64.3	36.7	22.1	58.8	30.9	0.040	0.40	0.23	0.25
1986	59.8	281.9	111.7	67.7	34.2	101.9	48.4	0.038	0.42	0.21	0.25
1990	110.7	491.4	193.8	113.0	60.2	173.2	87.6	0.037	0.38	0.20	0.25

[a] Values are expressed in billions of current dollars except for ratios.
[b] Gross interest paid on debt less interest earned on reserves.
[c] Exports of goods and services.
[d] Debt less the level of reserves.
[e] Surplus.

levels of amortization resulting from shorter private maturities require larger gross capital inflows and repayments. These in turn result in high debt service ratios compared even with scenarios involving a larger debt.

Harder financial terms are therefore of two types with distinct effects: higher interest costs that become embodied in larger net finance requirements and shorter maturities that imply more loan activity for a given debt. In part D of Table 4, the former contribute to a terminal debt that is 25% greater than in the base projection; the latter implies an almost constant real loan volume between 1980 and 1986, even though the current account deficit has halved relative to gross product.

Part E presents a composite of all these factors. It reflects dramatically the sensitivity of the debt to a series of small, but reinforcing, changes in the external environment as well as domestic policies. The terminal debt of $602 billion is almost three times greater than the 1990 value in part A. Real gross and net loan requirements increase at an annual rate of about 5% over the decade. The current account deficit merely stabilizes rather than showing dramatic improvement, and the debt service ratio hovers at a level indicative of considerable continuing vulnerability.

These scenarios convey a dual message. On the one hand, they make clear that regular trade growth at rates realized during the 1970s and continued access to foreign capital markets in comparable terms to those of the last decade combine to make the debt manageable. Part E is clearly the most realistic, if only because a stronger performance on current account would reflect itself in increased imports, not debt reduction. Even with its larger requirements, indebtedness slows markedly in comparison with the experience during the last decade, increasing in real terms by about 50% during the 1980s, about one-third the earlier rate.

This capacity to meet current obligations depends on an international economic environment that remains favorable and open. No large international sacrifice is implied because no significant increase in export–income or savings–income ratios is necessary. External finance continues to supplement domestic capital accumulation in only gradually diminishing proportion.

There is another and less optimistic interpretation. Modest reduction in trade growth can easily translate into much larger increases in indebtedness. Even a 6% export growth, with all the other conditions of part E unchanged, implies a terminal debt 37% higher and a corresponding debt service ratio of 0.58. The long-run dynamics are very sensitive to small changes, as one can see: an 11% reduction in export growth alters the panorama considerably.

In the short term, it is the capital account that dominates. Even with an interval of slower export growth in the next few years, the Latin American debt could be manageable. Use of reserves, import substitution, and somewhat slower product growth could keep the increase in debt within bounds. The critical requirement is continued creditworthiness that permits compensating borrowing. The increased needs are not dramatic. Export growth, while it cumulates impressively, does not make a large dent in foreign-exchange requirements in the near term. However, export performance has influenced the supply of private loans. A decline in export growth, whatever the long-term prospects, could then limit access to capital markets and provoke more immediate difficulties.

Prospects for developing-country exports in the next few years are not very promising. For 1981, one estimate of OECD import performance projects a real decline of 2%. Thereafter, even with recovery, import growth fails to average 7% through 1985. The pessimistic scenario is for an average annual growth in the next few years of less than 3% [see p.6 of World Financial Markets (1980)]. Between 1980 and 1985, the 1980 *World Development Report* projects a high case export growth of 6.1% for middle-income oil importers [see p.7 of World Bank (1980)].

The looming question, already signaled by some banks, is whether capital may not be available in amounts sufficient to bridge the gap. *World Financial Markets* estimates an annual supply increase—at current inflation rates—of no more than 15%. Banks are more reluctant to lend as developing countries' loans mount to a large multiple of their net worth. United States banks have already significantly reduced their growth in commitments in the last two years. At the same time, Morgan Guaranty sees non-oil-developing countries' requirements expanding at rates ranging downward from 22 to 16.5% between 1981 and 1985 [see p.8 of World Financial Markets (1980)]. Price, in the form of larger premiums, does not seem to equilibrate this market, although very recent Brazilian experience provides some contrary evidence. Still, supply is discontinuous: banks would curtail lending even more as a liquidity crisis occurs. Credit is most available to those who need it least.

For Latin America as a region, a 15% increase in finance—if it materialized—might suffice. There would be a reduced rate of economic expansion, but not as severe for Latin America as for other countries. Beyond the level of reserves, and the greater flexibility of productive structures that permits substitution for imported inputs, there is another special factor that enters into the projections. That is the progressively smaller weight of aggregate petroleum imports for the non-oil-producing countries of the region because of the new prominence of Mexico and Peru as oil exporters. Indeed, net imports of oil for the group as a whole have now been converted to a small export surplus.

It is precisely this new heterogeneity among countries of the region that reduces the usefulness of aggregate projections. They can provide an overview and guide to needed international policies. They fall short in their implications for internal measures because national circumstances vary. Corresponding to the more rapid growth of Mexican oil revenues, for example, has been an above-average import elasticity. Mexican debt policy between 1977 and 1982 more closely conformed to an active use of external finance for growth rather than adjustment.

In the last analysis, the debt problem is national rather than regional. Export revenues of some countries are not available to service the obligations of others. Despite some direct Mexican and Venezuelan assistance to the small countries of Central America and the Caribbean to help compensate for oil price increases, the record of regional cooperation in coping with the post-1973 deficits is a modest one. CEPAL's attempt to encourage a regional safety net found few supporters.

For this reason, we shall now turn to a closer examination of the current Brazilian experience. It typifies the oil-importer adjustment dilemma better than a hypothetical regional aggregate.

A. Brazil: A Liquidity Crisis?

Brazil accrued its debt of almost $60 billion at the end of 1980 in the two phases characteristic of other principal Latin American borrowers. Before the oil crisis, external finance was a strategic element in the "economic miracle," permitting a significant increase in the investment ratio without restraint upon consumption growth. After 1973, Brazil turned from debt-led growth to growth-led debt: foreign loans were contracted to offset the current account deficits associated with successful efforts to sustain high rates of growth. Despite the turbulence of the external environment, Brazilian gross domestic product increased between 1974 and 1980 at an average rate of about 7%, which is above the historical trend.

It is inherent in debt financing that mounting amortization and interest payments progressively reduce the real resources transferred by the same volume of loan activity. Debt growth from $12.6 billion at the end of 1973 to the almost $60 billion at the end of 1980 was offset by net interest costs that expanded much more than proportionally from $500 million to an estimated $6.9 billion in 1980. Annual amortization payments rose from $1.7 to $7 billion, a smaller increase because loan maturities initially lengthened from their pre-1973 terms and inflation intervened.[8] In the next few

---

[8] Values for the end of 1980 have been taken from estimates of Manufacturer's Hanover Bank, published in *Euromoney,* April Supplement, 1981, p. 4, and *International Financial Statistics* (International Monetary Fund, 1980).

years, payments will go up faster. Whatever initial advantage derived from inflation has disappeared, moreover, as interest rates have come to reflect, more fully, and perhaps overcompensate for, inflationary expectations. Because loans from private sources now represent about 90% of the gross inflow, flexible rates apply to a progressively larger proportion of the debt.

The adjustment path to higher oil prices that Brazil selected has postponed, but can not cancel, the real burden. Because Brazil is the largest developing country importer of oil, the effect of higher prices is large: at current consumption levels, a $5 increase in the price per barrel translates into $1.5 billion in added foreign-exchange requirements. But with accelerating momentum, the debt itself has added new vulnerability. Each percentage point in interest rate means about $500 million in net costs, and market rates have reached new high levels in 1980 and 1981. Mounting amortization requirements must also be refinanced.

That is why, despite an impressive export performance in 1980, when receipts rose by more than 30%, Brazil faces an apparent classic liquidity crisis in 1981. Significant reduction of reserves and an increase in short-term debt managed to reduce borrowing requirements in 1980. They cannot be counted on much longer.

What is of interest here is not so much the outcome of this particular drama but three more general issues. The first reiterates the dominant role of a continuing supply of capital, rather than increased export earnings, in alleviating the crisis. The second is the relationship of the terms of such finance to Brazilian economic policies. The third is the implication of short-term liquidity pressures for medium-term debt strategy.

An emphasis upon the importance of the capital account in meeting short-term foreign-exchange requirements is easily justified from the magnitudes involved. Brazil, now and for the next few years, faces current account deficits of between $12 and $15 billion, to which the trade deficit (including nonfactor services) is likely to contribute no more than about $5 billion, less than half the total. In addition, prospective amortization should add close to $10 billion to gross financial needs. Compared with total borrowing that will have to aggregate between $15 and $20 billion, expected increments in export earnings are offsets of $4 to $5 billion, assuming very substantial growth.

In other words, an increase in the debt is required. It will take some years of sustained increases in export receipts to alter this arithmetic. In the near term, gross loans will not fall so very short of export proceeds. Net inflow of credit will amount to about half of gross borrowing. That translates into a debt that will continue to show rapid increase—a doubling perhaps in nominal terms over five years, a rise in real terms of more than 40%. The principal source of the new finance will have to continue to be private commercial banks.

Thus far, the vulnerability of Brazil has been reflected in the greater spreads it has paid to induce continuing credit flows. Spreads that were less than 1% in the fall of 1979 have mounted by the spring of 1981 to as much as 2.5%. This excludes fees. Such a deterioration in terms far exceeds the rise for developing countries as a whole. *Euromoney's* index of weighted public spreads goes up by about 50% between the end of 1979 and the end of 1980.[9]

Because of the higher rates that have been necessary, Brazil has been conscious of the link between its economic policies and its creditworthiness. Indeed, the simultaneous need to satisfy a watchful and increasingly preoccupied international constituency and more vocal domestic interests has contributed to the schizophrenia and ineffectiveness of such policies. Delfim Neto's initial liberalization package of December 1979 helped to persuade creditors of his orthodox intentions, until accelerating inflation began to have the opposite effect. Continued emphasis upon excessive wage adjustment as a culprit in inflation (when its incidence in industrial costs is limited) is again a bow to more conservative preferences.

Attention has focused on instruments even more than outcomes. The apparent acceptance of a lower rate of domestic growth to improve the balance of payments is illustrative. However, if the balance of payments is at issue, the various measures to increase export subsidies, accelerate minidevaluations, and control imports are likely to prove at least as effective. Slower growth may be justifiable for other purposes but not on balance of payments grounds, especially in the medium term.

In the short term, more debt is the principal way to deal with what may be an excessive debt. This short-term need for additional finance is true even when the crisis eventually ends in debt renegotiation. Consolidation of debt usually does not substantially alter initial vulnerability or eliminate creditor hesitance. That is why the list of debt renegotiations contains large sets of multiple entries as countries are forced into default again. Only 17 countries account for 47 multilateral debt renegotiations between 1956 and 1980; of the 5 single experiences, 4 have occurred since the middle of 1978 and may yet result in repetitions. [see Table 1 and discussion in Hardy (1981).]

Two exceptions to this propensity for relief to be temporary may be noted. One is a rescheduling that is generous enough to lead to a signifi-

---

[9] *Euromoney's* index was first published in October 1980 and is available for higher and intermediate-income developing countries.

cant reduction in the debt burden. The other escape is a definitive change in export prospects.

In the case of Brazil, and most other oil-importing debtors, neither exception applies. This places a premium on medium-term economic management to reduce vulnerability. The essential character of the requisite strategy is clear: an increasing ratio of exports to income; an increasing ratio of savings to income; a reduction of energy consumption and substitution of new energy sources; and a continued use of external finance. These measures over time are compatible with economic growth, while reducing current account deficits and increments to the outstanding debt.

V. CONCLUSION

The emphasis in this chapter has been on the constructive potential of external financing for Latin American development during the difficult period of adjustment to higher oil prices after 1973. Whether that potential is realized depends on the future availability of private loans on favorable terms and not merely the past access. It also depends on the domestic policies of debtor countries.

In emphasizing that growing indebtedness, albeit at a slower rate, remains an essential part of the solution rather than the problem, I do so mindful that external debt is not a panacea. Eventually, and now, sooner than later, amortization and interest costs must flow back. There is always the danger that they will come due when export prospects are bleak. In the last analysis, the debt problem is a trade problem. A less rapid growth of future exports for debtor countries will frustrate what otherwise would have been a sound debt strategy.

Reliance on debt can also complicate and distort the economic policy of borrowers. Real exchange rates are susceptible to disequilibrium as the capital account assumes an importance greater than the trade account. In a first phase, undervaluation is used to stimulate internal demand for external credit by canceling fears of devaluation. As the rate is held fixed, despite internal inflation, in order to stimulate continuing capital flow, it becomes subject to overvaluation. The rate can be sustained, even at the prejudice of exports and correct medium-term debt management, because the volume of borrowing meets foreign-exchange requirements. Disequilibrium cannot resist indefinitely. An expected devaluation will reduce capital inflow and soon make devaluation necessary. Then the cycle begins again. When one adds in the role of externally financed reserve accumulation on domestic credit creation and the lulling effect of postponed rather than immediate adjustment to changed relative prices, the adverse possiblities become even more daunting.

There is thus a delicate and difficult balance inherent in development through debt. Many Latin American countries are far embarked upon such a path. For them, solution and problem are intertwined. Careful domestic management and a more certain international economic environment are both needed, lest the solution of the 1970s turn into the major problem of the 1980s.

REFERENCES

Aronson, J. D. (ed.) (1979). *Debt and the Less Developed Countries,* pp. 103, 203, 205. Boulder, Colorado: Westview Press.
Batista, P. N., Jr. (1980). *Participação Brasiliera no Mercado Financeiro Internacional: Custo e Perfil da Dívida Externa, 1968–1779,* pp. 10, 58. Rio de Janeiro: Fundação Getulio Vargas (March).
Cleveland, H. van B., and Brittain, W. H. B. (1977). "Are the LDCs in over their heads." Foreign Affairs (July).
Economic Commission for Latin America (ECLA) (1965). *External Financing in Latin America,* p. 188. (United Nations.)
Fishlow, A. (1981). "Latin American External Debt: Problem or Solution?" Unpublished.
Hardy, C. (1981). "Rescheduling Developing Country Debts, 1956–1980: Lessons and Recommendations." Working Paper No. 1, Overseas Development Council (March).
Inter-American Development Bank (1979). *Economic and Social Progress in Latin America.*
International Monetary Fund (1980). *International Financial Statistics Yearbook.*
International Monetary Fund (1982). *World Economic Outlook,* p. 170.
National Foreign Assessment Center (1979). "Non-OPEC LDCs: External Debt Position."
World Bank (1979). *World Debt Tables.*
World Bank (1980). *World Development Report.*
World Bank (1981). *World Debt Tables.*
World Financial Markets (1980). Morgan Guaranty Bank.

Department of Economics
Yale University
New Haven, Connecticut

Part III

Stabilization and Growth

Chapter 8

Macroeconomic Disequilibrium and Short-Run Economic Growth in Developing Countries*

Nathaniel H. Leff and Kazuo Sato

I. INTRODUCTION

Much of the analysis of economic growth in the less developed countries (LDCs) has taken place in a long-term perspective, emphasizing such structural elements as rates of capital formation, technical progress, and labor-force reallocation. These factors are clearly important determinants of long-term potential growth. In less developed as in more developed economies, however, the actual level of annual GNP and its growth are determined largely by short-run macroeconomic conditions. Consequently, considerable importance attaches to the ways in which a less developed economy achieves macroeconomic adjustment from a situation in which *ex ante* (desired) investment may exceed *ex ante* savings.

* An abbreviated version of this chapter was published by the *Review of Economics and Statistics* (May 1980); we thank the editor for permission to present the extended version here.

167

What happens in such a case is especially pertinent because alternative adjustment mechanisms have different impacts on economic growth. And if the adjustment processes that are less costly in terms of output expansion do not function effectively in the LDCs, other processes will operate, with ensuing consequences for the economy's growth path. Many developing economies appear to be subject to macroeconomic disturbances and ensuing growth cycles. An analysis of their economic growth in terms of short-term dynamics may therefore provide a useful complement to the more conventional long-run models of economic development.

Despite its analytical and policy importance, the subject of the short-run macroeconomics of developing countries has, until recently, received relatively little attention from researchers. Moreover, much of the earlier work in this general area focused on monetary and balance-of-payments stabilization, with relatively little attention directed to the subject of short-run national income per se. The past few years, however, have seen an important upsurge in analytical work on LDC macroeconomics.[1] This chapter is part of the emerging perspective in development economics. It presents an aggregate model for analyzing macroeconomic instability and short-run growth in developing countries. Although the model is built on standard *IS/LM* theoretical lines, an important empirical finding is that macroeconomic adjustment in the real sector of some developing countries differs from the professional expectations that may be prevalent in more developed countries. This observation leads us to a reconsideration of the macroeconomics of the developing economies and, particularly, of some features of short-term growth that affect the long-run expansion path. Our analysis also shows why these economies are often subject to chronic inflation and macroeconomic dependence on foreign-capital inflows.

We begin by formulating the macroeconomic adjustment in the real sector in the form of *IS* equilibrium (Section II). We then estimate the aggregate investment and saving functions with time-series data for six developing countries. The parameter estimates suggest that the macroeco-

---

[1] In addition to pressing real-world problems, this upsurge seems to have been sparked in part by the contributions of Shaw (1973) and McKinnon (1973). The literature is now too vast to be surveyed here; but for representative recent contributions, see Taylor (1979), Blejer and Fernandez (1978), and Behrman and Hanson (1979). One reason for the earlier relative neglect of short-run macroeconomics in the development literature was an assumption that semiindustrialized economies were too "fragmented" for macro analysis to apply. Because of some features of industrial organization in these economies, however, capital markets and product markets are in fact more integrated than has sometimes been supposed (Leff, 1976).

nomic adjustment process in these countries is characterized by instability because aggregate investment tends to be chronically more buoyant than aggregate saving (Sections III and IV). Section V shows how monetary factors can serve as stabilizing elements but also why they lead to a trade-off between inflation and real growth in the short run. Further, because money and credit supplies are connected to the economy's foreign balance, foreign-capital inflow has a powerful impact both on the real and on the monetary sectors of the economy (Section VI). This observation indicates another channel of macroeconomic adjustment, namely, the effect of real credit availability upon production through the supply of working-capital requirements. Because of this connection, short-run growth performance is intimately linked with macroeconomic adjustment (Section VII). Finally, our analysis indicates that the macroeconomics of these developing countries show strikingly classical properties, in that saving (domestic and foreign) is an ultimate determinant of long-run growth via its short-run impact on the macroeconomic equilibrium and stability (Section VIII). We conclude by discussing some implications that Latin America's experience in this area may hold for developing countries in other regions.

II. POSSIBLE MACROECONOMIC ADJUSTMENT MECHANISM: *IS* EQUILIBRIUM

We begin with the obvious proposition that, eventually, macroeconomic equilibrium must be established in LDCs just as much as in more developed economies. An LDC may in fact face a serious disequilibrium situation in which, perhaps because of supply shocks, government policy changes, and other exogenous factors, *ex ante* (desired) investment tends to exceed *ex ante* saving. What sort of a macroeconomic adjustment mechanism operates in eliminating this disequilibrium is especially pertinent because alternative adjustment mechanisms may have different impacts on the subsequent path of economic growth.

Ex post, the gross national product identity holds

$$Y = C + I + X - M, \tag{1}$$

where C is the (private and public) consumption, I the gross domestic capital formation, X the exports (including factor income from abroad), and M the imports (including factor payments to foreigners). An equivalent statement of (1) is the *IS* identity

$$I = S + F, \tag{2}$$

where S is gross domestic saving defined by

$$S = Y - C \tag{3}$$

and F is foreign-capital inflow defined by

$$F = M - X = I - S. \tag{4}$$

Should our proposition be true, (1) and (2) hold not only as *ex post* identities but also as equilibrium conditions. The latter implies that commodity markets are cleared at equilibrium prices. But what happens if *ex ante* investment exceeds *ex ante* saving at prices that prevailed in the preceding period? If foreign-capital inflow F is elastically supplied to the LDC, its internal adjustment problem is mitigated to a great extent because any excess of I over S is simply filled by F. However, because large components of foreign-capital inflow (e.g., aid and direct foreign investment) are exogenously determined, the LDC cannot rely on F as an equilibrating variable.

If output is flexible and responds to demand stimulus in the short run (within the given period), then I and S adjust to establish the equilibrium level of Y, given the exogenously imposed level of F. If this Keynesian channel of adjustment is effective, I and S respond to ΔY, the change of GNP, over the level in the preceding period. In semiindustrialized economies that do not have large non-market-subsistence sectors, supply rigidities may not be too pervasive to negate such adjustment.[2]

In some cases, however, supply may not be sufficiently responsive, and price changes may have to take over the role of macroeconomic adjustment. In other words, the aggregate price level rises under the pressure of excess demand for goods, which is represented by the excess of *ex ante* I over *ex ante* $S + F$ (evaluated at the previously prevailing price level).[3] For price inflation to eliminate the aggregate demand–supply gap, the investment function and/or the saving function must be responsive to the rate of inflation. If these functions shift with the right signs and magni-

---

[2] V. K. R. V. Rao (1952), in an influential paper, urged the view that, because of the short-run supply inelasticities assumed to prevail in the underdeveloped countries, output would not grow much in response to increases in aggregate demand. Hence, Keynesian multiplier models would be of little relevance for the determination of real output growth in the LDCs. Subsequent research has, however, disclosed considerable evidence of excess capacity in the industrial sectors of developing countries and of supply-responsive behavior in their agriculture. Nevertheless, a reluctance to utilize Keynesian models of short-run income determination for analytical purposes in developing countries has often persisted (Myint, 1965).

[3] This rise is over and above any autonomous increase in the aggregate supply price (via wage increases, etc.).

tudes, inflation can act to clear commodity markets and thus induce a convergence to macroeconomic equilibrium.[4]

Interest-rate changes, an adjustment mechanism familiar from more developed economies, are not very relevant in LDCs. For doctrinal and political reasons, the governments in these countries generally do not permit interest rates to move sufficiently to clear the financial markets (Shaw, 1973; McKinnon, 1973). Rather, the monetary authorities create new credit more or less independently of domestic saving, often in response to the government deficit. Credit creation, in turn, influences domestic investment because firms in LDCs are generally very dependent on credit for financing.

Considering the possible influence of contemporaneous variables upon the economy's saving and investment decisions, we may specify the saving and investment functions as

$$S = a_1 \Delta Y + a_2 \dot{P} + a_3 S_{-1} + a_0, \tag{5}$$

$$I = b_1 \Delta Y + b_2 \dot{P} + b_3 \Delta CR + b_0, \tag{6}$$

where ΔY is the change of real GNP over the preceding period, $\dot{P}$ the rate of inflation $\Delta P/P_{-1}$, and ΔCR the change in the real volume of credit over the preceding period. Specification of the S_{-1} term in (5) reflects the possibility of partial adjustment in saving behavior (Leff and Sato, 1975). Effects of other predetermined variables are subsumed in the constant terms a_0 and b_0.[5] Equations (5) and (6) hardly constitute a detailed macro model of a developing economy. However, they do permit us to analyze the impact of key macroeconomic varibles on short-run growth ΔY and inflation $\dot{P}$.

As for the signs of the coefficients of (5) and (6), we expect a_1 and a_3 to be greater than 0. The sign of a_2, however, is ambiguous because the saving behavior of the private and public sectors in response to inflation may

---

[4] Some clarification may be necessary concerning our treatment of price inflation. In developing countries (generally small and open economies), prices of traded goods are determined by world market conditiions. However, the non-traded-goods sector including many import-substituting activities, may be sizable enough to leave the overall domestic price level largely insulated from external conditions, so that the rate of inflation can be considered as endogenously determined. In addition, a question of timing is involved. The domestic prices of a country's traded goods are completely determined exogenously only to the extent that the country has a stable equilibrium exchange rate. Disequilibrium in the exchange market may create medium, and long-term pressures to establish such a rate; but in the short run, the country's parity may be "out of line." This chapter is concerned with these short-run conditions during which the country's price level is not exogenously determined.

[5] Foreign saving may also be a significant determinant of saving and investment in LDCs. Possible effects of F will be discussed later.

be very different.[6] An increase in $\dot{P}$ may cause forced saving in the private sector but could also reflect government dissaving, which is being covered by issue of nominal money. In (6), we expect $b_1 > 0$ because ΔY is included as a reflection of possible accelerator effects and the impact of current output growth on rates of return to capital and the incentive to invest. The rate $\dot{P}$ also enters this short-run investment function because of the possibility of profit inflation and ensuing higher rates of return. It may also be positively related to expectations of such changes and to capital gains. Thus, $b_2 > 0$. As the increase in real credit positively influences investment, we have $b_3 > 0$.

The *IS* equilibrium is obtained by substituting (5) and (6) into (2) and solving for the endogenous variables. First, observe that the change in real credit is not independent of $\dot{P}$. Assume, for example, that the nominal supply of credit *PCR* is exogenously determined by the monetary authorities. Then,

$$\Delta CR = \Delta PCR/P_{-1} - (CR_{-1})\dot{P}, \tag{7}$$

and the *IS* equation yields

$$(b_1 - a_1)\,\Delta Y + [b_2 - b_3(CR_{-1}) - a_2]\dot{P} = a_0 - b_0 - b_3\,\Delta PCR/P_{-1} \\ + a_3 S_{-1} + F. \tag{8}$$

In the fixprice system, we take $\dot{P} \equiv 0$; and (8) determines the change in real output. As is well known, the stability of the equilibrium requires $b_1 < a_1$; i.e., that investment be less responsive to changes in Y than is saving.

In the flexprice system, on the other hand, we assume that the change in output is autonomously determined, e.g., by supply capacity, and the necessary macroeconomic adjustment is established via price-level changes. The stability of the equilibrium requires that $b_2 - b_3(CR_{-1}) < a_2$, i.e., that investment be less responsive (net of the indirect effect of inflation in eroding real credit) to price changes than is saving.

More generally, when both the aggregate output level and the aggregate price level are flexible and operate as adjusting variables, the *IS* equilibrium alone is not sufficient to determine the two endogenous varibles. Another equilibrium condition that connects ΔY and $\dot{P}$ must be introduced (see Section III). Whatever that condition may be, however, the stability of the *IS* equilibrium is suspect unless both stability conditions just indicated are satisfied. That is , if investment responds more than saving to

[6] In principle, price changes might affect saving by redistributing income toward groups with different marginal propensities to save. In fact, it has sometimes been suggested that inflation leads to higher saving in developing countries.

changes in output and/or in prices, it must be difficult to eliminate the initial *IS* gap to which the economy is subject. We shall now examine this question empirically, by specifying and estimating the saving and investment functions for a sample of developing countries.

III. SAMPLE ESTIMATES OF THE SAVING AND INVESTMENT FUNCTIONS

Our primary interest at this point of our research is to test whether or not the *IS* equilibrium is stable. Therefore, in order to avoid undue complications, we discuss only the highly aggregated level that does not distinguish the private and public sectors on both the saving and investment side. It goes without saying that the public and private components of investment and saving may respond differently to income growth and to price changes. From the perspective of macroeconomic adjustment, however, what matters is the behavior of the aggregates.

By the nature of available data, the unit period is one year. In order to keep the project manageable, the model has been estimated for only six countries: Argentina, Brazil, Chile, Costa Rica, Israel, and Taiwan. The first three countries have a long history of macroeconomic instability; the other countries are included in the sample to give a broader perspective on parameter estimates and the nature of the adjustment process. All data except ΔCR were taken from the country tables of the World Bank. The observations for ΔCR were computed from data in the IMF's *International Financial Statistics*.[7] The observations are for the years 1950–1973. All variables except $\dot{P}$ were expressed in local currency units. As the reader will readily note, (5) and (6) are both specified in real terms. All nominal variables are deflated by the deflator implicit in the World Bank's data for the aggregate GNP series.

Equations (5) and (6) are estimated by a two-stage least squares (TSLS) method. In addition to S_{-1} and F, which are predetermined or exogenous variables, several outside instruments were used in the first stage of the estimation. Variables, S, I, ΔY, $\dot{P}$, and ΔCR were treated as endogenous.[8] Whenever the presence of heteroscedacity was indicated by the

---

[7] The credit variable employed is domestic credit, approximated by the total money supply less international reserves. Changes in domestic credit rather than in the total money supply are relevant here because, owing to changes in international reserves, credit may move differently over time than the total money supply. Domestic credit, however, is more directly relevant for domestic investment decisions (Guitian, 1973).

[8] The nominal supply of credit may be an endogenous variabale in a larger model that encompasses our real sector. Also, as indicated in (7), ΔCR is affected by the endogenous variable $\dot{P}$.

Goldfeld–Quandt (1965) test, the equation was estimated using a weighting procedure. Under the assumption that the variance of the error term in those equations increased with the square of Y, each observation was weighted by the inverse of the square root of the annual trend value of Y. Finally, because R^2 is not meaningful for TSLS estimates, that statistic is not presented. Our focus in any case is not on the goodness of fit of the individual equations or on using them for numerical simulation, but rather with the qualitative properties of the overall macroeconomic system.

Table 1 presents TSLS estimates of the saving function (5). The parameter estimates for the ΔY term in the saving equation indicate considerable diversity among the different countries, ranging from a coefficient of 0.69 in Costa Rica to coefficients that are clearly insignificantly different from zero in two countries. The latter results do not reflect misspecification, for Eq. (5) is based on standard economic theory. "Negative" results in econometric research on behavioral patterns in the LDCs may also involve substantive findings concerning those economies. Thus pa-

TABLE 1

Parameter Estimates and Summary Statistics for the Savings Equation[a]

Country	Coefficient on[b]				
	ΔY	$\dot{P}$	S_{-1}	a_0	D–W[c]
Argentina	0.276	492.598	0.931	18.892	2.36
	(1.50)	(0.97)	(12.07)	(0.12)	
Brazil	−0.012	−64.602	1.175	7.718	1.99
	(0.04)	(1.11)	(4.62)	(0.54)	
Chile	−0.336	−32.966	0.944	395.969	2.32
	(0.80)	(0.12)	(3.91)	(0.94)	
Costa Rica[d]	0.685	300.220	0.892	−39.065	2.42
	(3.29)	(0.74)	(7.57)	(0.73)	
Israel[d]	0.656	215.102	0.540	−1.460	2.10
	(2.93)	(0.33)	(3.59)	(0.01)	
Taiwan	0.555	2.385	1.031	−2.179	1.50
	(1.71)	(0.31)	(9.55)	(1.67)	

[a] $S = a_1 \Delta Y + a_2 \dot{P} + a_3 S_{-1} + a_0 + u$.
[b] Absolute values for the t ratios are in parentheses.
[c] Durbin–Watson statistics.
[d] Estimated with a weighting procedure to eliminate heteroscedasticity.

rameter estimates that differ from the values that may be expected on the basis of experience in the more developed countries may best be approached analytically with the perspective of a cross section, random coefficient model (Kelejian, 1974) rather than dismissed with a prioristic dogmatism.[9] The parameter estimates for the inflation term in the savings equation are insignificantly different from zero in all countries.[10] Thus our results contradict the contention that, behaviorally, inflation leads to higher aggregate saving in these developing countries.[11] Finally, the lagged savings term is significant in all countries, indicating that saving in these countries is a strongly autoregressive phenomenon and is heavily dependent on previous behavior. For Brazil and Taiwan, the coefficient on S_{-1} exceeds unity, which suggests that, in those countries, the S_{-1} term may reflect a trend parameter, which, as a consequence of institutional changes in the course of the development process, shifts the saving function upward over time.

Table 2 presents TSLS estimates of the investment function (6).[12] The current change in income ΔY has a powerful effect on investment in all countries. The coefficient on the income term cannot, of course, be inter-

[9] In particular, the coefficients on the ΔY term that are insignificantly different from zero appear only for Brazil and Chile—countries with a long history of inflation. Protracted experience with inflation in these countries before the onset of our sample period appears to have led to special behavioral patterns, which yield the zero coefficients that we observe on the ΔY term.

[10] Identical results were also obtained for the effects of inflation when the variable was specified in the form of the acceleration rather than the level of inflation. It might be more appropriate to specify, not the annual level of inflation, but the rate of acceleration or deceleration of inflation from previous levels to which economic agents had adjusted. Accordingly, we reestimated Eq. (5), deleting $\dot{P}$ and specifying instead an inflation-acceleration variable—the difference between current inflation and a running average of inflation in the two previous years. The inflation-acceleration variable was not statistically different from zero in any country. Note that results from other studies indicate rapid convergence of expected to actual rates of inflation in LDCs.

[11] Note that Eq. (5) does not constitute a true test of the "forced saving" hypothesis. Properly specified, that hypothesis posits a positive relation between saving and *unanticipated,* rather than actual, inflation (Boulding, 1957, see also Barro, 1977).

[12] The Durbin–Watson statistics shown in Table 2 indicate the presence of positive serial correlation in the residuals for Argentina and Taiwan. Serial correlation in an equation's error term does not lead to bias or inconsistency but does result in inefficient estimates. The Cochran–Orcutt transform can be used to correct for serial correlation; but with moderately trended independent variables, the Cochrane–Orcutt transformation *increases* the variances of the standard errors, particularly in small samples (Maeshiro, 1976). Consequently, rather than run the alternative risk of committing a type I error, we will ignore inefficiency, particularly because the *t* ratios for the specific parameter estimates discussed in the text for those two countries appear to be unambiguous.

TABLE 2

Parameter Estimates and Summary Statistics for the Investment Equation[a]

Country	ΔY	$\dot{P}$	ΔCR	b_0	D–W
		Coefficient on[b]			
Argentina	1.465 (2.65)	4908.23 (2.97)	1.682 (2.19)	146.511 (0.24)	1.41
Brazil	1.451 (7.42)	168.265 (3.34)	1.223 (2.80)	2.196 (0.11)	1.83
Chile	2.351 (2.94)	219.86 (3.05)	−0.660 (1.10)	488.910 (0.70)	1.88
Costa Rica[c]	2.354 (3.86)	3718.03 (4.02)	2.734 (2.15)	42.186 (0.29)	1.75
Israel	2.557 (5.52)	2299.43 (1.03)	−0.326 (0.63)	366.140 (0.78)	2.56
Taiwan	2.824 (3.11)	−41.454 (1.21)	−0.183 (0.14)	2.238 (5.19)	1.25

[a] $I = b_1 \Delta Y + b_2 \dot{P} + b_3 \Delta CR + b_0 + u$.

[b] Absolute values for the t ratios are in parentheses.

[c] Estimated with a weighting procedure to eliminate heteroscedasticity.

preted as a marginal propensity to invest, for ΔY, rather than Y, is the variable that is specified on the right-hand side of (6).[13]

Table 2 shows a positive response of investment to inflation in four countries (Argentina, Brazil, Chile, and Costa Rica). Finally, the parametric estimate for the ΔCR term is significant in three countries. In most countries, however, ΔCR and ΔY are highly correlated, so it is difficult to distinguish between their separate effects. Consequently, a more accurate conclusion from the results of Table 2 is that investment in these countries responds very buoyantly to current economic expansion, whether of ΔY or of ΔCR, as well as to $\dot{P}$.

By comparing Tables 1 and 2, we note that the parameter estimates for the ΔY and $\dot{P}$ terms, the variables that both the savings and investment

[13] A short-run investment function might also include I_{-1}. We do not specify this term for theoretical reasons: the flow of actual investment expenditures in LDCs depends heavily on immediate short-run conditions such as the availability of credit and the supply of imports (effects that we expect to capture with the ΔCR and ΔY terms). In any case, in order to examine the sensitivity of our results to the particular form of (6), we also experimented with equations that included I_{-1}. The properties of the *IS* system did not change.

functions have in common, are generally very dissimilar. The very different saving and investment responses to the same economic stimuli do not support the view that in LDCs the decision to invest conditions the decision to save, for both decisions are undertaken interdependently by the same economic agents. Rather, our results indicate the independence of saving and investment responses, and hence the importance of financial intermediation, which enables individual firms, households, and government agencies to make investments in excess of their own saving. From an aggregate perspective, of course, such behavior is possible only because of credit creation and foreign-capital inflow.

IV. DESTABILIZING *IS* ADJUSTMENT

As noted earlier, two potential adjustment mechanisms are changes in real output ΔY and price inflation $\dot{P}$. Table 3 shows the impact multipliers of these adjustment mechanisms. In order to standardize in terms of the units of measurement, the multipliers are presented in the form of elasticities.

Table 3 contains an important negative finding. The mechanisms for short-run adjustment proposed earlier generally do not operate in these countries. Indeed, the response to changes in ΔY is destablizing: if an initial excess of investment over saving leads to an increase in ΔY, the be-

TABLE 3

Elasticities of Impact Multipliers for Some Potential Macroeconomic Adjustment Mechanisms[a]

Country	$e_{S,\Delta Y}$	$e_{I,\Delta Y}$	$e_{S,\dot{P}}$	$e_{I,\dot{P}}$	$e_{I,\dot{P}CR_{-1}}$[b]
Argentina	0.053	0.292	0.059[c]	0.608	0.728
Brazil	−0.005[c]	0.571	−0.117	0.285	0.546
Chile	−0.069[c]	0.463	−0.001[c]	0.434	−0.410
Costa Rica	0.205	0.574	0.023[c]	0.228	0.137
Israel	0.479	0.777	0.025[c]	0.111	−0.036[c]
Taiwan	0.218	1.057	0.007[c]	−0.114	−0.013[c]

[a] Elasticities were computed using the parameter estimates of Tables 1 and 2 and the means of the variables in question. For example, for the ith country, $e_{S,\Delta Y} = \hat{a}_1/(\bar{S}/\Delta \bar{Y})$.

[b] This column, which shows inflation's indirect effect on investment via erosion of real credit, was computed as $\dfrac{\hat{b}_3}{\bar{I}/\bar{P}\bar{CR}_{-1}}$.

[c] Relevant parameter estimate is smaller than its standard error.

havioral response is such that I rises more than S, to increase the size of an initial gap. Similarly, for inflation to act as a stabilizer would require that $e_{S,\dot{P}} > e_{I,\dot{P}}$. The fourth and fifth columns of Table 3 show that this condition is satisfied only in the case of Taiwan. In the remaining five countries, the elasticities indicate that far from operating to clear the goods market, the responses of S and I to $\dot{P}$ are also destabilizing. Thus these results indicate that once macroeconomic instability begins in these economies, the parameters of the aggregate saving and investment functions are such that strong pressures exist for its persistence.

Does the effect of inflation on real credit [see (7)] have an impact on I that is sufficiently strong to restore IS equilibrium? To check this point, compare the fourth column with the fifth and sixth columns, which give the net effect of inflation taking account of credit erosion. This modificiation does help Brazil and, to a lesser extent, Argentina, though not enough to offset the instability induced by the ΔY terms.

Because most of the countries in our sample are chronically unstable economies, the destabilizing properties of the mechanisms we have considered are not surprising. Rather this finding indicates that our model has been able to replicate the macroeconomic reality of these countries. Our negative results raise two questions, however. First, can we maintain our fundamental proposition that a macroeconomic equilibrium is established in LDCs? Indeed, one might argue that these countries are in a permanent state of disequilibrium, never satisfying $I = S + F$ as an equilibrium condition. This may in fact be true in the case of Chile, which has experienced chronic rates of high inflation. Its saving function lacks significant contemporaneous terms that can serve as adjusting variables; and because its investment function gives significant coefficients for the output and price changes, one may infer that it is investment that prevails in the IS identity.

In all other countries of our sample, however, estimation of the model's equations yields at least one significant coefficient for the ΔY and $\dot{P}$ terms. The existence of well-determined parameter estimates with signs in accordance with a priori expectations suggests that some mechanisms do exist that move these economies toward macroeconomic equilibrium, for if these economies were simply drifting randomly and were perpetually far from equilibrium, one could hardly obtain significant coefficients in estimating the basic macroeconomic functions (Portes and Winter, 1978, p. 9). This observation and our previous IS results lead to our second question: what processes do operate to establish macroeconomic equilibrium in these LDCs? Before considering that issue, however, it is necessary to close the model.

V. CLOSING THE MODEL

The *IS* equation can be written as[14]

$$a_3 S_{-1} + F = (b_1 - a_1) \Delta Y + \left[\frac{b_2 - b_3 \overline{CR}_{-1} - a_2}{\overline{Y}_{-1}} \right] \dot{P} \overline{Y}_{-1}$$
$$+ b_3 \frac{\Delta PCR}{P_{-1}} + (b_0 - a_0). \tag{9}$$

The first term on the right-hand side of (9) shows the impact of changes in real output on *IS* equilibrium; the second term shows the direct and indirect effects of price changes; and the third term shows the effect of changes in nominal credit, whose magnitudes are taken as exogenously determined. Table 4 presents the *IS* equations obtained with TSLS estimation for the countries in our sample.

As Table 4 indicates, the *IS* locus is positively sloped in the $(\Delta Y, \dot{P} Y_{-1})$ plane for Argentina, Brazil, and Taiwan. Thus, in these countries, investment is more responsive to both output growth and inflation than is saving.

In order to determine the particular levels of ΔY and inflation that are established in the economy, we require an additional equilibrium condition, the *LM* locus. Because considerable analytical and empirical research is already available on the monetary sector in developing countries (Vogel, 1974; Wong, 1977), our discussion here can be brief.

Following this earlier research, we assume that the economy's portfolio demand for real-money balances depends on the output level and on

TABLE 4

The IS Loci in Six Developing Countries[a]

Country	Locus
Argentina	$0.931 S_{-1} + F = 1.189 \Delta Y - 0.134 \dot{P}(\overline{Y}_{-1}) + 1.682 \Delta PCR/P_{-1}$
Brazil	$1.175 S_{-1} + F = 1.463 \Delta Y - 0.101 \dot{P}(\overline{Y}_{-1}) + 1.223 \Delta PCR/P_{-1}$
Chile	$0.944 S_{-1} + F = 2.717 \Delta Y + 0.141 \dot{P}(\overline{Y}_{-1}) - 0.660 \Delta PCR/P_{-1}$
Costa Rica	$0.892 S_{-1} + F = 1.669 \Delta Y + 0.328 \dot{P}(\overline{Y}_{-1}) + 2.734 \Delta PCR/P_{-1}$
Israel	$0.540 S_{-1} + F = 1.901 \Delta Y + 0.345 \dot{P}(\overline{Y}_{-1}) - 0.326 \Delta PCR/P_{-1}$
Taiwan	$1.031 S_{-1} + F = 2.269 \Delta Y - 0.427 \dot{P}(\overline{Y}_{-1}) - 0.183 \Delta PCR/P_{-1}$

[a] The *IS* locus for each country was computed from Eq. (9) using the parameters of Tables 1 and 2. The constant terms are suppressed.

[14] In order to standardize dimensions and permit comparisons between countries, the coefficient on the price change term has been scaled by deflation with the mean of Y_{-1} for each country in the sample.

the expected rate of inflation (which affects the real rate of interest). Thus,

$$M/P = A Y^{c_1} \exp(-c_2 \pi), \qquad c_1 > 0, \quad c_2 > 0, \tag{10}$$

where M denotes nominal money balances and π the expected rate of inflation. Equation (10) can be transformed into the following incremental form:

$$c_1 \Delta Y + Y_{-1}\dot{P} - Y_{-1}(\Delta M/M_{-1}) = c_2 Y_{-1} \Delta \pi. \tag{11}$$

Hence the *LM* locus is negatively sloped.

The economy's full equilibrium holds at the intersection of the *IS* and *LM* loci, determining ΔY and $\dot{P}$. It can be shown that it is necessary that the *LM* locus cut the *IS* locus from below if full equilibrium is to prevail despite the negatively sloped *IS* locus. Needless to say, the parameter estimates on the ΔY and/or the $\dot{P}$ terms in *LM* equation must be statistically well determined. The work of Wong (1977) and Vogel (1974) provides empirical evidence on this point.[15] In particular, c_1 must be less than the ratio of the coefficient of ΔY to that of $\dot{P}Y_{-1}$ in the *IS* equation of Table 4.[16]

VI. SUPPLEMENTARY MACROECONOMIC ADJUSTMENT MECHANISMS

As noted earlier, one way of alleviating chronic excess demand in the real sector of these countries is foreign-capital inflow. Foreign saving assumes a stabilizing role here analogous to that played by inventory change in taking up *ex ante* saving–investment gaps in the closed-economy models for more developed countries.

Complications for such an adjustment mechanism may occur, however, if domestic saving and investment are functions of F (Areskoug, 1973) and react perversely from the viewpoint of macroeconomic adjustment. Further, it is not certain that F will be available in the requisite amounts. An exchange-rate devaluation may permit foreign borrowing such as IMF drawings and/or a reversal of earlier domestic capital flight. But if devaluation is not implemented or does not work quickly enough, net capital inflow may actually decline further because of additional capi-

[15] Vogel's estimates show that this requirement is not met by Chile only among the four Latin American countries in our sample, again suggesting that Chile suffers from chronic macroeconomic disequilibrium.

[16] This condition is necessary but not sufficient. The complete stability conditions for *IS/LM* equilibrium in LDCs are discussed in Sato (1978).

tal flight. Under such conditions, an additional adjustment mechanism is required, both for internal equilibrium and to meet external pressures.

In practice, this additional adjustment mechanism usually involves reducing the growth of the domestic credit stock. If the monetary authorities restrict the rate of nominal credit expansion below the rate of price increase, a decline in real credit will occur, at least in the short run, by erosion of real cash balances. In addition, exchange-rate devaluation, if implemented, also reduces the growth of real domestic credit by raising the domestic prices of traded goods (Cooper, 1971). To the extent that devaluation is successful in improving the balance of payments in LDCs, it is in fact usually associated with a decline in the growth of domestic credit (Connolly and Taylor, 1976). In the present context, such economic and/or policy processes that reduce ΔCR or turn it negative are relevant for achieving *internal* macroeconomic stability. The mechanism works through two channels.

First, lower ΔCR may reduce investment growth, inducing a movement toward *IS* equilibrium. Table 2 does, in fact, show a strong positive relation between current *I* and ΔCR in half the countries in our sample. More generally, the growth of real output in many LDCs appears to depend directly on an increasing supply of real credit. This is because changes in the availability of credit for working (circulating) capital help determine the rate of utilization of the existing stock of fixed capital and of land. Apart from its effects on agricultural and industrial output in general, credit is critical for financing production of consumer durables and residential construction, two sectors whose output is especially important in the modern sector of developing countries.[17] Because of these conditions, credit expansion or contraction has particularly potent effects on ΔY in developing countries.[18] Consequently, if the processes just outlined lead to $\Delta CR < 0$, ΔY is likely to decline. And with the growth of income reduced, Tables 1 and 2 tell us that investment will fall more than saving, thus narrowing the *IS* gap and reducing inflationary pressures. Note especially that this channel of adjustment is supplementary to money-market effects discussed in the preceding section. It focuses on the impact of credit conditions in the production process father than in the public's portfolio allocations.

[17] Concerning the relatively large quantitative significance of residential construction in the GNP of the less developed economies, see Grebler and Burns (1976), especially pp. 112–113.

[18] In view of the chronic excess demand for real credit in most LDCs, we interpret changes in ΔCR as mainly reflecting shifts in the supply rather than in the demand for credit. We focus on the contemporaneous effect of ΔCR on ΔY because of the zero-year gestation period that finance for working capital has on current output.

The economic and political costs of stabilization via ΔCR and ΔY, however, may be too high to make complete operation of this process feasible (see Section VII). In such a case, three other options are available for dealing with the problem of internal balance in these countries. First, government policy may restrain investment directly and thus avoid having the economy encounter serious disequilibrium in the first place. The government may be able to exert influence most effectively on its own spending. Consequently, control of public-sector I and S emerges as a major potential instrument of macroeconomic policy. This stabilization role for fiscal policy may, of course, conflict with allocational objectives. Second, government policies may attempt to elicit sufficient F to ensure stability. Such policies may focus on providing a hospitable environment for private foreign investment or other forms of foreign-capital inflow. This approach amounts to an effort to endogenize F via government policy, partly in order to satisfy the needs of macroeconomic balance. Third, macroeconomic adjustment may depend on mechanisms that work with longer lags than those we have considered with our short-run focus. This would imply, however, that an inflationary gap continues unabated in the meantime. And the longer the period before adjustment occurs, the greater the cumulative gap and, presumably, the cost of ultimate adjustment.

VII. MACROECONOMIC ADJUSTMENT AND SHORT-RUN GROWTH

Maintaining macroeconomic stability per se may have no intrinsic merit. On the contrary, as Schumpeter emphasized, economic growth occurs as a side effect, so to speak, of an economy's adjustment from a state of macroeconomic disequilibrium. The possibilities for substantial real growth to result from a situation of an *ex ante* excess of I over S are limited in the LDCs, however, which are often supply-constrained economies. More importantly in the present context, the mechanisms used for achieving stability themselves have important implications for economic growth.

Thus in the absence of the other possibilities just discussed, LDCs may be forced to rely on using ΔCR as an instrument for achieving internal balance. The objective in turning ΔCR negative is to lower aggregate investment more than aggregate saving. But the process works also by having ΔCR reduce producers' working capital and, hence, the growth of output and income. The losses in income (and employment) may be particularly great if the structural parameters are such that macroeconomic adjustment requires proceeding so far as to turn ΔY negative! Moreover, adjustment through ΔCR and ΔY is likely to be especially painful politically, for the burdens will probably not be shared equally by all segments of the country's population. Consequently, the process may not be carried sufficiently far to achieve stabilization. And, as the poor growth experience of countries like Argentina and Chile indicates, continuing with high rates of inflation is no panacea for high rates of increasing real-output growth.

In a dynamic perspective, our analysis also helps clarify some effects that follow from changes in foreign-capital movements. From Eq. (9), we know that an increase in F shifts the *IS* locus outward, whereas a decline in F has the opposite effect. How the result is divided between changes in ΔY and in $\dot{P}$ depends on the coefficients of the *IS* loci in individual countries.[19] In addition, increases in F may clearly lead to an increase in ΔCR, both because of the effects of F on base money and because an eased balance-of-payments situation may induce the authorities to relax domestic monetary policy. Thus F affects ΔY not only by providing additional saving and complementary imported inputs to the real sector of the economy (as stressed by the two-gap model) but the external sector also helps determine the expansion of domestic real credit and, hence, the supply of working capital for the productive process.

Because F affects both the monetary and the real sectors of these economies, their growth process is heavily dependent on foreign-trade and capital movements. The periodic recurrence of episodes of monetary stabilization, devaluation, and recession can be readily understood in this context. As we have seen, the parameters of the saving and investment functions impart an accelerationist bias to inflation in these economies. But if foreign lenders and investors are averse to high rates of inflation, foreign-capital inflow is inversely related to $\dot{P}$. Further, under a regime of fixed-exchange rates, export growth and, hence, capital-service capacity and foreign borrowing (Kapur, 1977) also depend negatively on $\dot{P}$. Thus stabilization episodes can be interpreted as periods in which the *IS* and *LM* loci are shifted toward the origin, reducing $\dot{P}$ in order to increase F and promote higher ΔY subsequently. This would lead to a pattern of cyclical fluctuation in ΔY, as is in fact often observed in the growth process of these economies.

Similarly, periodic efforts to reduce the rate of inflation via changes in ΔCR as a domestic policy objective may reinforce this cyclical pattern. Because of the distributional pressures previously alluded to, these episodes often exacerbate an internal political crisis. They may also involve a confrontation with foreign lenders such as the IMF. These institutional

---

[19] A more complete model would disaggregate F into its various components, which may well have different effects on S and I (Halevi, 1976). Also, much depends on the mix of policies used to effect the real transfer of F (Areskoug, 1973).

features, however, should not obscure the fact that what is occurring economically in these episodes is the establishment of macroeconomic equilibrium through heavy reliance on F and ΔCR as adjustment mechanisms.

VIII. CONCLUDING REMARKS

Our analysis permits some general conclusions concerning the macroeconomics of these developing countries. The parameters of the aggregate saving and investment functions in these economies are such that they generate inflation at a self-sustaining and accelerating rate. Investment is easily stimulated: inflation, economic growth, and credit expansion all have buoyant effects on investment. Investment is important for growth, however, mainly in raising the economy's potential output over time. Actual short-run increments to aggregate production depend heavily on the expansion of real credit, which provides working capital and helps determine the degree to which the economy's fixed capital and land are actually utilized. But changes in the supply of real credit are also a key mechanism for macroeconomic stabilization, for interest rates are often pegged at levels too low to be effective for adjustment purposes. Because of the twofold role of ΔCR in the system, economic growth in these countries becomes very sensitive to the achievement of short-run macroeconomic stability.

Increasing investment may not be a great problem for these economies, but stimulating saving clearly is, for saving is less responsive both to ΔY and to $\dot{P}$ than is investment. Saving enters the system in a number of important ways. First, last year's saving shifts outward this year's *IS* locus, permitting higher rates of income growth. Moreover, domestic saving is important in these economies not only for the reason often stressed in the development literature: to release factors of production for capital formation. Saving is also crucial for abating aggregate demand pressures and facilitating macroeconomic equilibrium without stabilization constraints on growth. That is, current saving responses affect the slope of the *IS* locus and, hence, the way in which macroeconomic changes are divided between inflation and real-output growth. Thus larger current savings reduce the inflationary impact of a given level of investment and credit expansion. Consequently, saving determines how far investment and income can rise before leading to intolerable rates of inflation and external imbalance and thus to contractionary measures.[20]

---

[20] Thus Rao seems to have been right in his suggestion that Keynesian growth models that focus on increasing aggregate demand may be of limited policy relevance in the LDCs, but for the wrong reason. The problem is not rigidities and price inelasticity in the supply of goods but rather the fact that saving is less responsive to current economic changes than is investment.

We observe, then, a system characterized by some surprisingly classical features. Saving ultimately determines investment by setting the limit on how far investment can expand.[21] Further, changes in real credit play a central role both in facilitating income growth and in macroeconomic adjustment. Note that changes in credit availability can be interpreted as the primal of interest-rate changes in an economy characterized by pervasive credit rationing. Hence the multiple effects of ΔCR in moving the system also reflect classical patterns.

More precisely, these are Wicksellian economies. Aggregate investment is hyperactive relative to saving, which adjusts sluggishly to current economic changes. Underlying this situation, however, is the artificial inflexibility of the interest rate, which is pegged below market-clearing levels. The general picture that emerges from our study is of economies that are prone to macroeconomic instability. Indeed, because of the parameters of the saving and investment functions, economic growth in these countries is *structurally* biased toward inflation.[22]

Finally, for the same *IS* structural reasons, these economies are also heavily dependent on foreign-capital inflow. This external dependency may be viewed as reflecting nothing more than the algebra of the absorption approach to the balance of payments (Alexander, 1952) in economies in which the level of domestic saving is "too low." This situation, however, reflects more than a problem at a point in time. Viewed in dynamic terms, the problem is more serious, for investment is persistently more buoyant than saving. Thus our results indicate why the expansion path in these economies is chronically dependent on foreign-capital inflow. Moreover, in a dynamic perspective, a continuing flow of F prompted by recurring short-term pressures can lead to important stock effects and steady-state dependence.

This macroeconomic dependency on F has not been noted in the voluminous literature on external dependency in LDCs. Its effects, however, are far-reaching, encompassing both the real and the monetary sectors of the economy.

The policy implications are clear for a less developed country. If it wants to avoid the pattern of macroeconomic dependency and a growth process that involves recurring episodes of accelerating inflation followed by deflation via ΔCR, it should avoid inflation at the outset. More specifi-

---

[21] One may wonder how representative our findings are for developing countries in general. Cross-section estimates for large samples of countries indicate that, similar to our time-series results for a small number of LDCs, inflation and economic growth have a greater effect in stimulating investment than in stimulating saving (Thirlwall, 1974, pp. 210, 218; Singh, 1975, pp. 133 and 146).

[22] Note that this *IS* "structural inflation" differs from an earlier usage of that term in LDCs. The earlier view emphasized alleged inelasticites in the supply of food, foreign exchange, and public finance (see, for example, Felix, 1961).

cally, our analysis suggests two means to this end. First, control over public investment emerges as an important policy instrument for maintaining internal balance. Second, the independence of investment from saving, which we have observed, is facilitated by excessive credit creations in economies where interest rates are held at artificially low levels. Higher interest rates would avoid the chronically Wicksellian pattern that we noted by controlling investment and, perhaps, also by eliciting more domestic saving. Thus the economic costs associated with pegged interest rates in LDCs go far beyond the often-cited losses owing to static and dynamic allocational inefficiency. Far more serious are the macroeconomic effects: the aggregate output losses owing to insufficient saving and excessive investment that lead to a pattern of stop–go growth. Hence our results add force to the proposals of Shaw, McKinnon, and others, made from a different perspective, on the importance of a well-conceived financial policy for economic development.

These conclusions may appear excessively conservative, but the alternative of macroeconomic dependency and recurring inflation and growth cycles also imposes far-reacching costs on less developed countries.

A POSTSCRIPT

The Latin American experience with its long history of inflation provides a basis for some speculations concerning possible future trends in other developing countries.

Although the Latin American countries are often classified together with the other developing economies, there is an important difference. The larger Latin American countries achieved political independence and control over their monetary and fiscal policies, not in the post-World War II period, but in the nineteenth century. This is in contrast with the situation in the other less developed areas that until relatively recently, had their aggregate demand policies made for them by their colonial masters. Further, in the larger Latin American countries, political and economic conditions were such that national autonomy in macroeconomic policy making led to a pattern of chronic inflation.[23] We surmise that, with the passage of time from independence, similar conditions may prevail in the larger developing countries outside of Latin America. As traditions of monetary and fiscal orthodoxy wane, political conditions similar to the

---

[23] See, for example, Hirschman's (1963) analysis, which includes a discussion of the causes of inflation in Chile. Leff (1968, Chapter 9) presents a model of how the policy-making process helped generate large budget deficits and credit expansion in Brazil. See also Thirlwall (1974, pp. 220–231) for a brief survey of inflation in Latin America and his discussion of the association between inflation and low growth.

Latin American pattern may assert themselves, leading to similar credit and aggregate demand policies in the larger countries. There are indications that this process of convergence has already begun, with perceptibly higher rates of inflation in many Asian and African developing countries in their second decade of independence as compared with their first decade.

Our focus here, however, is not on the forces that initiate or propagate inflation in developing countries. Rather we are concerned with what happens once an inflationary history and inflationary expectations have been created. Two possibilities are apparent. One is that, as economic agents gain experience with inflation, the values of key macroeconomic parameters will change, causing inflation to take on its own momentum. Thus it may not be by chance that of the six countries in our sample, only in Argentina, Brazil, and Chile does ΔY have no significant impact on savings (see Table 1). This difference in parameter values from the other countries may reflect changed behavior owing to the impact of inflation on returns to savers. Our sample size may be too small to permit a firm statistical conclusion that parameter values in the Latin American countries are unique, reflecting a long experience with inflation. The second possibility is less problematic, however. Once inflation begins and reaches unacceptable levels, reducing it has very high costs in developing countries in terms of increased dependence on foreign capital and lower income and employment growth.

The foregoing discussion, with its suggestion of the advantages of avoiding inflation in developing countries, may appear distressingly unprogressive, until we review the economic (and political) experience of developing countries that have followed an inflationary path. Albert Hirschman's analytical history of inflation in Chile is useful here. Inflationary rates of credit expansion began in Chile as the country attempted to attain various economic and social objectives. As the process continued, however, rational expectations and class mobilization developed with a vengeance, and disinflation became progressively harder. Further, by 1963, when Hirschman wrote his study, most of the technical insights and political strategies that have since become available for dealing with inflation had already been generated. Nevertheless, for the reasons just mentioned, the country has subsequently experienced continuing high inflation and a low rate of long-term economic growth. And, with the wisdom of hindsight, the comment cited in Hirschman (1963, p. 243) about "the uncanny ability of Chile to avoid both dictatorship and runaway inflation" seems to have been premature. A similar pattern of high inflation, low growth, and unhappy political evolution has also characterized Argentina. The same syndrome has been present as well in another Latin American country that is not in our sample, Uruguay. Brazil has been able to avoid the low-growth feature of this syndrome, which has afflicted the other chronically inflationary Latin American countries, but that was because of special reasons that we cannot pursue here.[24]

We have just noted that the costs to developing countries of embarking on an inflationary path may be higher than they anticipate. Pointing this out will hardly change the course of events, however, and the scenario just sketched may well unfold. As the postindependence period proceeds for non-Latin American developing countries, their policy makers may become less inhibited with inflationary policies. We may then witness a generalization to the larger developing countries of what has previously been a characteristically Latin American phenomenon: chronic inflation and high dependence on foreign-capital inflow to achieve macroeconomic equilibrium. What makes this prospect even less attractive is that, as just noted, in most of the chronically inflationary Latin American countries, this pattern has also been associated with low growth.

If the less developed countries in other regions do embark on a Latin American-type inflationary path, the analytical and policy problems of economic development will shift closer to the focus we propose here. Our model also indicates the policy implications for the *more* developed countries if the scenario is realized. Foreign lenders are more willing to lend to developing countries that show rapidly increasing exports; and the rate of growth of import supply is in any case greatly affected by a developing country's rate of export growth. Consequently, if less developed countries do follow an inflationary path, it is especially important that the more developed countries maintain high rates of income and import growth and open their import and capital markets to the less developed countries.

ACKNOWLEDGMENTS

We are grateful to the Faculty Research Program of the Columbia Business School, which supported part of Leff's work, and to Shekhar Shah and John Millar for research assistance. We also thank Nicholas Carter of the World Bank for supplying necessary data. Finally, we are grateful to seminars at Columbia, New York University, and Princeton; and to Michael Connolly, Keith Johnson, W. Arthur Lewis, John Millar, Anthony Thirlwall, and especially, Kaj Areskoug for helpful comments on an earlier draft. We bear sole responsibility for any errors.

---

[24] Two sets of conditions are especially pertinent. First, econometric results not presented show that, unlike the case in Argentina and Chile, the short-run impact of ΔCR on both ΔY and I was significant. Hence Brazil's policy makers had available relatively potent and fast levers for reducing inflation without disproportionate loss of economic growth. Second, because of conditions arising from Brazil's large size and long industrial history, the country was generally able to maintain relatively buoyant import supply and foreign-capital inflow.

REFERENCES

Alexander, S. S. (1952). "Effects of a Devaluation on a Trade Balance." *IMF Staff Papers* **2** (April), 263–278.

Areskoug, K. (1973). "Foreign Capital Utilization and Economic Policies in Developing Countries." *Review of Economics and Statistics* **53** (May), 182–189.

Barro, R. (1977). "Unanticipated Money Growth and Unemployment in the United States." *American Economic Review* **67** (2) (March), 101–115.

Behrman, J. R., and Hanson, J. A. (eds.) (1979). *Short-Term Macroeconomic Policy in Latin America*. Cambrige, Massachusetts: Ballinger Pub.

Blejer, M. I., and Fernandez, R. B. (1978). "On The Output–Inflation Trade-Off in an Open Economy." *The Manchester School* **46** (June), 123–138.

Boulding, K. E. (1957). "Some Reflections on Inflation and Economic Development." In *Contribuicões a Analise do Desenvolvimento Econômico*, pp. 61–68. Rio de Janeíro: Agir.

Connolly, M., and Taylor, D. (1976). "Testing the Monetary Approach to Devaluation in Developing Countries." *Journal of Political Economy* **84** (August), 849–859.

Cooper, R. N. (1971). "Currency Devaluation in Developing Countries." *Princeton Essays in International Finance* (June).

Felix, D. (1961). "An Alternative View of the 'Monetarist'–'Structuralist' Controversy." In *Latin American Issues* (A. Hirschman, ed.), pp. 81–94. New York: Twentieth Century Fund.

Goldfeld, S. M., and Quandt, R. E. (1965). "Some Tests for Homoscedasticity." *Journal of the American Statistical Association* **60** (June), 539–547.

Grebler, L., and Burns, L. S. (1976). "Resource Allocation to Housing Investment: A Comparative International Study." *Economic Development and Cultural Change* **25** (October), 95–122.

Guitian, M. (1973). "Credit Versus Money as an Instrument of Control." *IMF Staff Papers* **20** (3) (November), 785–800.

Halevi, N. (1976). "The Effects on Investment and Consumption of Import Surpluses in Developing Countries." *The Economic Journal* **86** (December), 853–858.

Hirschman, A. O. (1963). "Inflation in Chile." *In Journeys toward Progress*, pp. 161–223. New York: Twentieth Century Fund.

Kapur, I. (1977). "The Supply of Euro-Currency Finance to Developing Countries." *Oxford Bulletin of Economics and Statistics* **39** (3) (August), 173–188.

Kelejian, H. H. (1974). "Random Parameters in a Simultaneous Equation Framework: Identification and Estimation." *Econometrica* **42** (May), 517–528.

Leff, N. H. (1976). "Capital Markets in the Developing Countries, The 'Group' Principle." In *Money and Capital in Economic Growth and Development* (R. I. McKinnon, ed.), pp. 97–122. New York: Dekker.

Leff, N. H., and Sato, K. (1975). "A Simultaneous-Equations Model of Savings in Developing Countries." *Journal of Political Economy* **83** (December), 1217–1228.

Leff, N. H., and Sato, K. (1980). "Macroeconomic Adjustment in Developing Countries: Instability, Short-Run Growth, and External Dependency." *Review of Economics and Statistics* **62** (May), 170–179.

Maeshiro, A. (1976). "Autoregressive Transformation, Trended Independent Variables, and Autocorrelated Disturbance Terms." *Review of Economics and Statistics* **58** (November), 497–500.

McKinnon, R. (1973). *Money and Capital in Economic Development*. Washington, D.C.: The Brookings Institution.

Myint, H. (1965). "Economic Theory and the Underdeveloped Countries." *Journal of Political Economy* **73** (5) (October), 477–491.

Portes, R., and Winter, D. (1978). "The Demand for Money and for Consumption Goods in Centrally Planned Economies." *Review of Economies and Statistics* **60** (February), 8–18.

Rao, V. K. R. V. (1952). "Investment, Income, and the Multiplier in an Underdeveloped Economy." *Indian Economic Review* (February). Reprinted in A. N. Agarwala and S. P. Singh, *The Economics of Underdevelopment*, pp. 205–218. London and New York: Oxford Univ. Press, 1963.

Sato, K. (1978). "A General Disequilibrium Model of Output, Money, and Prices in Developing Countries," mimeo.

Shaw, E. S. (1973). *Financial Deepening in Economic Development*. London and New York: Oxford Univ. Press, 1973.

Singh, S. K. (1975). *Development Economics, Some Findings*. Lexington, Massachusetts: Lexington Books.

Taylor, L. (1979). *Macro Models for Developing Countries*. New York: McGraw-Hill.

Thirlwell, A. (1974). *Inflation, Saving and Growth in Developing Countries*. New York: St. Martins Press.

Vogel, R. C. (1974). "The Dynamics of Inflation in Latin America, 1950–1969." *American Economic Review* **64** (March), 102–114.

Wong, C.-H. (1977). "Demand for Money in Developing Countries," *Journal of Monetary Economics* **3** (January), 59–86.

NATHANIEL H. LEFF
Graduate School of Business
Columbia University
New York, New York

KAZUO SATO
Department of Economics
State Univeristy of New York at Buffalo
Amherst, New York

Chapter 9

Investment, Inflation, and Employment: A Macroeconomic Framework

Constantino Lluch

I. INTRODUCTION

Inflation is a mechanism to redistribute income during a process of growth whereby more of the extra output than would otherwise goes to the earners of noncontractual incomes. This is the central point of the contribution by Georgescu-Roegen (1970) to the study of inflations in Latin America.[1] Because of that, he argues, inflationary processes (prolonged declines in the value of money in terms of goods and services) always go hand in hand with relative price changes and the fixing of some nominal prices: of basic foodstuffs, credit, labor, housing, and public utili-

[1] The contribution by Georgescu-Roegen (1970) is important in the context of monetarist versus structuralist explanations of inflationary processes in Latin America. The link between inflation and distribution was, of course, recognized much earlier. Keynes (1923) devoted the first chapter of his tract to an account of how the business class, earners, and rentiers were affected by the breakdown of price stability after the Great War.

191

ties. In this context, it matters little whether inflation is anticipated or not. More important is the fact that some population groups can do little to protect themselves against anticipated inflation, and therefore nothing much depends on whether their anticipations turn out to be right or wrong. The link between inflation and distribution, through changes in relative prices, implies also that inflationary processes affect the amount and the structure of investment. Thus inflations and their associated monetary events do affect output and its distribution in the long run.

Georgescu-Roegen wrote "in terms of 'structures' in the tradition of the French School of Francois Perroux" (1970, p. 560). His lead has not been followed as much as it deserves. This chapter follows that lead with some formal analysis, although the formalization is not carried out to the study of inflationary processes. It is only a first step, concerned with the nature of the temporary equilibrium at each stage of the process of inflation. Also, all commodities are aggregated into GDP, further limiting the scope of the work by Georgescu-Roegen. This is done to emphasize the importance of disaggregation over time, in his analysis.

There is a need to disaggregate over time, to conduct the analysis in terms of periods, because the distributional impact of inflationary processes follows from not everyone and everything adjusting within one period, even as long as a year or two. More basically, if inflation might generate abnormal, *ex post* profits, the analysis should not assume them away, as happens with conventional interpretations of the income accounts. In them, the value of output is the income of factors of production, and factors get paid their marginal product. Clearly, this obscures the timing and nature of income generation. Some personal incomes today were fixed in nominal terms in the past (for example, income from loans at a fixed interest rate); others are generated by forward-looking contracts (for example, payments to labor at the beginning of a production period, made upon the expectation of profits at a later date); still others are residual incomes (the realized, current profits that may or may not be equal to the expected profits sustaining past production, employment, and investment decisions). Without the distinction between contractual and residual incomes, it is hard to formalize the role of uncertainty and risk in production and investment plans; to examine the impact of financial institutions upon economic growth and the distribution of its benefits; and to study inflation and distribution.

The drawback of period analysis is its arbitrariness: how to know which variables are jointly determined now and which ones change only from period to period, and according to which rule. The temptation looms large to aggregate sufficiently over time and to rule out rigidities and lags as "second-order effects." Because it is not known whether, indeed, only effects of secondary importance are ignored through aggregation over time, it is worthwhile to pursue the work of Georgescu-Roegen and also to accumulate case studies with attention to institutional detail and the sequence of historical events. This chapter follows the first route.

An important contribution to macroeconomic analysis with price rigidities over the relevant period has been made by Malinvaud (1977, 1980). This work is motivated by the frequent observation in advanced industrial economies that quantities adjust faster than prices; by the need to avoid simplistic, partial equilibrium links in the analysis of unemployment (like the statement that employment will increase if the real wage falls); and by the need to explain stagflation. This chapter follows an alternative formulation of rigidities. In the short run, the quantities of goods transacted are given by past decisions, whereas labor incomes follow from current decisions by firms about how much output is profitable to bring to market in the next period. Prices are such that the current output market clears— with the important simplification that all output is sold, so that there is no undesired inventory accumulation. This formulation of short-run rigidities is probably better suited to the study of temporary equilibrium in less advanced economies experiencing substantial price increases. Also, it fits the view of experienced commentators about credit, wages, and prices; and it provides a first step to integrate the analysis of a once-for-all price change with that of inflationary processes.

This chapter is structured as follows. In Section II, the accounting is set out, together with assumptions about the timing of decisions about production, investment, and employment; and the timing of transactions in the output and labor markets. The main link between stocks and flows is the identity at current prices equating household saving with changes in household wealth. In Section III, equilibrium conditions in the markets for goods, labor, and credit are derived. Overall equilibrium values are obtained for the nominal rate of interest, the price level, the real wage, and employment, given the rate of inflation expected by firms. The current price level, relative to the one last period, gives the current rate of inflation. For the last period, firms may or may not have guessed the current rate correctly. A graphical representation of overall equilibrium is given in the figures. In Section IV, its comparative static properties are examined. Also, some limitations of the analysis are pointed out, with suggestions for further work. In particular, the analysis deals with a one-period rate of inflation, not with a sequence of rates—an inflationary process. An appendix contains the model of the representative firm on which the decisions on employment and investment are based.

II. INCOME AND WEALTH ACCOUNTS

Table 1 contains the wealth accounts of the agents we are considering: the central bank, commercial banks, firms, and households. The central bank holds assets F, which are a liability of the government. It also holds liabilities $R = \gamma(D + Z)$, which are the commercial bank reserves. A single reserve requirement ratio γ is assumed to apply to both household deposits D and firm deposits Z at commercial banks. The other liability is the amount of currency outstanding M, which is assumed to be held only by households.

The commercial banks' consolidated balance sheet has two assets: credit to firms B and reserves at the central bank R. It also has two liabilities (Z and D) and a balancing item N_B, denoting the net worth of the banking sector.

Firms hold physical assets $P_k K$, valued at current prices, and deposits at banks. They are liable for bank borrowing and their net worth is denoted by N_F.

Households hold deposits D and currency M; own banks and firms, so that the networth from both is a household asset $N = N_B + N_F$; and both items make up their total wealth A. The overall consolidated balance

TABLE 1

Balance Sheets

Central bank			
Government debt	F	Bank reserves	R
		Currency outstanding	M
Commercial banks			
Credit	B	Firm deposits	Z
Reserves	R	Household deposits	D
		Net worth	N_B
Firms			
Physical assets	$P_k K$	Debt	B
Deposits	Z	Net worth	N_F
Households			
Deposits	D	Wealth	A
Currency	M		
	N		

[2] Households count the liabilities of the government to the central bank as part of their wealth. This sidesteps a long controversy about the proper definition of private wealth. The justification for this is the short shrift given to savings behavior in this chapter, to concentrate attention on other matters.

sheet implies that $A = F + P_k K$, so that household wealth is equal to government debt plus the value of capital.[2]

How do the current balance sheets in Table 1 relate to the ones one period ago (denoted by the same symbols with a bar below each)? The changes between both must be linked to income flows over the period, and this requires conventions about the timing of production and investment decisions and the timing of transactions. Usually, timing conventions are such that everything occurs simultaneously within a time period, on grounds of aggregation over a large number of firms and households: each may have different production and payment periods, but this does not matter in the aggregate because production, investment, and market transactions occur continuously. This justification is not convincing. The average of a large number of production periods is not zero. If such periods are relevant for borrowing decisions, the hiring of labor, or the computation of profits, they should not be allowed to vanish in the aggregate. In addition, it is desirable to have timing conventions that allow the share of profits to vary with inflation[3] and that show as a gain from inflation the ability to "borrow now and repay later in devalued currency" (Georgescu-Roegen, 1970, p. 579).

I shall adopt the following conventions on transactions and their timing: (a) the output sold today at price P is the result of past production decisions and it is denoted as $\underline{X}$; (b) the capital stock in existence K is the depreciated stock from the last period $(1 - \delta)\underline{K}$ plus gross investment $\underline{I}$, decided upon in the past and successfully carried out; (c) current labor payments WL correspond to the current output and investment decisions about the quantities (X, I) that will come to market next period; (d) those labor payments are part of the bank credit to firms; it is the part held in firm deposits at banks Z; and as workers spend their paychecks quickly, it shall be assumed that $Z = WL$; (e) commercial banks pay no interest on deposits nor receive any interest from reserves held at the central bank, so iB is the income they will get next period on account of the current bank credit outstanding B; today, the operating receipts of commercial banks are $\underline{iB}$, the interest payments contracted one period ago; (f) for simplicity, there is only one nominal interest rate i without distinction between short- and long-term credit; (g) also for simplicity, it will be assumed that banks and firms distribute the same proportion λ of their operating profits.

These conventions incorporate many assumed rigidities in the short run. Most notable is the link between labor payments and firm deposits at banks. This is a crude representation of the liquidity requirements familiar from the theory of the firm under finance constraints (Vickers, 1968). In

---

[3] This is desirable so that factor shares are not determined only by technological conditions, cost minimization, and full employment.

empirical applications, a proportionality coefficient with the dimension of time should be included into $Z = WL$ to match the observed orders of magnitude of labor payments versus firm deposits. Relative constancy over time of such coefficient would add plausibility to the assumed link between bank credit and labor payments.

To proceed, let us adopt the simplest rule of valuation of capital: $P = P_k$. Current firm profits are then

$$\Pi = P\underline{X} - (1 + i)\underline{WL} - i(\underline{B} - \underline{WL}) - \delta P\underline{K}$$
$$= P\hat{\underline{X}} - \underline{WL} - i\underline{B},$$

with $\hat{\underline{X}} = \underline{X} - \delta\underline{K}$. Profits are the value of output $P\underline{X}$; net of repaid working capital $(1 + i)\underline{WL}$; other interest payments $i(\underline{B} - \underline{WL})$; and depreciation allowances $\delta P\underline{K}$.

Current receipts by households Y are

$$Y = WL + \lambda i\underline{B} + \lambda\Pi,$$

the sum of wages, distributed interest, and distributed profits. Substituting Π, we obtain

$$Y = WL + \lambda\Pi_g,$$

where $\Pi_g = \Pi + i\underline{B} = P\hat{\underline{X}} - \underline{WL}$, which is current profits, gross of interest payments (i.e., the value of net output minus past labor costs incurred to produce it).[4]

To complete the chosen accounting conventions, it is necessary to link current household receipts to changes in household wealth. This link is

$$sY + (\Delta P)\underline{K} = \Delta A,$$

where $\Delta P = P - \underline{P}$, $\Delta A = A - \underline{A}$. The change in nominal household wealth has two components: savings out of current receipts at the rate s and capital gains $(\Delta P)\underline{K}$. No theory of the saving rate[5] need be offered at this stage, which deals with accounting only. Note that[6]

$$\Delta A = F + (\Delta P)\underline{K} + P\,\Delta K,$$

---

[4] Under these accounting conventions, current household receipts are equal to the value of net output transacted only by chance. Adding and subtracting Π_g, we obtain

$$Y = P\hat{\underline{X}} + \Delta(WL) - (1 - \lambda)\Pi_g,$$

where $\Delta(WL) = WL - \underline{WL}$. Thus $Y = P\hat{\underline{X}}$ only if the increase in the wage bill is equal to undistributed profits gross of interest payments. It will be seen later that this is an equilibrium condition in the output market if the government debt has not changed.

[5] It can be thought of as an average of rates from different income sources or as a function of wealth and the rate of interest. Later on, in the study of temporary equilibrium, more rigidity will be assumed by making s constant in the short run.

[6] From Table 1, $\Delta A = \Delta D + \Delta M + \Delta N$; $\Delta N = (\Delta P)\underline{K} + P(\Delta K) + \Delta R - \Delta D$; and $\Delta R + \Delta M = \Delta F$.

which yields

$$sY = \Delta F + P(\Delta K),$$

i.e., saving out of current household receipts can be allocated only to the accumulation of physical capital or government debt. This is the *present* accounting link between magnitudes determined by decisions taken in the past and by decisions taken now on the basis of expectations about the future. Economic forces can be imposed upon such a link to construct a simple notion of economic equilibrium. This will be done in the next section.

Note that government has been reduced to a very limited role: to put a limit to money creation through the issue of debt. Taxation or interest payments on the public debt are ignored because they would add formal complications at this stage and divert attention away from the main point.

III. EQUILIBRIUM

A. Output

Equilibrium in the output market requires that the available supply for consumption purposes be equal to the quantity demanded. The simplest demand[7] and supply functions are

$$PC^d = (1 - s)Y, \qquad C^s = \underline{X} - \underline{I},$$

where $C^i, (i = d, s)$, stands for consumption demand and supply. The

---

[7] The aggregate demand $(1 - s)Y/P$ has a peculiar feature. It represents, to the extreme, the income effect of an increase in the price level through its effect upon distributed profits. To see this, recall that current household receipts are

$$Y = WL + \lambda \Pi_g, \qquad \Pi_g = P\hat{\underline{X}} - \underline{WL}.$$

Thus, for a given saving rate and a real wage bill, a higher price level yields a higher real income Y/P through the increase in real profits Π_g/P. In the plane (P, C), aggregate consumption demand appears to have a positive slope!

The income effect of an increase in the price level is probably important in practice, although not as much as in the chosen representation of aggregate demand. In empirical applications, more general representations should be used. In general,

$$PC^d = (1 - s_W)WL + (1 - s_K)\lambda \Pi_g, \qquad s_j = s_j(i, \hat{\pi}, A/P),$$

where $j = W, K$ and $\hat{\pi}$ is the expected rate of inflation.

The positive association between the saving rate and the equilibrium price level noted later (the inflationary effect of thriftiness, so to speak) follows from this narrow representation of aggregate demand.

value of excess demand is

$$P(C^d - C^s) = (1 - s)Y - P(\underline{X} - \underline{I}),$$

which, after some manipulation,[8] can be written as

$$P(C^d - C^s) = \Delta(WL) - \Delta F - (1 - \lambda)\Pi_g. \tag{1}$$

This proves the following proposition.

Proposition 1. Under the accounting and timing conventions in Table 1, there exists equilibrium in the output market if and only if the increase in the wage bill is equal to the increase in government debt plus undistributed profits, gross of interest payments to banks. If the wage bill increases by more, there exists excess demand; if by less, excess supply.

The particular disaggregation over time specified here yields an operational measure of disequilibrium. It also yields the jump in the price level that is necessary to clear the output market. Consider the equilibrium condition in (1):

$$\Delta(WL) = \Delta F + (1 - \lambda)\Pi_g,$$

with $\Pi_g = P\underline{X} - \underline{WL}$. Therefore, the price level that clears the output market is the one that makes undistributed profits, gross of interest payments to banks, equal to the difference between the extra wage bill and the extra government debt. Such price level P is given by

$$(1 - \lambda)P\underline{X} = \underline{WL} - \lambda\underline{WL} - \Delta F,$$

and by comparison with $\underline{P}$, the equilibrium jump in the price level is found. Conditions for price stability can also be obtained.[9]

The equilibrium condition in (1) may be useful in organizing data, but it is not by itself very informative about the equilibrium values of the endogenous variables of interest: employment, the real wage, the rate of interest, and the price level. Let $\underline{C} = \underline{X} - \underline{I}$, the available supply for con-

---

[8] The process is $P(C^d - C^s) = Y - \Delta F - (\Delta K)P - P(\underline{X} - \underline{I}) = P\dot{\underline{X}} + \Delta(WL) - (1 - \lambda)\Pi_g - \Delta F - (\underline{I} - \delta\underline{K})P - P\underline{X} + P\underline{I} = \Delta(WL) - \Delta F - (1 - \lambda)\Pi_g$.

[9] Equilibrium in the output market one period ago, assuming that λ is constant over time, implies that

$$(1 - \lambda)\underline{PX} = \underline{WL} - \lambda\underline{\underline{WL}} - \Delta\underline{F},$$

where double bars denote two period lags. Then $P = \underline{P}$ if and only if the ratio of current to past output (the output growth factor) is equal to $\underline{a}(a - b - \lambda)/(\underline{a} - \underline{b} - \lambda)$, where $a = WL/\underline{WL}$, the growth factor for the wage bill; $b = a \Delta F/WL$, the increase in the government debt as a proportion of the wage bill times the wage bill growth factor; and where bars denote the same ratios, lagged one period.

sumption purposes. How have $(\underline{X}, \underline{I})$ been determined? Similarly, how is current employment determined in view of the future (X, I)?

If the market for output is in equilibrium under the simplest demand assumption, then

$$\underline{C} = (1 - s)[wL + \lambda(\hat{\underline{X}} - \underline{WL}/P)],$$

where $w = W/P$. For any given $(L; s, \lambda)$, there exists a negative association between the equilibrium values of the real wage and the price level. Given $(L, w; \lambda)$, there exists a positive association between the saving rate and the equilibrium price level. Such inflationary pressure from thriftiness will be found in practice when the income effect of an increase in the price level dominates all others. This is the case reflected in the simple representation of aggregate consumption demand adopted here.

In any case, nothing has been said about the determination of the real wage and the level of employment. For this, it is necessary to examine the working of the labor market. The peculiarity of the analysis that follows is the assumed connection between labor costs and the part of bank credit to firms. The nominal rate of interest is then an argument in the demand function for labor.

B. Labor

In the Appendix, the current demand for labor by a representative firm is obtained from the maximization of the present value of expected profits. In the simplest one-period problem, labor is demanded up to the point where the real wage is equal to its adjusted marginal product. The need to adjust the marginal product by a proportionality factor follows from the timing conventions adopted here. Labor is paid currently, but output is sold with a one-period lag. Under these circumstances, the coefficient of adjustment applied to the marginal product of labor is the ratio of the inflation factor (the expected inflation rate plus unity) to the effective interest factor (the effective interest rate plus unity). The effective interest rate is the ratio of interest payments to the firm's balance sheet.[10]

Even in the simple one-period case, the coefficient of adjustment need not be unity. Furthermore, changes in the nominal rate of interest need not be fully compensated by changes in the expected inflation rate, so that the coefficient of adjustment is, in general, negatively associated with the nominal rate of interest. The implication is that, in the (w, L) plane, the labor-demand schedule is represented by a family of curves with the nom-

---

[10] Alternatively, the effective interest rate is the nominal rate of interest divided by the ratio of the firm's net worth to its outstanding debt plus unity.

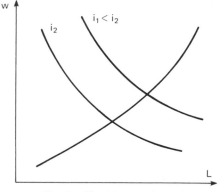

Fig. 1.   The labor market.

inal rate of interest as a shift factor. Curves closer to the origin correspond to higher interest rates: for the same real wage and expectations
about inflation, less labor will be demanded the higher the nominal rate of
interest.

In the Appendix, a more complex case is also considered. With a planning horizon of two periods or more, the representative firm must also
choose an investment plan, the optimal additions to its present capital
stock. This represents an additional source of current labor demand under
the assumption that the representative firm produces that addition itself.
If the net marginal product of capital exceeds the real, effective nominal
rate of interest, the investment is undertaken.[11] A higher nominal rate of
interest in this case is an added reason for a reduction in the quantity of
labor demanded at a given real wage.

The excess demand function for labor is

$$L^{\mathrm{d}}(w, i) - L^{\mathrm{s}}(w), \tag{2}$$

with $L_1^{\mathrm{d}} < 0$; $L_2^{\mathrm{d}} < 0$; $L_1^{\mathrm{s}} > 0$. The labor market is represented graphically
in Fig. 1.

In equilibrium, $L^{\mathrm{d}} = L^{\mathrm{s}} = L$. In this chapter, what matters most are
the equilibrium properties of

$$z = wL,$$

the equilibrium real wage bill, or "working capital," because it appears in

---

[11] But note that, in general, investment orders are not carried out to the point where the
net marginal product of capital is equal to the effective interest rate. The representative firm
will balance a higher investment order on future output against the lower, residual supply for
consumption purposes; and it has some notion of the consumption demand it will face in the
future.

the excess demand function for output and for credit via the assumed link between the wage bill and part of the bank credit to firms. In equilibrium, working capital is a negative function of the nominal rate of interest, i.e.,

$$z = z(i), \qquad z'(i) < 0.$$

This expression can be easily specified for particular production and labor supply functions, using the results in the Appendix, but here it is needed only in this general form.

C. Output and Labor: The *CC* schedule

The equilibrium condition in the output and labor markets can now be written as

$$\underline{C} = (1 - s)[z(i) + \lambda(\hat{\underline{X}} - \underline{WL}/P)]. \tag{3}$$

Given (s, λ), an increase in the rate of interest i is associated with a fall in consumption demand through the fall in the real wage bill (by assumption, working capital). To compensate for such a fall, a higher price level is needed, corresponding to a higher level of distributed real profits, gross of interest payments to banks. The schedule CC in Fig. 2 is the locus of all equilibrium pairs (i, P) such that both output and labor markets are in equilibrium, so that (3) holds.

The importance of the CC schedule lies in its positive slope: it provides a rationale for a positive association between the nominal interest rate and the price level, for given output, saving out of current household

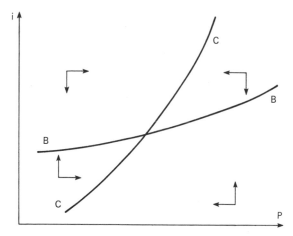

Fig. 2. Overall macroeconomic equilibrium, with dominant income effect of a change in the price level: the stable case.

receipts, and proportion of distributed profits. Different points in the CC schedule correspond to different levels of employment and investment (i.e., future output). Given expected inflation, higher current interest rates curtail output growth.

The role of expected inflation in (3) and the corresponding CC schedule have not yet been considered. The higher the inflation factor $P/\underline{P}$ (the inflation rate, relative to one period ago, plus unity), the higher the distributed profits, i.e., the second term in brackets in (3). Presumably, the higher would also be the rate of inflation expected to hold one period hence. This is expansionary in the sense that $z(i)$ is larger than otherwise. Therefore, the higher would be the increase in the rate of interest necessary to clear the current output market. Inflationary expectations, therefore, will tend to produce a steeper CC schedule. By the same token, if such expectations are suddenly broken, to the extent that this is contractionary (i.e., $z(i)$ is smaller than otherwise), anything may happen to the level of the nominal rate of interest consistent with short-run equilibrium. Conceivably, if contraction is strong enough, a boost to demand through lower rates of interest may be required. This would result in a negatively sloped CC schedule.

Expectations about future inflation play an important role on the shape of the CC schedule[12] and, thus, in short-term macroeconomic equilibrium. In what follows, all results are understood to be conditional on a given expected inflation rate.

The positive slope of the CC schedule follows from the assumed income effect of an increase in the price level, which results in increased consumption demand from higher profits. This is an unconventional assumption, leading to a paradox. Nonetheless, it may be relevant in practice. At the very least, it poses an empirical question that requires further work: Does the income effect of a price increase dominate possible contractionary effects? Such contraction of consumption demand may come from many sources. The adjustment of nominal wages may not be immediate, as assumed in the previous section. This may imply a fall in the real wage bill through price increases. If the increase in profit incomes goes into saving or into demand for foreign output, there would then be a fall in domestic consumption demand. To maintain equilibrium in the output and the labor market, the nominal rate of interest would then have to fall, so that CC would be negatively sloped.

An alternative source of contraction in consumption demand as the result of the price increase is the real wealth effect. If A/P is an argument in

---

[12] Presumably, expectations about future prices depend very much on particular circumstances. This adds to the need for case studies of particular stabilization episodes, an effort too often dismissed as anecdotal.

aggregate consumption demand, it follows from the definition of household wealth that

$$A = \underline{A} + \Delta A, \qquad \Delta A = \Delta F + P(\Delta K)$$

and, therefore,

$$A/P = \Delta K + (\underline{A}/P) + (\Delta F/P).$$

A higher price level reduces A/P, given $(\Delta K, \underline{A}, \Delta F)$, and thus it would reduce aggregate consumption demand. The schedule CC will again be negatively sloped if the real wealth effect is strong enough.

The implications of policies affecting the interest rate or the level of prices in the short run are very different, depending on the slope of the CC schedule. In what follows, the unconventional assumption (a positive CC schedule) will be explored further, to highlight the difference that a positive CC makes and the need to determine CC in practical applications.[13] The conventional case (a negatively sloped CC) will also be considered.

Short-run macroeconomic equilibrium requires the existence of another link between (i, P) besides CC. Two possibilities are apparent, and, given the accounting constraints in Table 1, mutually exclusive. The first attributes primary economic importance to household decisions about desired wealth, so that banks accommodate these decisions and the increase in government debt. There would then exist a desired household wealth $(A/P)^d$ and a desired composition, which implies a desired $(\Delta K, \Delta F/P)$, for any given $\underline{A}/P$, past wealth at current prices. The second possibility attributes primary economic importance to decisions by banks and firms about credit and its allocation, so that household wealth would then be the accommodating variable, given the increase in government debt.

Since Keynes, the first possibility has occupied most professional attention, with the consequent relative lack of emphasis upon the economic behavior of banks. This chapter focuses on a very simple representation of the second possibility (the credit approach), on the grounds that its neglect has gone too far, particularly in inflationary situations where the question of credit availability at subsidized interest rates is central to the

---

[13] For future use, note that points above the CC schedule in Fig. 2 denote equilibrium in the labor market and excess supply in the output market; points below, equilibrium in the labor market and excess demand in the output market. Under the assumption of the dominating income effect of changes in the price level, P would be increasing under excess supply and falling under excess demand in the output market. These anomalous adjustment hypotheses illustrate one more aspect of the importance of the slope of the CC schedule in practical applications.

Note that if $s = s(i)$, $s'(i) > 0$, a positively sloped CC would be flatter than the CC corresponding to a constant s.

study of the distributional impact of inflation. This is particularly important in Latin America, as emphasized by Georgescu-Roegen (1970).

D.   Credit

The demand for credit by firms is determined by their chosen ratio of net worth to debt, their demand for working capital, and their reactions to unanticipated price changes. Let the ratio of net worth to debt be ϕ, a given constant, and let us ignore the impact of mistakes (differences between current prices and the last period expectation of current prices). If $Z = WL$ is working capital, the total demand for credit by firms can be read off their balance sheet in Table 1 as

$$z(i) + K = (1 + \phi)B^{\mathrm{d}}/P.$$

Given $z'(i) < 0$, on the grounds given in the Appendix, this implies a negative relationship between real credit demand and the nominal rate of interest (given, also, the expected rate of inflation).

The supply of credit is determined by the allocation of total bank assets between reserves and loans to firms. Assume that there exists a desired loan-to-reserve ratio $h(i)$ such that

$$B^{\mathrm{s}} = h(i)R, \qquad h'(i) > 0.$$

The excess demand for credit is $B^{\mathrm{d}} - B^{\mathrm{s}}$, and equilibrium in the credit market is characterized by

$$z(i) + K = (1 + \phi)h(i)R/P. \tag{4}$$

From Table 1, $R = F - M$. For a given R (i.e., exogenous determination by the government and the Central Bank of F and M), Eq. (4) determines BB (Fig. 2) and the locus (i, P) such that the market for credit viewed as a stock is in equilibrium. From an equilibrium pair (i, P), let the rate of interest fall. Then $h(i)$ falls and $z(i)$ increases. The new price level that clears the credit market is lower than before. The locus BB in Fig. 2 is upward sloping. Points above the BB schedule represent an excess supply of credit at a given price level; points below, excess demand. The simplest adjustment hypothesis is that the nominal rate of interest tends to fall in the region above the BB schedule and to increase in the region below it.

E.   Overall Equilibrium

Figure 2 assumes that the CC schedule is steeper than the BB schedule. Under the simple hypothesis about the adjustments of (i, P) outside

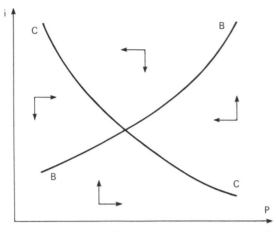

Fig. 3. Overall macroeconomic equilibrium when increases in P reduce current aggregate consumption demand.

equilibrium adopted here, Fig. 2 represents the case of stable, short-run, macroeconomic equilibrium. It follows that if the income effect of a change in the price level dominates aggregate consumption demand, it should dominate enough for equilibrium to be stable. It is not known how empirically relevant the adjustment hypotheses are, whether, in fact, markets adjust under the assumed assignment rules. Therefore, not much should be made of the unstable case in which the BB schedule is steeper than the CC schedule. But one region of instability is of potential practical interest: when i is too small to clear the credit market and P (or income) too small to clear the current market for consumption goods.

Figure 3 contains a more conventional representation of overall macroeconomic equilibrium in the short run: the case of a negatively sloped CC schedule. Through unspecified (but easy to specify) lagged adjustments in the labor market or real wealth effects, let either or both of the following hold:

(i) $z = z(i, P)$, $z_i < 0$, $z_P < 0$,
(ii) $s = s(P)$, $s' > 0$.

Assume that the contraction in consumption demand, through these channels, from an increase in P exceeds the expansion from the increase in profits. Then, consider an equilibrium pair (i_0, P_0) and a higher $P > P_0$, for $i = i_0$. This reduces consumption demand below the market clearing $\underline{C}$, and a compensating expansion through $i < i_0$ is required to restore equilibrium. Thus, CC slopes downward. To the right of CC, P is too high, there exists excess supply of output, and there is a tendency for P to fall. The opposite holds to the left of CC.

Overall equilibrium in this case is stable, as shown by the simple assignment rules represented by the arrows in Fig. 3.

IV. COMPARATIVE STATICS

Figures 2 and 3 represent short-run macroeconomic equilibrium in two situations: under a dominant income effect of a change in the price level and, a more conventional case, where an increase in the price level reduces current aggregate consumption demand. In both cases, the equilibrium is conditional on the expected inflation rate[14] and also $(s, \lambda, \phi; R)$. Given the supply of output available for consumption purposes, macroeconomic equilibrium determines the price system at which decisions by firms (about the distribution of *ex post* profits and the hiring of labor for future production), by banks (about the distribution of their assets between loans and reserves), and by households (about how much of current receipts to save) are compatible with each other.

The equilibrium pair (i, P) is associated with a real wage and a level of employment such that the labor market is in equilibrium (see Fig. 1). It was previously noted that there may be rigidities in the short-run money wage and that this is an important factor toward a downward-sloping CC schedule. Again, more elaborate representations of the labor market are beyond the scope of this chapter, which is concerned only with the fundamental aspects of macroeconomic equilibrium under the quantity rigidities that follow from differences in the timing of production and exchange and that give rise to *ex post* profits and to distributional impacts from a change in the price level.

It is useful to consider the effects of changes in $(s, \lambda, \phi; R)$ upon the equilibrium pair (i, P). Policy operates, in part, through the first set of variables. Therefore, comparative static effects are an important component of policy evaluation. Table 2 contains, in schematic form, the responses in the schedules (CC, BB) and the equilibrium values (i, P) to an increase in $(s, \lambda, \phi; R)$. The results in Table 2 illustrate the importance, in theory, when a change in the price level has a dominant income effect. In that case, all comparative static results are counter intuitive: thriftiness is

---

[14] Price expectations figure prominently in the Appendix. They enter in all first-order conditions for a maximum of present value of profits. In Figs. 2 and 3, the expected inflation rate $\hat{\pi}$ was ignored. The links between expected and actual inflation rates, the level of profits, and the mistakes in planning made by the representative firm need to be studied as part of the analysis of inflationary processes. Such analysis is beyond the scope of this chapter.

TABLE 2

Comparative Static Effects upon (i, P) of Increases in $(s, \lambda, \phi; R)$

	Change in[a]			
Increase in	*BB*	*CC*	*i*	*P*
For Fig. 2				
s		+	+	+
λ		−	−	−
φ	+		−	−
R	+		−	−
For Fig. 3				
s		−	−	−
λ		+	+	+
φ	+		−	+
R	+		−	+

[a] *Notes:* (1) A plus sign attached to a change in (BB, CC) denotes a shift to the right; a minus sign, a shift to the left. (2) A plus sign attached to a change in (i, P) denotes an increase in the equilibrium value; a minus sign, a decrease. (3) The signs under (i, P) are also the signs of the reduced-form equilibrium differentials with respect to $(s, \lambda, \phi; R)$.

inflationary; money creation deflationary. Decreases in the price level have not been observed often in Latin America. But this is not sufficient evidence to dismiss Fig. 2 and the first half of Table 2 as cases without any practical relevance. The main reason is, of course, that the equilibrium (i, P) in Fig. 2 can hardly be identified with actual data: it is very difficult to argue that the credit market clears in practice, so that there is no excess demand for credit at the regulated bank interest rates. But if such excess demand exists and if it does so for long periods, the proper use of Fig. 2 (or its counterpart, the unstable case) is to place the observed values into the appropriate region of disequilibrium and to examine tendencies toward short-run equilibrium coupled with across-period shifts in the equilibrium schedules (BB, CC). The first half of Table 2 is then quite compatible with sustained inflation, in practice. This chapter will not deal with such processes. It only illustrates the importance of the CC schedule and the fact that the income effect of a price increase has been relatively neglected. In particular, consider the impact of a larger public sector deficit financed through the creation of money, so that R is higher than otherwise. In Fig. 2, this implies a shift to the right in the BB schedule, so that the equilibrium price level rises proportionately to the increase in R for each rate of interest. Otherwise, the credit market would not clear: the demand for credit by firms $z(i) + K$ would be smaller than the supply of credit $(1 + \phi)h(i)R/P$. At the higher price level, though, there would now be excess demand for output, as read from the *CC* schedule, because of the higher *ex post* profits. The elimination of this excess demand would require disposal of the available supply of consumption goods at (both) a lower price level and rate of interest. This is the paradox of the deflationary impact of money creation when the increase in *ex post* profits results in an increase of aggregate demand.

The second half of Table 2 is much more familiar. A "normally behaved" *CC* schedule produces the links expected intuitively between the expansion of high-power money, interest rates, and the price level. The relevance of the second half of Table 2 does not lie in the verification of familiar results via credit market equilibrium. It lies, rather, in showing the potential real effects of monetary policy through the rate of interest. To which extent interest and credit determine the growth path of Latin American economies is the major empirical question that might be answered through the elaboration of the tools sketched in this chapter. These tools are still very primitive: the short-run constancy of the saving rate, the ratio of distributed profits, and the ratio of debt to equity are devices for exposition. How they respond to changes in the rate of interest is the major unanswered question for empirical analysis.

APPENDIX. INVESTMENT ORDERS AND DEMAND FOR LABOR

A model of a representative firm deciding on investment, employment, and production can be set out as follows: Profits for the next period $t + 1$ expected at present t are[15]

$$\Pi(t + 1, t) = P(t + 1, t)\hat{X}(t + 1) - Z(t) - i(t)B(t),$$

where $P(t + 1, t)$ is the price expected at t to hold at $t + 1$; $\hat{X}(t + 1) = X(t + 1) - \delta K(t)$, the net output at $t + 1$; $Z(t) = W(t)L(t)$, the current payments to labor; and $i(t)B(t)$ are the contractual interest payments made at $t + 1$ but fixed in nominal terms at t.

In the balance sheet in Table 1, assume that $\phi B = N_F$. Then

$$(1 + \phi)B(t) = P(t)K(t) + Z(t),$$

by the assumption that variable costs are working capital and end up as

---

[15] Similarly, current profits as expected one period ago are

$$\Pi(t, t - 1) = P(t, t - 1)\hat{X}(t) - Z(t - 1) - i(t - 1)B(t - 1)$$

and they differ from realized current profits by

$$\nabla\Pi(t) = [P(t) - P(t, t - 1)]\hat{X}(t),$$

where $P(t)$ is the current price. The mistake $\nabla\Pi$ is neglected in this analysis.

deposits of firms at banks. Substituting $B(t)$ into $\Pi(t + 1, t)$, we obtain

$$\Pi(t + 1, t) = (1 + \hat{\pi})PX_1 - \rho WL - \beta PK,$$

where the subscript t for the current variables (P, W, L, K) has been dropped for convenience; $\hat{\pi}$ is the expected inflation rate between t and $t + 1$; $X_1 = X(t + 1)$; ρ the effective interest rate factor, and β the effective rate of depreciation defined as

$$\rho = 1 + i(1 + \phi)^{-1}, \qquad \beta = \delta(1 + \hat{\pi}) + i(1 + \phi)^{-1}.$$

Given to the firm are $(P, W, i; K)$, if perfect competition is assumed, together with fixed plant and equipment in the short run. The problem of the firm is to choose L to maximize $\Pi(t + 1, t)$, given the production function with a one-point lag $X_1 = F(K, L)$. Labor is employed up to the point where its adjusted marginal product equals the real wage, i.e.,

$$[(1 + \hat{\pi})/\rho]F_L(K, L) = w, \qquad w = W/P.$$

The coefficient of adjustment is the ratio of the expected inflation factor to the effective interest factor. If the expected rate of inflation equals the ratio of interest payments to total assets, so that $\hat{\pi} = i(1 + \phi)^{-1}$, the coefficient of adjustment is unity. If it is less, the marginal product of labor would exceed the real wage in equilibrium, so that labor demand would be smaller, at the same real wage as before. Similarly, if $\hat{\pi} > i(1 + \phi)^{-1}$, more labor would be demanded at the same real wage. At any real wage, then, the demand for labor increases with $(\phi, \hat{\pi})$ and declines with the nominal rate of interest i. This decline is the response emphasized in the text, Fig. 1.

To consider optimal additions to the capital stock, a longer horizon is required. Investment can be represented as an order of the representative firm against its future output X_1. This fiction cuts across problems of aggregation over firms, the existence of a current market for investment goods, and so on. Also, it takes part of future output away from the supply for consumption purposes. The fiction, nonetheless, simplifies matters considerably and throws light on the effect of increases in demand for investment upon the current demand for labor. But, with investment produced by the representative firm, it is natural to drop the assumption of perfect competition in the output market: the representative firm should balance an increase of the investment order against the reduced available consumption supply, given its expectations about the state of future consumption demand.

The size of the "investment order" is chosen to maximize the present value of a stream of expected profits. For our purposes, a two-period horizon illustrates the principles involved. If $(\hat{\pi}, i)$ are constant over the planning horizon and we define

$$\Pi = (1 + \hat{\pi})PX_1 - \rho WL - \beta PK,$$

$$\Pi_1 = (1 + \hat{\pi})P_1 X_2 - \rho W_1 L_1 - \beta P_1 K_1,$$

the problem is to choose $(L; L_1, I)$ such that

$$\Pi + (1 + i)^{-1}\Pi_1$$

is maximized, subject to

$$X_1 = F(K, L), \qquad X_2 = G(K_1, L_1),$$

$$K_1 = (1 - \delta)K + I, \qquad X_i = I_i + C_i^e \qquad (i = 1, 2).$$

Let ψ be the Lagrangian associated with $X_1 = C_1^e + I$, the output allocation constraint for the next period. Then, a subset of the first order conditions is

$$(1 + \hat{\pi} + \psi/P)F_L = \rho w, \tag{5a}$$

$$(1 + i)\psi/P_1 = (1 + \hat{\pi})(G_K - \delta) - i(1 + \phi)^{-1}, \tag{5b}$$

$$F(K, L) = I_1 + C_1^e. \tag{5c}$$

These three equations can be solved for $(L, I_1; \psi)$, ignoring the planned demand L_1 that appears as an argument in G_K. Therefore, there exists a link between the current labor demand and the investment order. If investment is perceived as profitable,

$$G_K - \delta > i(1 + \phi)^{-1}(1 + \hat{\pi})^{-1},$$

the net marginal product of capital is higher than the effective nominal rate of interest adjusted for expected inflation. The multiplier ψ/P is the discounted value of the difference, and enters into the marginal product of labor [Eq. (5a)]. This means that profitable investment shifts to the right the demand curve for current labor at a given real wage. There are now two reasons for the negative association between the demand for labor and the rate of interest: the adjustment to F_L discussed earlier and the further adjustment through the profitability of investment.

The results in this Appendix justify the representation of the labor market given in Fig. 1.

ACKNOWLEDGMENTS

I greatly benefited from conversations with A. Braverman, D. Papageorgiou, M. Selowsky, and A. B. Treadway; from written comments on a previous draft by M. Kohn, Y. Plessner, and L. Taylor; and from comments of participants at the Bar-Ilan symposium and seminars at the World Bank and Boston University.

REFERENCES

Georgescu-Roegen, N. (1970). "Structural Inflation-Lock and Balanced Growth." *Economies et Sociétés, Economie Mathematique et Econométrie, Cahiers de L'I.S.E.A.* **4** (3) (March), 557–605.

Keynes, J. M. (1923). *A Tract on Monetary Reform.* New York: MacMillan.

Malinvaud, E. (1977). *The Theory of Unemployment Reconsidered.* New York: Wiley.

Malinvaud, E. (1980). *Profitability and Unemployment.* London and New York: Cambridge University Press.

Vickers, D. (1968). *The Theory of the Firm: Production, Capital and Finance.* New York: McGraw Hill.

Development Research Department
The World Bank
Washington, D.C.

Chapter 10

Inflation and Growth: Lessons from the Argentine Experience

Juan Carlos de Pablo

I. INTRODUCTION

According to the cost-of-living index, the overall level of prices in Argentina rose 0.22 times between 1914 (i.e., the beginning of the First World War) and 1939 (i.e., the beginning of the Second World War), which implies that during those 25 years the annual rate of inflation was on average 0.8%. (In fact, in 1939 the overall level of prices was lower in absolute terms than the observed level in 1918, namely, at the end of the First World War.) On the other hand, the overall level of prices rose 1715 times between mid-1945 and mid-1975, which implies an average annual rate of inflation of 28% during these 30 years. Last, but (unfortunately) not least, the overall level of prices rose 139 times between mid-1975 and mid-1979, which implies, on average, an annual rate of inflation of 245% during these 4 years.

Four decades of steady inflation, at high and, moreover, at extremely variable rates, seem enough to explain why "we" (i.e., the Argentines)

213

hold the unofficial title of "teachers of the world"[1] on how to survive and profit under inflation,[2] although, given the previously mentioned performance, we cannot say anything constructive about how to stop inflation.[3]

As far as the twentieth-century growth performance of Argentina is concerned, Díaz Alejandro (1970) asserted:

"It is common nowadays to lump the Argentine economy in the same category with the economies of other Latin American nations. Some opinion even puts it among such less developed nations as India and Nigeria. Yet, most economists writing during the first three decades of this century would have placed Argentine among the most advanced countries—with Western Europe, the United States, Canada, and Australia (at the turn of the century the Argentine per capita income was about the same as those of Germany, Holland, and Belgium, and higher than those of Austria, Spain, Italy, Switzerland, Sweden, and Norway). To have called Argentina 'underdeveloped,' in the sense that word has today, would have been considered laughable. Not only was per capita income high, but its growth was also one of the highest in the world."

An apparently different picture emerges from national accounts.[4] Total real GNP rate of growth was 4.8% per annum during the period 1900–1929 and 3.9% during the period 1900–1939; the corresponding per capita rates of growth were 1.4 and 1%, respectively. These figures, together with the rate of growth of 4% per annum for the period 1945–1975, imply that the rate of growth of total real GNP has been constant so far during the century. However, the per capita rate of growth has been significantly *higher* during the last decades (about 2.5% per annum) because a sharp reduction in the rate of growth of population[5] took place since the early thirties. (The reconciliation between Díaz Alejandro's statement and the previously mentioned national accounts estimates lies in the fact that during the twentieth century the rest of the world grew at a faster rate than Argentina.[6])

[1] Brazil and Chile have also had high rates of inflation for several decades.

[2] Notice that in order to survive under inflation you have to know what inflation is all about, whereas in order to profit from inflation you have to find an economic unit that does *not* know what inflation is about.

[3] Antiinflationary programs were implemented in 1952, 1959, 1962, 1965, 1967, 1973, and 1976 (these years correspond to the beginnings of the respective programs).

[4] My thanks to M. Brodersohn for his explanation on this point.

[5] This growth occurred because of a decline in the birth rate and also because of a reduction in immigration.

[6] An alternative explanation is, of course, that Argentine's national accounts estimates are wrong.

A simple regression between the rate of inflation as the independent variable and the rate of growth of GNP as the dependent will be meaningless in the case of total GNP (because the long-term rate of growth of the Argentine economy has been fairly constant) and will show a *positive* association in the case of per capita GNP. But, because this kind of naive econometrics is not very illuminating,[7] the issue of the influence of inflation on growth will be presented from the predictions offered by economic analysis based on the behavior of the government observed in the Argentine case, given the existence of inflation, and the corresponding behavior of the private sector.

The chapter is divided into four main sections. The first section surveys the costs of inflation; the second section elaborates one of the costs of inflation, namely, *repressed* inflation; the third section analyzes the relationship between inflation and growth; and the fourth section suggests that the movement from repressed to open inflation lies along the road to sustained price stability. The chapter ends with a brief summary and conclusions.

II. THE COSTS OF INFLATION

You may ask why this section is not entitled "Benefits and Costs of Inflation" (after all, there exists a literature on the *optimum* — not always zero — rate of inflation). The answer, derived from the Argentine experience, is that once inflation has been under way for a long period, the (perhaps) initial benefits (i.e., a wealth transfer from holders of financial assets to the rest of the community, given the unexpected inflation) just evaporate. For this reason the present section will concentrate on the (unfortunately) permanent costs of inflation.

The costs of inflation can be classified into three broad categories. The first corresponds to the traditional argument, namely, the tax on cash balances. Currency and demand deposits are, as is well known, non-interest-bearing forms of money, in contrast to time deposits. Because money creation is not equiproportionally distributed according to individual money holdings, in an inflationary economy the private cost of holding non-interest-bearing forms of money increases and, consequently, its de-

---

[7] A less naive approach would attempt to find out that rate of inflation that maximizes the rate growth of per capita GNP, given the fact that during the last 5 years, in addition to extremely high rates of inflation, Argentina experienced an absolute decline in per capita real income.

mand is reduced in real terms[8] (the cost of inflation arises from the difference between the social cost of producing money, almost nil, and the private cost of holding it, high indeed).

The tax on cash balances is the only cost of inflation in an economy in which (i) the future rate of inflation is forecast with certainty and (ii) all inflationary pressures are incorporated into prices without restrictions. I know of no economy in the world in which these two characteristics hold (certainly not in the Argentine case), and accordingly, attention will be paid to each one of the costs.

Forecasting the future rate of inflation correctly is crucial under inflation, except in a perfectly indexed economy (i.e., one in which *everything* is adjusted to a single price index automatically, instantaneously, and equiproportionately); and forecasting implies not only a guess concerning the future evolution of the overall level of prices but also the (generally more difficult) task of anticipating future changes in relative prices from the individual economic unit point of view.

Forecasting the future rate of inflation correctly is also extremely difficult (that is why good forecasting, from the private point of view, is extremely good business). Let me illustrate the point with a single example: assume, for a moment, that you are a teacher and your students are the board of directors of a company that is considering whether to borrow a loan at a fixed nominal interest rate. The decision will obviously be adopted in real terms, so that a forecast of the future rate of inflation[9] is needed. Invite your students to write in a paper just a number, namely, the *ex ante* rate of inflation for, say, the next month, and plot the results on the blackboard. My experience in Argentina is that, from people exposed to the same economic situation, you will find expected price increases from, say, 2% to, say, 10%.

From the forecasting point of view, the costs of inflation arise from two sources: on the one hand, from the uncertainty derived from "pure"

---

[8] Money, as a percentage of GNP, which was about 60% during the twenties (i.e., under price stability), diminished to less than 10% in March 1976 (i.e., a month in which prices rose by 50%).

With regard to disaggregation of money into interest- and non-interest-bearing varieties, note that in October 31, 1979, currency amounted to just 13.6% of money, demand deposits to just 14.1%, and the rest, namely, 72.3%, was "something," which, in the traditional macroeconomic literature, could be classified as bonds but which, in practice, is an almost perfect substitute for "money."

Baez (1979) analyzed in the Argentine case the change in the M1/M2 or M1/M4 relationship as a result of changes in the rate of inflation, finding empirical support for a priori results.

[9] What is required, more precisely, is the future price increase of the product the company sells.

forecasting errors (which implies, for instance, that in such an environment investment projects are realized just when the internal rates of return are extremely high); on the other hand, from the uncertainty derived from the (to a certain extent) unexpected inflation-induced changes in economic policy.[10]

Under the inflation-as-a-tax approach, inflation is neutral in the sense that, except in the case of the increased cost of holding money, relative prices coincide with those that would exist under price stability. Moreover, uncertainty over the future rate of inflation causes some *ex post* changes in relative prices.

But although all this is strictly true, there is more to the problem because, as will be shown in the next section, in practice, relative prices change, in addition to nonmonetary causes, as a direct consequence of inflation-induced changes in economic policy or, more precisely, of *repressed* inflation. (My feeling is that this is by far the greatest cost of inflation.)

III. REPRESSED INFLATION

In the mid-sixties, money was introduced in the up-to-that-point-barter neoclassical growth theory.[11] From the point of view of this chapter, the relevant question is the following: Does a change in the rate of growth of the money supply affect the rate of growth of the economy? In the relevant literature, the answer is negative, at least in the steady-state sense.[12]

The reason for this unfortunate result (would it not be wonderful if the rate of growth of an economy could be increased without bounds by just printing money?) is that in neoclassical growth theory the rate of growth of the economy is determined by *real* factors, namely, the rate of growth of population and the rate of technological change. This means that the issue of the neutrality of money in the literature refers to whether or not the change in the rate of growth of the money supply affects real variables

[10] This is not necessarily a counterexample of rational expectations. In its strong version, the rational expectations hypothesis maintains that the minister of economics has a model and that the population knows it; but because the basic idea of rational expectations seems to be that the minister of economics is not cleverer than the population, a weak version can be postulated, namely, the one in which the minister has no model and that the population knows it (in other words, that the population does not know what the future rate of inflation will be and that the minister does not know it either).

[11] An extensive literature grew out of the pioneer papers of Tobin (1965), Sidrauski (1967a,b), and Johnson (1966).

[12] Sato's (1963) numerical exercise showed, however, that transitions are very important in terms of the calendar.

such as the capital–labor ratio of the economy, the *level* of income, and the *level* of consumption.

One important assumption of the money and growth literature is "government neutrality," i.e., the minister of economics does not adopt any measure that, besides reducing the rate of inflation in the short run, distorts *relative* prices.[13] The question is then the following: What is the relationship between inflation and growth when the government represses inflation? This important question will be answered in Section IV of this chapter, because in the present section, as necessary background, a "stylized version" of the Argentine experience during the fifties and sixties is presented.[14]

Since Argentina has a mixed economy, namely, one in which the government sets the value of key parameters, according to which the private sector operates following their *private* calculations, the analysis begins with the assumption that inflation originated in government. Despite the fact that the final result is the same, from the decision-making point of view it is worth differentiating between "passive" distortions (i.e., changes in relative prices resulting from the fact that, in the presence of inflation, the government did not do something that it *ought*[15] to have done) and "active" distortions (i.e., modifications in relative prices resulting from the fact that the government did something that, according to the same principle, it ought not to have done).

Among the most significant examples of passive distortions, the tax and judiciary systems are worth mentioning. Within the first—in the corporation income tax—the depreciation of capital goods at historical costs and the deduction of nominal interests paid illustrate the point very neatly[16]; and the latter case can be illustrated by the lack of adjustment of the value in pesos under dispute between the time of the beginning of a trial and the time when sentence is delivered (years, very often).

---

[13] The rate of inflation is at best reduced just in the short run. The *ceteris paribus* long-run rate of inflation is higher because the cost of the distortion in terms of resource allocation has to be added to the price increase that results from the restoration of relative prices. Moyano Llerena (1958) showed that, after the elimination of price controls, the relative price of controlled commodities rose with respect to noncontrolled commodities, when compared with the precontrol era, which is not difficult to understand in view of the supply shift away from the controlled sectors.

[14] More details relevant to the following discussion in this section can be found in de Pablo (1980a). The period chosen here is the one during which distortions were greater.

[15] This is meant in the sense of something that good economic analysis would strongly recommend.

[16] Some of the issues connected with taxation in an inflationary environment have recently been discussed by Hamada (1979).

Notice the significant *lack of neutrality* of inflation, given the previously mentioned behavior of the government. In this context, inflation enters directly into the heart of individual decision making. The manager of a firm who is considering the acquisition of a single capital good out of several alternatives available consults his engineer about the physical productivity of each of them; but at the same time, he consults his tax adviser about the reduction in taxes of each one of the alternatives because it is clear that the rankings of before- and after-tax profits of each one of the models do not necessarily coincide (lack of indexing of depreciation charges in general lowers the privately optimal lifetime of capital goods).

In the case of the judiciary system, the impact is analogous. Even if I know that I am wrong in the dispute, I have great economic incentives to go to trial because, in the absence of indexing, the one who, from the legal point of view, wins the trial is, from the real point of view, the one who loses it, and vice versa.

Active distortions, on the other hand, result from different varieties of direct price controls. Relative prices are changed, either because the government tries to control all prices—in practice this is impossible (some prices are controlled and the rest are free)—or because the government deliberately tries to control just some prices ("basic" commodities, such as bread, milk, and medicines and/or rents, exchange rates, interest rates, and public utility rates).

Some of the costs of active distortions have been extensively analyzed in the literature (i.e., rationing, black markets, reduction in quality, fiscal deficits induced by lower-than-necessary public utility rates, balance-of-payments difficulties resulting from currency overvaluation; the final disappearance of the commodities in those markets that are unable to evade control). But, again, it is clear from the Argentine experience that, in practice, this is just part of the story. The other part (and, in my opinion, a very important part) arises from the *endogeneity* of policy making in the presence of inflation, particularly given the sort of inflation-induced governmental behavior just surveyed ("G-inefficiency"?). The point will be developed in more detail in the next section, but it seems worthwhile to present now the application of price controls to different experiences.

If you are the manager of a firm that operates in a country whose government has a "board of prices" and you know that changes in controlled prices are not decided on technical grounds alone (because relevant information is insufficient, because human nature is weak, etc.), where would you allocate your scarce resources, namely, your time, your efforts, your imagination, to improve the technology, to develop new markets, etc., or to pay a close look at the board's activities, particularly so that it does not freeze the prices of the products you sell and that it does freeze the prices of the products you buy?[17] The answer is obvious: it all depends on the most profitable alternative from the *private* point of view.

Our concern, however, refers to the social implications of the previously mentioned behavior of the private sector. What are the (unfortunate[18]) implications from the social point of view and, particularly, from the point of view of the rate of growth of the economy; and what of the fact that the most profitable activity for the managers of an economy is to maintain favorable connections with the board of prices? As with many good questions, the precise answer is "God only knows." But, judging from the Argentine experience, I am absolutely convinced that, if it were possible to measure the effect under consideration, the resulting loss will not be negligible.

IV. INFLATION AND GROWTH

In the previous section a number of examples derived from the Argentine experience were given to illustrate the distortions originating in the governmental behavior in the presence of inflation. By distortions I mean measures of economic policy that generate a set of relative prices different from the one that would have produced an open inflation; and when I say distortions I am clearly implying that the price structure under open inflation is, at least from the resource allocation point of view, the price structure that ought to exist.[19]

Because the main objective of this chapter is to discuss the relationship between inflation and growth, it is necessary to show that the previously mentioned distortions result in a reduction in the rate of growth of the economy and not merely in a once-and-for-all permanent reduction of the level of GNP of the economy. The demonstration, obviously, will not have the neatness of, say, the factor price equilization theorem; but I expect to be clear enough to convince (most of) the reader(s).

---

[17] The "partial equilibrium" of most entrepreneurial proposals is striking (the exchange rate is too low, say exporters; interest rates are too high, say debtors; taxes are extraordinarily high, say tax payers, etc.). Is this a fallacy of composition? Not necessarily; in my opinion it is profit maximization, as the concept is used and taught in the business schools, namely: "if someone else, one way or the other, pays the costs, it is OK with me."

[18] See the controversy among Waugh (1944), Oi (1972), and Samuelson (1972), concluding that it is impossible to increase social welfare by *generating* price oscillations.

[19] From the income distribution point of view, the issue is debatable, although again, the Argentine experience is almost a textbook case of the fantastic costs of trying to "improve" income distribution through changes in the price structure [a detailed analysis of the last Perónist attempt is presented in de Pablo (1980a)].

For clarification, the arguments concerning the reduction of the rate of growth of the economy will be divided into two groups. In the first set, the more orthodox arguments will be included, the most important aspect being the way in which the "stop-and-go" characteristic of this inflation-induced economic policy enters into the decision-making process of the private sector of the economy; the other set corresponds to the already mentioned issue of "G-inefficiency." In both cases the impact on the rate of growth of the economy is thought of in terms of the variables that determine the rate of growth in the literature, namely, the rate of growth of population and technological change in the neoclassical tradition and the savings and output–capital ratio in the Keynesian fashion.

Distortions do not last forever, but because distortions are a fantastic (although transitory) source of private profits, the questions the profit maximizer asks are how long distortions will last and, accordingly, what is, from the private point of view, the extent of optimal resource reallocation (think, for instance, of the impact on private investment of the existence of currency undervaluation, currency overvaluation, negative real interest rates, etc.). In other words, any rational decision maker anticipates the "stop and go" characteristic that inevitably occurs in an inflation-induced economic policy like the one under consideration. Nevertheless, in practice, one does not often find project evaluations in which prices are computed over the cycle.[20]

It is clear (to me, at least) that this behavior of the private sector reduces the rate of growth of the economy. This is so, in terms of the Keynesian approach for instance, because it is likely that it reduces the saving ratio of the economy and *surely* because it reduces the output–capital ratio of the economy because it diminishes the social productivity of investment.[21]

Another reason that the class of inflation under consideration diminishes the rate of growth of the economy is "G-inefficiency." "G-inefficiency" is not a resource-free activity; on the contrary, it absorbs the best brains the firm has because, from the private point of view, it is the most profitable activity. But, because human capital in the firms is a scarce resource, this allocation has a negative effect from the social point of view.

[20] This consideration is not independent of the second class of argument to be discussed, namely, the endogeneity of policy making. Very often those who benefit from a distortion are concentrated, whereas those who are harmed are dispersed; in these conditions, the forces for and against a change in economic policy are not balanced. This aspect, in my opinion, explains some *ex post* myopic maximization, because some of the entrepreneurs, calculating that enough pressure on the government will result in distortions being maintained forever, allocate funds according to current relative prices.

[21] In the Chenery and Strout (1966) two-gap model computations, the (marginal) output–capital ratio of the Argentine economy was found to be among the lowest in the world.

(Following the neoclassical approach, the inefficiency of skilled labor that results from repressed inflation reduces the rate of growth of the economy because it lowers the rate of technological change.)

V. FREE INFLATION: THE ROAD TO SUSTAINED PRICE STABILITY

The significant costs of inflation in general and of repressed inflation in particular provide great incentives for eliminating it.[22] The objective of this section is not to present a detailed analysis of feasible and successful antiinflationary programs (among other reasons, because, as I have said earlier, the Argentines have no credibility whatsoever in this regard) but to consider briefly a single issue, namely, whether the most convenient strategy for the elimination of repressed inflation is through a process by which repressed inflation is transformed overnight into price stability or through a stepwise approach in which the earlier stages of the program are dedicated to transforming inflation from a repressed variety to free inflation.[23]

The nature of the issue should be clarified. If the purpose of eliminating inflation is to end the costs of inflation and if one of the most important costs of inflation is its lack of neutrality, it follows that price stability necessarily changes the productive structure, income distribution, etc.; and this effect is independent of the shock versus gradualist characteristics of different antiinflationary programs.

The issue, then, is whether the previously mentioned necessary change and the corresponding *learning process* of the economic unit are accomplished in a cheaper way, from the social point of view, when achieved simultaneously with price stability or whether it is better to spend some time in a context in which inflation continues (the rate of inflation, measured by official price indexes, may even increase temporarily) but in which, because of a gradual transformation from repressed inflation to open inflation, relative prices will look like the ones that would

[22] See Feldstein (1979) for a reexamination of the cost–benefit analysis of disinflation when the negative impact of nonneutral inflation on the rate of growth of the economy is taken into account.

[23] Both alternatives have been tried experimentally in Argentina, the former, starting in 1967, using the Krieger Vasena (or Moyano Llerena?) program, and the latter starting in 1976, with the Martinez de Hoz program (see de Pablo (1972, 1974) for an analysis of the Krieger Vasena program).

exist under price stability. (Notice that the real problem is to go from repressed inflation to price stability in the former case and from repressed to open inflation in the latter, as compared with free inflation changing into price stability.)

The Argentine experience suggests that the latter alternative is better because the transformation of inflation from repressed to open in no way complicates the road to sustained price stability (although it clearly complicates next month's indexes), and on the contrary, it is very helpful because it "teaches" the economic unit how to operate in an economic environment in which relative prices are not distorted, as they are under price stability.[24]

VI. CONCLUSIONS

The inhabitants of Argentina have been exposed to rates of inflation of 8% per year (as in 1968), 8% per month (as in 1977), and even of more than 8% per week (as in June 1975 and March 1976). Accordingly, we lead the world in this subject (although the gap between Argentina and the rest of the world has diminished in the past few years).[25]

What lessons can be derived from this basic course of "Argentinomics for foreigners"? (1) In inflationary economies governments do a lot more (harm) than just printing money; (2) as a result, inflation is nonneutral from the resource allocation point of view; (3) accordingly, the incentives for eliminating inflation increase; and (4) the process from repressed to open inflation lies on the road to sustained price stability.[26] An additional lesson, for the happy few countries that so far have not entered the club of inflationary economies: do not be soft on inflation during the early stages; do *anything* (short of killing people) that is necessary to stop inflation.[27] As an Argentine, I know what I am talking about.

[24] This theory is very unpopular, especially among the partial equilibrium lovers. Time and again the economic unit points out that elimination of distortions increases the rate of inflation, a complaint that is inevitably illustrated by prices of the products they buy but never by the prices of the products they sell.

[25] Not surprisingly, the quality of interpretation of inflation as a subject has improved significantly in the international literature. Compare, for instance, the Bronfenbrenner and Holzman 1963 survey on inflation, with, say, the Laidler and Parkin 1975 survey.

[26] See Ramos (1978) for a very interesting list of conclusions derived from the recent Chilean experience.

[27] In the same fashion, Lindbeck's (1976) proposal for the eleventh commandment reads as follows: "Do not *start* an inflation."

ACKNOWLEDGMENTS

I want to thank R. Ffrench-Davis and D. Schydlowsky for their helpful comments.

REFERENCES

Baez, J. C. (1979). "Estimacion de los Componentes de la Demanda de Dinero." *Centro de Estudios Monetarios y Bancarios.* Banco Central de la Republica Argentina, *Estudios Tecnicos* **38** (June).
Bronfenbrenner, M., and Holzman, F. (1963). "Survey of Inflation Theory." *American Economic Review* (September).
Chenery, H. B., and Strout, A. M. (1966). "Foreign Assistance and Economic Development." *American Economic Review* **56** (September), 679–733.
de Pablo, J. C. (1972). *Politica Antiinflacionaria en la Argentina, 1967–70.* Buenos Aires: Amorrortu Editores.
de Pablo, J. C. (1974). "Relative Prices, Income Distribution and Stabilization Plans: The Argentine Experience, 1967–70." *Journal of Development Economics* **1** (3) (December).
de Pablo, J. C. (1980a). *Cuatro Ensayos Sobre la Economia Argentina.* Buenos Aires: Macchi Ediciones.
de Pablo, J. C. (1980b). *Politica Economica Perónista, 1973–76.* Buenos Aires: El Cid Editor.
Díaz Alejandro, C. F. (1970). *Essays on the Economic History of the Argentine Republic.* Cambridge, Massachusetts: MIT Press.
Feldstein, M. S. (1979). "The Welfare Cost of Permanent Inflation and the Optimal Short-Run Economic Policy." *Journal of Political Economy* **87** (4) (August), 749–768.
Hamada, H. S. (1979). "Financial Theory and Taxation in an Inflationary World: Some Public Policy Issues." *The Journal of Finance* **34** (2) (May), 347–369.
Johnson, H. G. (1966). "The Neoclassical One Sector Growth Model: A Geometrical Exposition and Extension to a Monetary Economy." *Economica,* **33** (131), 265–287.
Laidler, D. E. W., and Parkin, M. (1975). "Inflation: A Survey." *Economic Journal* **85** (December), 741–809.
Lindbeck, A. (1976). "Stabilization Policy in Open Economies With Endogenous Politicians." *American Economic Review* **66** (2) (Papers and Proceedings) (May), 1–19.
Moyano Llerena, C. M. (1958). "Viente Años de Controles." *Panorama de la Economia Argentina* **1** (6) (September), 218–224.
Oi, W. Y. (1972). "The Consumer Does Benefit from Feasible Price Stability: A Comment." *The Quarterly Journal of Economics* **86** (3) (August), 494–498.
Ramos, J. (1978). "Inflacion Persistente, Inflacion Reprimida e Hiperstanflacion. Lecciones de Inflacion y Estabilizacion en Chile." *Desarrollo Economico—Revista de Ciencias Sociales,* **18** (69) (April–June), 3–48.
Samuelson, P. A. (1972). "The Consumer Does Benefit from Feasible Price Stability." *The Quarterly Journal of Economics* **86** (3) (August), 476–493.
Sato, R. (1963). "Fiscal policy in a Neoclassical Growth Model: An Analysis of Time Required for Equilibrating Adjustment." *Review of Economics Studies* **30** (February), 16–23.
Sidrauski, N. (1967a). "Rational Choice and Patterns of Growth in a Monetary Economy." *American Economic Review* (May), 534–544.
Sidrauski, N. (1967b). "Inflation and Economic Growth." *The Journal of Political Economy* **75** (December), 796–810.

Tobin, J. (1965). "Money and Economic Growth." *Econometrica* **33** (4) (October), 671–684.
Waugh, F. V. (1944). "Does the Consumer Benefit from Price Instability?" *The Quarterly Journal of Economics* **58,** 602–614.

University of Buenos Aires
Buenos Aires, Argentina

Chapter 11

Economic Stabilization and Structural Change: The Chilean Economy after 1973

Alejandro Foxley

In this chapter the economic policies of Chile after 1973 are evaluated. As is well known, after the military coup of September 1973, Chile embarked on a radical experiment in economic orthodoxy. This consisted in the application of a monetarist stabilization program and deep structural reforms reflecting a neoconservative, free-market philosophy. The main elements in the former were monetary control, fiscal discipline, and deregulation of prices; the latter consisted of privatization of most economic activities previously performed by the government, of the development of a private capital market where financial resources were to be transferred, and of a drastic opening up of the economy to international trade.

Our evaluation of the Chilean experiment deals with three aspects: the macroeconomic results, the stabilization program, and the structural changes brought about by the new economic policies. In Section I we give and briefly discuss some macroeconomic results in the period 1974–1979. Section II describes the stabilization program and its various phases. Section III deals with the long-term structural component of the policies. Section IV summarizes the conclusions.

I. MACROECONOMIC RESULTS

A brief summary of the macroeconomic results for the period 1974–1979 in Chile can be found in Table 1. Results give mixed signs: the rate of inflation decreased from over 300% at the moment of the coup to around 40% after five years of stabilization program. The fiscal deficit was all but eliminated by 1979, and the balance of payments was brought under equilibrium after 1976. On the other hand, the current account showed a deficit for all years except 1976, with higher deficits after 1977.

Growth performance was modest, GDP per capita grew at less than 1% a year between 1974 and 1979, but this average hides higher growth rates during the last three years, a clear sign of recuperation from the recession that implied, at its height, a loss of 10% of GDP in 1975. The rate of investment stayed low during stabilization, the average rate of gross investment over GDP being 11.2% for the period 1974–1979, which compares unfavorably with a historical rate of between 15 and 16%. Employment stagnated and because the labor force grew more than 10% in the period, unemployment rose sharply, reaching over 16% of the labor force in 1976 and stabilizing around 14% thereafter. Real wages and salaries fell close to 40% during the stabilization program and after six years were still 18% below levels for 1970.

Summing up, the stabilization program was able to reduce inflation, eliminate the fiscal deficit, and accumulate foreign reserves through foreign loans and good export performance. A deep recession in 1975–1976 explains modest achievements in terms of real GDP growth rates. But a significant recuperation took place after 1977. This was matched by low investment and negative results in terms of employment and income distribution. In order to obtain a better understanding of how these results were achieved, we shall discuss in more detail, in the next section, the stabilization policies and the various phases that can be distinguished in the period 1974–1979.

II. THE STABILIZATION PROGRAM AND ITS PHASES

The stabilization program in Chile can be separated into four phases.[1] The first we call ''deregulation;'' the second consists of the so-called

---

[1] For a good description of the policies and their interrelationship with social behavior and ideology, see Moulian and Vergara (1979a, b).

TABLE 1

Macroeconomic Indicators: Chile

Year	GDP per capita[a]	Consumer prices[b]	Fiscal deficit[c]	Balance of payments[d]	Balance of payments current account[d]	Investment rate[e]	Unemployment rate[f]	Real wages and salaries[g]
1970	100.0	36.1	2.9	226.1	−159.9	15.0	6.1	100.0
1974	102.4	369.2	8.0	−54.2	−254.3	13.0	9.2	65.1
1975	89.3	243.3	2.9	−297.5	−532.3	10.7	13.4	62.9
1976	91.4	197.9	2.0	485.7	159.5	9.8	16.3	64.8
1977	97.6	84.2	1.5	−7.0	−551.4	10.6	14.0	71.5
1978	101.7	37.2	0.8	545.8	−776.6	11.3	13.9	76.0
1979	106.8	38.9	—	803.6	−685.3	12.9	13.8	82.3

[a] ODEPLAN, *Cuentas Nacionales de Chile*. 1970 = 100. The figures for 1978 and 1979 correspond to provisional estimates for GDP.

[b] CPI, by Cortázar and Marshall (1980).

[c] Ministerio de Hacienda, *Exposición sobre el Estado de la Hacienda Pública*, January 1978, and ODEPLAN, *Cuentas Nacionales de Chile*. Percentages of GDP.

[d] Central Bank of Chile, in Ffrench-Davis (1979a). Figures in millions of 1977 dollars.

[e] ODEPLAN, *Cuentas Nacionales de Chile*.

[f] Meller *et al.* (1979).

[g] University of Chile, Taller de Coyuntura.

shock treatment; the third centers on curbing expectations; and the fourth corresponds to the global monetarist approach. The main economic indicators for all four phases are given in Table 2, where trends for the various phases can be easily identified.

Phase 1: Deregulation, September 1973–March 1975

The main objective of phase 1 was to restitute market mechanisms in an economy with extended controls and severe imbalances. Setting prices right was the first task, and this was done by devaluing domestic currency and by freeing up prices, except for 30 products whose prices were deregulated more gradually. The exchange rate was devalued by 230% between September and October 1973. A second objective of the policy was to reduce the public sector deficit by decreasing government expenditures and increasing taxes. The main tax changes consisted of the introduction of a 20% value-added tax, while at the same time several direct taxes affecting capital were reduced or eliminated: the tax on corporate profits was reduced and the net wealth and capital gains taxes were eliminated. Additional contractions in demand were pursued by reducing the rate of expansion in money supply and by a contraction in real wages.

Other objectives consisted in preparing the ground for long-term structural changes. Policy measures in this area were various. They consisted in restituting to previous owners private property that had been taken over by workers or intervened in by the government. Previously expropriated American companies, mainly in the copper sector, were compensated for a presumed underpayment. New norms liberalizing imports and requirements for foreign investment, proposing across-the-board tariff reductions, setting the rules for a privatization of public enterprises, and stimulating the development of a private capital market were enforced. Collective bargaining was suppressed and labor union activities were severely curtailed.

The course followed by the main macro variables is given in Table 2. The abrupt deregulation of prices led to a monthly rate of inflation of 87.6% in October 1973, whereas the average rate between January and September had been 14.6%. But the dramatic upsurge in prices, reflecting previous repressed inflation and a price overshoot after deregulation, was not followed by similarly high rates in the next months. In fact, the price increases stabilized around 14% a month during this phase, a rate similar to that prevailing in the last year of the Allende government.

As a result of free prices, firms were stimulated into replenishing their low level of stocks, a result of strict price controls and high inflation throughout 1972 and 1973. Industrial production expanded in the last quarter of 1973 but stabilized at a lower level during 1974, as is readily observed in Table 2. In early 1975, clear recessionary signs were present: industrial production in the first quarter was 15% below that of the last quarter of 1974. The recession was the consequence of a drastic reduction in real-cash balances in the last quarter of 1975, as can also be seen in Table 2 when comparing the expansion of nominal money supply and that of prices. The increase in prices almost tripled the increase in the quantity of money. Monetary contraction was reinforced by a fall in real wages that reached over 40%.

The unemployment rate was rapidly responsive to the new policies: during the first three months it doubled, reaching 7% in the last quarter of 1973. It stayed around 9.5% throughout 1974 and jumped to 13.3% in the first quarter of 1975.

The recession was not more severe during 1974 mainly because of an expansionary fiscal policy, in spite of stated objectives to the contrary. Public investment increased, particularly in the first semester. It was hoped, at this stage, that a reduction in public subsidies and employment could bring the fiscal accounts in balance, without resorting to reductions in public investment. In July 1974 a new finance minister who did not share this view attempted to reverse the expansionary trend by curtailing budget expenditures by 15% and public employment by 50,000 persons. At the same time subsidies to public enterprises were ended. It was this contractionary fiscal policy, sustained while the rate of inflation was accelerating and other components of aggregate demand were falling, that generated the more severe recession of early 1975.

One of the main concerns during this phase was the balance of payments. The policies designed to reduce the external sector deficit paid off in a rather brief period of time. During the first semester of 1974, there was already a net accumulation of reserves, a result of rapid export expansion aided by unusually high prices for the main Chilean export, copper, and by the large devaluation of late 1973.

The exchange-rate policy during this period followed the fluctuations in the price of copper. The policy consisted of unannounced minidevaluations several times per month. When the price of copper was high, as in the first semester of 1974, the exchange rate tended to lag behind domestic inflation. Real devaluations took place when the copper price fell, as was the case in the second semester of 1974.

Tariff reductions were announced at the beginning of 1974. They were to take place in a period of three years, with a maximum target of 60% for nominal tariffs. This maximum target was reduced to 35% in 1975, with a minimum of 10%, which was targeted for 1978. The program was imple-

TABLE 2

Phases in Stabilization Program: Chile 1973–1979

Year		CPI[a]	BP[b]	IIP[c]	UNEM[d]	PCU[e]	ER[f]	TAR[g]	ERM[h]	$M_1{}^i$	M_2	$i_{nom}{}^k$	$i_r{}^l$	w^m
Phase 1														
1973	II	51.9	—	106.3	3.1	73.9	—	—	—	32.1	31.8	—	—	—
	III	64.3	—	101.2	—	91.4	9.2	—	—	49.3	49.2	—	—	—
	IV	128.5	—	122.5	7.0	99.3	30.1	94.0	58.4	45.4	45.7	—	—	—
1974	I	45.3	59.5	109.8	9.2	106.9	29.6	92.3	56.9	63.2	64.2	—	—	64.3
	II	46.6	180.3	113.8	10.3	126.3	32.9	76.3	58.0	30.9	29.9	—	—	64.5
	III	46.8	-3.9	111.0	9.4	78.4	33.3	67.0	55.6	28.1	27.8	—	—	63.7
	IV	44.7	-375.6	109.7	9.7	62.0	37.1	67.0	62.0	28.1	30.8	9.6	-24.4	68.5
1975	I	46.5	-189.3	93.1	—	57.8	45.0	54.7	69.6	44.8	51.9	9.6	-49.3	64.9
Phase 2														
1975	I	46.5	-189.3	93.1	13.3	57.8	45.0	54.7	69.6	44.8	51.9	9.6	-49.3	64.9
	II	67.8	-82.5	88.8	16.1	57.1	46.7	52.0	71.0	25.0	38.7	16.5	-23.4	60.4
	III	41.4	44.1	73.5	16.6	56.1	45.2	47.7	66.8	45.0	57.2	19.7	178.4	63.2
	IV	29.4	-47.0	85.2	18.7	53.1	44.9	44.0	64.7	38.2	35.1	12.8	65.7	63.1
1976	I	36.4	136.6	90.4	19.8	56.6	44.3	40.7	62.3	37.2	39.8	14.6	18.2	62.1
	II	38.8	94.4	93.5	18.0	69.2	40.5	36.7	55.4	22.8	38.9	14.7	56.4	63.0
Phase 3														
1976	II	38.8	94.4	93.5	18.0	69.2	40.5	36.7	55.4	22.8	38.9	14.7	56.4	63.0
	III	33.1	134.1	97.1	15.7	70.3	33.6	33.0	44.7	34.7	48.3	11.8	40.9	65.1
	IV	20.0	103.7	100.3	13.6	58.2	34.2	32.3	45.2	26.8	29.1	12.5	101.2	68.8
1977	I	21.4	48.6	98.1	13.9	65.5	32.7	24.3	40.6	45.1	58.3	11.3	52.9	71.7
	II	20.8	7.7	105.4	13.0	62.2	29.0	23.2	35.7	22.9	28.7	7.8	34.5	69.3
	III	13.5	-59.3	107.9	12.8	54.5	29.5	21.6	35.8	14.4	16.6	6.3	23.9	71.7
	IV	12.7	-3.6	104.9	13.2	56.5	31.7	18.5	37.6	11.8	13.7	7.3	45.9	71.7

Year		CPI^a	BP^b	IIP^c	UNEM^d	PCU^e	ER^f	TAR^g	ERM^h	M_1^{i}	M_2^{j}	i_{nom}^{k}	i_r^{l}	w^m
1978	I	8.7	270.5	103.9	14.7	56.4	33.1	15.3	38.2	30.2	32.2	5.9	47.6	74.8
	II	9.4	129.7	117.1	12.8	59.3	34.5	14.1	39.4	17.1	18.3	5.0	28.3	75.1
	III	9.8	107.6	119.7	13.7	63.6	34.3	13.2	38.8	6.6	15.9	4.7	14.0	76.9
	IV	6.6	109.5	117.5	14.8	68.2	34.5	12.2	38.7	9.8	21.1	5.5	52.9	77.1
1979	I	6.6	339.9	122.1	16.5	85.5	33.8	11.4	37.7	21.7	24.2	4.4	29.8	81.0
	II	7.7	211.8	123.2	12.5	92.6	34.1	10.5	37.7	9.9	9.0	4.0	19.6	82.2
Phase 4														
1979	II	7.7	211.8	123.2	12.5	92.6	34.1	10.5	37.7	9.9	9.0	4.0	19.6	82.2
	III	11.0	289.4	126.0	12.5	89.0	33.7	10.2	37.1	7.2	13.3	4.0	-1.2	83.3
	IV	9.0	206.8	125.2	12.7	96.4	31.8	10.2	35.0	11.3	11.2	4.0	23.9	82.8
1980	I	6.7	411.9	126.2	—	118.4	30.5	10.2	33.8	16.6	13.9	4.1	23.9	86.7
	II	7.5	150.3	128.0	—	92.7	28.9	10.2	32.4	13.9	9.8	3.1	10.0	89.1
	III	6.4	228.5	131.5	11.8	95.5	27.8	10.2	30.6	7.2	12.5	2.9	9.9	88.4
	IV	7.7	-15.3	130.8	10.7	89.7	26.2	10.2	28.8	13.7	14.3	3.0	6.2	92.6
1981	I	4.3	-192.3	129.7	11.3	83.0	75.3[n]	10.2	27.8[n]	12.4[n]	19.2[n]	3.6	37.7	92.9
	II	2.8	-207.7	132.9	9.0	79.6	24.0[n]	10.2	26.4[n]	13.1[n]	14.6[n]	3.5	36.1	94.5
	III	2.3	-3.9	134.4	10.5	78.3	23.5[n]	10.2	25.9[n]	-4.2[n]	13.3[n]	3.5	36.1	97.5
	IV	1.6	-181.9	120.2	13.5	75.2	—	10.2	—	5.4[n]	3.9[n]	3.7	49.4	102.2

^{a} CPI: Consumer price index rate of growth (Cortázar and Marshall, 1980).

^{b} BP: Net accumulation of reserves balance of payments in millions of dollars (Central Bank).

^{c} IIP: Index of industrial production seasonally adjusted (Sociedad de Fomento Fabril).

^{d} UNEM : Rate of unemployment for Gran Santiago (Economics Dept., University of Chile).

^{e} PCU: Price of copper, U.S. cents per pound (Central Bank).

^{f} ER: Real-exchange rate, pesos per dollar, in December 1978 prices.

^{g} TAR : Average nominal tariffs (Central Bank).

^{h} ERM: Real-exchange rate for imports (real-exchange rate corrected for changes in tariffs) (R. Ffrench-Davis, 1979a).

^{i} M_1: Rate-of-growth nominal money supply, defined as currency plus demand deposits (Central Bank).

^{j} M_2: Rate-of-growth nominal money supply, defined as currency plus demand and time deposits (Central Bank).

^{k} i_{nom}: Thirty-day nominal interest rate (Central Bank).

^{l} i_r: Yearly equivalent of 30-day *real* interest rate (Central Bank and CPI by Cortázar and Marshall, 1980).

^{m} w: Real wages and salaries index based on CPI^a and official figures for nominal wages and salaries (Instituto Nacional de Estadísticas (INA). Base 1970-10).

^{n} Index of wages and salaries with 1970-100.

mented gradually during 1974 and early 1975. The cost of imports decreased sharply during the first semester of 1974, when compared with previous levels, but stabilized thereafter because of compensating devaluations.

Changes in the financial market allowed for the establishment of private financial companies that operated with no more restrictions than a maximum monthly interest rate of 25%. The interest rate for banks (which at the time were part of the public sector) was under control and fixed at 9.6% per month. This discrimination in favor of private financial companies was deliberate in order to stimulate a transfer of funds away from the government and toward the private sector.

By the end of 1974, the rate of inflation had stabilized around 45% per quarter, production figures were showing a decline, and the price of copper fell sharply, which was reflected in a loss of reserves of $375 million in the last quarter alone. The devaluations (30% in December 1974 and an additional 40% in March 1975) were responsible for an increase in the rate of inflation from 9% in December 1974 to 21.4% in April 1975. All these results can be observed in Table 2. This bleak picture of recession, accelerated inflation, and balance-of-payments crisis led to a change in policies. Phase 1 was over. A shock treatment was called for if the negative trends were to be reversed.

Phase 2: The Shock Treatment, April 1975– June 1976

The new policies consisted of a contractionary shock on demand and a deepening of structural reforms. The demand shock was administered through various channels. Government expenditures were to decrease by 15% in the domestic component and 25% in the imported component. Total expenditures in fact fell by 27% in real terms in 1975, with public investment being reduced by half. Tax revenues were to increase by imposing a surcharge on the income tax and eliminating exemptions in the value-added tax. Public enterprises' rates were also sharply increased. Real wages were additionally reduced by changing the benchmark against which compensation for cost-of-living increases was calculated. A makework employment program was created (the so-called Minimum Employment Program) and a subsidy for firms hiring new workers was established to compensate for the negative effects of the recession.

The deepening of long-term structural changes was pursued by three simultaneous channels: more privatization of public enterprises, including the banks that were auctioned at the beginning of this phase; additional stimulus to the development of a private capital market by freeing interest rates charged by banks (once they had been transferred to private hands);

and an acceleration in the speed and a lowering of the levels programmed for reductions in external tariffs.

A study of the evolution of the main indicators shows mixed results. The rate of increase in the price level diminished from 17% a month during the first semester of 1975 to 9% in the second semester. At the same time, the loss of reserves was curbed during the second semester, a consequence of a dramatic fall in imports and a continued expansion in nontraditional exports that, at least partially, compensated for the big loss in copper export revenues. By the end of 1975, the balance of payments was still in deficit, but the trend was encouraging in that the deficit during the second semester had reached only $5 million. The situation continued to improve in 1976 because the demand for imports was depressed by the recession and exports were still growing fast, whereas the price of copper was slowly recuperating and inflows of short-term capital from abroad increased. The balance of payments showed a surplus of almost $500 million during 1976.

On the negative side, the policies generated a huge recession. Industrial production fell by 35% in the third quarter of 1975 compared with the same period in 1974. Unemployment rose to 19.6% in early 1976, in spite of public make-work employment programs that were fully effective at this time. These results can be seen in Table 2.

The exchange-rate policy in this phase is discontinuous. After large real devaluations at the beginning of 1975, the exchange rate remained fairly constant except at the end of the period, when it lagged behind domestic inflation, perhaps because of the trend to higher inflation rates in the first semester of 1976 (11.7% per month) as compared with the previous six-month period (9% a month). A constant value for the exchange rate was matched by a continued tendency to lower tariffs, as can be observed in Table 2. As a result, the cost of imports was slowly reduced.

Financial and monetary policies offered interesting results. Financial deregulation led to an increase in real interest rates from -23% in the second quarter of 1975 to 178% in the third quarter. This abrupt increase generated a cost shock to firms that accentuated the stagflationary effects that had originated in other policy measures, such as demand contraction and devaluation. Monetary policy, on the other hand, was complicated by the drastic reduction in the demand for imports that resulted in accumulation of reserves in the private sector, with an expansionary effect on the monetary base. This is the reason that the monetary shock was really sustained only during the second quarter of 1975.

Unhappiness with a recession that was deeper and longer than expected and the upsurge in inflation during the first semester of 1976 led to a new change in policies. The strategy to contain inflation was modified and it was expected that, as a result, inflation would fall and the economy would begin a recuperation in the level of economic activity. Phase 3 was inaugurated with the announcement in June 1976 of a Program of Economic Recuperation.

Phase 3: Curbing Expectations, June 1976– June 1979

The antiinflation strategy in Phase 3 changed the emphasis from demand contraction to curbing cost pressures and expectations. In June 1976, the peso was revalued 10% and a 30-day preannounced value for future exchange rates was established as a way of influencing inflationary expectations. The exchange rate was revalued again in March 1977. In February 1978, this policy was extended: the value of the exchange rate was announced for the next 11 months. This new approach was complemented by more drastic tariff reductions. Between December 1976 and December 1977, the maximum desired tariff went down gradually until an across-the-board maximum tariff of 10% was established as a target to be achieved in 1979, automobiles being the only exception. The movement toward free trade was reinforced by the withdrawal of the country from the Andean Pact and by a gradual, but systematic, deregulation of external capital flows that began in October 1977 and was completed in 1979.

Revaluation of domestic currency had a rapid impact on expectations and on the rate of inflation, which decreased to 4.9% in August 1976, only to increase again to 7 to 8% in the following months. However, the medium-term trend was clear: quarterly rates decreased from 40% for the second quarter of 1976 to 13% in the third and fourth quarters of 1977 (accumulated rate for a three-month period). The downward trend continued in 1978, as can be seen in Table 2. The quarterly rate of inflation stabilized between 7 and 9% until the end of phase 3, in June 1979.

The reduction in the rate of inflation encouraged an expansion in real wages because nominal wages were indexed to previous inflation. Real wages increased by 5% in the second semester of 1976 compared with the first semester. This was a factor that helped industrial production, which showed an upward trend all through this phase. Unemployment went down from 16 to 13% and stayed at that level in 1978 and 1979 (see Table 2).

The balance of payments was subject to contradictory forces during this phase. In 1976 it showed a surplus in spite of the negative effect of revaluation on the trade accounts: the depressed demand for imports predominated and was helped by an increasing inflow of foreign loans, in such a way that a balance-of-payments surplus was generated. In the second semester of 1977, the situation was reversed, owing to the accumulated effect of two revaluations plus a higher demand for imports originating in the expansion of domestic production. A fall in copper prices of

13% with respect to the first semester added to the forces that created a current account deficit of $500 million in 1977. To counteract the tendency, the exchange rate was devalued twice in 1977 (in September and December) and again in 1978. Given the program of tariff reductions and the compensating effect of devaluations, the cost of imports did not change much in the period. External inflows of capital accelerated, facilitating the accumulation of reserves, as figures for BP in Table 2 show. The high level of reserves by mid-1979 made possible the transition to phase 4.

Phase 4: Global Monetarism Since June 1979

Phase 4 corresponds to a stage in which tariff reductions were completed. No import duties were above 10%, except for cars. Reserves were increasing, the fiscal deficit had all but disappeared and the economy continued giving signs of recuperating from the recession. At this point, in June 1979, the exchange rate was first devalued by 5.7% and then fixed. Given that the economy was now open to international trade, it was hoped that the rate of price increases in the world economy would automatically regulate domestic inflation. After a lag, the latter should approach the former. When this happens, there will be no need for further adjustments in the exchange rate. Global monetarism provides full automaticity to adjustment mechanisms in the economy.

Results in this phase are illustrative of the way automatic adjustment operates in practice. A fixed exchange rate plus the elimination of the fiscal deficit worked in favor of a reduction in the rate of inflation to 9.5% in December 1981. On the other hand, for 2½ years starting in June 1979 domestic inflation was consistently above world inflation. The trend can be clearly observed in Table 2. The practical consequence of this, given a fixed nominal exchange rate, was that the real exchange rate appreciated by almost 30% in the period, as seen in Table 2, column 6. The loss of competitiveness implied by this figure resulted in rapidly expanding trade and current accounts deficits, which were to be equivalent to 10.7% and 15.1% of GDP by the end of 1981. The deficit resulted in a loss of reserves, reduced capital inflows, and sharp increases in the yearly rate of interest that went to 50% in real terms during the last quarter of 1981 (Table 2, column 12).

High interest rates and loss of competitiveness were responsible for a deep recession that began in the fourth quarter of 1980. A year later, industrial production fell at a rate of 8% for the year, when quarterly figures are compared. At the same time unemployment went up once again. It reached 13.5% of the labor force in Santiago and 12.4% nationally. But if those employed in the "Minimum Employment Program" are included (earning less than 30 dollars a month), national unemployment reached 17% in September 1981 and deteriorated even more thereafter.

Recession, accompanied by a reduced inflow of external loans, high interest rates, and high indebtedness on the part of most firms, increased bankruptcies and bank failures. The government was forced to take over four banks and four financial companies on the verge of collapse. A deep financial crisis overtook most of the productive sector. After three years, the "miracle" seemed to be running out of steam.

III. STRUCTURAL CHANGES[2]

Having examined the course of short-term stabilization policies, it is now time to evaluate some of the long-term changes in the Chilean economy since 1973. We shall refer to three different long-term policy actions: privatization of the economy, opening up to trade, and changes in the composition of production and distribution of income.

A. Privatization

One of the basic elements of the new economic policy consisted in a drastic change in the role assigned to economic agents in Chile. The state gradually decreased in importance. This was attained by means of a reduction in public expenditures and a more limited presence of the state as a producer and as a developmental agent.

As can be seen in Table 3, fiscal expenditures as a proportion of GDP dropped from 25.8% in 1974 to 19.7% in 1979. This was accompanied by a policy of privatization of public enterprises, which meant that out of 507 public enterprises in 1973, only 15 would remain in government hands by 1980.[3] The state also diminishes its developmental role, an outstanding characteristic of its action since the creation of the "Corporación de Fomento." This developmental role increased considerably during the governments of Frei and Allende, as can be seen from the figures of public employment by activity in Table 4. The withdrawal of the state from development assistance affected mainly small producers in the agricultural, mining, and industrial sectors as well as the process of agrarian reform that not only came to a stop but was, in fact, reversed by the return of a significant share of expropriated land to former owners, as will be seen later. Where the state left the field, the private sector—either domestic or foreign—entered. Particularly important was the growth of private financial institutions.

Organized labor was excluded from this picture. Not only wages were

[2] This section is based on Foxley (1982).

[3] CORFO, Gerencia de Normalización and *El Mercurio*, February 27, 1980. The figures correspond to firms owned by CORFO.

TABLE 3

Fiscal Expenditures and Fiscal Deficit[a]

Year	Total expenditures excluding public debt	Fiscal deficit
1970	22.7	2.9
1971	27.1	9.3
1972	29.1	12.2
1973	40.8	27.7
1974	25.8	8.9
1975	19.4	2.9
1976	17.6	2.0
1977	18.6	1.5
1978	19.7	0.8

[a] Values are given as percentages of GDP. *Sources:* Ministerio de Hacienda and ODE-PLAN. The 1978 figures include our estimate of nominal GDP.

controlled and, in fact, drastically curtailed in real terms, but no collective bargaining was allowed, strikes were forbidden, and no mechanism existed for the participation of labor in economic decisions. Only in 1979 was a labor plan implemented to regulate, under conditions of subordination of workers to the employers, the functioning of labor unions and allow for a very restricted form of collective bargaining. The privatization of the economy implied a massive transfer of resources toward the private sector, particularly toward financial firms and large industrial enterprises. This transfer of resources was made possible by the particular form taken by the processes of privatization, of market liberalization, and of inflationary control.

Thus, privatization of state enterprises occurred in extremely advantageous conditions for the new owners. In Table 5 we estimate the implicit

TABLE 4

Employment in the Public Sector[a]

Year	Administrative services	Development institutions	Social services	Public enterprises	Total
1964	32.3	28.5	49.6	49.6	209.9
1970	46.1	44.3	133.8	55.8	280.0
1974	52.8	69.5	178.3	59.5	360.2
1978	46.2	34.4	176.9	35.9	293.3
Variation					
1964–70	6.1	7.6	6.0	2.0	4.9
1970–74	3.5	11.9	7.4	1.6	6.5
1974–78	−3.3	−16.1	−0.2	−11.2	−5.0

[a] Values are given in thousands of persons and annual variation rates. *Source:* Ministerio de Hacienda.

TABLE 5
Subsidy in the Sale of State Enterprises[a]

Discount rate					
1974–1978	1979–1983	Sale value	Value of assets in 1978	Subsidy	Subsidy as percentage of asset value
10	10	496.1	731.8	235.7	32.2
25	15	533.0	731.8	198.8	27.2

[a] The figures are in millions of 1978 dollars and correspond to a sample of 41 enterprises and banks representing around 60% of the firms auctioned. The value of the sale, updated to 1978, assumes a four-year payment period for the industrial firms and eight quarters for banks, with interest rates of 10 and 8%, respectively. *Source:* Dahse (1979) and CORFO, Gerencia de Normalización.

subsidy for those who bought these public assets. The subsidy turns out to be equivalent to 30% of the firms' actual worth and up to 40 and 50% of the purchase value.[4] The low sale price was influenced by the state's urgency to sell and for doing so in a moment of deep recession and high interest rates, a point at which the short-term profitability of the enterprises decreased. Given these circumstances, only those firms with liquid resources or access to cheap foreign credit were in a position to buy the auctioned enterprises. Something similar occurred in the agricultural sector, in which the policy was to return a fraction of the lands expropriated during agrarian reform to their original owners. Another part was subdivided into individual plots and handed over to peasants. By April 1979, 30% of the expropriated land had been returned to the former owners and 35% had been assigned in individual plots to peasants and small farmers. Moreover, by June 1978, nearly 40% of these lands had been sold or leased by peasants to third parties as a consequence of the high cost of credit and reduced technical assistance.

Thus, the privatization of manufacturing firms as well as that of the land reform sector implied a transfer of assets, generally undervalued, either to former owners, in the agricultural case, or to business groups in the industrial and financial sectors. The foregoing tendency was reinforced by the particular form taken by the process of market liberalization. Thus the liberalization of the foreign-credit market was only partial. A ceiling was imposed on foreign borrowing, as a percentage of the value of assets. Given that only large enterprises and the better established banks and financial institutions had access to cheap, rationed external credit and that domestic interest rates were much higher, this constituted a source of large profits for banks and larger firms. Zahler (1979) esti-

[4] The calculation was made based on the figures of Dahse (1979) for a sample of 41 enterprises, as explained in the note to Table 5.

mated the profit for those enterprises that had access to external credit in the period 1976–1979 to be on the order of $800 million. These profits arose from the high differential in interest rates, taking into account expected devaluation, between foreign rates (from 6 to 11%) and domestic interest rates in dollars (between 11 and 42%).

On the other hand, the process of market liberalization did not follow uniform rules with regard to factor and goods prices. Upon the drastic freeing up of prices followed by wage contraction, a strong bias against labor set in, as can be seen in Table 6. The drastic fall of the relative price of labor with respect to wholesale prices, export, and industrial prices is obvious from an inspection of Table 6. The relative reduction in wages reached between 50 and 60% in 1976 and was still between 30 and 40% during 1978.

These sets of relative prices are extremely favorable to productive enterprises, particularly those in export activities. Undoubtedly it allowed them to absorb a good part of the greater costs associated with the severe 1975–1976 recession and it provided a cushion that facilitated adjustment to increased external competition resulting from lower tariffs. The effect of changes in relative prices is reinforced by consideration of the reduction in the employer's contribution to social security. The accumulated effect of both factors on the cost of labor can be observed in the third column of Table 7.

Given labor productivity increases, the incidence of labor costs for the industrial producer dropped from 15.8% of the gross value of production in 1970 to 10.2% in 1978, as indicated in the last column of Table 7.

Another important way in which resources were transferred to large business firms came about as a by-product of the policy of economic stabilization. This policy was characterized by a strict monetarist, closed-economy approach. The policy sought stabilization through partial use of

TABLE 6

Prices and Wages[a]

Year	Remunerations/ wholesale prices	Remunerations/ export prices	Industrial remunerations/ industrial prices
1970	100.0	100.0	100.0
1974	49.7	50.3	57.5
1975	40.0	36.3	46.7
1976	40.5	45.3	53.5
1977	52.2	60.7	67.2
1978	57.9	57.9	73.1

[a] 1970 Indexes = 100. *Sources:* Second column—Instituto Nacional de Estadísticas (INE), *Indice de Sueldos y Salarios* (ISS) and Indice de Precios Mayonistos (*IPM*), national products; third column—INE, *ISS*, Exchange rate and Ffrench-Davis (1979b); fourth column—INE, *ISS*, Industrial Sector and Industrial *IPM*.

TABLE 7
Productivity and Labor Costs in the Industrial Sector[a]

Year	Wages	Cost of labor	Physical productivity	Cost of labor/ over gross value of production
1970	100.0	100.0	100.0	15.8
1974	57.5	59.9	99.6	9.5
1975	46.7	47.6	77.1	9.8
1976	53.5	54.5	94.9	9.1
1977	67.2	67.6	103.7	10.3
1978	73.1	70.5	109.6	10.2

[a] *Sources:* Second column—INE, *ISS,* Industrial sector and industrial *IPM;* third column—wages plus the employer's contribution to social security. The actual rate of contribution effective for 1974 was considered, as calculated by ODEPLAN, *Cuentas Nacionales de Chile* and was varied for the years listed according to the rates of the Service of Social Security. Fourth column—ODEPLAN, and employment by sectors figures from ODEPLAN; fifth column—for 1970, ODEPLAN, *op. cit.* and for the other years, it is calculated using cost of labor and physical productivity.

the instruments at its disposal: principally the reduction of money supply, real wages, and the fiscal deficit.

The approach was successful in producing a sharp drop in effective demand and in reducing real wages. Prices increased without any relation to demand because the impact of expectations and costs was difficult to gauge in a situation that passed rapidly from "repressed" inflation to open inflation. Consequently, high inflation continued far longer than expected. The economy entered a prolonged phase of recession with high inflation, a period characterized by generalized market disequilibrium. Market imbalances surfaced in the form of sharp and intermittent movements in relative prices.

Anyone with enough liquidity to react quickly to these fluctuations in relative prices benefited from those movements, as did, obviously, anyone with special access to economic information that would allow him to predict correctly those movements or to know ahead of time of any corrective measures planned by the government.

The economic groups that controlled the country's large firms and financial sector took full advantage of these opportunities for speculation. Market disequilibria and high inflation lasted over five years, long enough for those groups to corner for themselves the speculative gains available in different markets.

In short, beginning in 1973, the operation of the Chilean economy fundamentally changed, not only because the economic roles assigned to different participants changed, but also because the dynamic processes of adjustment to a new economic model made possible the real transfer of resources to industrial–financial groups. These groups took advantage of this resource transfer, using it to acquire a dominant position in the country's productive apparatus, as will be shown next.

B. Transition from a Closed to an Open Economy

At the end of 1973, the average nominal tariff on imports to Chile was 94%. By June 1979, a gradual policy of tariff reductions brought nearly all tariffs down to a uniform 10%, except for automotive vehicles. The process of tariff reduction, which took a little over five years, was part of a general liberalization of restrictions on foreign trade: elimination of nontariff barriers and a reduction on limits to foreign investment, foreign credit, and foreign-exchange transactions. At the same time, the government attempted to maintain an exchange rate that would favor Chilean exports. The government also sought to encourage exports by exempting exported goods from the across-the-board value-added tax on all products sold in Chile and from export customs duties.

Policies designed to open the economy were resolutely put into effect from 1974 to 1976. By the end of six years, the Chilean economy was well on its way to becoming an "open" economy with few barriers to international trade. Here we shall briefly review the principal changes that occurred as a result of the transition from a closed to an open economy.[5]

One of the objectives of liberalizing imports was to encourage the development of an export sector. Lower tariffs reduced the cost to the Chilean producer of intermediate goods. An increase in the volume of imports would raise the equilibrium exchange rate for the dollar, creating an exchange rate more favorable to export growth.

The policy of export stimulation was also helped by the low wage rates that prevailed during the period and by special tax exemptions on exports. The policy was also aided by an excess capacity in the industrial sector, which resulted from the antiinflation program.

The growth of exports in the period was undoubtedly significant. Normalizing for the price of copper, total exports rise from 15% of GDP in 1970 to 18% in 1977. Nevertheless, the greater success was obtained in the growth of nontraditional exports, as shown in Table 8. During the period 1974–1979, nontraditional exports tripled. This was accompanied by export diversification. If copper is excluded from total exports, to avoid

---

[5] What follows is based on studies by Ffrench-Davis (1979a) and Vergara (1980).

Alejandro Foxley

TABLE 8

Imports and Exports[a]

Goods	1970	1974	1978	1979
Imports				
Food consumption	107.4	85.5	115.7	130.2
Nonfood consumption	191.6	236.8	410.7	528.7
Capital	550.2	336.3	566.6	668.7
Intermediate	1055.2	1769.7	1533.8	1925.9
Intermediate, including oil, wheat, and maize	907.4	1099.6	940.9	1117.8
Total	1904.4	2428.3	2626.8	3253.5
Exports				
Traditional	1897.0	2257.1	1233.6	1695.2
Semitraditional	93.2	174.5	226.7	293.3
Nontraditional	225.9	273.2	644.9	897.5
Total	2216.1	2704.8	2105.2	2886.0

[a] Figures are in millions of 1977 dollars. *Source:* Ffrench-Davis (1980).

the effect of excessive price fluctuations, industrial exports rose from 59% of total exports in 1974 (excluding copper) to 65% in 1978.[6]

As regards imports, they grew rapidly after 1978, as seen in Table 8. The expansion was particularly significant for imports of nonfood consumption goods, whose growth rate is over 100% between 1974 and 1979. On the other hand, imports of capital goods fell during the recession and only in 1978 did they recuperate to 1970 levels. A similar behavior is observed when looking at intermediate imports.[7]

What impact did the opening of the economy have on the structure of production, particularly in the industrial sector? The manufacturing sector suffered the simultaneous impact of recession and tariff reduction, which negatively affected production levels, as can be observed in Table 9.[8] Both effects are not easy to separate. Yet, based on Vergara's study, we constructed Table 9 in which we grouped sectoral data that will allow us to distinguish among sectors depending on how they have been affected by the opening up to trade and by recession, respectively. In category A we classify those sectors that were simultaneously affected by falls in domestic demand and by tariff reduction. In these sectors production decreased and imports increased, giving way to a marked desubstitu-

[6] Only exports of goods are considered in these figures.

[7] Oil, wheat, and maize are excluded from this observation.

[8] The customs duties reduction started to be an important factor only in 1976. See Ffrench-Davis (1979a).

TABLE 9

Opening Up to World Markets: Effects on the Industrial Sector[a]

Sector	Production	Imports	Exports	Domestic demand	Import substitution
(A) *Affected by opening and fall of internal demand*	−2.5	4.7	22.6	−1.8	−11.2
Textiles, clothing and footwear (321, 322, 323, and 324)	−0.6	6.1	46.0	−1.2	−3.4
Industrial inputs (351, 354, 361, and 382)	−5.9	4.8	24.2	−3.3	−22.2
Others (342 and 385)	−2.2	2.8	−7.4	−0.6	−9.1
(B) *Affected by opening to trade*	−1.1	8.7	23.3	2.0	−17.7
Electronic equipment (3832)	−1.1	14.0	−15.4	6.7	−27.2
Transportation material (384)	−1.2	6.9	46.5	2.2	−14.4
(C) *Affected by the fall in internal demand*	−1.6	−7.0	5.8	−3.0	8.0
Intermediate for construction (369, 371, and 381)	−1.5	−6.0	12.9	−2.9	6.7
Unvulcanized rubber and plastics (355 and 356)	−1.9	−16.4	−8.7	−3.6	13.2
(D) *Oriented to exports*	2.9	−9.2	11.4	−0.7	6.4
Timber (331)	4.4	−29.9	15.4	2.9	11.4
Paper (341)	0.6	2.4	10.0	−8.5	−2.0
(E) *Others* (311, 312, 313, 314, 352, 362, 3833, and 390)	2.1	4.8	17.1	1.7	−1.4
Total	0.2	1.6	15.3	−0.6	−1.4

[a] Numbers in parenthesis are the identity codes according to the United Nations, *International Standard Industrial Classification of all Economic Activities* (ISIC). Figures are given as annual variation rates 1969/70–1978. *Source:* Vergara (1980). Domestic demand was measured as a proxy by the difference between production plus imports minus exports. The last column indicates the variation in the coefficient of domestic production over total supply.

tion of imports. Therefore, this is a case of sectors that were affected simultaneously by falls in demand and by import liberalization. This group includes textiles, shoes, and clothing, as well as some intermediate inputs for industry. Category B includes those activities where, in spite of an increase in domestic demand, production fell. At the same time, imports increased significantly. These are sectors typically affected by the opening up to trade. This group includes the electronic industry and transportation, among others.

Category C consists of intermediate inputs for construction and rubber and plastics. These sectors were mainly affected by recession rather than by tariff reduction. This may be verified by observing that, in the face of contraction in demand, both imports and production decreased, but the former fell even more sharply. Category D represents export-oriented activities that successfully adjusted to lower tariffs, like wood and paper. In category E, whose principal component is food, beverages, and tobacco, we include sectors where both production and imports grew.

In brief, empirical evidence indicates that trade liberalization caused (a) significant export expansion; (b) a change in the composition of imports, in which the most rapid growth is observed in the imports of non-food consumption goods; (c) a differentiated impact of tariff reduction on the various branches of industry; and (d) stagflation in industrial employment accompanied by a slow recuperation in industrial output levels. Undoubtedly this adjustment process was helped by the remarkable fall in wages with respect to the exchange rate and to industrial prices, as was seen in Table 6. By this means, the industrial sector was able to absorb part of the impact of increased external competition. There is also some evidence that firms hedged against foreign competition by becoming importers of competitive products [See Ffrench-Davis (1979a)]. On the other hand, a greater specialization in production is evident in some industries, as a way of increasing production efficiency in order to meet the import challenge [See Vergara (1980)]. Another factor that facilitated the adjustment was the access to foreign loans.

It is perhaps too early to make a definite assessment of the impact of trade liberalization in Chile. Although the process of tariff reduction ended in 1979, the appreciation of domestic currency that results from a fixed exchange rate established in June 1979 (given that domestic inflation more than doubles external inflation) is further reducing effective protection in the industrial sector. A final evaluation must wait until these effects have sorted themselves out.

C.   Changes in the Composition of Production and Income Distribution

Up to this point, we have analyzed the main changes in the economy's operation that resulted from policy reforms begun in 1973. These changes, privatization and greater degree of openness to foreign trade, no doubt have repercussions on the structure of production and on patterns of income and wealth distribution. But the effects are slow to take form. Given the short period of time that has passed, we can now observe only the emerging outlines of some of the tendencies.

In Table 10 we show the composition of production and employment

TABLE 10

Production Composition and Employment[a]

Sector	1970		1974		1978	
	Production	Employment	Production	Employment[b]	Production	Employment[c]
Agriculture	9.7	22.6	9.1	18.3	10.2	19.3
Mining	10.7	3.2	11.6	3.7	12.0	3.4
Industry	26.0	17.8	25.7	18.5	22.7	16.1
Construction	5.0	6.9	4.8	5.7	2.8	4.0
Energy and transportation	6.4	7.4	6.8	7.6	7.1	7.3
Commerce (trade)	22.3	12.1	21.9	12.7	23.6	16.7
Services[d]	19.9	30.0	20.1	33.4	21.6	33.3
Total	100.0	100.0	100.0	100.0	100.0	100.0

[a] Figures are given as percentages. *Sources:* Production columns—ODEPLAN, *Cuentas Nacionales;* employment columns—ODEPLAN, *Antecedentes sobre el Desarrollo Económico Chileno 1960–1970.*

[b] Corresponds to the 1975 survey. There is no information for 1974.

[c] Corresponds to the 1977 survey, which is the last information available.

[d] Excludes housing property.

for the principal productive sectors. The primary sectors increased their relative importance in production from 20% in 1970 to 22% in 1978. In spite of its greater importance in production, the participation of the primary sectors in employment fell from 26% in 1970 to 22.7% in 1978.

On the other hand, the manufacturing sector dropped its relative importance in GDP, as would be expected, because it was the most heavily protected sector before the tariff reforms and was at the same time affected by reductions in domestic demand. The industrial sector participation in GDP fell over 3 percentage points between 1970 and 1978. In employment, the reduction is close to 2 percentage points. The reduction of industrial employment continues as a tendency even after 1976, when industrial production began to recuperate.

The most dynamic sectors in the period are commerce and services. Jointly considered, their participation in production rose from 42% in 1970 to 45% in 1978. One out of two jobs in the economy was generated in these sectors by 1978.[9] The importance achieved by the service sectors is such that their participation in production and employment is higher than

[9] This happened in spite of the fact that employment in education and health were reduced. The employment in "other services," instead, increased by 21% between 1975 and 1977.

TABLE 11

Distribution of Household Consumption by Quintiles: Greater Santiago, Chile[a]

	Share of total consumption	
Quintiles	1969	1978
I	7.7	5.2
II	12.1	9.3
III	16.0	13.6
IV	21.0	20.9
V	43.2	51.0
Total	100.0	100.0

[a] *Source:* Instituto Nacional de Estadísticas (INE), Chile, Encuesta de Presupuestos Familiares, 1969, and Encuesta de Presupuestos Familiares, 1978.

that of all productive sectors jointly considered (agriculture, mining, and industry). On the other hand, infrastructure and construction activities decreased in importance. The latter reduced its participation in production by half.

Summarizing, the changes in the structure of production and employment are meaningful in spite of the short time that has transpired. Part of these changes does not reflect modifications in the productive capacity but only in the degree of utilization of that capacity.[10]

The direction of the changes is clear: the production of primary goods and commerce and services grow at a significant rate; industry and the sectors of infrastructure at a very slow pace. These unbalances in sectoral growth, if persistent, will probably end up modifying permanently not only the productive structure but also income distribution patterns.

Distributive changes are strongly influenced by the high unemployment rate and the fall of real wages. The simultaneous reduction in employment and wages generates a regressive distribution of income, a proxy for which we consider household consumption expenditures by income brackets. The figures are given in Table 11 and point to a concentration of consumption in the high-income brackets.[11]

[10] Of course, to the extent that idle capacity is maintained as such for an extended period in some sectors, it may become a signal for further expansions to be oriented toward other activities, those where the "new" demand is concentrated.

[11] This information, which is in accord with wages and employment data, contradicts official statements that the income distribution in 1978 would not be significantly different than that of 1970. According to a study by Heskia, the distribution improved even in the worst recession years. For a criticism of the results of Heskia, see Cortázar (1980).

On the other hand, empirical evidence shows a marked stratification in consumption. Imports of nonessential consumption goods, which grew about 300% between 1970 and 1978, are highly concentrated in the highest 20% of the families. These families consume nearly 60% of total imported nonessential consumption [see Ffrench-Davis (1979a) and INE; data for 1978]. The trickling down in consumption to other income groups is scarce, being almost negligible for the lower 20% of the families.

Contrasted with the expansion of luxury consumption that was concentrated in high-income groups, essential food consumption per family for the poorer groups shows a reduction of 20% in real terms between 1969 and 1978.[12] Instead, the consumption per family of the same basic food products for the high-income groups grew slightly. This marked dualism in consumption seems to be an essential characteristic of the model. It is in agreement with the changes and with the income distribution patterns previously discussed.

IV. CONCLUSIONS

The Chilean economy, in the period 1974–1979, was simultaneously subjected to a process of economic stabilization and transition toward a free market economy.

In the first aspect, a substantial decrease in the rate of inflation was attained, the balance of payments was adjusted accumulating international reserves, and, after passing through a deep recession, the economy showed signs of recuperating toward the levels of production of 1970.

Other indicators, however, showed negative results: high unemployment persisted in the seventh year of application of the policy, distribution of income and household expenditures was regressive, investment levels were low, and the deficit in the current account of the balance of payments is still growing, as is external debt. These indicators cast a shadow on the growth potential of the model, as it has been applied in Chile, and in its capacity to absorb labor in productive activities.

But macroeconomic indicators are only the more visible, and perhaps they are the less important part of the revolutionary process of change in the Chilean economy in this period. The process of transition to a free-market economy implied that, simultaneously with the antiinflationary policy, deep structural reforms were carried out: a drastic privatization of the economy; a quick opening of the economy to world markets; and a massive transfer of resources to the modern sector of industry and finance. As a consequence of the latter, powerful conglomerates with

[12] INE, *Encuesta de Presupuestos Familiares*, 1969 and 1978.

ample economic and political influence emerged. This is one of the outstanding traits of the industrial organization scheme to arise from the experiment.

The conglomerates, or "economic groups," are, in fact, the new actors in the process of development. They increasingly control industrial assets, as well as those of banks and financial institutions. Also, they are the dynamic agents in the process of industrial adjustment to face foreign competition. These conglomerates are the ones that relate to international private banks and control the large proportion of the flow of external loans.

The other basic modification in the functioning of the Chilean economy refers to the radical opening up to world markets. This process did not result in as deep a breakdown of the industrial sector as could have occurred. Although several industrial branches suffered significant losses in markets and industrial employment fell, other activities seem to have adapted successfully.

The financial opening, which goes together with the commercial opening, helps to overcome the problems derived from the recession and the transition to the open economy. Nevertheless, it has distorting effects in other aspects. It prolongs the price stabilization period as it becomes the most important source of monetary expansion. At the same time it reinforces the tendency toward asset concentration as it gives differentiated access to cheap external credit (in comparison with domestic credit), mainly to large enterprises of the modern sector, and makes it possible to keep an undervalued exchange rate that coexists with large deficits in trade flows.

Production adjustment, as a result of the opening up of the economy, is just beginning to show. As expected, new production patterns are oriented toward expanding primary producing activities (mainly copper mining and agricultural and forestry products) and exports.

However, the most dynamic sectors are commerce, financial activities, and personal services. The first two are stimulated by expanded foreign trade and by the development of the capital market. Demand for personal services grew as a consequence of the rapid expansion in income for high-income groups. At the same time that the productive structure changed, a higher degree of asset and income concentration was observed.

What type of economy emerges from the deep structural changes undertaken in Chile after 1973? Certainly, what we have is an open economy, with more specialization and, potentially, with higher incentives for efficiency in domestic production. It is also an economy that is more vulnerable with respect to changes, shocks, and fluctuations in the international economy. It is, on the other hand, highly dependent on the availability of private external credit in order to balance the current account deficit.

A salient feature of the model is the wide dispersion in income and consumption patterns between the rich and the rest of the population. With respect to consumption, a marked stratification is produced. The "deprivation horizon" is a reality for low-income groups, as is "the opulent consumer society" for the high-income sectors.

This is only one of the unsolved problems. Other persistent problems are extremely high unemployment and low investment. In the political sphere, the model has not been able to solve the inherent contradiction between economic freedom, a basic objective of the model and of the Friedmanian "ideal," and the political authoritarianism that accompanies it. After all, facing the dilemma, it seems that the Chilean model has certainly chosen capitalism but has forgotten all about freedom.

REFERENCES

Cauas, J., and Saieh, A. (1979). "Política Económica 1973–1979." *Boletń del Banco Central* (621) (November).

Cortázar, R. (1980). "Remuneraciones, Empleo y Distribución del Ingreso en Chile 1970–1978." *CIEPLAN* (3), Santiago, (June).

Cortázar, R., and Marshall J. (1980). *Indice de Precios al Consumidor el Chile: 1970–1978. Colección Estadios CIEPLAN* (4), Santiago (November).

Dahse, F. (1979). *Mapa de la Extrema Riqueza.* Santiago: Editorial Aconcagua.

Departamento de Economía, University of Chile (1978). *Comentarios sobre la Situación Económica,* 2nd Semester.

Díaz Alejandro, C. (1981). "Southern Cone Stabilization Plans." In *Economic Stabilization in Developing Countries* (W. Cline, S. Weintraub, eds.). Washington, D.C.: The Brookings Institution.

Ffrench-Davis, R. (1979a). "Políticas de Comercio Exterior en Chile: 1973–78," mimeo, CIEPLAN.

Ffrench-Davis, R. (1979b). "Indice de Precios Externos y Vabr Real del Comercio Internacional de Chile." *Notas Técnicas CIEPLAN* (15).

Ffrench-Davis, R. (1980). "Liberalización de Importaciones: la Experiencia Chilena en 1973–1979." *Colección Estudios CIEPLAN* (4), Santiago (November).

Ffrench-Davis, R., and Arellano, J. P. (1980). "Apertura Financiera Externa, la Experiencia Chilena," mimeo, CIEPLAN.

Foxley, A. (1980). "Stabilization Policies and Stagflation: the Cases of Brazil and Chile." In *World Development* (A. Foxley and L. Whitehead, eds.), Special Issue, "Economic Stabilization in Latin America: Political Dimensions." London and New York: Oxford University Press.

Foxley, A. (1981). "Stabilization Policies and Their Effects on Employment and Income Distribution." In *Economic Stabilization in Developing Countries* (W. Cline and S. Weintraub, eds.). Washington, D.C.: The Brookings Institution.

Foxley, A. (1982). "Towards a Free-Market Economy: Chile 1974–1979." *Journal of Development Economics* (February).

Friedman, I. (1981). "The Role of Private Banks in Stabilization Programs." In *Economic Stabilization in Developing Countries* (W. Cline and S. Weintraub, eds.). Washington, D.C.: The Brookings Institution.

Herrera, J. E., and Morales, J. (1979). "La Inversión Financiera Externa: el Caso de Chile 1974–1978." *Colección Estudios CIEPLAN* (1). Instituto Nacional de Estadisticas (1979). *Encuesta de Presupuestos Familiares* **3** (May).

Instituto Nacional de Estadísticas (INE) (1979). "Encuesta de Presupuestos Familiares, 1969 and 1978." *El Mercurio* (February).

Meller, P., Cortázar, R., and Marshall, J. (1979). "La Evolución del Empleo en Chile 1974–1978." *Colección Estudios CIEPLAN* (2).

Moulian, T., and Vergara, P. (1979a). "Estado, Ideologia y Politicas Económicas en Chile 1973–1978." *Colección Estudios CIEPLAN* (3).

Moulian, T., and Vergara, P. (1979b). "Politicas de Estabilizacion y Comportamientos Sociales: la Experiencia Chilena, 1973–1978." *Apuntes CIEPLAN* (22) (November).

Prebisch, R. (1978). "Estructura Socioeconómica y Crisis del Sistema." *Revista de la CEPAL,* 2nd Semester.

Vergara, P. (1980). "Apertura Externa y Desarrollo Industrial en Chile: 1974–1978." *Colección Estudios CIEPLAN* (4), Santiago (December).

Zahler, R. (1979). "Repercusiones Monetaries y Reales de la Apertura de la Economía Chilena 1975–1978." *Revista de la CEPAL* (April).

CIEPLAN
Santiago, Chile

Part IV

Technology

Chapter 12

Fostering Technological Mastery by Means of Selective Infant-Industry Protection

Larry E. Westphal

I. INTRODUCTION

A number of cross-country comparative research studies on the relationship of trade policy to industrialization have been completed over the past decade. Although there are important differences of detail in the conclusions reached, the various syntheses of this research all agree on one central conclusion: greater uniformity of incentives across activities and higher levels of export achievement—individually and in combination—are associated with improved industrial performance as measured by the growth of manufacturing output expressed in either domestic or world prices.[1] This conclusion is often interpreted in the following terms: though modest levels of promotional incentives to infant industries may be in

[1] See, for example, Little *et al.* (1970), Balassa and associates (1971), Bhagwati and Krueger (1973), Balassa (1978), Bhagwati (1978), Krueger (1978), Bhagwati and Srinivasan (1978), and Krueger (1980).

255

order, the closer the policy regime is to free trade, the better the industrial performance is because a free-trade regime necessarily means uniformity of incentives vis-à-vis trading opportunities and empirically appears to assure the requisite high levels of export achievement.

The foregoing interpretation admits of the possibility that the "optimal" policy regime may depart significantly from free trade in the treatment of some industries because it does recognize the possible need for measures to promote the development of infant industries. But there has been very little empirical research focused on issues directly relevant to the promotion of infant industries. To my knowledge, none of the underlying country studies [including Westphal and Kim (1982)] traced the evolution of particular infant industries over time to see what lessons might be drawn, nor do any of the syntheses provide an empirically grounded discussion of appropriate means and levels of infant-industry promotion. The central question concerning infant-industry promotion thus remains largely unanswered. The question is, "Under different measures that could be used to promote the development of infant industries, what are the benefits, what are the costs, and do the former exceed the latter?" Obviously, infant-industry promotion is warranted only if its benefits exceed its costs, and the promotional measure that should be used—if any should—is that which yields the greatest excess of benefits over costs.

An *infant industry* is any newly established type of activity for which the economy's existing endowment of skills and human capital does not provide immediate technological mastery. *Technological mastery* consists in command over technological knowledge as manifested in the ability to use it effectively. The costs of infant-industry development are thus the costs of acquiring technological mastery, and the benefits are those associated with the attainment of increased technological mastery. The question of whether infant industries ought to be given promotional incentives turns on whether there would otherwise be adequate incentives for the acquisition of increased technological mastery, which in turn depends on whether individual producers realize all of the socially relevant costs and benefits of their own technological effort and whether they evaluate costs and benefits in a manner consistent with social objectives.

It is not possible to make a quantitative assessment of the need for— or, more generally, of the merits of—infant-industry promotion without empirical evidence concerning costs and benefits. But, even were such evidence available, it would not be conclusive. To assess the need for promotion requires knowledge of what would happen (or, for an *ex post* assessment, of what would have happened) under various alternatives with regard to the provision of promotional incentives. Such knowledge comes only in the form of predictions that cannot be verified directly, except perhaps in the case pertaining to the alternative actually followed. In any event, because they require the comparison of alternatives, at least one of which is counterfactual, estimates of costs and benefits are of uncertain reliability. Thus there may always be legitimate disagreement about the need for infant-industry promotion, but the scope for disagreement is, at present, magnified by the lack of empirical evidence.

The remainder of this chapter reviews the evidence that does exist, for the purpose of framing some hypotheses about policies to promote infant industries. The evidence with which I am concerned is of two types. First, as a result of recent research on technological change in developing countries, there is considerable information about the nature of the costs and benefits of infant-industry development, together with a tentative indication of the magnitude of the costs. Second, the recently completed cross-country comparative research gives a basis for stating some tentative lessons about the promotion of infant industries by means of trade policies. These lessons concern both the merits of protecting infant industries from imports and the efficacy of fostering infant-industry exports. To give the lessons substance, they will be illustrated by the experience of the Republic of Korea, the developing country I am most familiar with.

II. THE NATURE OF INFANT-INDUSTRY COSTS AND BENEFITS

As just indicated, infant-industry costs are the costs of acquiring technological mastery in newly established activities. The benefits are increases in the productivity with which the economy's resources are employed as a result of technological changes brought about by applying the newly acquired technological mastery. It is often thought that the costs are small, on the grounds that infant industries are typically established through transfers of production technology from abroad. But the costs of acquiring technological mastery include more than the price that is paid for imported technology. They also include what is needed in order to assimilate the technology.

The extent of indigenous effort involved in the assimilation of technology has only recently begun to be appreciated, as case studies have been undertaken of technological changes that have occurred within firms in newly established industries. These case studies have shown that "manufacturing technology is characterized by a considerable element of tacitness, difficulties in imitation and teaching, and uncertainty regarding what modifications will work and what will not" (Nelson 1979, p. 18). That is, important elements of the technology appropriate to a particular situation can be acquired only through effort to adapt existing technological knowledge to that situation. To bring any venture to fruition—in particular, to establish a new production activity—requires a great deal of iterative problem solving and experimentation as the original concept is refined and given practical expression, and this sequential process lasts for as long as changes continue to be made in the operation of the venture. Research at the firm level has demonstrated that this process can continue indefinitely, that it is central to the acquisition of technological mastery, and that it produces technological changes that greatly increase productivity.

Dahlman and Fonseca (1978), for example, examined the technological history of an integrated Brazilian steel producer whose first plant was established under the equivalent of a turnkey contract. In order to increase the plant's production capacity, the firm gradually built up its technological mastery through a carefully managed process of selectively importing technical assistance where needed to supplement its own engineering efforts. As a result, the plant's capacity was more than doubled from its initial nominal rating through a sequence of capacity-stretching technological changes, which took place over seven years. Because these changes required very little additional capital investment and no additions to the work force, they more than doubled the plant's total factor productivity. Moreover, the acquisition of the increased technological mastery initiated by this process eventually enabled the firm to design and execute further additions to its capacity and to sell technical assistance to other steel producers, principally in Brazil, but elsewhere in Latin America as well.

More generally, firms have been found to undertake substantial technological effort in order to achieve a wide variety of technological changes.[2] These changes include stretching capacity through various adaptations (as in the example just cited), breaking bottlenecks in particular processes, improving the use of by-products, extending the life of equipment, making accommodations to changes in raw material sources, and altering the product mix. Some of the firms studied appear to have followed explicit technological strategies aimed at specific long-term objectives; others seem merely to have reacted defensively to changes in their circumstances or to obvious needs to adapt imported technology. In turn, some of the firms have undertaken no appreciable technological ef-

[2] The largest block of firm-level research has been carried out under the auspices of the Regional Program of Studies on Scientific and Technical Development in Latin America, jointly sponsored by the Inter-American Development Bank, the United Nations Economic Commission for Latin America, and the United Nations Development Program. For a review of this research, see Katz (1978) and Chapter 13.

fort and so have experienced no technological change.[3] There have not yet been a sufficient number of case studies to generalize about the determinants of the extent and direction of technological effort by individual firms, though it is apparent that economic forces have an impact, as do characteristics peculiar to individual firms and types of technology.

Most of the technological changes uncovered in this research may be characterized as minor, in the sense that they do not create radically new technologies but rather adapt existing ones. Nonetheless, as shown by the example of the Brazilian steel plant, a sequence of minor technological changes can have a pronounced cumulative effect on productivity. In fact, judged in terms of their impact on the productivity with which the economy's resources are employed, the cumulative sequence of technological changes that has been observed to follow the establishment of a new activity may be more important than the initial establishment of the activity. This possibility has not been explored, as far as I know, but it is consistent with what has been learned about the process of technological change in the industrialized countries.

Studies of major technological changes in these countries have found it useful to distinguish between what Enos (1962) refers to as the *alpha* and *beta* stages. The former includes all of the effort leading to and including the introduction of a radically new technology. The latter covers all of the subsequent minor technological changes undertaken to modify and adapt it. In his own analysis of the development and diffusion of six new petrochemical processes between 1913 and 1943, Enos found that the cumulative reduction in production cost per unit achieved during the beta stage was greater than the initial reduction obtained in the alpha stage. Studies of other major technological changes show them to have followed the same pattern: the economic impact of replacing the old technology by the new is generally less than the cumulative impact of the gradual improvements made after its introduction.

The assimilation of a new technology imported from abroad is a major technological change from the standpoint of a developing economy. The initial transfer is parallel to Enos's alpha stage. The comparable beta stage is the subsequent, gradual improvement in the productivity with which the technology is used. But the significance of the beta stage in assimilating a technology transfer appears to be far greater than is suggested by the analogy. To introduce a radically new technology into the world requires mastery of that technology; in contrast, to import a technology does not require complete mastery of it, certainly not at the outset. Indeed, the

---

[3] For an example and a highly illuminating discussion of why technological effort is not automatically or necessarily undertaken, see Bell *et al.* (1980).

case study research suggests that it is in the beta stage that most of the increase in technological mastery is achieved.

Part of the impact of that increase is reflected in higher productivity using the particular technology, but much of the impact spills over into related activities. For example, the mastery gained in assimilating one technology enables greater indigenous participation in subsequent transfers of related technologies, thereby increasing the effectiveness with which they are assimilated. In more general terms, increased mastery gained through experience with previously introduced technologies contributes to an economy's capacity to undertake independent technological efforts, which may be to replicate or adapt foreign technologies or to create new technologies. Further evidence of the achievement of technological mastery in a number of semiindustrial countries is found in the fact that they are exporting technology to other developing countries, and doing so on an increasingly expanded scale (Lall, 1980).

To summarize the preceding discussion: A number of firms in developing countries have been found to engage in a purposive technological effort to increase productivity and accommodate changing circumstances, an effort that typically takes place in the context of day-to-day operations outside that of formal research and development. Such effort appears to be a primary means of acquiring technological mastery and is the principal reflection of its acquisition. Moreover, such effort has been found to produce large increases in productivity, which translate into substantial reductions in domestic resource costs vis-à-vis foreign-exchange savings (or earnings).[4] Judging from various case studies in addition to that of the Brazilian steel producer previously cited, it may not be exceptional for the unit domestic resource cost of production in a particular type of activity to fall at an annual rate of around 10% during the first five to ten years of production.

Insofar as the cost of infant-industry development is the cost of providing experience needed to gain technological mastery, it is reflected in reductions over time in the unit domestic resource cost of production. In addition to providing valuable insights into how technological mastery is achieved in relation to processes of technological change, the research on technological change at the firm level in developing countries implies that

---

[4] Domestic resource cost per unit of foreign-exchange savings (or earnings) is the appropriate indicator of changes in productivity. Properly measured, it incorporates changes in the use per unit of output of all inputs. In order to determine foreign-exchange savings (or earnings) in net terms, both output and internationally traded inputs are valued at border prices. Factor and other nontraded inputs are valued at shadow prices, which properly reflect relative scarcities. For a lucid exposition of the domestic resource cost indicator, see Bruno (1972).

this cost can be quite high, to the extent that unit domestic resource costs of production may initially be more than twice what can be achieved on the basis of less than a decade of experience. But this research clearly cannot be taken to mean that experience *necessarily* leads to greater technological mastery and hence to increased productivity. Whether experience produces these results depends crucially on the extent and character of directed effort to capitalize upon it by undertaking technological changes, and such effort is by no means automatically forthcoming. Nor should this research be considered to suggest that all infant industries must depend equally on internal experience to gain technological mastery or that all infant industries initially realize levels of productivity that are equally low relative to what can be attained over time.

Infant industries can obtain technological mastery by means other than their own internal experience. Most importantly, mastery acquired in relation to one type of activity can—to varying degrees, depending on the similarity of the underlying technologies—be applied in relation to other types of activities. Thus, as indicated earlier, preceding generations of infant industries provide benefits to succeeding generations by augmenting the economy's technological mastery. The use of existing technological mastery by an infant industry reduces the cost of its development by raising the level of productivity with which it starts. Indeed, the use of know-how derived from previous experience in closely related types of activity sometimes provides immediate technological mastery, making the newly established activity internationally competitive at its inception.

Infant industries can also benefit from foreign technological mastery. But the important lesson from research on technological change at the firm level, as from other research more directly focused on international transfers of technology, is that technological mastery cannot be achieved through the passive reception of technology imports.[5] As stated previously, the capacity to use technology effectively results from the effort that is associated with the assimilation of technological knowledge. Although transfers of technology can assist the process of assimilation, they cannot wholly substitute for it. Nonetheless, through direct foreign investment, infant industries can be developed solely on the basis of foreign technological mastery; domestic assimilation of the technology can then proceed over time by gradually increasing the involvement of local manpower in various aspects of the industry's operation. However, it is an open question whether direct foreign investment provides a generally applicable means of greatly minimizing or even avoiding the costs of infant-

---

[5] For further discussion, see Stewart (1979) or Dahlman and Westphal (1981).

industry development. Case studies of firms created with direct foreign investment have uncovered increases in productivity equally as large as those found in domestic firms. In fact, the Brazilian steel producer discussed previously started as a joint venture involving Japanese interests.

To conclude: There clearly is no basis for expecting the costs of infant-industry development to be the same irrespective of the type of activity,[6] the industrial base that exists at the time of its inception, or the manner in which it is established. The case study research that was just summarized can thus be used only to infer that infant-industry costs may sometimes be quite high. The inference is unfortunately weakened by the fact that none of the case study research with which I am familiar makes clear whether the observed increases in productivity led to international competitiveness or to something more or less than "best practice" levels of productivity. Thus, none of this research has attempted to quantify infant-industry costs directly in terms of the implied level of promotional incentives.

Nevertheless, the research does suggest that, even for an "efficient" infant industry, the domestic resource cost of production—evaluated at prices that properly reflect relative scarcities—might initially be as much as twice the value of the foreign exchange saved (or earned), with up to a decade being required to bring costs down to competitive levels. Assuming that production subsidies are used, the implied starting rate of subsidy in relation to value added is as much as 50%. Alternatively, assuming that protection is the instrument of infant-industry promotion, the rate of effective protection implied at the start of production is as much as 100%.[7] These rates greatly exceed those that are either explicit or implicit in the policy advice derived from the syntheses of cross-country comparative research cited previously.

III. CONVENTIONAL PRESCRIPTIONS VERSUS ACTUAL PRACTICE

Conventional prescriptions about promotional incentives for infant industries concern both the measures to be used and the appropriate magnitude of the incentives. In regard to choosing among measures, there are well-known theoretical arguments against using protection to promote infant industries. Baldwin (1969) provides a particularly compelling state-

---

[6] Because it appears obvious, I do not seek to rationalize the point that the costs of gaining technological mastery are unlikely to be equal for different technologies.

[7] Throughout this chapter, reference is to the rate of effective protection after downward adjustment to remove the effect of currency overvaluation, i.e., to the so-called net rate [see Balassa and associates (1971, pp. 324 ff)].

ment of the theoretical case, by first indicating that the problems of infant industries are not necessarily peculiar to them alone and then demonstrating that protection may easily fail—where "more direct and selective policy measures" would succeed—either to offset these problems or to induce the appropriate behavior.

In fact, many governments do employ direct and selective policy measures to promote infant industries, though the policies appear frequently not to be "first best:" preferred access to credit on preferred terms may be interpreted as a means of overcoming imperfections in capital markets and differences in private and social evaluations of risk; use of public enterprises or the sanctioning of cartels or monopolies, as a means of ensuring that the returns from technological effort are appropriable; industrial planning that includes such things as project identification and preliminary feasibility studies, as a means of subsidizing the acquisition of initial technological information; sharing in the costs of labor training and "research and development," as a means of promoting the direct outlays necessary to achieve socially "optimal" levels of knowledge and training; etc.

Nonetheless, nearly all of the same governments also protect their infant industries against imports. And, whether for practical reasons or otherwise, a number of economists have strongly argued in favor of some degree of infant-industry protection. Balassa (1975), for example, gives a particularly detailed and complete set of policy prescriptions derived from the cross-country comparative research. He argues for modest levels of infant-industry protection and, thus, advocates a two-tier system of protection: uniform effective protection at no more than 10–15% (p. 375) for all manufacturing activities other than infant industries for which "exceptional cases aside, it does not appear likely that rates of effective protection more than double those for mature industries would be warranted on infant industry grounds" (p. 376).[8] In addition, protection to individual infant industries should be temporary, according to a preannounced schedule that declines to the level of the first tier over a period of, say, five to eight years.

In another paper also concerned with deriving policy implications from the empirical evidence, Balassa (1978, p. 50) further argues against "differential [or, deliberately discriminatory] treatment to particular manufacturing industries," and states that exceptions from the two-tier system "should be made only in cases when it is well established that an industry generates substantially greater (lesser) external economies than

[8] Reference here is to "potential" effective protection rates; "realized" rates may, of course, be less in some activities and to that degree need not be uniform.

the average" and "in the form of direct measures [e.g., direct subsidization of research and development] rather than higher rates of protection." As do many other researchers in the field, Balassa (1978, p. 50) bases his argument against "tailor-made" [or, "made-to-measure," in Corden's (1980) terminology] protection on "ignorance as regards interindustry differences in social benefits."

But, not only do most governments protect their infant industries, many appear to rely on protection as the principal instrument of promotion by granting infant industries effective protection at rates well in excess of 20 to 30%. Included among the latter are the governments of some of the most successfully industrializing countries. The effects of initially giving much higher protection to infant industries have by no means always been inimical to successful industrialization. I have not tried to document this observation formally with the care and precision needed, but I am quite certain that it can be supported by the historical experience of at least several countries. For example, the Republic of Korea (or South Korea; hereafter referred to simply as Korea), widely touted for its outward-looking strategy, appears to have used quite high initial rates of infant-industry protection with successful results—success here being indicated by the rapid achievement of international competitiveness by a number of the industries that have been so promoted.[9] High starting levels of protection have also been associated with the successful development of various infant industries in other semiindustrial economies, in Latin America and elsewhere. (It should not go unnoticed that the indicator of success that is being used here is far removed from even a crude assessment of net benefits, but it is the only readily available indicator.)

Additionally, some countries—for example, Korea—appear to have fostered the rapid achievement of international competitiveness by infant industries that, on deliberately discriminatory grounds, were initially granted whatever levels of effective protection were required to secure an adequate market for their output as well as a satisfactory rate of return on investment. (In Korea, "tailor-made" infant-industry protection has typically been afforded via quantitative restrictions on imports, with starting levels of effective protection of as much as 100%.) This obviously does not necessarily imply that differential treatment and high levels of protection are the "optimal" means to promote infant industries; but, signifi-

[9] Evidence of the use of infant-industry protection in Korea is given in Westphal and Kim (1982), which is summarized in Westphal (1978). In turn, there is a variety of circumstantial evidence of its successful results, some of which is given in these papers, albeit not in a form that makes the case as directly as it might be made. Definitive evidence in this regard may be forthcoming from ongoing research by two of my World Bank colleagues, Garry Pursell and Yung W. Rhee, who are engaged in an exhaustive analysis of Korea's export performance.

cantly, it does imply that differential treatment and high levels of protection may effectively be used to promote infant industries.

It is not my purpose to inquire why most governments appear to favor protection as the principal instrument of infant-industry promotion or to argue that they are correct in this respect. Instead, I simply want to establish that infant-industry protection can "work" in the sense of fostering the rapid achievement of internationally competitive levels of productivity. This is admittedly a weak conclusion, for it does not even follow that the benefits of infant-industry protection necessarily exceed the costs in those cases where protection works. Moreover, infant-industry protection has not always worked. As will be shown later, the cross-country comparative research provides a possible explanation for this. And, for governments that choose to rely on protection as the principal instrument of infant-industry promotion, this research also suggests how the conventional prescriptions can be reformulated to take account of the possible need for very high initial rates of effective protection. The reformulation leaves intact the most important element of the two-tier system of protection advocated by Balassa, though it does prescribe highly selective differential treatment to infant industries chosen on deliberately discriminatory grounds.

IV. REFORMULATION OF THE PRESCRIPTION FOR INFANT INDUSTRIES

Hereafter I shall be concerned with the question: How should protection be applied if it is to be the principal instrument of infant-industry promotion? The rest of the chapter thus assumes that protection is the chosen instrument. In addition, following from the previous discussion of the costs of infant-industry development, it will be assumed that the costs of acquiring technological mastery are sometimes sufficiently great to require effective protection at rates close to 100% in order initially to ensure adequate infant-industry incentives. Do these assumptions imply that all or a very large subset of the not-yet-established potential infant industries should simultaneously be given effective protection at such high rates?

The results of the cross-country comparative research clearly indicate that the answer is no. The countries that have followed this approach are those that have opted for an inward-looking strategy of extensive import substitution. These countries by and large have experienced considerably poorer industrial performance than those that have pursued a more outward-looking strategy involving greater selectivity in import substitution and more attention to the promotion of export growth. Nonetheless, as

previously indicated, some of the latter countries—certainly Korea—
have used the same means to promote selectively chosen infant industries
as have been used on a more wholesale basis by the former countries.

The comparative evidence does not definitively establish that the promotion of fewer infant industries at a time results in the more rapid
achievement of international competitiveness. Nor does it demonstrate
that faster achievement of international competitiveness by infant industries is largely responsible for superior industrial performance. Other elements associated with the difference between inward- and outward-looking orientations are almost certainly of greater importance. To cite but
one such element: in company with many other commentators, Díaz Alejandro (1975) maintains that the debilitating effects of the "stop–go" macroeconomic policies stemming from poor overall export achievement are
among the most important factors in explaining the relatively poor performance that seems to attend an inward-looking orientation. But, regardless of its relative contribution, accelerated productivity improvement in
infant industries should, in virtually all plausible circumstances, lead to
faster-paced industrial growth overall.

Thus the real question is whether greater selectivity (i.e., the promotion of fewer infant industries at a time) results in infant industries that
either immediately upon their establishment are more efficient or after
their establishment experience more rapid gains in efficiency, efficiency
being judged by comparing domestic resource costs with foreign-exchange savings (or earnings) at prices that properly reflect relative scarcities. In view of the paucity of empirical evidence having a bearing on this
question, it delimits a priority area for further research, though various
arguments can be made to suggest why the number of infant industries
simultaneously being promoted ought to affect the speed with which efficient production is reached. For example, greater selectivity in import
substitution undoubtedly accompanies the delay in construction of initial
plants until the market has grown to an appropriate size; it permits scarce
investment resources to be concentrated in one or a few sectors at a time
and thereby enables greater exploitation of economies of scale and of the
linkages among closely interrelated activities. Greater selectivity equally
allows the concentration of scarce entrepreneurial resources and technical talent and thereby avoids spreading the agents of technological change
so thinly that no industry has the critical mass that may be necessary to
initiate a sustained process of efficiency improvement through the acquisition of technological mastery. These arguments imply that the warranted degree of selectivity depends on "initial conditions" within a particular country, including the overall size of its economy and the
availability of high-level manpower of various types.

To summarize: absolute protection to infant industries appears to offer a viable means of fostering rapid industrial development, but only if a relatively small number of infant industries are promoted at any one time. "Absolute" protection here means whatever is necessary to secure an adequate market for the industry's output as well as a satisfactory rate of return on investment. Absolute protection reflects the efficiency of the industry; thus, the level of absolute protection is something that can only be determined "endogenously," for example, by basing protection on import quotas (but see the qualification regarding sales for use in the production of exports that appears in Section VI). As regards the precise number of infant industries that it is warranted to promote simultaneously, not much can be said without further research.[10]

V. THE EVIDENCE RECONSIDERED

Absolute, selective infant-industry protection is consistent with low and uniform effective incentives to all other industrial activities.[11] Indeed, the cross-country comparative evidence indicates that applying low, uniform effective incentives to activities that are not being selectively promoted is critically important, because it both avoids capricious discrimination among these activities and benefits export activity. All syntheses of the evidence agree on this fundamental point, as they also concur on the importance of incorporating other incentive measures together with protection in evaluating an industrial policy regime and of distinguishing between the two aspects of the structure of incentives. Of the latter, *industry-bias* refers to the variance of the structure as regards the degree to which differential incentives are given to different activities; *trade-bias*, to the overall effect of the structure as regards the encouragement given to import substitution (or domestic sales) vis-à-vis export activity.

Bhagwati and Srinivasan (1978), for instance, in seeking to answer why "the superior-export-performance countries do better compared with both their own earlier growth performance under restrictive trade regimes and other countries with inferior export performance" (p. 17), observe: "It would appear that the pattern of incentives, and hence of ex-

[10] Observe that the level of aggregation at which industries are delineated matters a great deal in this regard.

[11] "Effective incentives" extends the effective protection concept to incorporate the impact of all incentive policy instruments, including such measures as cash subsidies, preferential interest rates, and direct tax reductions, in addition to protection and whatever other measures are actually employed in a given setting. A quantitative implementation of this concept is found in Balassa's (1971) measure of the effective subsidy rate.

port promotion, is less skewed [with respect to both trade- and industry-bias] in practice than the chaotic pattern of import-substituting incentives under the restrictive trade regimes'' (p. 17); thus, ''one could argue'' that the more ''neutral'' incentives found under the liberalized trade regimes must provide some of the explanation for the greater efficiency of the industrialization process that is empirically associated with the export-promoting strategy (pp. 18–19). By stating the case in such cautious terms (''one could argue''), Bhagwati and Srinivasan apparently seek to distance themselves from those [including Westphal (1978)] who have in fact argued the case. But, even so, Bhagwati and Srinivasan in effect appear to accept its basic validity.

It would nonetheless be wrong to conclude that neutral incentives lead to superior performance, and not merely because industrial incentive policies provide only a part of the explanation for better performance. Equally important is that some degree of industry-bias is warranted on infant-industry grounds. In this respect, the selectivity with which infant industries are promoted appears to be of far greater consequence than the relative magnitude of the effective incentives initially granted to them. This result holds irrespective of the part played by protection in the provision of effective incentives. In turn, as previously indicated, absolute and selective protection to infant industries appears to have been effective in fostering the rapid achievement of international competitiveness in at least one (if not more) of the ''superior-export-performance'' countries. Correspondingly, the single most important policy prescription emanating from past cross-country comparative research on trade policy in relation to industrial strategy concerns, not the treatment of infant industries *per se*, but rather the efficacy of giving low, uniform effective incentives (hence protection also) to all industrial activities except a small number that are being promoted on infant-industry grounds.

This is a paradoxical conclusion. Countries that have followed a strategy of wholesale import substitution have undoubtedly done so, among other reasons, in the expectation that it offers the best means to promote the development of infant industries. Yet, by providing very high effective incentives to a large number of infant industries simultaneously (and indiscriminately), they have failed in effect to provide adequate incentives to any one infant industry relative to all other industrial activities, including the other infants. In fact, the degree of industry-bias in favor of any one infant industry in an inward-looking economy may well be far less than that in an outward-looking economy that has practiced greater selectivity in the promotion of infant industries and provided low, uniform effective incentives to activities that are not being selectively promoted.

Though further research is needed to confirm it, the result appears to be that the infant industries of the inward-looking economies are by and large retarded relative to those of the outward-looking economies. Consequently, simultaneous promotion of a large number of infant industries "from the start" does not necessarily lead over time to greater breadth and depth of industrialization; the sequenced, selective promotion of subsets of these industries may, over the same period of time (which need not be very long), nurture the same industries to greater efficiency.

VI. EXPORT PERFORMANCE

Low levels of effective incentives—in particular, low levels of effective protection to domestic sales—for activities other than those being selectively promoted are also required in order to avoid an antiexport trade-bias and thereby to ensure adequate export performance. Indeed, the improbability of there being adequate export performance if effective incentives discriminate against exports vis-à-vis domestic sales is perhaps the most robust finding from the cross-country comparative research.[12] Owing to the practical difficulty of subsidizing exports at high rates and the likelihood that large subsidies would in any event invite retaliation from overseas, provision of adequate effective incentives to exports relative to domestic sales precludes anything more than low nominal protection to the latter because export subsidies of one kind or another are required to offset whatever protection is given to domestic sales. Again, as a practical matter, satisfactory export performance has also been shown empirically to necessitate access at world prices for tradable inputs used in export production and zero or very low exchange-rate overvaluation, the latter to ensure that the prices of nontradable inputs are appropriate (Balassa, 1978).[13]

The only effective way to guarantee that exporters pay no more than world prices for tradable inputs, including those that they purchase from

---

[12] There is, of course, one exception: namely, an export tax is optimal for commodities facing less than infinitely elastic foreign demand. However, this exception does not apply in practice for the case of most manufactured exports, though the exercise of monopoly power is warranted for products subject to import restrictions overseas.

[13] Unless there is justification for temporary additional incentives to enter new foreign markets, exports ideally should receive incentives equal to those given to domestic sales in relation to value added. However, implementation of the polices indicated here often has the effect of giving higher effective incentives to exports; production for domestic sale does not necessarily benefit from access to tradable inputs at world prices and may not be fully compensated for this by the nominal protection that it receives.

domestic producers, is to give them unrestricted access to and tariff exemptions on imported inputs (together with exemptions from indirect taxes on all inputs).[14] Thus domestic producers of intermediate and capital goods should be denied any protection against imports that would be used in the production of exports.[15] For all industries—including selectively promoted infant industries—protection should be given, if at all, for only that part of their output that is *not* sold for use in the manufacture of exports.[16] To reflect this in the ensuing discussion, it is necessary to introduce several terms: *indirect exports* will denote that part of an industry's output that is sold for use in the manufacture of exports; *non-export-related sales* will denote an industry's total sales less its export-related sales, i.e., less its exports and its indirect exports.

Industries that have attained internationally competitive levels of productivity are responsible for the bulk of export-related sales under the "optimal" industrial incentive policy regime. The prescription that adequate effective incentives be provided to exports relative to domestic sales applies to these industries and is further implemented by providing low nominal protection to their non-export-related sales, something that, in principal, is easily accomplished (given the proper exchange rate) by virtue of their efficiency. In turn, it might be expected that giving absolute protection to non-export-related sales by selectively promoted infant industries would, in the absence of high offsetting subsidies, preclude their exporting, either directly or indirectly (i.e., by sales to exporters). However, certainly in Korea, this is not the case.

Infant industries in Korea begin exporting—both directly and indirectly—at a very early stage, often at once, notwithstanding that these sales do not receive subsidies sufficient to offset the absolute protection

[14] Even with slight protection in the domestic market and low currency overvaluation, unrestricted access to and tariff exemptions on imported inputs lead to a bias in favor of using imported as opposed to domestically produced inputs in the production of exports. To offset this bias, the Korean government provides the full range of its export incentives to producers of inputs supplied to exporters.

[15] Satisfactory export performance clearly requires that exporters be permitted to import capital goods without any restrictions, so that they are able to use the most appropriate production methods. However, this may not preclude levying modest tariff rates on such imports. In most industries, capital charges account for a small proportion of total production cost (particularly in comparison to intermediate input costs). Thus giving capital goods producers modest protection against imports of capital goods by export manufacturers would generally have only minor effects on the cost competitiveness of exports. Such protection may be justified by the unique role of capital goods production in acquiring technological mastery.

[16] This is the qualification to the meaning of absolute protection to which I referred in the concluding paragraph of Section IV.

that is granted only to non-export-related sales.[17] For infant industries in Korea (as elsewhere), effective incentives, including all of those measures for which quantification is possible, are far greater for non-export-related sales than for export-related sales. But many of these industries are either monopolized or operate as cartels, which implies that export-related sales may be explained in terms of discriminating monopoly.

The theory pertaining to discriminating monopoly indicates that non-competitive firms may find it profitable to sell some of their output at world prices even though these prices are less than the prices received for non-export-related sales.[18] The theory states that a monopoly or cartel that sells the same product in several distinct markets will allocate its sales so as to equate marginal revenues across markets, one to another and to the marginal cost of production. As a result, there will be an inverse relation between the prices charged and the demand elasticities in the various markets. On the highly plausible assumption that the elasticity of demand for non-export-related sales is less than the elasticity of demand for export-related sales,[19] the price in the protected segment of the domestic market will exceed the border prices for direct and indirect exports.[20] Thus, assuming that protection enables separating the market for non-export-related sales from the markets for export-related sales and that the separable costs of entering into export activity are negligible, a monopolized or cartelized industry that acts to maximize its total profits may reasonably be expected to engage in export-related sales up to the point where the marginal cost of production equals the marginal revenue from these sales and to adjust its production and non-export-related sales accordingly.

There is evidence that the Korean government has sanctioned non-competitive market structures in order to elicit export-related sales from infant industries.[21] Moreover, the government has at its disposal several

---

[17] Direct exports from selectively promoted infant industries never appear to have accounted for more than at most a quarter of Korea's manufactured exports. (Comparable information is not available with regard to indirect exports.)

[18] For the application of this theory to international trade, see Corden (1967), Pursell and Snape (1973), White (1974), or Caves (1978).

[19] Note that the "small-country assumption," under which the country is assumed to be a price-taker in international markets, implies that export demand is infinitely elastic. On this assumption, the derived demand for indirect exports is also, in essence, infinitely elastic.

[20] Border prices for direct and indirect exports are not equal; respectively, they are the FOB export price and the CIF import price.

[21] The sheltering of non-export-related sales as a means of encouraging export-related sales has not gone unnoticed by other observers of the Korean scene; see, for example, Krueger (1978, Chapter 12).

policy instruments that, in combination, may be used to stimulate direct and indirect exports from noncompetitive infant industries. Chief among these is the export targeting system, which applies to both direct and indirect exports and under which indicative export targets are set jointly by the government and the various exporters' associations (virtually every industry of any consequence has an exporters' association). And subsidies to export-related sales sometimes appear to have been jointly negotiated simultaneously with export targets.[22] But the government's leverage over these industries derives primarily from its control of the banking system and, thereby, of credit rationing. Preferential access to credit for financing of fixed investment as well as working capital has been a potent instrument in the promotion of new industrial activities.

VII. INFANT-INDUSTRY EXPORTS

I do not know for certain whether other governments similarly encourage infant industries to engage in export-related production; it is nonetheless pertinent to analyze the costs and benefits associated with infant-industry exports (here taken to include both direct and indirect exports), for there is evidence that export activity can tremendously hasten the process and greatly reduce the costs of achieving technological mastery. But before turning to this evidence, it is necessary to indicate that there may also be costs. These costs stem from the fact that an infant industry may practice discriminatory pricing such that export-related production leads to an increase in the price at which non-export-related sales are made. Granted that an infant industry experiences a low level of efficiency, cross-subsidization of sales at border prices by non-export-related sales at higher prices is required unless there are offsetting subsidies, as there typically appear not to be.

It is widely appreciated that protection imposes real costs on domestic consumers, at least in the short run. These costs may be increased by the practice of discriminatory pricing on the part of infant industries. Under the usual assumptions, including that economies of scale are not substan-

---

[22] One of these subsidies operates through the "wastage allowance" that is permitted when determining tariff-free raw material imports for use in export-related production. To subsidize direct and indirect exports, this allowance is usually in excess of actual wastage. Because profits can be earned by using the excess imports to produce goods for sale on the protected segment of the domestic market, control over the amount of tariff-free imported inputs allowed in relation to the volume of export-related sales (and hence, implicitly, over the amount of excess imports) gives the government a means to influence the division between export-related and non-export-related sales.

tial in relation to the size of the market for non-export-related sales, export-related production that results from discriminatory pricing can be shown to impose greater costs on domestic consumers: that is, compared with a situation in which the industry produces only for non-export-related sales, production for export-related sales leads to lower non-export-related sales (even though total output rises) and, thereby, to a price for non-export-related sales higher than that which would obtain were there no export-related production.[23]

This result depends critically on the assumption that there are no economies of scale to be exploited through export activity. But most industries are characterized by increasing returns to scale up to a nonnegligible size. And developing countries sometimes appear to establish individual industries well before the market for non-export-related sales has attained the size at which increasing returns are exhausted. In such cases and to the degree that it is associated with larger scale production, even with discriminatory pricing, export activity can reduce unit costs of production and thereby lead to domestic prices lower than those that would prevail in its absence. It is therefore not unreasonable to expect that export-related production, though associated with discriminatory pricing, may sometimes lower the costs imposed on domestic consumers by the promotion of infant industries.

But, this consideration aside, it is very likely that infant-industry exports will yield sizable net benefits because export activity appears to accelerate the acquisition of technological mastery and hence to hasten productivity improvement and efficiency gains. Insofar as they result from inadequate technological mastery (as opposed to the exercise of monopoly power), the costs imposed by infant-industry protection are transitory and diminish over time as technological mastery is acquired. Anything that accelerates the attainment of technological mastery also quickens the pace at which the costs of infant-industry protection decline. Correspondingly, even if infant-industry exports initially impose additional costs, owing to the practice of discriminatory pricing, they can nonetheless yield substantial net benefits over time as a result of their effects leading to more rapid productivity improvement and efficiency gains.

There are various grounds for asserting that export activity must lead infant industries to realize faster technological change. To the degree that efficiency improvement and other forms of technological change derive from experience in production and in capacity expansion, export activity must necessarily lead to greater technological change if it is associated with greater volumes of production over time. But the direct effects of

---

[23] For the reasoning leading to this result, see any of the following references: Corden (1967), Pursell and Snape (1973), White (1974), and Caves (1978).

export activity in both enforcing and fostering technological mastery are undoubtedly the most important. As to enforcing technological mastery, exporting, whether directly or indirectly, requires the ability to meet world standards in matching specifications given by the type and quality of product involved. In turn, as to fostering technological mastery, efforts to maintain and increase penetration in overseas markets lead to the gradual upgrading of product quality. In addition, and perhaps most important, there is clear evidence from Korea as well as from elsewhere that exporters enjoy virtually costless access to a tremendous range of technological improvements that are diffused to them through various activities of the buyers of their exports [see Westphal *et al.* (1981)]. Not only do buyers contribute product designs and help to install or improve methods of quality control, they also contribute to achieving greater efficiency and lower costs through such things as suggesting changes in individual elements of production processes and improvements in the organization of production within plants and in management techniques more generally.

A strong case can thus be made that the promotion of infant-industry exports provides an effective means to hasten the achievement of international competitiveness. The argument may not pertain, however, to exports from infant industries created by establishing subsidiaries of multinational corporations, for there is no assurance that the activities of these firms will contribute to domestic human capital formation or in other ways yield real externalities through the diffusion of technological mastery to local producers. (In this respect it is pertinent to note that most of Korea's exports are produced by wholly local firms.) In any event, further research is needed to verify that export activity induces faster technological progress, as well as to examine whether and how export activity conditions the direction of technological change and to demonstrate that infant-industry exports do indeed result in positive net benefits over time to the economy as a whole.

VIII. CONCLUSION: IMPLICATIONS FOR INDUSTRIAL STRATEGY

The foregoing discussion provides one possible reason why the industrial sector in a country like Korea, following an outward-looking strategy, performs so well; namely, the possibility that its selectively promoted infant industries exhibit superior performance as a result of their export activity. This is by no means to suggest that it is the only possible reason. But, if valid, its relative importance must increase as the time period of analysis lengthens because the number of infant industries that achieve international competitiveness can be expected to increase with the length of the time period, as can the relative contribution of these industries to the economy's total industrial production.

The questions that remain concern how the choice of infant industries for selective promotion affects industrial performance. Does it make any difference which industries are selected; if so, how should infant industries be chosen? The issues involved in the selection of infant industries appear to be far more complex than those relating to how they are to be promoted. Comprehensive discussion of these issues must therefore be left to future research. But several issues do deserve brief discussion here.

Potential infant industries are by no means similar in their need for selective promotion, which is most likely to be warranted where the costs of acquiring technological mastery are quite high. But selective promotion is warranted only if the benefits of attaining technological mastery appear to outweigh the costs, and then only if the necessary technological effort is unlikely to be undertaken by individual producers in the absence of selective promotion. Many potential infant industries can—and therefore should—be established without selective promotion. This is particularly true for those that can benefit from previous experience in closely related types of activity. Indeed, many of the most successful infant industries in Korea have not benefited from selective promotion, including a number of important export industries. Thus it is critically important not to discriminate against the development of infant industries that are not being selectively promoted. This is, in fact, one of the strongest arguments for low, uniform effective incentives—in particular, low and uniform effective protection to non-export-related sales—for all activities except those being selectively promoted. It provides an equally strong argument against the use of quantitative import restrictions (as opposed to tariffs), as well as against the use of various forms of restrictive controls on new undertakings.

It must also be recognized that the choice of infant industries for selective promotion is not something to be done without regard to existing circumstances or without active consultation between government and prospective producers. Choices must be made with a view to existing levels of technological mastery and to the transferability of technological mastery across successive generations of infant industries. A substantial expenditure of effort in searching for and making use of technological and economic information is needed to make sound choices. Much of this effort should be, and often is, undertaken by prospective producers, but their forecasts of costs and benefits require independent appraisal. Furthermore, choices should be subject to revision in the light of additional information and experience gained in successive phases of identification and implementation. Indeed, it is to be expected that some mistakes will be made in the initial identification of particular types of activity as being suitable for selective promotion. It is therefore very important to recognize mistakes and take remedial action quickly, as well as to learn from past mistakes in making future choices. These and many other considerations imply that selective infant-industry promotion requires a high level of competence in its administration. Such competence can be learned, but it is apparent that conditions conducive to its being learned and effectively applied are not present in all countries.

Finally, what importance should be attached to trading possibilities in the choice of infant industries for selective promotion? Even granted that comparative advantage is not innate but is acquired through effort to achieve technological mastery, it does not follow that trading possibilities should be neglected. What is remarkable in this respect about a country like Korea is that infant industries often appear to be selectively promoted on the grounds of their export potential, whereas infants selectively promoted on other grounds are also expected to develop exports, either directly or indirectly. Moreover, the Korean government has, on several occasions, put aside its initial plans for selectively promoting particular industries when additional information indicated that they would not achieve international competitiveness within a reasonable length of time.

These may be the most important distinguishing characteristics of an export-promoting strategy. In turn, as already suggested, the efficacy of this strategy might also be found in the impact of export activity on the speed with which technological mastery is acquired and the pace at which technological change takes place. These observations could provide a large part of the explanation for why such a pronounced difference in growth performance is associated with a strategy of export promotion as contrasted with one of import substitution. But further research is needed to confirm that the dynamics of technological change are indeed central to understanding this difference and that the implications for industrial policy conform to the reformulation of conventional prescriptions previously given.

IX.   POSTSCRIPT

To the degree that the foregoing arguments rest on what I believe underlies Korea's successful industrialization, it is important to give explicit recognition to the fact that Korea's industrialization appears recently to have faltered somewhat. In particular, substantial difficulty has been encountered in developing its most recent set of infant industries, which are in the so-called heavy industries. What I know about the situation suggests that the difficulty stems from the Korean government's initial decision to promote too many infant industries at once and from its subsequent—and newly acquired—reluctance to abandon or radically revise its plans on the basis of information and experience accumulated over time. Thus, Korea's recent problems may provide additional evidence to support the need for selectivity in the promotion of infant industries.

ACKNOWLEDGMENTS

The author is a member of the Economics and Research Staff of the World Bank. The views and interpretations in this chapter are his and should not be attributed to the World Bank, to its affiliated organizations, or to any individual acting in their behalf. The author gratefully acknowledges comments on previous versions of this paper from B. Balassa, J. de Melo, B. de Vries, A. Krueger, S. Teitel, and M. Wolf, as well as from various participants at the Bar-Ilan University symposium.

REFERENCES

Balassa, B. (1971). "Development Strategies in Semi-Industrial Countries: Outline and Methodology (revised)," mimeo. Washington, D.C.: World Bank.

Balassa, B. (1975). "Reforming the System of Incentives in Developing Countries." *World Development* **3**, 365–382.

Balassa, B. (1978). "Export Incentives and Export Performance in Developing Countries: A Comparative Analysis." *Weltwirtschaftliches Archiv* **114**, 24–61.

Balassa, B., and associates (1971). *The Structure of Protection in Developing Countries.* Baltimore, Maryland: Johns Hopkins Press (for the World Bank and the Inter-American Development Bank).

Baldwin, R. E. (1969). "The Case against Infant-Industry Tariff Protection." *Journal of Political Economy* **77**, 295–305.

Bell, M., Scott-Kemmis, D., and Satyarakwit, W. (1980). "Learning and Technical Change in the Development of Manufacturing Industry: A Case Study of a Permanently Infant Enterprise." Science Policy Research Unit Working Paper, unnumbered. Brighton, Great Britain: University of Sussex.

Bhagwati, J. (1978). *Foreign Trade Regimes and Economic Development: Anatomy and Consequences of Exchange Control Regimes.* New York: National Bureau of Economic Research.

Bhagwati, J., and Krueger, A. O. (1973). "Exchange Control, Liberalization and Economic Development." *American Economic Review* **63**, Papers and Proceedings, 419–427.

Bhagwati, J., and Srinivasan, T. N. (1978). "Trade Policy and Development." In *International Economic Policy: Theory and Evidence* (R. Dornbusch and J. A. Frenkel, eds.). Baltimore, Maryland: Johns Hopkins University Press.

Bruno, M. (1972). "Domestic Resource Costs and Effective Protection: Clarification and Synthesis." *Journal of Political Economy* **80**, 16–33.

Caves, R. E. (1978). "International Cartels and Monopolies in International Trade." In *International Economic Policy: Theory and Evidence* (R. Dornbusch and J. A. Frenkel, eds.). Baltimore, Maryland: Johns Hopkins University Press.

Corden, W. M. (1967). "Monopoly, Tariffs, and Subsidies." *Economica, New Series* **34,** 50–58.

Corden, W. M. (1980). "Trade Policies." In *Policies for Industrial Progress in Developing Countries* (J. Cody, H. Hughes, and D. Wall, eds.). London and New York: Oxford University Press (for the World Bank).

Dahlman, C. J., and Fonseca, F. V. (1978). "From Technological Dependence to Technological Development: The Case of the Usiminas Steel Plant in Brazil." IDB/ECLA/UNDP/IDRC Regional Program of Studies on Scientific and Technical Development in Latin America, Working Paper No. 21. Buenos Aires: Economic Commission for Latin America.

Dahlman, C. J., and Westphal, L. E. (1981). "The Meaning of Technological Mastery in Relation to Transfer of Technology." *The Annals of the American Academy of Political and Social Science* **458,** 12–26.

Díaz Alejandro, C. F. (1975). "Trade Policies and Economic Development." In *International Trade and Finance: Frontiers for Research* (P. Kenen, ed.). London and New York, Cambridge University Press.

Enos, J. L. (1962). "Invention and Innovation in the Petroleum Refining Industry." In *The Rate and Direction of Inventive Activity: Economic and Social Factors,* National Bureau of Economic Research. Princeton, New Jersey: Princeton University Press.

Katz, J. (1978). "Technological Change, Economic Development and Intra and Extra Regional Relations in Latin America." IDB/ECLA/UNDP/IDRC Regional Program of Studies on Scientific and Technical Development in Latin America, Working Paper no. 30. Buenos Aires: Economic Commission for Latin America.

Krueger, A. O. (1978). *Foreign Trade Regimes and Economic Development: Liberalization Attempts and Consequences.* New York: National Bureau of Economic Research.

Krueger, A. O. (1980). "Trade Policy as an Input to Development." *American Economic Review* **70,** Papers and Proceedings, 288–292.

Lall, S. (1980). "Developing Countries as Exporters of Industrial Technology." *Research Policy* **9,** 24–52.

Little, I., Scitovsky, T., and Scott, M. (1970). *Industry and Trade in Some Developing Countries: A Comparative Study.* London and New York: Oxford University Press (for the Development Center of the Organization for Economic Co-operation and Development).

Nelson, R. (1979). "Innovation and Economic Development: Theoretical Retrospect and Prospect." IDB/ECLA/UNDP/IDRC Regional Program of Studies on Scientific and Technical Development in Latin America, Working Paper No. 31. Buenos Aires: Economic Commission for Latin America.

Pursell, G. and Snape R. H. (1973). "Economics of Scale, Price Discrimination and Exporting." *Journal of International Economics* **3,** 85–92.

Stewart, F. (1979). "International Technology Transfer: Issues and Policy Options." World Bank Staff Working Paper No. 344. Washington, D.C.: World Bank.

Westphal, L. E. (1978). "The Republic of Korea's Experience and Export-Led Industrial Development." *World Development* **6,** 347–382.

Westphal, L. E., and Kim, K. S. (1982). "Korea." In *Development Strategies in Semi-Industrial Countries* (B. Balassa and associates, eds.). Baltimore, Maryland: Johns Hopkins University Press (for the World Bank).

Westphal, L. E., Rhee, Y. W., and Pursell, G. (1981). "Korean Industrial Competence: Where It Came From." World Bank Staff Working Paper No. 469. Washington, D.C.: World Bank.

White, L. J. (1974). "Industrial Organization and International Trade: Some Theoretical Considerations." *American Economic Review* **64,** 1013–1020.

Development Research Department
The World Bank
Washington, D.C.

Chapter 13

Technology and Economic Development: An Overview of Research Findings

Jorge M. Katz

I. INTRODUCTION

Until recently, the student of development economics was inclined to think that industrial firms opening up in developing countries would normally replicate similar undertakings implanted a few years (or decades) earlier in more mature industrial societies. It was also taken for granted that the industrial organization, i.e., the degree of vertical integration, the patterns of subcontracting, etc., associated with any particular manufacturing venture would also somehow replicate the industrial organization of the original undertaking.

The notion of the "technology shelf" stocked in libraries and archives of universities and manufacturing firms of the developed world and just waiting to be used by any odd LDC was the standard idea with which economists approached the study of the industrialization process of developing nations. Moreover, such a view was frequently complemented by the assumption of an almost complete passiveness on the part of the recipient society, as if no domestic adaptation efforts worth taking into

281

account could be expected to emerge during the process of industrial transfer.[1]

Today very few people would doubt that such a mechanical description of the industrialization process of LDCs leaves more unanswered questions than those that it helps to clarify. This is so for at least two sets of reasons. On the one hand, the argument rests on a highly unrealistic perception of what a technology and its associated industrial organization actually are. On the other hand, such a view of the process does not capture the very large differences that prevail among LDCs in terms of economic maturity in general and, more specifically, in terms of availability of domestic engineering and entrepreneurial skills, which, in a gradual and steady way, adapt the technological and organizational "blueprints" received from abroad to the local environment. We intuitively perceive that such adaptation efforts, when they exist, can end up by giving birth to a new, rather different, and highly idiosyncratic "production function."

Concerning the first of these topics, i.e., the unrealistic description of what a technology and its associated industrial organization are supposed to be, economists have recently began to notice that "to the extent that imitation is not trivial, the idea of an industry-wide production set, the elements of which are accessible to all firms, is a misleading abstraction" and that "to the extent that technologies are not well understood, sharply defined invention possibility sets are a misleading concept and interaction between learning through R&D and learning through experience is an important part of the invention process" (Nelson, 1978).

A similar kind of awareness concerning the rather idiosyncratic nature of the industrial organization fabric likely to develop in association with a given industry and, therefore, the likelihood of there being rather large intercountry differences in this respect is also gaining ground in the profession. After studying the Taiwanese machine-tool industry, Amsden (1977) wrote: "A striking feature of the structure of machine-tool production in Taiwan was, and continues to be, a low degree of specialization and a high degree of vertical integration. The all-purpose nature of operations in the smaller firms has been very pronounced. Larger firms have engaged in even more activities which are ancillary to the production of

---

[1] Curiously enough, such basic theoretical background was common to both the neoclassical and the "dependency" school. For either one of them, "technology" was something "produced" by developed industrial nations and all that was left to the developing countries was a "correct" or "incorrect" selection and negotiation for its purchase. It is now increasingly clear that both schools of thought missed a very important link in the story, i.e., the "domestic component" involved in each and every action related to the incorporation of new technical knowledge in any given industry or society. One of the main lessons gained from our recent research is that the utilization of technical knowledge normally carries with it the need for the generation of additional technical knowledge.

machine-tools. In industrialized countries such activities would typically be sub-contracted" (Amsden, 1977).

In other words, the standard textbook notion of the production function as an exogenously given, completely specified, easily duplicatable, and internationally transferable set of engineering and organizational rules and "blueprints" that tends to be rather similar across countries is now recognized to be an oversimplified tool of economic analysis that fares rather badly when we begin to explore the actual evolution of industrial production in any given society.

As far as the second topic is concerned, i.e., the differences in industrial and technological achievements among LDCs, it is becoming increasingly apparent that, *pari passu,* with the expansion of the share and complexity of the manufacturing sector, a group of developing countries—now frequently referred to as the NICs (new industrializing countries)—is attaining standards of industrial and technological sophistication that set them quite apart from the LDC group in general. Some of these countries have, in recent years, experienced a dramatic increase in their exports of manufactures—many of them of a fairly complex technological nature—and are nowadays profiting from their initial significant successes as exporters of technology under the form of licenses, engineering services, sales of complete plants through turnkey operations, etc.[2]

As in other fields of contemporary economics, some new thinking and a comprehensive body of new, hard empirical evidence seem to be strongly needed in this field if we are to make further progress. In particular, the theory of innovation has yet to come to grips with the fact that important localized knowledge creation efforts are carried out in a number of developing countries. The rate and nature of such technological efforts as well as the role of micro and macro variables in shaping entrepreneurial behavior in this respect should clearly receive priority in any research agenda concerned with long-term growth.[3] On the other hand, the theory of economic development needs to incorporate the fact that some of the developing nations have in the postwar period built up fairly strong industrial sectors, many of which are nowadays reducing the technological gap that separated them from common international practices

---

[2] Recent papers concerning technological exports by some of the developing nations have shown countries with so different an import-substitution strategy as Argentina, Korea, Taiwan, and India attaining very impressive performances in this respect. See Katz and Ablin (1976), Rhee and Westphal (1978), and Lall (1979).

[3] Nelson and Winter are breaking new and important ground in this territory on the basis of an ongoing research program that has already produced most interesting results. See, for example, Nelson and Winter (1977a, p. 36) and also Nelson and Winter (1977b).

and are gradually gaining competitiveness in the world trade scenario, not just on the basis of lower wages, but also on the basis of an indigenously generated and/or locally adapted technology. The old infant-industry argument as well as the whole debate concerning protection and the notion of dynamic comparative advantages seem to be calling for a fresh and careful reexamination. As in the previous case, this is a subject that has received insufficient attention in recent years.[4]

The purpose of this chapter is to explore two different sets of questions related to the technological performance of some of the largest Latin American countries. On the one hand, we examine whether or not manufacturing firms in LDCs employ a technology—or production function—that closely resembles the one employed by firms producing similar commodities in more developed industrial societies. On the other hand, we pose a somewhat similar question concerning, not the technology itself, but its changes through time, i.e., the rate of technical progress. Is there any reason to believe that the nature of technological change incorporated by firms or industries in LDCs somehow replicates that incorporated by comparable firms and industries in more mature societies?

In attempting to answer then two questions, we expect to throw some light on various aspects of the theory of technological change in developing nations and on the broader fields of industrialization, trade, and development.

During our examination of these questions, we shall make extensive use of some of the research findings obtained in the course of a five-year-long exploration into the economics of technological change carried out in Latin America by a team of economists and engineers. Individual firm, as well as industrywide and macro, studies were carried out in several Latin American countries in order to study: the rate, nature, determinants, and consequences of the observed technological changes incorporated by selected firms and industries through time. Some of the collected evidence comprises the empirical ground underlying this chapter.

Section II considers the first of the previously mentioned questions. Conventional theory has taken for granted that the answer is an easy one, i.e., that the technological package employed by manufacturing firms in LDCs constitutes a mere replica of the technical and organizational routines used at some prior point in history by industrial firms in developed nations. We shall argue throughout this chapter that, in most real-life situations, such a view grossly oversimplifies the case and constitutes a

---

[4] It is interesting to observe how little attention the infant-industry argument has received in all of the large-scale research efforts carried out during the sixties by Little, Scitovsky, Balassa, and others. A well-stated critique of such neglect is put forward by Westphal in Chapter 12.

wrong description of the manufacturing world. Production functions significantly differ among firms and countries, turning productivity comparisons, as well as the growth accounting exercises, into rather misleading simplifications of what is actually going on.

In what sense are we saying that "production functions" are significantly different? Assume that we define *technology* in a rather broad sense to include all bits and pieces of technical knowledge or information indicating how to carry out a given economic activity. Such a package of technical knowledge and information is related to at least three different aspects of the activity: (a) the design or specification of the product or service, (b) the production process, or basic technology, to be employed, and (c) the industrial organization, i.e., the degree of vertical integration, patterns of subcontracting, etc., most convenient for accomplishing the purpose.[5]

For reasons that are examined in Section II and that have to do, among other things, with the relative size of the market, with the availability (or lack of) a network of specialized subcontractors, with relative factor prices, with government-induced market distortions, etc., manufacturing firms in LDCs normally employ a technology that is substantially different from the one employed by a firm producing a somewhat similar product in a developed society. The observed differences become all the more significant, not in relation to the product design itself, but with respect to the other two items of the stated trilogy, i.e., the production process and the way production is organized. "Batchlike" discontinuous processes of varying, but relatively low, degrees of automation, a high degree of vertical integration, a rather low level of subcontracting, etc., are all ubiquitous features of the Latin American manufacturing scenario. Contrariwise, continuous-flow process of a much more highly automated nature, low vertical integration, a great deal more specialization and subcontracting, etc., immediately catch the eye when one examines comparable firms and industries in the United States, Europe, or Japan. To put it succinctly: the whole "mode of production" is significantly different.

After stressing the idiosyncratic nature of manufacturing technology in an LDC environment and the rather important differences between such technology and the one employed by comparable firms in more de-

[5] When dealing with the concept of technology, economists normally think in terms of item (b), wrongly omitting the other two items. Pack (Chapter 16) shows that the lion's share of productivity differentials between comparable industrial firms in developed and less developed countries is not to be explained by differences relating to the basic production process but rather by major differences in item (c), i.e., industrial organization technology. Unfortunately, the profession has very little to say in this respect.

veloped nations, Section III proceeds to show that technical change in an LDC industrial scenario is also bound to be significantly different from the one incorporated by industrial firms in more mature societies. On the one hand, we should expect this to be so as a consequence of the observed differences concerning the production function itself. On the other hand, LDCs are characterized by peculiar features of their own, such as unduly high rates of tariff protection, acute raw material scarcities, market imperfections, and bottlenecks affecting the physical design of manufacturing plants and industrial complexes, that continuously flash specific signals to the industrial entrepreneurs. Such signals induce particular and idiosyncratic patterns of technological response on the part of manufacturing firms. Summarizing, in a very precise manner, many of the research findings obtained during the course of our research, Freeman wrote:

> [Various] empirical studies of technical change in industry [he is refering to those carried out as part of the IDB/ECLA/UNDP Regional Programme of Research in Science and Technology] have demonstrated conclusively that firms do respond to changes in their environment by redirecting their efforts at technical change. . . . It was discovered that the type of technical change which was sought and introduced varied both with major changes in factor costs and with changes in the competitive environment. When one plant was the sole supplier the emphasis was on speed of output, but, when competitors entered the market and surplus capacity appeared, the emphasis changed to product quality. Changes in wage costs, material costs, etc. similarly led to re-direction and change of emphasis in technical effort. Such a response is more likely when the change is dramatic and therefore clearly perceived (Freeman, 1978).

In each one of the previously mentioned areas, product design, process engineering, and industrial organization, the firm will normally search for incremental units of technical knowledge or information with which to upgrade its daily operation. Such technological searches will not, however, be exogenously determined as most neoclassical growth models tend to assume, neither will they follow routes identical to the technological search processes that take place in plants in a developed-country environment. Rather, the specificity of each economic setup will make a definite imprint of its own upon the technological efforts carried out at the firm level. We argue in Section III that the technological path of a given industrial plant is evolutionary in nature and should be studied as a time-dimensional process, not as a state or condition. The rate and nature of technical change, as well as the type of innovations and productivity advances to be sought by a given enterprise at a certain point of time, strongly depend on: (a) strictly microeconomic forces emerging from the specific history of such firm; (b) market variables describing the competitive environment in which the firm operates; (c) macroeconomic forces characterizing the broad parameters of the system in which both the firm and industry are inmersed, and finally (d) the evolution of the knowledge frontier, or "state of the art," at a worldwide level.

II. FIRMS, TECHNOLOGY, AND INDUSTRIAL ORGANIZATION IN DCs AND LDCs

Let us start with a rather simple question: Is there any reason to believe that a "representative" firm in any given branch of manufacturing production in an LDC utilizes a technology that somehow replicates the one employed by a comparable firm in a mature industrial society? Or, in other words, is there any a priori reason to accept that manufacturing firms producing somewhat comparable goods in DCs and LDCs tend to use different factor intensities of a similar technology?

Although observed differences in production functions between firms in DCs and LDCs tend to be more significant in some branches of manufacturing than in others—this seems to be so, for example, in mechanical engineering industries as compared with process industries—we shall argue in this section that the answer to our question is negative across the industrial spectrum. Indeed, production functions significantly differ between firms, on the one hand, for reasons inherent in the notion of technology itself as a package of technical information and, on the other hand, for circumstances emerging from the specificity of each particular social and physical environment in which a given technology is brought into operation. Let us examine these two sets of reasons separately.

A. Irreplicability of the Technical Knowledge Package

The first major reason why we cannot realistically expect any given manufacturing firm to have access to a package of technical information that is an exact replica of a similar package previously employed by somebody else comes from the notion of knowledge itself as a factor of production. Unlike other factors, this one is frequently incompletely specified, i.e., it leaves room for ad hoc solutions and unforeseen procedures not completely described *ex ante*. As a consequence of this condition, it cannot be entirely replicated. Neither can it be easily transferred. Knowledge accumulated through experience becomes an important part of the technical information package in any identifiable technology.

In order to explore this point further, we shall briefly deal with a central concept of production theory, i.e., that of the production possibility set. This concept and its subset of efficient elements, the production function, constitute one of the pillars upon which the theory of the firm has been constructed.

The production possibility set constitutes the domain of all the production activities that are technically feasible for a given producer. As Nelson and Winter put it: "In the conventional production set the boundary is the abyss of the unknown and the impossible."[6] The difference between what is "known" and what is "technically possible," requires further examination.

Koopmans, Debreu, and others have modeled the production set in terms of activities. An activity is "a way of doing things," each one subject to fixed input–output coefficients, perfect divisibility, and constant returns to scale. Intuitively, we observe that an implicit assumption underlying the notion of an activity is that each one is related to a certain body of knowledge or information, that is, to a certain routine or program, that indicates stepwise how the activity is to be performed. Thus, underlying the notion of the production possibility set is the amount of knowledge or technical information economic agents have at their disposal.[7] Such information will determine: (a) the subset of activities known to the agents and (b) the routine or program to perform it.

The problem with this specification of the production possibility set is that it is much too clean. When technical knowledge or information is taken as yet another input to the production process, it does not seem realistic to specify such input in a dichotomous way, either as being there or not being there altogether. Rather, it seems only natural to allow for learning and upgrading, that is, for a gradual and steady increment in the knowledge base inherent to any activity in the set—"for a process, not a condition," as Hirschleifer (1973) put it. Nelson and Winter quite correctly argue that such a sharp distinction between the technically possible

---

[6] Nelson and Winter (1980d). Throughout this section, I shall draw rather heavily on this (to my knowledge) unpublished paper. I thank the authors for giving me access to an early version of this most stimulating monograph.

[7] The notion of the production set admits of the creation of new technology. It does so, however, in a rather peculiar form. Research and development has to be thought of as one more activity belonging to the set. For such purpose, we have to assume that "there is a discrete moment of time when R&D is completed and it springs forth like Minerva, into the production set. Unless this is assumed the sharpness of the model is broken" (Nelson and Winter, 1980d). There are obvious reasons to be worried with such a description of the knowledge creation process as a rather dichotomous phenomenon in which the gradual resolution of uncertainty and successive levels of accomplishment are essentially absent.

and impossible activities constitutes a legacy of modeling relatively static situations, i.e., optimal terminal points (Nelson and Winter, 1977a,b).

The basic limitation of conventional theory in handling production situations in which technical knowledge and information become part of the story can now be seen intuitively. The boundaries of the production set cannot be taken as sharp and clean. Rather, they should be thought of as blurred and uncertain. Activities might be known to a greater or lesser extent, depending on the complexity and sharpness of specification of the body of knowledge itself, as well as on the initial knowledge base of the economic agent, its learning efforts, and the time span along which such efforts have been taking place.

Once we leave behind the neat distinction between the technically possible and not possible activities, we venture into a world in which there are differences, small or large, in the quantity and quality of the package of technical information commanded by any two procedures performing the same activity, i.e., firms can be thought of as accomplishing an essentially comparable job but following different engineering routines. Each of the routines will have an unspecified component of ad hoc technical knowledge "produced" by its user in order to fulfill all those steps of the routine that were not completely specified *ex ante*.

Consider now a second set of reasons on account of which production functions in DCs and LDCs are likely to be significantly different. These relate to environmental differences that make it technologically impossible or economically unprofitable to replicate in an LDC environment the technological package of a more mature industrial society.

B. Differences in Environmental and Operating Conditions between Developed and Less Developed Countries

1. PLANT SIZE AND CHOICE OF TECHNIQUE

With very few exceptions, most industrial firms operating in LDCs are just a tiny fraction, between 1 and 10%, of the size of their counterparts in developed nations. For example, a "representative" Latin American firm producing automobiles could turn out anywhere between 20,000 and 100,000 units per annum. A machine-tool manufacturer would produce from 100 to 500 lathes per year, whereas a petrochemical plant producing polyethylene would produce anywhere between 10,000 and 120,000 tons per annum.[8] Only in recent years have some Brazilian firms seemed to be moving up in order to reach internationally competitive scales. (This is, however, certainly more the exception than the rule throughout the re-

[8] Evidence of this can be obtained from various sources. See, for example, Baranson (1971), Watanabe (1979), and Mitra (1979).

gion.) Industrial firms producing similar commodities in mature industrial societies would normally be ten (or more) times larger.

We shall argue here that such differences in plant size induce many differences in the way in which products are actually produced. The same point has been made recently by Morley and Smith (1979) after studying a sample of Brazilian manufacturing firms: "When we looked closely at the way products are actually produced we could see why production methods may be insensitive to relative factor prices. It seems clear that economies of scale and technical considerations dominate technical choice almost regardless of factor prices."

Continuous-flow, high automated technologies that would normally be the technology of choice for a new industrial undertaking in a developed country environment are frequently ruled out from the start by firms operating in LDCs for at least two different reasons. First, such technologies normally involve a rate of output that is well beyond the size of the local market. Furthermore, such plants frequently embody a level of operational and maintenance complexity that cannot be handled by the locally available engineering and technical skills.

Instead, LDC's manufacturing firms usually settle for a discontinuous technology and for a much lower degree of automation than that adopted by DCs' firms. The choice of a discontinuous, not highly automated technology certainly has a major impact upon such aspects as (1) plant layout, (2) type, cost, etc., of equipment and machinery to be installed, (3) overall organization of production (degree and patterns of subcontracting, etc.), and (4) overall number of workers, as well as the proportion of direct to indirect labor that it will be economic to employ. Such a choice will also affect the size of the economies of scale that can eventually be captured by the firm as well as the rate and nature of the various technological changes that the manufacturing plant can incorporate through time.

In other words, not only will the physical configuration of the plant be rather different, but also the sources of efficiency growth (possibilities for capital–labor substitution, economies of scale, rate and nature of technical progress, etc.) will be dramatically at variance with those underlying the operation of a countinuous-flow manufacturing unit.

In spite of the fact that almost any dichotomous classificatory scheme (continuous versus discontinuous processes, automated versus nonautomated technologies, etc.) is bound to create some difficulties when we use it to examine a distribution that, in fact, is organized along a continuum, we shall develop the argument of this section by comparing two polar cases: on the one hand, that of a highly automated, continuous-flow technology and, on the other hand, the alternative option of a discontinuous, less automated process for the production of a comparable commodity.

Obviously, most real-life situations are not as clear cut as the two extreme options to be examined here. Discontinuous technologies in which partial sections of the plant have been transformed for continuous operation or manufacturing plants that produce a similar commodity with very different degrees of automation have been found in our exploration of the Latin American manufacturing scenario. However, and for the sake of argument, we shall examine here two "stylized" extreme situations. Consider first the case of a continuous-flow production unit.

Manufacturing plants of this sort frequently are *product-specific,* i.e., their "layout" is organized along a sequence or order imposed by the various technical transformations that have to be carried out for the purpose of producing a given product. The sequence of technical transformations is always the same, and this is what decides the factory "layout." In manufacturing units of this sort, the rate of output is usually rather large, as it frequently happens that continuous-flow technologies are employed to produce massively commercialized products. Common features of a plant of this kind are:

(1) The preproduction planning of the "line" is extremely detailed and complete. There is low *expost* flexibility concerning both the product design and the production process.

(2) The activities and technical transformations systematically proceed along a "direct" route, thus minimizing delays and downtime. The production cycle is minimized as the production "line" is balanced and activities are individually coordinated to the level of the micromovement.

(3) The handling of raw materials and stocks of work in progress is also minimized. Inventories as well as storage spaces have to be balanced in conjunction with the overall production "line."

(4) The product tends to be highly normalized and most of the equipment has a rather specific nature, i.e., is specially designed to fulfill particular tasks or combination of tasks.

(5) There is relatively little "on-the-job decision making," thus *direct* labor skills and supervisory requirements are relatively less important than in discontinuous production units.

In spite of its various potential advantages, in particular concerning economies of scale and minimum production cycle, a continuous-flow production technology is not always necessarily the cheapest available way of production. On the one hand, plants of this sort normally make relatively large investment outlays. Unit capital costs tend to be rather large if the equipment is less than fully utilized. On the other hand, a stop anywhere along the "line" can bring the whole line to a halt; thus, unplanned delays tend to be rather expensive. For both reasons, a continuous-flow technology can be far from economic in situations in which a steady rate of full-capacity utilization is not guaranteed.

In contrast, discontinous process plants are very different indeed. The plant "layout" is organized in "shops" in which the order is flexible and varies as the situation requires. Such factories are frequently involved in the production of goods or services in small runs or in response to individual orders. Different products can be simultaneously produced. In this setup, the product proceeds from one "shop" to the next moving around the factory, i.e., the plant is not designed following the successive technical transformations demanded by the product but rather by "groups" of somewhat similar machines. Plants of this sort have some of the following features in common:

(1)   The capital equipment is less expensive and of a more general nature than that required by a continuous-flow technology. There is less need for "backup" equipment (which is normally kept idle for replacement purposes in continous-flow production units).

(2)   There is a great deal of flexibility in the way in which a given job is performed. Given that all of the machines of a certain type can perform a particular task, the actual work load is assigned to whatever machine happens to be available. Also, similar transformations can be performed with different machines.

(3)   The transport of raw materials, components, subassemblies, etc., between "shops" becomes an important part of the production process. It is, also, a significant source of bottlenecks, waiting periods, and other forms of slack. The production cycle is not minimized and there is ample room for actually reducing it by carefully rearranging the physical distribution of jobs in the plant.

(4)   Given that the product is not highly standardized, on-the-job decision making is relatively important. "Custom-ordered" changes are normally admitted. Workers' skills in setting up the machines, preparing jigs and tools for the job, etc., and in actually carrying out the task become very important indeed. The same tends to be true of supervisory skills.

From both these descriptions we notice that continuous and discontinuous technologies correspond to very different "production functions." This is so regardless of the actual degree of automation embodied in a given plant design. In either case, a production unit can be designed to embody a relatively high or relatively low degree of automation, depending on the specific conditions of a given environment, i.e., relative factor prices, availability of electronic process control skills, etc. We can, however, intuitively perceive that both the physical configurations and the *modus operandi* of continuous and discontinuous technologies will differ quite substantially, independently of the degree of automation.

We can now close this section by briefly summarizing its central point. Owing to large differences in market size, manufacturing firms operating in LDCs frequently tend to operate on the basis of discontinuous-flow technologies and a relatively low degree of automation. Consequently, both the physical configuration of the plant—its layout, the number and nature of the machines actually employed, etc.—as well as the *modus operandi* of the firm—its forms of industrial organization, patterns of subcontracting, etc.—will be significantly different from those employed by firms in DCs operating on the basis of continuous-flow manufacturing units. It is rather misleading to think that both techniques are different factor intensities of a similar production function. A fairly different "mode of production" is embodied in each one of them and straightforward comparisons between them should be handled with care.

2. ROUNDABOUTNESS, SKILLS, AND FURTHER TECHNOLOGICAL DIFFERENCES BETWEEN DEVELOPED AND LESS DEVELOPED COUNTRIES

Throughout the previous section we argued that, owing to large differences in size, we should a priori expect firms in developed and less developed countries to operate with different production functions, not just with different techniques emerging from the same function, i.e., different factor intensities of a given technology.

Thus far we have looked at one possible source of differences among manufacturing firms in DCs and LDCs: size. We shall now examine yet another set of reasons why the technological *modus operandi* of manufacturing firms in DCs and LDCs are likely to be significantly different. We refer to the degree of vertical integration and to the extent and nature of subcontracting employed in either case.

The empirical evidence on this account is scanty but rather conclusive. It shows that: (1) Manufacturing firms in LDCs make much less use of subcontracting than their counterparts in DCs, i.e., they choose to operate with a much higher degree of vertical integration than that normally chosen by comparable firms in DCs.[9] (2) The degree of subcontracting

---

[9] Besides Amsden's (1977) research results, which illuminate this point in relation to the Taiwanese machine-tool industry, a similar pattern of limited subcontracting in the capital goods industries in developing countries is discussed by Pack in Chapter 16. Identical results have been found in various studies carried out in Latin America and Asia. See, for example, Castaño *et al.* (1980) and Watanabe (1979).

seems to increase over time, but not at a very fast pace.[10] On the contrary, the time span needed for a reasonably efficient network of subcontractors to emerge and develop in any particular branch of manufacturing seems to take the better part of two (or even three) decades. In this respect, the experience of LDCs does not seem to be significantly different from the earlier ones of England, the United States, and, more recently, Japan [e.g., Allen (1970)].

Subcontractors tend to develop from large industrial firms. Former technicians and workers of large manufacturing firms frequently become independent subcontractors for such companies, using second-hand equipment and technology obtained from them.[11]

So much for the empirical evidence. At the conceptual level, the subject of subcontracting, which is, of course, central to the classical view of the long-term development process has not received a great deal of attention in the modern literature. In principle, it is to be expected that a given entrepreneur will not engage in subcontracting unless the marginal cost of internal coordination of production exceeds the marginal cost of external coordination minus the difference between the marginal cost of internal and external production. In other words, the difference in production costs due to external, rather than internal, production should exceed the (presumably) higher cost of coordinating external suppliers for the entrepreneur to be attracted by the prospect of subcontracting. The trouble with this general formulation of the problem is that is does not carry us very far in the understanding of the actual problems underlying the subcontracting decision.

Classical economics teaches us that the cost of external production should, in principle, be lower than that of internal supply in all those cases in which a market is large enough to take advantage of the benefits of specialization and dynamic economies of scale. Clearly, this constitutes the core of Adam Smith's (1776) contention that the degree of "roundaboutness" employed in production is a direct reflection of the size of the market. Large enough markets permit further division of labor and this, in turn, allows for a group of complex processes to be tranformed into a succession of simpler processes, some of which lend themselves to the use of specialized machinery. Such machinery is also an outcome of the expansion of the market in as much as the existence of a large market induces innovative efforts in the development of new capital goods. In Smith we find not just economies of scale in the static sense but, rather, a mixture of

---

[10] Research now in progress in the metalworking industries of Argentina, Brazil, Venezuela, etc., indicates that the subject of subcontracting is becoming important. In this respect, see Castaño *et al.* (1980).

[11] An interesting example of this can be seen in Katz *et al.* (1978).

economies of scale and "learning by doing," in a dynamic framework. His view of the problem becomes clear when he writes:

> This great increase in the quantity of work, which, in consequence of the division of labour, the same number of people are capable of performing, is owing to three different circumstances; first, to the increase in dexterity in every particular workman; secondly, to the saving of time which is commonly lost in passing from one species of work to another; and lastly, to the invention of a great number of machines which facilitate and abridge labour and enable one man to do the work of many (p. 7).

Thus, we notice that in the classical formulation the division of labor, resulting from the expansion of the market brings about an enhancement of skills, a savings of time, and the development and introduction of specialized machinery.

For various reasons, this formulation of the problem does not seem to convey the complete story. The available evidence seems to indicate that it is not exclusively on the basis of straightforward cost differentials that entrepreneurs make decisions concerning subcontracting. Rather, questions of quality of supply (indeed, of *stability* of quality standards) as well as considerations of uncertainty in delivery, fare very highly indeed among the reasons frequently quoted by large industrial firms in LDCs for maintaining a high rate of vertical integration, i.e., a low level of subcontracting.[12]

Now, quality standards and reliability are not easily obtained in societies in which engineering and entrepreneurial skills are in very short supply. The fact that such talents require a rather long gestation period probably explains why even in those few LDCs with large enough markets of their own, such as Brazil or India, the growth of subcontractors has proceeded at a very low pace, nowhere reaching levels comparable to those prevailing in mature industrial societies.

Comparing India and Japan and trying to explain why subcontracting has not proceeded at a comparable pace, Baranson (1967, pp. 68–69) wrote:

---

[12] Questions of quality and uncertainty of supply could be explicitly incorporated into a probabilistic model comparing the expected cost of internal with the external supply, this last weighted by the probability of failure due to low quality and by the likelihood of subcontractors not meeting required deadlines.

Exploring the magnitude and problems of subcontracting in the Philippine automobile industry, Watanabe recently wrote: "Anywhere in the developing world, and even in industrialized countries, parent firms in subcontracting almost invariably face three major problems: high cost of production, inadequate quality of work and unreliable delivery" (Watanabe, 1979).

The following are some of the outstanding reasons on account of which India has not been able to develop an infrastructure of subcontractors comparable to the Japanese one:

    a.   Shortage of engineers and technicians experienced at adapting techniques to the available equipment and raw materials.

    b.   Lack of skilled personnel capable of operating the equipment and of maintaining minimum standards of industrial discipline.

    c.   Absence of an industrial organization flexible enough to make room for the efficient utilization of small firms as complementary to modern industrial complexes.

    d.   Limited size of the local market and small rates of growth.

Thus, coming now full circle from the classical argument, we notice that, in spite of the fact that skills and industrial organization are bound to improve with the division of labor and the expansion of the market, their initial shortage might very well constitute a major barrier to the further division of labor. In other words, even if in the long-run engineering and entrepreneurial skills could improve *pari passu* with the expansion of the market, in shorter periods of time—and here we might well be speaking of a few decades—lack of certain skills may block the expansion of a suitable network of subcontractors and therefore foreclose the possiblity of large manufacturing firms enjoying economies of scale and specialization comparable to those normally enjoyed by industrial firms in developed nations.

Summarizing, two major sets of reasons force industrial firms in LDCs to operate with a much higher degree of vertical integration, i.e., with a lower degree of subcontracting, than the one normally chosen by comparable firms in DCs: (a) smallness of the domestic market and (b) structural deficiencies in the supply of engineering and entrepreneurial skills. For both reasons, manufacturing firms in LDCs are likely to have both a manufacturing and an organizational technology that will be significantly different from the one employed by comparable firms in DCs.

3.   Other Sources of Technological Differences between Developed and Less Developed Countries

Size and initial lack of qualified subcontractors are two of the main reasons why manufacturing firms in LDCs normally find it technologically impossible and economically unprofitable to replicate the technology employed by firms in DCs. They are by no means the only explanations that can be found of the fact that firms in LDCs normally operate on the basis of a highly idiosyncratic technological package, clearly different from the one employed by comparable firms in more advanced industrial societies.

Other explanations, some of them of the sort that can be derived from conventional price theory, can be found as well. Let us briefly consider them.

Substitution Effects

Various substitution effects play an active role in inducing firms in LDC's to adopt different production techniques than those normally employed in more developed countries. Substitution effects could result from policy-induced government intervention, which can be a major source of the relative price distortions that ultimately influence technological choice, or from an "autonomous" cause, i.e., derived from differences in resource endowments or other such "natural" sources.

Under the heading of "policy-induced" substitution effects, we include all those forms of substitution among different types of machinery and/or raw materials, particularly those that result from tariffs on imported goods, quotas, distorted exchange rates, outright prohibition of access to certain imputs, etc., all of which have been shown to affect seriously the choice of technique by Latin American industrial firms.[13]

As far as "autonomous" factor substitition is concerned, relative price differentials between capital and labor are probably the major source of technological differences between firms in LDCs and DCs that needs to be taken into account.[14]

A much lower degree of automation, implying more universal machines, manual rather than electronic process control devices, etc., more labor-intensive transportation within the plant, less sophisticated maintenance technology, and so on are all standard features of Latin American manufacturing industries. The available empirical evidence clearly shows that the choice of technique has been, and still is, highly sensitive to factor price differentials.

Physical Bottlenecks and Other Technical Constraints

The literature of recent years, from Rosenberg (1960, 1978) to David (1975) and including various industry and individual plant studies carried out in Latin America,[15] tends to show that a given original engineering de-

---

[13] See, in this respect Canitrot (1977), and Teitel (1981). Various case studies of the IDB/ECLA/UNDP Program present empirical evidence confirming the fact that the choice of technique seems to reflect factor price differentials between countries; among them Lucángeli and Fidel (1978); Pearson (1976); and Sercovich (1978).

[14] This is, of course, the standard case examined by Sen in his famous book *Choice of Techniques* (Sen, 1960).

[15] For an introductory general survey, see Katz (1978) and Lucángeli and Cibotti (1980).

sign places a set of technical constraints upon potential expansions and plant modernization schemes. The examples single out steel mills and petrochemical complexes as particular cases in which unbalanced sectional expansions as well as previous technical choices seriously affect the range of technical options from which manufacturing firms have to choose.

We can now close this section by briefly restating its central point. Size, lack of subcontractors, policy-induced and autonomous substitution effects, physical bottlenecks emerging from prior technological history, etc., all seem to play a role in making DCs' technological package, i.e., product designs, production processes, and patterns of industrial organization, far from replicable in LDCs' environments. Rather, manufacturing firms in LDCs built up their operations on the basis of highly idiosyncratic technologies that reflect the nature and intensity of local market imperfections, prevailing physical scarcities, factor price differentials, degree of development of the network of subcontractors, size of the market, etc. Rather than assuming identical production functions across countries, it becomes necessary to continue exploring the actual production conditions of individual societies to better explain the international productivity differentials.

Having looked at choice of technique, let us now turn to changes of technique through time, i.e., technical progress.

III. THE PRODUCTION FUNCTION FOR NEW TECHNICAL KNOWLEDGE

A. In-House Engineering Activities

If production functions significantly differ across firms, then the introduction of changes in the engineering routine of any given firm will normally involve a certain amount of "custom-ordered" specificity. This being the case, there is reason to expect firms to engage in technological search activities the purpose of which would be generation of additional technical information useful within the plant.

In this section we shall examine the evolutionary nature of such a knowledge-generation process. We would like to throw some light on questions such as: Which sections or activities within the plant will have as their major task that of "producing" new technical information? How would the size and nature of such activities be influenced by company-specific as well as by market and general macroeconomic forces?

Consider first the question of knowledge-generating activities performed at the individual firm level. Three broadly defined categories of engineering and technical activities have been previously identified: product design, process engineering, and industrial organization of production.

It should be noted that we are talking about technical activities that might or might not be performed by formally organized departments or sections within the firm. The same set of technical functions will be present even if a formal structure is absent. They are carried out by the entrepreneur in small family enterprises and are gradually decentralized and covered by specialized personnel when the firm acquires larger size and complexity. In this section we shall look at their nature, the time sequence of their individual development, their specific input requirements, the different forms of output they normally produce, etc.

In dealing with "in-plant" knowledge-generation activities, it becomes important once again to distinguish between firms employing a continuous-flow production process and those operating with a discontinuous technology. Also, it is important to know whether we are examining homogenous products produced for stock or, on the contrary, "custom-ordered" goods or services. Very significant differences exist in these cases in terms of stability of product design, flexibility of the production process, and industrial organization of production at large.

Let us first consider each of the three technical functions on an individual basis before bringing up their interdependencies.

1. PRODUCT DESIGN AND SPECIFICATION

Being responsible for answering the question of *what* to produce, the product design department, or the design function in the case where a formally organized department does not exist within the firm, constitutes the first technical function to be fulfilled in any given enterprise. The product design department employs different design techniques, such as building of prototypes, pilot plant experimentation, etc., with the aim of attaining a final product design that minimizes engineering complexity, input content, etc.

The engineering knowledge generated by this department takes the form of product specifications, drawings, and so forth, specifying different aspects of the product to be manufactured. Also, this technical department has, as a standard job, the generation of incremental units of technical information on the basis of which the original product design is upgraded, improved, or modified.

Economic as well as technical considerations influence the technological search efforts carried out by design personnel. On one side, product-differentiation and/or cost-reduction needs imposed by competitive pressure can be frequently traced back as underlying the activities of the product design personnel. On the other hand, newly received technical information, coming from service department statistics, trade journals, academic publications, and the like, could point toward the need to redesign specific parts and components and/or to produce them with different raw materials or under different physical conditions. Typical of the technical efforts carried out by product design engineers are product simplification studies, standardization and normalization of parts and components, and substitutions among raw materials. As we shall see later many of these technical efforts involve a great deal of interaction between the product design staff and members of the process engineering and industrial organization departments.

2. PROCESS ENGINEERING

The process engineering section of the firm is responsible for answering such questions as *how, by whom,* and *where* should the product be produced. For such purpose, it has to choose both the equipment and the labor force, including the size and skills of the crew, to be used in production. This is the group within the plant that has the responsibility for studying the production cycle in order to reduce it whenever possible. Also, it explores all potential "output-stretching" capabilities embodied in the existing equipment (Maxwell, 1979), as well as the relationship between raw materials and the production process itself. Pilot plant experimental work as well as time and motion studies constitute some of the technological search efforts carried out by this engineering department. There is a great deal of cumulative learning underlying the functioning of this office. It gradually has to acquire capabilities for registering and interpreting technical parameters describing the behavior of the production process under different operative circumstances. The acquisition of such capabilities constitutes a very major step in terms of organizational structure, incorporation of electronic equipment for the collection and processing of technical information, and skill enhancement associated with the understanding of the production process.

3. INDUSTRIAL ENGINEERING: PLANNING AND CONTROL OF THE OVERALL PRODUCTION OPERATION

A third technical department with a major role in technological matters is the one responsible for the planning and control of the overall production operation. This technical section of the plant, normally called the industrial engineering department, is the one that has to issue a formal production plan stating *when* each action should be performed, in *which* machine or equipment, and using, *what* externally acquired parts and components. Also, it is the industrial engineering personnel who decide on the "batch" size, the loading program for the available machinery, the degree and patterns of external subcontracting, the level of inventories, etc.

Given the central role fulfilled by the planning and control department, it has a rather large scope for introducing changes in the engineering routine followed by the plant. In actuality, such departments operate on the basis of a long-term plan, a short-term action program, and a control function that monitors whether the current operation is proceeding as expected.

Contrary to the other two technical sections, which have very precise knowledge-generating activities whose output can be explicitly identified as a set of "blueprints," production instruction sheets, etc., the planning and control department has a less obvious knowledge-generating function but, nonetheless, an important one. This department has to issue, on a daily, weekly, etc., basis, the production plan of the firm. Far from performing a static, allocative exercise, this department fulfills a dynamic role, constantly adjusting the plant's operation to the everchanging signals emerging from the marketplace.

Having answered the first of the previously stated questions; i.e., which kind of technical activities are knowledge-generating activities within a plant, let us now examine both the inputs and outputs of such activities and their interdependencies.

As previously stated, the nature of the production process—whether a continuous-flow operation as opposed to a discontinuous process—as well as the type of product—a homogeneous commodity produced for stock as opposed to an individually ordered "tailor-made" good or service—will influence both the role played by the previously mentioned technical departments as well as the specific inputs and outputs associated with them.

In the case of a homogeneous commodity produced in a continuous-flow "line," as is the case with the production of automobiles, petrochemical products, etc., we have a rather inflexible product design as well as a tightly specified production process, none of which can be significantly modified. The preproduction engineering efforts, related to both product design and process specification, are very detailed as is the overall planning of the plant's operation. A great deal of *ex ante* technical effort is put into balancing the production line, and the time and motion studies required for such purpose are very precise and detailed down to the level of the micromovement. Given such a degree of prespecification of the production routine, the amount of preparatory work for each position in the "line" is rather large, whereas the actual working time involved in each one is relatively less significant. Time and motion specialists, programmers, and other such skilled personnel are employed in order to specify *ex ante* each activity.

Contrary to this picture, discontinuous technologies, frequently related to the production of goods and services in response to individual orders, tend to be organized in "isles," or "centers" rather than in "lines." Such production areas are organized around a specific type of machine, i.e., lathes, drills, etc. The production of airplanes and ships, as well as the ubiquitous activities of stamping, forging, and machining belong to this type of industries.

In most of these cases, the product is not tighly specified and admits ad hoc changes. So does the production equipment, which, in general, is of a more universal nature than in the previous case. Production planning is done almost every time a given product is manufactured. There is significant motivation for reducing the duration of the production cycle, which is now highly dependent on the amount of time that is employed in "transport" operations as well as waiting in between "isles." Contrary to the former case, *ex ante* preparation time is comparatively smaller than actual working time.

Keeping in mind the present dichotomy between continuous and discontinuous technologies, let us now take a new look at the "in-house" knowledge-generating activities. Intuitively we perceive that the three previously described technical departments will have different responsibilities and will fulfill different roles.

In the case of a continuous-flow plant, product design blueprints as well as production routines are spelled out in great detail and on an *ex ante* basis. Almost each and every part, component, or production subroutine is treated with equal thoroughness. Both product design and process engineering efforts take a very different form in discontinuous process industries. Following what engineers call the "ABC method," careful attempts are made at designing some 20–30% of the total number of parts and components that belong to a given product design, leaving the remaining 70–80% of the total list of parts and components relatively less attended.[16]

[16] Parts and components of a given product design, as well as the respective production routines, are classified according to their relative weight in total cost. It is then observed that only a small proportion, usually less than 20% of the total list, accounts for close to 80% of total cost. Those items are classified as "category A" and are the ones that receive the most attention as far as design and production methods are concerned. There is a "category B," which usually comprises an additional 20% of the total list of parts and components and ab-

Thus, in a discontinuous process plant, there is a lot more ad hoc decision making done at the shop level. This introduces a set of skill requirements at the actual machine level that significantly differs from those typically demanded by a continuous-flow operation. Skillful craftsmen with decades of experience in each particular job are substitutes for job programmers and time and motion specialists.

Also, the industrial engineering department of continuous and discontinuous plants carry out rather different activities. In the latter case, the office is responsible for issuing a maching-loading program, the purpose of which is the minimization of waiting periods between jobs and capacity underutilization emerging from imbalances between stations. By definition of continuous-flow operation, the production "line" is balanced *ex ante*, the production cycle is minimized from the beginning, and no such similar job, i.e., machine-loading program, needs to be done at all.

To conclude this discussion, let us briefly consider the interdependencies among the previously described technical departments. In most real-life situations, the design of a given product, the substitution of one raw material for another in its production, etc., are far from independent from the way in which the product is to be manufactured. On the other hand, different parameters of the production process are strongly correlated with the product's quality, reliability, and general performance. Thus, it is frequently observed that "in-house" knowledge-generating efforts demand mixed groups in which product design engineers, personnel from the process engineering department, and members of the production planning office interact rather extensively to develop a new product design and/or production engineering routine. Normally, one of the three departments will lead the technological research effort—which one depends on whether the search entails a new product, a new production method, or a change in the organization of production—but there seems to be consensus that a firm's successful technology generation normally involves a combined effort from all three of these technical offices.

The next subsection will examine further the nature of the "in-house" knowledge-generation process likely to occur in any given firm or industry.

---

sorbs yet another 10–15% of the producer's cost. Some of these items, but not all of them, receive individual attention from the product design and process engineering teams. The remaining items, a rather large number, but accounting for only a minute fraction of total cost is called "category C." Either standard versions of the items in the category are available in the market—nuts, bolts, screws, etc.—or unsophisticated "in-house" designs, are employed. See ILO (1966) and McGraw-Hill (1949).

B.   An "Evolutionary" Metaphor of the "In-House" Technology-Generation Process

Firms, markets, and macroeconomic systems and technologies are dynamic entities that change through time and therefore a frequent restating of their interdependencies is called for. Let us briefly look at them from the perspective of the "received theory" of technical change before we present a rather simple metaphor describing various aspects of firm behavior as far as "in-house" knowledge-generation efforts are concerned.[17]

1. FIRMS

Research in the field of technology has clearly followed a microeconomic strand over the last decade. The old paradigm in which technological change was exogenously applied to a firm has now given way to a new micro theory in which companies have an endogenously determined "technological research path," Various authors[18] have, in recent years, examined what an "optimal research path" would be like under conventional profit-maximizing assumptions, explicitly showing that the *direction* of technical change would be in accordance with factor scarcities as perceived by the entrepreneur. Assuming technical change to be exclusively of the cost-reducing variety, with the innovation possibility frontier (IPF)[19] being given and constant, it is not surprising that companies would push their research efforts in any one direction up to the point where the marginal return from such efforts equals the marginal cost (Katz, 1976). In spite of the fact that there is quite a lot to be learned from this sort of modeling of the innovation process, a fair number of unresolved questions

---

[17] It should be noted that the overall rate of technical progress attained by any given enterprise includes both the technical knowledge generated externally to the firm by equipment and raw material suppliers as well as the technical knowledge produced "in-house" by its own technical staff. This subsection deals exclusively with "in-house" technology-generation efforts, thereby covering only part of the firm's technological history.

[18] The decade of the 1960s was rather rich in research efforts concerning the theory of induced innovation; see, for example, Ahmad (1966), Kennedy (1964), and Fellner (1961). In contrast with the previously mentioned authors the contributors of the 1970s were interested in the dynamic extension of the notion of induced research. Binswanger (1974), as well as Evenson and Kislev (1975) have been some of the outstanding contributors to the debate.

[19] The concept of the IPF (innovation possiblity frontier) was used by Kennedy, in his famous article, as an analytical tool with which to explore "induced" technological research efforts (see, Kennedy, 1964).

remain.[20] Furthermore, several authors have pointed out the rather stringent nature of some of the assumptions underlying the basic paradigm.[21]

Leaving aside the standard profit-maximization metaphor, other micromodels of the research process have been discussed in the literature. Nelson and Winter do not particularly quarrel with the idea of "the quest for profit being a good first approximation of a firm's objectives, but rather with the formalization of behavior as profit *maximization*" (Nelson and Winter, 1979). They argue that "maximization of profits presumes that the choice set is given and that the firm knows this set and the profit consequences of choosing any element." Rather, they prefer to assume that at any given time firms operate with technologies as good as any they know but that they dedicate research and imagination to searching for better things to be doing. "In particular, it must not be presumed that the process is so effective that the full set of alternatives can be explored cheaply and quickly" (Nelson and Winter, 1979).

Cyert and March (1963) as well as Rosenberg (1969) have argued that the search process is "problem-oriented."

> My primary point is that most mechanical productive processes throw off signals of a sort which are both compelling and fairly obvious. Indeed, these processes when sufficiently complex and interdependent involve an almost compulsive formulation of problems. These problems capture a large proportion of the time and energies of those engaged in the search for improved techniques (Rosenberg, 1969).

None of the previously mentioned authors, however, details the type of engineering search efforts likely to be carried out by manufacturing firms under different micro and macro circumstances. Neither do they specifically have in mind cases in which market distortions, physical scarcities, protection, etc., are as extreme as they have been shown to be in most Latin American manufacturing industries.

Given the situation as just outlined, consider it useful to begin by presenting a verbal exposition of some observed patterns. We feel that such "pretheoretical" approach might clean up the ground for future theoretical efforts.

Industry and individual firm studies seem to indicate that an "evolutionary sequence" tends to prevail as far as "in-house" technological research efforts are concerned. Such a sequence appears to begin with research efforts in the area of product design, being followed by process

---

[20] See, for example, the note by Nordhaus (1973).
[21] See, for example, Nelson and Winter (1974).

engineering search activities. Third in the sequence, and in many cases a good number of years along the line,[22] production planning and industrial engineering research projects are considered. This sequence seems to be significantly affected both by micro and macro variables such as the size of the firm and its rate of growth, the diversity and sophistication of the product mix, the continuous or discontinuous nature of the technology, the extent and type of competition, and the level of engineering skills available in the plant.

Let us examine the sequence in more detail. The first thing a firm must have is a product with which to approach a given market. Most products produced by Latin American firms are not new, i.e., they were previously produced elsewhere by firms in more developed societies. By the time these products are brought in any of the Latin American markets, one, two, or even more decades have already passed from the product's first worldwide introduction. In the meantime, the original version has gone through a number of stages, which are associated with design simplification, standardization of production methods, dissemination of technical information among producers and consumers, etc.

Such dissemination of the technical information explains why in a fair number of cases, which range from foodstuffs and textiles to agricultural and transport equipment, successful local imitations have been arrived at by skillful craftsmen or technicians.[23] Licensing and product design transfers within the framework of multinational corporations constitute other major channels through which access is obtained to the original product designs which are the starting point of most of the Latin American manufacturing markets.

In spite of such externally conditioned origins, technological research efforts in the area of product design seem to appear rather early in the technical history of many of the manufacturing firms examined. Only a

---

[22] Two studies of individual firm technological behavior in the context of Argentina showed that it was only at a late point during the second decade of production activities that both companies could confidently handle industrial organization and production planning questions with rather large technological implications. Both firms could tackle product engineering efforts much before that. In the series of IDB/ECLA/UNDP studies, see Katz *et al.* (1978) and Castaño *et al.* (1980). A similar pattern emerges from a case study concerning a Mexican chemical firm (see Pérez and Pérez Aceves, 1978).

[23] A large number of locally designed products can be identified in the Latin American manufacturing scene. The ingenious combination of separate pieces of technology frequently constitutes the basis of an indigenous technological design. For example, a horse-powered harvest machine and the power plant of a passenger vehicle were used by an imaginative local mechanic in designing a complex agricultural machine. Creative sequences of this sort, based on the assembly of already available pieces of technology, are rather frequently found in the larger Latin American countries.

few years after start up, firms seem to begin developing "in-house" technical skills related to product engineering. On the basis of such skills, they, first, adapt and improve the original design and, second, start using product differentiation strategies as part of their competitive behavior. The limited "life-cycle" of many industrial products,[24] as well as the relatively low incentive to search for cost-reduction innovations, given the rather high protection granted to industrial firms, appear as major explanations of the fact that product design engineering capabilities seem to develop at a somewhat earlier stage. We have observed that firms engage in such research efforts much before they can exhibit significant technical strength in other areas. Prototypes and pilot plant experimentation for product design purposes seem to appear well before time and motion studies or other such tools of production engineering are employed by "in-house" technical personnel.

The previous statement should not be taken to mean that technological research in areas related to process engineering is entirely absent during the initial years of a firm's life. Rudimentary forms of research are almost invariably present during the "start-up" period (Clark *et al.* 1971). Also, substitution of one raw material for another, the introduction of new or improved products, etc., are activities that necessarily call for some research effort concerning both the production process and the organization of production.

We have noted, however, that a certain discontinuity frequently occurs in the technical history of firms as far as research efforts in the fields of process engineering and production planning are concerned. Such discontinuity seems to be associated with a major change in attitude toward questions of quality control, tolerance limits, preventive maintenance, and other such technical matters. In many cases, such changes of attitude seem to be related, both to a significant reorganization of the firm's administrative structure, with the creation of a number of new departments, such as quality control, research and development, and tooling, and, to a major increase in the size and complexity and/or the degree of sophistication of the commodity produced. Both changes call for a rather different way of handling purchasing and inventories, machine-loading programs, plant space, quality control, etc. Process engineering and organizational skills acquired in an informal way during the initial years of company operation are found to be insufficient at that point, thus flagging the need for a radical change in departmental organization, data

---

[24] Consumer durables, pharmaceuticals, and many other manufacturing goods seem to exhibit life cycles that, roughly, oscilate between four and eight years. The duration of the life cycle in pharmaceutical products has been examined by various authors; see Cooper (1970).

gathering, and interpretation efforts. A whole new approach to engineering efforts frequently sets in after such discontinuity in the firm's technical development occurs, the most noticeable change being a drastic increase in the ratio of indirect to direct personnel.

2. MARKETS

In time markets also seem to experiment significant changes both in structure and in competitive atmosphere. Two "stylized" cases stand out from the various case studies undertaken in Latin America. In both cases, the market structures evolved endogenously through time. In case I, owing to the granting of an exclusive import license or to the early entrance of a large enough plant capable of catering for all (or most) of the domestic market, the prevailing market structure at the industry's starting point was that of a monopoly. Automobiles, the production of chemical and petrochemical products, etc., tend to reflect cases of this sort.

On the other hand, case II describes an entirely opposite situation, i.e., a starting point characterized by the existence of many small undifferentiated competitors. Such a situation has been shown to be a fair description of different branches of the metalworking sector (Castaño *et al.*, 1980), residencial construction, etc. (Vitelli, 1976).

In due time, both models evolved into situations of an oligopolistic nature. The protected monopolist did so as a consequence of the new entry induced by abnormally high profits.[25] That of the atomistic undifferentiated competitors is somewhat more complex. We have observed that either a financial and/or a technological advantage determines that at some point in the market's history one of the firms outgrows its fellow competitors, eventually becoming a market leader.

Technological research efforts are clearly influenced, both in their rate and nature, by the dynamics of the market's competitive structure. Protected monopolies have been seen to be relatively more associated with the technological research efforts of the "output-stretching" variety than to cost-reducing and/or quality improvement innovations. By the time the monopolistic advantage evolves into an oligopolistic confrontation, product-differentiation research efforts as well as a relatively stronger interest in cost-reducing innovations are likely to develop as well. Contrariwise, other things being equal, more competitive environments have been observed to lead to cost-reduction technological research efforts as well as to product-differentiation strategies.

Summarizing, there are reasons to expect product design research efforts to develop at a rather early stage in a firm's history. More competi-

---

[25] A model of this sort has been recently presented by Nelson and Winter (1980).

tive environments are likely to induce a stronger drive in this direction. On the contrary, monopolistic market situations enhance the search for output-stretching innovations rather than for quality improvements and/or product differentiation.

Obviously, we should not take these "trends" in a restrictive way as indicating that always, and as a matter of logical necessity, firms behave as suggested here. Similarly, there is nothing compulsory leading monopolistic firms to output-stretching innovations and more competitive ones into product-differentiation efforts. Cases can be found where such tendencies do not occur, and yet our generalization seems to be supported by various case studies.

3. MACROECONOMIC VARIABLES

It is scarcely a surprise to learn that firms' react to changes in macroeconomic variables by modifying their behavior. The magnitude of the change and the company's degree of perception seem to be rather crucial variables in determining the patterns of reaction.[26]

Consider the following observed behavioral relations:

(a)   Increases in the cost of new capital equipment, which occur, for example, as a consequence of a higher rate of interest or a currency devaluation, induce entrepreneurs to postpone major investment decisions. Simultaneously, the advantages of output-stretching technological research efforts are enhanced. Conversely, subsidies to capital expenditure, such as, for example, those that emerge from a cut in taxation or from the granting of an import license at a preferential exchange rate, increase the internal rate of return of a given investment project, thus reducing the likelihood of the firm's adopting an output-stretching strategy. Socially unjustifiable overextensions of the life cycle of outmoded equipment as well as equally unjustifiable anticipated plant scrapping decisions have both been detected during the course of our field work. The former can be interpreted as a rational private choice in the face of the observed relative prices of skilled engineering labor vis-à-vis new capital equipment (Fidel and Lucángeli, 1978; Canitrot, 1977). An increase in the rate of interest, other things being equal, can be expected to induce research efforts directed toward the reduction of the production cycle. Such efforts could be of the product engineering sort—simplification of design standardization, etc.—but would most likely be related to process engineering aspects (for example, reduction of transport operations between "stations" of a dis-

---

[26] Schwartz, in a very stimulating monograph, has recently examined the subject of perception, a topic that has thus far received too little attention from economists (Schwartz, 1979).

continuous process plant) or to production planning matters (such as, say, more adequate management of inventories of raw materials and components).[27]

(b)   In the same fashion, a rapid rate of demand expansion, occurring, for example, from various policy actions related to aggregate demand management, will most probably induce favorable expectations among entrepreneurs and therefore induce optimistic investment program in new plants and equipment. Such an expansionary business "climate" will reduce the likelihood of research efforts of the output-stretching variety, making the investment in new production facilities more likely.

(c)   Tariffs also seem to play a role in determining the direction of research followed by a given company. Sheltered from external competition, local firms feel somewhat less compelled to improve their product's quality. Obviously, there is still some incentive from domestic competition, but this is not necessarily a perfect substitute for the former. Output-stretching innovations, rather than product improvements, are more likely to occur in such market regimes.

(d)   Other features of the macro economy, besides tariffs, the rate of interest, the rate of expansion of the gross domestic product, the level of taxation, and subsidies to capital expenditure, will also influence micro-economic technological behavior. Two conditioning forces of major importance should be mentioned: first, availability and cost of skilled personnel, including long-term investments in education, training, etc., of the labor force; second, all those measures of direct support to individual companies' research efforts, such as tax incentives to research and development expenditure, and direct public participation (through universities, public research laboratories, etc.) in technology-generation programs.[28]

A final set of forces influencing firms' technological behavior is related to events of a scientific and technological nature taking place at the industry's knowledge frontier. Let us briefly examine them.

---

[27] After experiencing for many decades a negative rate of interest, the Argentine economy has in recent years switched to a regime with rather high positive interest rates. Various firms under study carried out research efforts of the sort indicated in the text, with the result that the production cycle could be reduced by as much as 30% in some cases.

[28] Most governments—both of the developed and less developed world—are presently involved in heavy subsidization of research and development expenditures. The decision to interfere in the "knowledge" market is a clear reflection of the fact that market forces cannot be expected to induce an adequate allocation of resources for the creation of new technology.

4. MOVEMENTS IN THE TECHNOLOGY FRONTIER

In the field of technology one frequently hears about the existence of "science-based" industries, which are defined as those in which "latent productivity evolves over time at a rate determined by outside forces [i.e., advances in fundamental physics or biology, etc., resulting from research at universities]" (Nelson and Winter, 1980a).[29]

Both the rhythm of expansion of the "best practice" frontier and the ease of imitation—both technical and legal—of the rapidly evolving technology are crucial aspects of the competitive atmosphere prevailing in such industries. There seems to be a consensus in the literature concerning the fact that "science-based" industries are characterized by rather elastic demand functions and by a product design and a production process that are both relatively flexible and therefore admit to quite significant ad hoc changes. Product engineering efforts are of fundamental importance even though standardization and normalization activities take place only after a few "generations" of the original product design have passed the test market. Process engineering and production planning efforts also tend to be rather flexible, as the experience indicates that frequent changes have to be introduced in both the equipment, which is of more universal nature, and the organization of production.

Obviously, "science-based" industries are still far from being accessible fields for LDCs firms. On the contrary, many other branches of manufacturing exhibit a much slower technological pace, cumulative improvements developing around a basically stable technology. The likelihood of LDC firms "catching up" with average international practices is considerably greater in these industries than in the former ones.

"In-house" technology-generation activities will no doubt reflect in various ways the relative distance between an industry's technology and the basic knowledge pool from which such an industry draws the scientific and technological principles that underlie its operation. An example in this respect is the extent to which mechanical engineering firms producing, say, machine tools, have been forced to introduce changes in the skill composition of their product design and process engineering departments in order to catch up with the trend to numerically controlled machine

---

[29] There is a certain "cross-fertilization" effect that needs to be mentioned at this point and that comes from the recent dramatic expansion of the electronic industry. Microprocessors and electronic process control equipment of all sorts are presently being adopted with great success by sectors as different as foodstuffs or textiles, thus making it possible for some of the advances in one of the "science-based" sectors to penetrate into the production process of "non-science-based" industries. Effects of this sort can also be found in other areas of manufacturing.

tools now rapidly evolving in the machine-tool sector as a consequence of contemporary developments in the electronic front (see Jacobsson, 1980).

We are now in a position to summarize our discussion concerning the determinants of "in-house" technology-generation efforts and to return to the basic question addressed in this section, i.e., are there reasons on account of which we should expect the pace, nature, etc., of technological change of any given firm in a LDC environment to be a close replica of that introduced by comparable firms in more developed industrial societies?

As we have seen, an evolutionary sequence seems to develop at the level of the individual firm as far as "in-house" knowledge-generation efforts are concerned. Such a sequence involves search, trial and error, and, above all, learning in a much more fundamental way than the one presently contained in the "received theory" of technical change. Product design capabilities, followed in due time by process engineering and production planning skills, seem to develop in a sequential order, absorbing the best part of one (or even two) decades of a company's technical history.

The market's competitive atmosphere, changes in macroeconomics parameters, and the exogenously given pace of advance of the knowledge frontier will send specific technical and economic signals that induce firms periodically to restate their technological research strategies. Obviously, the answers firms come up with are unlikely to be an exact replica of previously attained answers, as there is a great deal of specificity in the questions to which firms address themselves. Company histories as well as market relations and macroeconomic forces significantly differ across countries, and individual firm's research strategies will no doubt reflect such differences.

A final word on future research. Our discussion has shown how complex the problem of formalizing microeconomic behavior in the field of technology is. Further exploratory work in each one of the four interacting fields herein described seems to be needed in order to overcome the pretheoretical stage in which economists still dwell as far as understanding technology-generation efforts are concerned.

ACKNOWLEDGMENTS

The IDB/ECLA/UNDP Research Program of Studies on Scientific and Technological Development has been cosponsored by the Inter-American Development Bank, the Economic Commission for Latin America, and the United Nations Development Program. The long-standing support of these institutions is hereby acknowledged; obviously they are not to be held responsible for mistakes or personal opinions.

REFERENCES

Ahmad, S. (1966). "On the Theory of Induced Invention." *Economic Journal* **76** (302) (June) 344–357.

Allen, G. C. (1970). *British Industries and Their Organization*. London: Longman.

Amsden, A. (1977). "The Division of Labour is Limited by the Type of Market. The Case of the Taiwanese Machine-tool Industry." *World Development* **5** (3).

Baranson, J. (1967). *Manufacturing Problems in India: The Cummins Diesel Experience*, pp. 68–69. Syracuse, New York: Syracuse University Press.

Baranson, J. (1971). "International Transfer of Automotive Technology to Developing Countries." Unitar Research Reports, No 8.

Binswanger, H. (1974). "A Microeconomic Approach to Induced Innovation." *Economic Journal* **84** (December), 940–958.

Canitrot, A. (1977). "Method for Evaluating the Significance of Macro-economic Variables in the Analysis of Technology Incorporation Decisions." Working Paper No. 12, IDB/ECLA/UNDP Program of Studies on Science and Technology.

Castaño, A., Katz, J., and Navajas, F. (1980). "Etapas históricas y conductas tenológicas en una planta metalmecánica argentina," mimeo, Programa BID/CEPAL/PNUD de Estudios Sobre Ciencia y Tecnología, Buenos Aires.

Clark, M. E., de Forest, E. M., and Stechley, L. R. (1971). "Aches and Pains of Plant 'Start-up'." *Chemical and Engineering Progress* **67** (December).

Cooper, J. D. (ed.) (1970). *The Economics of Drug Innovation*. Washington, D.C.: American University.

Cyert, R., and March, J. (1963). *A Behavioural Theory of the Firm*. Englewood Cliffs, New Jersey: Prentice Hall.

David, P. A. (1975). *Technical Choice, Innovation and Economic Growth: Essarys on American and British Experience in the 19th Century*. London and New York: Cambridge University Press.

Evenson, L., and Kislev, G. (1975). *Agricultural Research and Productivity*. New Haven, Connecticut: Yale University Press.

Fellner, W. (1961). "Two Propositions in the Theory of Induced Innovations." *Economic Journal* **71**, 305–308.

Fidel, J. and Lucángeli, J. (1978). "Cost-Benefit of Different Technological Options in the Context of a Differentiated Oligopoly: The Case of the Argentine Cigarette Industry." Working Paper No. 18, IDB/ECLA/UNDP Program of Studies on Science and Technology.

Freeman, Cr. (1978). "Technical Change and Unemployment." Paper presented at the *Conference on Science, Technology and Public Policy, an International Perspective, University of New South Wales* (December), mimeo, Sussex.

Hirschleifer, J. (1973). "Where Are We in the Theory of Information." *American Economic Review* **63** (2) (May).

ILO (1966). Introducción al Estudio del Trabajo. Geneve: ILO.

Jacobsson, S. (1980). "Technical Change, Skill Requirements and Intervention Policies in the Machine Tool-Sector. The Case of Argentina" (outline of a doctoral dissertation for the University of Sussex, England), mimeo (March), IDB/ECLA/UNDP Program of Studies on Science and Technology.

Katz, J. (1976). *Importación de Tecnología, aprendizaje local e industrialización dependiente*. México: Fondo de Cultura Económica.

Katz, J. (1978). "Technological Change, Economic Development and Intra and Extra Regional Relations in Latin America." Working Paper No. 30, IDB/ECLA/UNDP Program of Studies on Science and Technology.

Katz, J., and Ablin, E. (1976). "From Infant Industry to Technology Exports. The Argentine Experience in the International Sale of Industrial Plants and Engineering Works." Working Paper No. 14, IBD/ECLA/UNDP Program of Studies on Science and Technology, Buenos Aires.

Katz, J. *et al.* (1978). "Productivity, Technology and Domestic Efforts in Research and Development." Working Paper No. 14. IDB/ECLA/UNDP Program of Studies on Science and Technology, Buenos Aires, ("July).

Kennedy, Ch. (1964). "Induced Bias in Innovation and the Theory of Distribution." *Economic Journal* **74** (295) (September) 541–547.

Lall, S. (1979). "Developing Countries as Exporters of Technology and Capital Goods. The Indian Experience," mimeo, Oxford (June).

Lucángeli, J., and Cibotti, R. (1980). "El Fenómeno Tecnológico Interno," mimeo, IDB/ECLA/UNDP Program of Studies on Science and Technology.

McGraw-Hill (1949). *Tools and Manufacturing Engineers Handbook.* New York: McGraw-Hill.

Maxwell, P. (1979). "Implicit R&D Strategy and Investment-linked R&D. A Study of the R&D Programme of the Argentine Steel Firm, Acindar, S.A." Working Paper No. 23, IDB/ECLA/UNDP Program of Studies on Science and Technology (March).

Mitra, J. D. (1979). "The Capital Goods Sector in LDCs. A Case for State Intervention?" World Bank Working Papers No. 343. Washington (July).

Morley, S. A., and Smith, G. W. (1979). "Adaptation by Foreign Firms to Labour Abundance in Brazil." *In Technological Progress in Latin America. The Prospects of Overcoming Dependency* (J. H. Street and D. D. James, eds.). Boulder, Colorado: Westview Press.

Nelson, R. (1978). "Innovation and Economic Development. Theoretical Retrospect and Prospect." Working Paper No. 31, IDB/ECLA/UNDP Program of Studies on Science and Technology, Buenos Aires (November).

Nelson, R., and Winter, S. (1974). "Neoclassical vs. Evolutionary Theories of Economic Growth. Critique and Prospects." *Economic Journal* (December).

Nelson, R., and Winter, S. (1977a). "In Search of a Useful Theory of Innovation." *Research Policy* **6**, 36.

Nelson, R., and Winter, S. (1977b). "Simulation of Schumpeterian Competition." *American Economic Review* (February).

Nelson R., and Winter, S. (1979). "Firm and Industry Response to Changed Market Conditions," mimeo, Institution for Social and Policy Studies, Yale University, Working Paper No. 788 (May).

Nelson, R., and Winter S. (1980a). "Organizational Capabilities in a Dynamic World," mimeo, Yale University.

Nelson, R., and Winter, S. (1980b). *The Schumpeterian Trade off Revisited,* Working Paper No. 834. Institution for Social and Policy Studies, Yale University, New Haven, Connecticut: mimeo.

Nordhaus, W. (1973). "Some Skeptical Thoughts on the Theory of Induced Innovation." *Quarterly Journal of Economics* **87**, 209–219.

Pearson, R. (1976). "Technology, Innovation and Transfer of Technology in the Cement Industry." Working Paper No. 9, IDB/ECLA/UNDP Program of Studies on Science and Technology.

Perez, L. A., and Perez Aceves, J. (1978). "Análisis Microeconómico de las Características del Cambio Tecnológico y del Proceso de Innovaciones. El caso de Furfural y Derivados, S. A. México," Working Paper No. 20. IDB/ECLA/UNDP Program of Studies on Science and Technology.

Rhee, Y. W., and Westphal, L. E. (1978). "A Note on the Exports of Technology from the Republics of Korea and Taiwan." Paper presented at the seminar on Technology and Development organized by the IDB/ECLA/UNDP Program of Studies on Science and Technology, Buenos Aires (November).

Rosenberg, N. (1969). "The Direction of Technological Change. Inducement Mechanisms and Focusing Devices." *Economic Development and Cultural Change* **18** (October).

Rosenberg, N. (1978). *Perspectives on Technology.* London and New York: Cambridge University Press.

Schwarz, H. (1979). "Perception, Judgment and Motivation in Decision Making. Hypothesis Suggested by a Study of Metalworking Enterprises in Argentina, Mexico and the United States," mimeo, Washington (November).

Sen, A. K. (1960). *Choice of Techniques,* 3rd ed. Fairfield, New Jersey: Kelly.

Sercovich, F. (1978). "Design Engineering and Endogenous Technical Change. A Microeconomic Approach Based on the Experience of the Argentine Chemical and Petrochemical Industries." Working Paper No. 19, IDB/ECLA/UNDP Program of Studies on Science and Technology.

Smith, A. (1776). *Wealth of Nations,* Book I.

Teitel, S. (1981). "Toward an Understanding of Technical Change in Semi-Industrialized Countries," *Research Policy* **10** (April), 127–147.

Vitelli, G. (1976). "Competition, Oligopoly and Technological Change in the Construction Industry. The Argentine Case," Working Paper No. 3, IDB/ECLA/UNDP Program of Studies on Science and Technology.

Watanabe, S. (1979). "Technical Cooperation between Large and Small Firms in Philippine Automobile Industry." World Employment Research Program, Geneva, ILO.

IDB/ECLA/UNDP Program of Studies
on Scientific and Technological
Development in Latin America
Buenos Aires, Argentina

Chapter 14

The Engineering Sector in a Model of Economic Development

Morris Teubal

The purpose of this chapter is to analyze some issues related to the role of the engineering (capital goods) sector in transmitting growth from an expanding primary goods export sector to the rest of the economy. One possibility explored in a previous paper (Teubal, 1980) is to divide the economy into three sectors: the primary sector, Sector X, whose growth in response to a growing world market generated possibilities, directly and indirectly, for the emergence and growth of other sectors; the engineering sector, Sector E, whose output of machines or intermediate inputs is directed toward satisfying the local demand created by the expanding primary sector (backward linkages) and where the production skill accumulated increases the effectiveness of resources invested in developing new techniques for the remaining sectors (spin-off);[1] the rest of the economy, Sector C, whose existing techniques cannot sustain domestic production but where an appropriate technique may be developed, thanks to the skills being accumulated in the engineering sector.

---

[1] In this chapter, the expression "engineering sector" has the same meaning as the term "capital goods sector" or "machinery-producing sector."

Section I summarizes the objectives and structure of the model and presents some of the conclusions derived in the original paper. In Section II, a more thorough discussion of the nature of the model relative to other growth models and of specific issues emerging from it will be undertaken. Attention will be given to the following: (i) the initial stimulus to growth; (ii) the focus of the analysis; (iii) endogenous technical changes; (iv) the importance of chronological time; (v) the time sequence of activities; and (vi) policy issues.

I. THE MODEL

A. Objectives

The first objective of the model is to formalize some of the roles that economic historians and development economists have assigned to the metalworking/machine-building sectors. It has been suggested that in this sector the skills (components) acquired (developed) while performing certain activities or tasks can then be fruitfully applied to other activities or tasks.[2] In our model, production skills help design activities, the former activity aimed at satisfying input demands from the primary sectors and the latter activity aimed at enabling the substitution of imports of other goods for domestic production.

A second objective of the model is to incorporate such a sector into a multisector model of the economy where some initial stimulus sets the growth process going in one sector and where a series of factors and parameters will determine whether or not the growth is transmitted to other sectors. The engineering sector will play a crucial role in this transmission.[3] In terms of our model, we ask ourselves under what conditions will a C sector emerge in our economy, the initial bottleneck being the absence

---

[2] Rosenberg (1963) uses the term "key sector" when describing the activities of the U.S. machine-tool sector in the nineteenth century. The sector developed and diffused technologies for a wide spectrum of metal-using, metal-forming activities. Diffusion involved the adaptation of a machine tool already developed for one sector to the specific needs of another. Any single adaptation enlarged the pool of skills and knowledge relevant for subsequent adaptations. Pack and Todaro (1969) and others refer to the role of the machine sector in adapting foreign technology to the local needs. Youngson (1959) refers to the role of machinery and implements firms in developing new techniques in response to changing world market conditions. For a survey of part of the literature, see Stewart (1978).

[3] Our model thus also gives a formal expression to the central issue discussed by the so-called Staple theories of export-led growth; see Watkins (1963), Baldwin (1956). For a good review, see Roemer (1970).

of a technique on the shelf that is appropriate to the conditions of our economy.

B. Description

A very short description will be presented here. Further details can be found in Teubal (1980).

1. PRIMARY SECTOR

It is assumed that our economy may influence the world price of its primary export and that world export demand grows at an exponential rate g at least until chronological time T when, under one interpretation of the model, it collapses. This specific interpretation will be adopted here because it fits well with an aspect of the model that we want to emphasize, namely, that the exogenous stimulus to growth is a temporary one, like a short-lived staple (see Section II.A for further comment). Alternatively, T may be considered as the planning horizon of entrepreneurs in the engineering sector, but this fits less well with our objective and it requires modifying the model somewhat (the central issue would be the time of appearance of Sector C rather than whether C will appear or not). It is also assumed that there exists perfect competition, surplus labor, and that the everlasting capital is acquired from abroad until t_1, when it begins to be supplied domestically (see the later discussion). Finally, production takes place under constant costs and these remain constant through time.[4] Under these conditions, the growth of the primary sector X is represented by the equation

$$x_t = x_o e^{gt}, \tag{1}$$

where x_t is primary sector output (exports) at time t.

2. ENGINEERING SECTOR

Sector E emerges at t_1 to supply inputs to the primary sector once the local market y_k^d is sufficiently large to enable unit production costs c_k to be lower than the fixed world price $\bar{p}_k$. There are static production economies of scale

$$c_k = a + y_k^{-\alpha}, \tag{2}$$

---

[4] Labor is being drawn at a constant wage $\bar{w}$ and the cost of capital to the sector is assumed to be constant through time. In particular, the shift to local production of capital goods is assumed not to be associated with a reduction in the price paid by the sector, which will be discussed later.

where y_k is the rate of output and α a positive parameter. This function is invariant through time. Exports are not possible and local demand for the infinite-lived capital is given by

$$y_k^d = \mu_x \, dx/dt = \mu_x g x_0 e^{gt}, \tag{3}$$

where μ_x is a fixed-capital-output coefficient. It follows that t_1 is defined by the equation

$$K_x^M \equiv \mu_x x_0 e^{gt_1} = 1/g(\bar{p}_k - a)^{1/\alpha}, \tag{4}$$

where K_x^M is the stock of imported capital in the primary sector at and beyond t_1. We assume that the machines sold after t_1 to the primary sector are priced at $\bar{p}_k$, their import cost to x.[5]

The sudden shift from imports to domestic production postulated in this model is an oversimplification of reality. It would be desirable to describe a gradual transition, but this would complicate the model without apparently modifying the nature of the results. Concerning exports of capital goods, it is reasonable to assume that nonprice factors and setup costs preclude exports at the early stage of this industry. The assumption that no exports are possible is, however, increasingly less realistic as time elapses beyond t_1 and the sector becomes more fully developed. In this paper, we concentrate on the emerging stages of the sector.

3. Sector C

Sector C represents the rest of the economy and, for simplicity, is assumed to be a consumption goods sector. Our country does not have a comparative advantage initially in producing these goods because the technique—identified here by the capital–labor ratio—which is available from the advanced countries is too capital-intensive and therefore inappropriate.[6] However, the production experience accumulated by Sector E enhances its design capabilities in respect to the techniques for Sector C. Specifically, the fixed design costs of developing technique k_c at t_2 are given by the expression

$$d(k_c, t_2) = \beta(k_c^A - k_c)/V(t_2), \tag{5}$$

where k_c^A is the C technique available on the shelf from advanced coun-

---

[5] This is profit minimizing, provided the discontinuous drop of marginal revenue at $\bar{p}_k$ makes it attain a level below the level of marginal costs at that point. A sufficient condition is an inelastic demand at that point, although this is not necessary.

[6] Inappropriateness could also derive from other factors, such as intensiveness in natural resources, that are not abundant in our economy.

tries, β a positive parameter, and $V(t_2)$ the design-relevant production experience accumulated in Sector E,

$$V(t_2) = \left(\int_{t_1}^{t_2} y_k(t) \, dt \right)^{\eta}, \tag{6}$$

η translating production experience to design capabilities.

4. EMERGENCE OF SECTOR C

Entrepreneurs make a cost–benefit analysis at t_1 to determine whether or not to introduce a technique for C, and if so, which k_c and at what t_2. We assume that there exists a monopolist E firm that extracts all the "surplus" from potential C producers, i.e., unit royalties $R(k_c)$ are given by

$$R(k_c) = 1 - C_c(k_c),$$

where 1 is the world price of C goods—the numéraire—and $C_c(k_c)$ the unit production cost when technique k_c is being used. Unit cost declines with k_c within an interval $(k_c^A, \underline{k}_c)$ and increases thereafter. Total royalties per period, until time T, the time of collapse of the primary sector, are discounted back to t_1 and compared with discounted, fixed development costs. Let

$$B(t_2, k_c) = R(k_c) \int_{t_2}^{T} y_c(t) \exp\left[-\rho(t - t_2)\right] dt \tag{7}$$

be accumulated royalties discounted back to t_2 at rate ρ, with $y_c(t)$ being the output of C at time t.

A technique will be developed for Sector C enabling the sector to be established if and only if there exists a technique k_c $(k_c^A > k_c > \underline{k}_c)$ and a time $t_2 > t_1$ such that

$$B(t_2, k_c) \geq d(t_2, k_c). \tag{8}$$

This condition can be elucidated by combining all the terms into two functions: $f(t_2, T)$, which includes all the t_2 terms, and $g(k_c)$:

$$f(t_2, T) = V(t_2) \int_{t_2}^{T} Y_x(t) \exp\left[-\rho(t - t_2)\right] dt, \tag{9}$$

$$g(k_c) = \beta(k_c^A - k_c)/m(k_c, \gamma)R(k_c), \tag{10}$$

where $Y_x(t)$ is the income of domestic factors in sector X, i.e., net of capital service charges paid forever on the stock of capital, and $m(k_c, \gamma)$ a sort of "multiplier" relating $Y_x(t)$ to the local demand for C goods, with γ the constant proportion of the income of domestic factors of all sectors spent on C goods. It depends, among other things, on the distribution of income.

The first function $f(t_2, T)$ is the product of the domestic value-added of the primary sector from the date when the technique is developed (t_2) until the collapse of the sector (at T) times the experience term V. Both elements favor the development of the new technique.

A rise in t_2 enables the accumulation of experience but it shortens the time left before primary exports collapse. The f function will therefore be bell-shaped with respect to t_2.

A necessary condition for the emergence of Sector C is

$$\max f(t_2, T) \geq \min g(k_c),$$

as shown in Fig. 1a. Figure 1b depicts a situation where no technique will be developed by that sector, so no Sector C will emerge prior to the collapse of X.

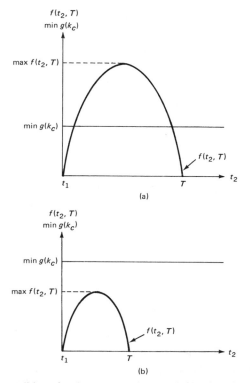

Fig. 1. Possible conditions for the (a) emergence and (b) nonemergence of Sector C.

C. Conclusions

Factors raising the $f(t_2, T)$ curve and lowering min $g(k_c)$ increase the probability of the emergence of Sector C. It turns out that there are a number of strategic variables.

1. SIZE OF LOCAL MARKET

The local market size is a main determinant of the profitability of introducing a technique into Sector C because exporting is inherently more difficult than selling to the local market. The main variables affecting it are: the rate of growth of exports g, the proportion γ spent on C goods, and the stock of imported capital in the export sector K_x^M. We shall deal with each one separately. For g, a higher rate of growth of exports implies a greater export sector income, a wider local market for C goods, and greater prospects for the emergence of this sector. For γ, its magnitude depends fundamentally on the distribution of income in the export sector. A more egalitarian distribution of income will, presumably, lead to a greater domestic market for C goods.[7] For K_x^M, a higher value implies greater capital service flows abroad and therefore a lower income received by domestic factors of production.

2. LEARNING ELASTICITY η

The elasticity coefficient relates the relevant aspects of production experience to design costs. In a sense, it refers to a transfer of skills from one activity to the other. A certain hierarchy of skills (maintenance and repair, production, design) underlies the approach followed in this chapter.

3. THE HORIZON T

There is a horizon T beyond which the primary sector ceases to be viable. A higher T shifts the $f(t_2, T)$ curve upward and to the right, thereby increasing the probability that a C technique will be profitable. This occurs for two reasons—one demand and one supply: (i) the primary sector will be earning income and spending it on C goods for a longer period of time; (ii) more design-relevant production experience can be accumulated in the engineering sector.

---

[7] This is the general impression one obtains from the case study literature on exports and economic development. Compare the case of wheat in Canada with sugar cane, copper, etc. A useful review of this issue can be found in Roemer (1970).

4. RETURNS TO SCALE IN SECTOR E

A higher level of α results in an earlier appearance of Sector E. This enables more production experience to be accumulated in this sector throughout the lifetime of the primary sector, thereby increasing the profitability of developing a technique for C.[8]

II. NATURE AND IMPLICATIONS OF THE MODEL

The three-sector model just presented is significantly different from the three-sector growth model I proposed some time ago (Teubal, 1971, 1973) and from neoclassical growth models generally. Although some of the latter incorporate the possibility of technical change or learning by doing, the description of these phenomena is invariably too simple and even trivial. The effect of learning, for example, is to reduce the production cost of *existing products* (Bardhan, 1970), a fact that is not the essential feature of sectors whose major characteristic is specialization in a specific technology, such as mechanical engineering or electronics, rather than in specific products. Such a feature is the capability of doing *new* things as spin-offs from current or past activity. In explicitly postulating such a sector, albeit in an extremely simple fashion, this model differs from other growth or development models.[9] Beyond this major characterization of the model, we find a series of characteristics that merit separate attention.

A. Growth-Initiating Factor (Initial Stimulus)

In our model, the stimulus to growth derives from an expansion in the world demand for the economy's primary product (demand pull). No sav-

---

[8] It should be noted here that α determines the *elasticity* of unit costs c_k with respect to output y_k, so a higher level of this variable, *ceteris paribus*, should be favorable to the developing country. Another crucial scale parameter not yet considered is the *level* of unit costs at a particular output level. A small firm contemplating producing such a good should be particularly interested in the level of unit costs at low levels of output, relative to the import price of the good $\bar{P}_k$. For a given elasticity of unit costs, the higher such a level—a variable associated with the *diseconomies of small scale*—the *less* favorable it will be for the emergence of Sector E. The cost function postulated in this chapter does not permit parameter variation of this variable because unit costs at zero outputs always tend to infinity.

[9] The fact that such sectors exist in reality also provides a justification for assuming that the learning and externality phenomena are concentrated in one or a small number of such sectors rather than presuming, out of ignorance, that they may be equally distributed among all sectors of the economy.

ing or capital accumulation is needed, even as an enabling factor, because we assume that capital can be rented from abroad. In contrast, most neoclassical models generally consider saving and capital accumulation as factors initiating growth (supply push).[10] In addition, by postulating the existence of a saving function and a constant rate of population growth, they imply that the stimulus to growth is a *permanent* one. A major feature of our model, on the other hand, is that the exogenous stimulus to growth is a *temporary* one: world demand, although first growing at an exponential rate, collapses for some unspecified reason at time *T*. Although there are other, more elegant, formulations for a temporary exogenous stimulus to growth, the main point remains that the environment of developing countries is subject to violent fluctuations. This implies that (a) it is not wise to rely on any particular exogenous growth stimulus for long and (b) the countries involved should develop capabilities for exploiting new growth opportunities once they arise.

B. Focus of Analysis: Environment and Bottlenecks

Our analysis focuses on the conditions for the emergence of Sector C, where the effective bottleneck is absence of an appropriate technique of production. Alternatively, we focus on the conditions assuring the *transmission of growth* from the primary sector. These conditions are expressed in terms of the following staple-theory-type *indirect* effects of export expansion: production linkage, consumption goods linkage, skill, and innovation. Neoclassical models, on the other hand, tend to focus on the very long run *steady state:* its characteristics, such as rate of growth, and the conditions assuring convergence of the factor accumulation path to a balanced growth path.[11]

Our concern for the transmission of growth from the sector receiving the initial stimulus stems from the nature of the environment facing our less developed economy. The issue arises as to what remains after the primary sector disappears or after its significance has been substantially reduced. This is a more fundamental issue than the issue of convergence toward, and nature of, the steady state.

---

[10] See the models of Solow (1956) and Uzawa (1964). Exceptions to this are the models of Bardhan (1970) and Findlay (1973, Chapter 5). In these models, although the opportunity to grow derives from expansion in world demand (as in our model), the process also requires saving and capital accumulation.

[11] A less common objective is describing structural change along the growth path of the economy; see Teubal (1971, 1973) and Findlay (1973).

C. Endogenous Technical Change

Unlike other formal models of growth or development, the present one stresses the primacy of technological innovation for the emergence of new sectors (beyond X and E). This enables the model to capture what seems to be a central fact: a series of microstudies of the last few years have shown quite convincingly that success in the transfer of technology to developing countries requires local adaptation of technology.[12] In other words, an active recipient of the foreign technology is required in order to adapt foreign technology successfully to local conditions. This is probably even truer with respect to technologies enabling—as in our model—the establishment of a new sector. The absence of a local capability to adapt foreign technology would represent, under those circumstances, a skill or know-how bottleneck to the establishment of such a sector.[13]

The analysis focuses on the supply and demand factors determining whether or not the appropriate technique will be developed. Both sets of factors are present here: Supply is represented by the accretion of production experience relevant to design, that is, a learning-by-doing phenomenon. Demand is represented by the growing *local* demand for C goods, a consequence of growing export proceeds and a sharp differentiation between the local and the world markets, specifically that at the early stages of development of C, the country cannot export.

Concerning the relevance of the skill acquisition process postulated, the importance of learning by doing has been consistently pointed out in the economic development literature. Lack of ability to invest in less developed countries is ascribed to the absence of experience with a modern sector (Hirschman, 1958). Cooper (1973) states that this type of skill creation is a basic ingredient to economic development and that market failure in providing enough opportunities, owing to externalities and risk, is a major cause of technological dependence. Leff's (1968) interpretation of growth and increasing sophistication of the Brazilian capital goods industry is very much based on just such a type of skill acquisition process. Activity sequences, such as production first, design later, as postulated in the model, are also encountered in the literature, including a shift from

---

[12] See Katz (1976) and the series of studies on adaptation and local generation of technology undertaken under the IDB-ECLA-UNDP Program. For a review of the program's findings, see Chapter 13 and Teitel (1981).

[13] The commissioning abroad of the required adaptation, although possible in principle, may be impractical for a number of reasons, at least within the relevant time framework. The reasons include lack of intimate knowledge of local needs and the high price the developing country would have to pay.

repair and maintenance activities on machinery and equipment to production of machinery parts and components.[14]

The sharp distinction between the local and foreign markets postulated in the model is due not only to transportation costs, but also to informational requirements on foreign markets, which demand time for acquisition; to the high setup (fixed) marketing and distribution costs
associated with exporting; to obstacles caused by a firm's lack of reputa-
tion; and to low and nonhomogeneous quality of products at the early
stages of the development of an industry. In this sense, a sharp difference
probably exists between staple exports and exports of certain categories
of industrial products.

D. The Importance of Chronological Time

In neoclassical models, chronological time does not play a role when
addressing the central issue dealt with: the nature of and convergence
toward the steady state. These depend on the parameters of the model
and are independent of the initial conditions of the economy—initial capital–labor ratio and (if desired) chronological time. In our model, chronological time is central because the exogenous stimulus to growth depends
on this variable, and specifically, it terminates at time T. The structure of
the model is such that the transmission of growth from the export sector
should also take place before T. It follows that initial conditions, which, in
our model, could be represented by the date of discovery of those natural
resources that the primary sector will exploit, play a central role. If the
"beginning" is late relative to T, then the chances that the development of
the export sector will lead to the emergence of C are correspondingly low.

E. Sequence of Activities

The time sequence of sectors that may appear in our model is the following: first, the primary exporting sector (Sector X), then the sector producing inputs for the primary sector (Sector E), and finally, a manufacturing consumer goods sector (Sector C). This structure is particularly useful
for analyzing the staple theory of export-led growth, namely, the condi-

---

[14] See Leff for examples within the Brazilian capital goods industry and Roemer for examples such as that of copper mining in Zambia. Israel Aircraft Industries is a good example
of a shift from repair of aircraft to production of parts and components, design of new components, and even of completely new aircraft. For an interesting link between preventive
maintenance activities and design activities in an Argentine steel plant, see Maxwell (1976).

tions under which export growth will be transmitted to the rest of the economy. It would be presumptuous, however, to ascertain that this is the optimum time sequence of activities for *all* developing countries or that historical experience has always conformed to this pattern. The potential significance of the model does not lie in the specific sequence postulated but rather in having attempted a conceptualization of the engineering sector and its incorporation into a broader model of economic development. There are some historical examples where elements of the pattern suggested in this chapter seem to be present.

(1)   In his study of the capital goods industries in Brazil, Leff (1968, pp. 118–29) states explicitly that their emergence occurred very early in Brazil's development, in response to the processing needs of primary products such as coffee, sugar, and cotton. The overall impression is that at least the emergence of the Brazilian capital goods industry is not the final stage of an industrialization process beginning with final consumer industries like textiles and food. The study also gives examples of spin-offs from the early activities of machinery-producing firms.

(2)   The development of Denmark and Sweden in the nineteenth century, as described by Youngson (1959), also includes aspects of machinery and implements firms developing in response to a rapidly expanding export sector (timber, dairy products, etc.). However, this development cannot be easily separated from the impulse derived from "the general development of industry," i.e., from manufacturing that was probably largely devoted, in that period, to satisfying local demand. This probably has also been the case in the economic history of other present-day developed countries.

However, despite these historical cases, there seems to be significant historical evidence favoring the "normal" pattern, where the production of consumer goods precedes that of capital goods. The model, we emphasize again, should therefore be regarded as one possible sequence among a set of sequences, one that need not be the most frequent one. The sequence postulated is presumably more realistic for the subset of cases where the external stimulus to growth (via export demand) was significant relative to the stimulus derived from the local market.

A specific criticism is that the pattern of structural change postulated in the model contradicts the import substitution industrialization (ISI) experience of developing countries in Latin America after World War II, where consumer or final goods development preceded the development of intermediate and capital goods. This is undoubtedly true, but two questions arise:

(1) The model presented is, at present, only a descriptive model, i.e., the time sequence of activities is that which appears in the absence of governmental policy. On the other hand, the ISI policy has been implemented by massive protection of the industrial sector as a whole. The historical record, therefore, need not contradict the results of the model. In particular, a tariff or production subsidy τ on C goods

$$\tau \geq c(k_c^A) - 1$$

imposed before t_1, the time of emergence of the E sector, would lead to the prior emergence of the C sector.

(2) The ISI policy was at least a partial failure. Contradiction of the historical record may, in this case, represent an advantage of the model rather than a disadvantage. Moreover, by highlighting the difference between the engineering sector and other sectors, the model suggests the need for *selective* government support directed to this sector rather than all-out support of (other) manufacturing.

F. Policy Issues

Some preliminary thoughts on the objectives and effects of policy are appropriate here in order to elicit comments. It is not clear what the objectives of policy should be because they depend on the decision makers' perceptions of the opportunities and risks to the economy beyond calendar time T. Although the descriptive part of this chapter focused on the emergence of C, the normative part may focus on attaining a sufficiently well developed engineering sector by T to enable the economy to adapt to the new environment confronting it—all this at a minimum cost to the economy.

One aspect of this is the time of emergence of the engineering sector. There are no unpriced benefits (externalities) in our model because we assumed that the engineering sector was a monopoly. However, we assumed that the beginning of this sector is the result of a myopic decision, i.e., it takes place once local demand for inputs to X is sufficiently great to enable unit costs to equal the world price. The economic value of the benefits from production experience—the spin-offs—are not taken into account. Therefore, the policy implications are similar to the case of externalities: the emergence of the engineering sector should be anticipated relative to the date it would begin operations under market forces. This conclusion is relatively standard and does not depend on the terminal value of the skills accumulated by this sector until T.[15]

---

[15] It depends on this terminal value being positive if no spin-off should take place prior to T.

In choosing the policy instruments to attain this objective, consideration should be given to the existence of differential learning affects. A production subsidy will unambiguously raise the production experience of
Sector E by

$$\int_{t_1'}^{t_1} y_k(t)\, dt,$$

that is, by the accumulated output of E goods between the anticipated
time of emergence t_1' and the original time $t_1(t_1' < t_1)$. The level of output
beyond t_1 will remain as before.[16] An equivalent tariff on imports, on the
other hand, has two opposite effects on production experience: first, a
positive effect from the anticipation of domestic production of E goods;
second, a negative effect from a substitution of capital goods by labor in
the primary sector.[17] The former refers to the $[t_1', t_1]$ period and the latter
takes place beyond t_1. The net effect on production experience is not
known without further specification of the model. We would expect it to
be generally lower than that resulting from an equivalent subsidy or even
to be negative. In the latter situation, tariff protection of the engineering
sector will *reduce* the spin-off that would result from this sector.

III.   FINAL REMARKS

We have commented on a three-sector model of an economy with an
engineering or machinery-producing sector. Differences and similarities
with other formal models have been analyzed. The pattern of structural
change and some policy issues have also been considered.

Additional work is required regarding the basic framework developed
up to now and with respect to policy issues. The existence of uncertainty,
especially with regard to the future world demand for primary exports,
should be explicitly modeled. This would improve on the assumption
made in this chapter, namely that the primary sector collapses at a specified future date T. The processes of capital accumulation and the balance-
of-payments constraint should also be introduced and the appropriate set
of policy measures favoring the engineering sector should be worked out.
A continuous effort should be made to relate the assumptions, structure,

---

[16] This occurs because the sector will continue to charge a price $\bar{p}_k$ to X producers, except when the marginal costs (associated with the quantity demanded at $\bar{p}_k$) *net* of subsidies
declines below marginal revenue.

[17] This will include both a pure substitution and an "output" effect owing to an increase
in the costs of primary production.

and conclusions derived from the model to the historical case studies and to the growing body of findings on innovation and development. Needless to say, the task of conceptualizing and formalizing an engineering sector or firm is still in its beginnings.

ACKNOWLEDGMENTS

The author greatly appreciates the comments of N. Gross, G. Hanoch, M. Syrquin, and participants of the Bar-Ilan Symposium.

REFERENCES

Baldwin, R. (1956). "Patterns of Development in Newly Settled Regions." *Manchester School of Economic and Social Studies* **24** (May), 161–179.
Bardhan, P. (1970). *Economic Growth, Development, and Foreign Trade*. New York: Wiley.
Cooper, C. (1973). "Science, Technology and Production in the Underdeveloped Countries: An Introduction." *Science, Technology and Development* (C. Cooper, ed.). London: Frank Cass.
Findlay, R. (1973). *International Trade and Development Theory*. New York: Columbia University Press.
Hirschman, A. (1958). *The Strategy of Economic Development*. Cambridge, Massachusetts: Yale University Press.
Katz, J. (1976). *Importación we Tecnología, Aprendizaje E Industrialización Dependiente*. Mexico: Fondo De Cultura Economica.
Leff, N. (1968). *The Brazilian Capital Goods Industry, 1929–1964*. Hartford, Connecticut: Harvard University Press.
Maxwell, P. (1976). "Learning and Technical Change in the Steel Plant of Acindar." IDB/ECLA/UNDP Program on Science in Technology, Paper No. 4 (December).
Pack, H., and Todaro, M. (1969). "Technological Change, Labor Absorption and Economic Development." *Oxford Economic Papers* **21** (November), 395–403.
Roemer, M. (1970). *Fishing for Growth*. Hartford, Connecticut: Harvard University Press.
Rosenberg, N. (1963). "Technological Change in the U.S. Machine Tool Sector, 1840–1910." *Journal of Economic History* **23** (December), 414–443; reprinted in *Perspectives on Technology*, Chapter 1. London and New York: Cambridge University Press, 1976.
Solow, R. (1956). "A Contribution to the Theory of Economic Growth." *Quarterly Journal of Economics* **70** (February), 65–94.
Stewart, F. (1978). *Technology and Underdevelopment*. New York: Macmillan Press.
Teitel, S. (1981). "Towards an Understanding of Technical Change in Semi-industrialized Countries." *Research Policy* **10** (April), 127–147.
Teubal, M. (1971). "Development Strategy for a Medium-Sized Economy." *Econometrica* **39** (September), 773–796.
Teubal, M. (1973). "Heavy and Light Industry in Economic Development." *American Economic Review* **63** (September), 588–596.
Teubal, M. (1980). "Exportacions de Bienes Primarios y Desarrollo Economico." Cuaderno No. 103, Serie Ocre, economia, Institute Torcuato DeTella; or "Primary Exports and

Economic Development: The Role of the Engineering Sector.'' Falk Institute, Discussion Paper No. 7915 (1980).

Uzawa, H. (1964). ''On a Two-Sector Model of Economic Growth II.'' *Review of Economic Studies* **30** (June), 105–118.

Watkins, M. (1963). A Staple Theory of Economic Growth.'' *Canadian Journal of Economics and Political Science* **29** (May), 141–158.

Youngson, A. J. (1959). *Possibilities of Economic Progress.* London and New York: Cambridge University Press.

Department of Economics
The Hebrew University
Mount Scopus
Jerusalem, Israel

Chapter 15

The Skills and Information Requirements of Industrial Technologies: On the Use of Engineers as a Proxy

Simón Teitel

I. INTRODUCTION

The transfer of technology requires agents capable of learning the relevant technical information and modifing it for adaptation to local conditions. The process includes information transfer in both codified and uncodified forms. The codified information will generally be available in written documents of various types: reports, drawings, specifications, manuals, etc. The skills necessary to comprehend these documents will be engineering and technical, i.e., those acquired in university-level engineering schools or middle-level technical schools.

The focus of this chapter is on the engineering skills involved in this process. At this stage, the approach will be largely conceptual and aimed at establishing the feasibility of using data on engineering labor in determining indicators for the skill and information content of industrial technologies transferred to less industrialized countries. More specifically, we

333

are concerned with identifying the role played by various types of engineering skills in the process of technology transfer and adaptation, including local technical change. An attempt is made to characterize the various industries according to the engineering skills they utilize as an indicator of the nature of their technological processes. We also try to characterize the level of technological development of the semiindustrialized countries (such as many in Latin America) on the basis of their stock and utilization of engineering manpower.

II. THE ENGINEERING ROLE

Engineers participate in the various phases of *interpreting* technical information, *modifying* that information to meet local needs and conditions, and *creating* new technical information by way of new or improved methods of producing existing products, creating new ones, or producing new materials, etc. These various roles played by engineers may take place in different organizational units, which vary, not only according to function, but by the nature of the industrial process involved. Engineers may be engaged in product design, maintenance and plant repair, manufacturing or production engineering, research and development, etc. Plant layout and time and motion studies leading to methods improvement are also, generally, well-established engineering functions. Even scheduling, programming, and quality control of production may be under engineering supervision, depending on the type of organizational structure followed.

It is to be expected that various types of engineering specialties will be employed in the manufacturing industries. On the one hand, engineers are required to deal with the technical information requirements of the particular processes important in each industry. Accordingly, we would expect, for example, to have a large proportion of chemical engineers in the chemical and petrochemical industries, and in the metal products industries, a high proportion of mechanical engineers is to be expected. Furthermore, in some industries we expect to find a high proportion of engineers dealing with a specific product specialty; for example, textile engineers in the textile and clothing industries. This type of engineering skill is of a more specific nature, that is, with less flexibility in its use than chemical or mechanical engineering skills. There is another type of engineering that is perhaps more "universal" and can be applied, in principle, to all industries or production processes. This is industrial engineering, which deals with changes in the time and space sequence of the methods utilized in all activities to increase output or reduce costs. It is thus likely that there will be a more even distribution across industries of this type of engineer than the others.

To put it a bit more formally, we expect that a high proportion of chemical engineers will be working in the chemical industries and, similarly, that a high proportion of the mechanical engineers will be working in the metalworking industries, while we would expect that practically all textile engineers will be employed in the textile and related industries and that industrial engineers will be more or less evenly distributed across the manufacturing industries.

III. CHARACTERIZATION OF THE INDUSTRIES BY ENGINEERING SKILLS

Table 1 shows the breakdown of engineering personnel as a proportion of total employment in the various manufacturing industries in the United States in 1970. We shall use this information to arrive at a classification or characterization of the industries on the basis of the type of engineering skills utilized. Some justification for the use of U.S. data as a standard is provided in Teitel (1976, 1981).

First we pose the question: *How are the industries ranked by their intensity of engineering employment?* Table 2 provides this answer: only seven industries have a proportion of engineers in their labor force that is above 3.3%, the average number of engineers per 100 persons engaged in manufacturing. These industries are: electrical machinery, with 8.4%; motor vehicles, with 7.3%; professional and scientific instruments, 6.3%; petroleum and coal products, 5.8%; metal products, 4.7%; machinery (excluding electrical), 4.6%; and chemicals and chemical products, 4.3%. The other industries have lower than the average proportion, including such industries as nonferrous metals, rubber products and plastics, iron and steel and paper and paper products.

Having become accustomed to characterizing industries by indicators measuring research intensity, it is natural to ask *whether these engineering-intensive industries are also the same one's with the highest rankings by research and development intensity measures.* An answer is given in Table 4, in which we compare the rankings given in Table 2 with two measures of research and development intensity, given in Table 3: R & D scientists and engineers per 100 employees and percentage of net sales devoted to R & D. As we can see, there is some correspondence and also some notable reversals. Motor vehicles, which ranks second in engineering intensity, ranks only fifth in R & D intensity, and chemicals, which ranks only seventh in engineering intensity, ranks second or fourth, according to the indicator chosen, in R & D intensity.

Although this evidence requires further analysis and the data are not strictly comparable, they point to an interesting possible conclusion: engi-

TABLE 1 *Engineering Personnel In U.S. Manufacturing, 1970[a]*

Industry	Total engineers	Civil and architects	Electrical/electronic	Mechanical	Industrial	Chemical	Metallurgical	Industry-specific	Other[b]
Manufacturing	33	1	8	6	6	2	1	3	6
Food and beverages	8			1	3	1			3
Tobacco and tobacco products	8	1	1	2	3	1			
Textile mill products	7			1	4				2
Clothing and fabricated textiles	2				2				
Leather and its products	3				2				1
Lumber and wood products	6			1	2				3
Paper and paper products	16	1	1	3	4	2			5
Printing and publishing	2				1				1
Rubber products and plastics	24	1	1	4	7	3			8
Chemicals and chemical products	43	2	2	5	6	24			4
Petroleum and coal products	58	5	3	7	4	28		5	6
Glass, stone, and clay products	19	2	1	2	5	2			7
Iron and steel	19	1	2	3	6	1	4		2
Nonferrous metals	27	1	3	4	7	1	7		4
Metal products (excl. machinery)	47	2	8	11	9	1	1	3	12
Machinery (excl. electrical)	46	1	4	16	9		1		15
Electrical machinery	84	1	48	8	14	1			12
Motor vehicles	73	2	9	16	12	1	1	28	4
Professional and scientific instruments	63	1	12	10	14	2		1	23

[a] Values are based on 1000 persons engaged. *Source:* Zymelman (1980).
[b] Includes rounding-off adjustments.

TABLE 2

U.S. Manufacturing Industries Ranked by Engineering Intensity[a]

Rank	Industry	Engineers in total employment (%)
1	Electrical machinery	8.4
2	Motor vehicles	7.3
3	Professional and scientific instruments	6.3
4	Petroleum and coal products	5.8
5	Metal products	4.7
6	Machinery (excluding electrical)	4.6
7	Chemicals and chemical products	4.3
8	Nonferrous metals	2.7
9	Rubber products and plastics	2.4
10–11	Iron and steel	1.9
10–11	Glass, stone, and clay products	1.9
12	Paper and paper products	1.6
13–14	Food and beverages	0.8
13–14	Tobacco and tobacco products	0.8
15	Textile mill products	0.7
16	Lumber and wood products	0.6
17	Leather and its products	0.3
18–19	Printing and publishing	0.2
18–19	Clothing and fabricated textiles	0.2
	Average	3.3

[a] *Source:* Zymelman (1980).

neers are employed to perform different tasks in different industries and engineering tasks may be more research-oriented in some industries and production-oriented in others.

The next related question we would like to ask is: *What type of engineers do these industries use? Is it possible to classify them according to engineering specialties?* For this, we turn to Table 5, which shows that, on average, i.e., for the manufacturing sector, the breakdown of the engineering specialties is as follows: electrical and electronic engineers constitute the largest group with 24.24% of the total engineering force employed in manufacturing; this group is followed by mechanical engineers and industrial engineers, both groups with 18.18%. "Other engineering," a catch-all group including unclassified specialties, also accounts for 18.18%. In fifth place are specific engineering specialties (including, presumably, such specialties as automotive engineers, and petroleum engineers), with 9.09%. The following group by size is that of chemical engi-

TABLE 3

Engineering and R & D Intensity of U.S. Manufacturing Industries

Industry	Engineers per 100 employees[a]	R & D scientists and engineers per 100 employees[b]	Net sales devoted to R & D (%)
Electrical machinery	8.4	3.9	7.5
Motor vehicles	7.3	2.0	3.5
Professional and scientific instruments	6.3	3.1	5.9
Petroleum and coal products	5.8	1.8	1.1
Metal products	4.7	1.0	1.2
Machinery (excl. electrical)	4.6	2.8	4.2
Chemicals and chemical products	4.3	3.8	4.1
Nonferrous metals	2.7	0.6	0.8
Rubber products and plastics	2.4	1.8	2.1
Iron and steel	1.9	—[c]	—[c]
Glass, stone, and clay products	1.9	1.4	1.9
Paper and paper products	1.6	0.6	0.7
Food and beverages	0.8	0.6	0.4
Tobacco and tobacco products	0.8	—	—
Textile mill products	0.7	0.4	0.5
Lumber and wood products	0.6	0.4	0.4
Leather and its products	0.3	—	—
Printing and publishing	0.2	—	—
Clothing and fabricated textiles	0.2	—[d]	—[d]

[a] *Source:* Zymelman (1980).

[b] *Source:* National Science Foundation (1973).

[c] Included with nonferrous metals as primary metals.

[d] Included with textile mill products as textiles and apparel.

neers with 6.06%, followed by civil engineers and architects and metallurgical engineers, both with 3.3% of the total.

Against this average pattern, is it possible to differentiate among the various manufacturing industries according to their use of engineering skills? Without referring to the group labeled "Other," because it may include a residual of otherwise unclassified specialties, we may point out the following features in the employment of engineers by industries. First,

TABLE 4

Ranking of U.S. Manufacturing Industries by Engineers and R & D Intensity[a]

Industry	Engineers per 100 employees[a]	R & D scientists and engineers per 100 employees[b]	Net sales devoted to R & D (%)
Electrical machinery	1	1	1
Motor vehicles	2	5	5
Professional and scientific instruments	3	3	2
Petroleum and coal products	4	6–7	9
Metal products	5	9	8
Machinery (excl. electrical)	6	4	3
Chemicals and chemical products	7	2	4
Nonferrous metals	8	10–12	10–11
Rubber products and plastics	9	6–7	6
Iron and steel	10	10–12[c]	10–11[c]
Glass, stone, and clay products	11	8	7
Paper and paper products	12	10–12	12

[a] *Source:* Zymelman (1980).

[b] *Source:* National Science Foundation (1973).

[c] Included with nonferrous metals as primary metals.

we note two *general features* of the breakdown by engineering specialties.

(a) A majority of the industries employ only a few of the engineering specialties. Without including consideration of the group of specific engineers (characteristic of particular industries), only 4 of the 19 industries include utilization of all engineering specialties. These industries are iron and steel, nonferrous metals, metal products, and motor vehicles. All these industries could be part of a designated "metal-based" group of industries.

(b) Only one engineering specialty cuts across all industries and is employed in all of them in substantial proportions: industrial engineers. This confirms our preliminary hypotheses about the existence of certain types of engineering skills of "universal" applicability, i.e., with no industry specificity.

Second, we note six specific features from the data presented in Table 6.

TABLE 5

Proportion of Engineering Specialties in Total Engineering Employment in U.S. Manufacturing Industry, 1970[a]

Industry	Civil and architects	Electrical/ electronic	Mechanical	Industrial	Chemical	Metallurgical	Industry-specific	Other
Manufacturing	3.03	24.24	18.18	18.18	6.06	3.03	9.09	18.18
Food and beverages			12.50	37.50	12.50			37.50
Tobacco and tobacco products	12.50	12.50	25.0	37.50	12.50			
Textile mill products			14.29	57.14				28.57
Clothing and fabricated textiles				100.0				
Leather and its products			16.67	66.67				33.33
Lumber and wood products				33.33				50.0
Paper and paper products	6.25	6.25	18.75	25.0	12.50			31.25
Printing and publishing				50.0				50.0
Rubber and plastics	4.17	4.17	16.67	29.16	12.50			33.33
Chemicals and chemical products	4.65	4.65	11.63	13.95	55.81			9.30
Petroleum and coal products	8.62	5.17	12.07	6.90	48.28		8.62	10.34
Glass, stone, and clay products	10.53	5.26	10.53	26.32	10.53			36.84
Iron and steel	5.26	10.53	15.79	31.58	5.26	21.05		10.53
Nonferrous metals	3.70	11.11	14.81	25.93	3.70	25.93		14.81
Metal products (excl. machinery)	4.26	17.02	23.40	19.15	2.13	2.13	6.38	25.53
Machinery (excl. electrical)	2.17	8.70	34.78	19.57		2.17		32.61
Electrical machinery	1.19	57.14	9.52	16.67	1.19			14.29
Motor vehicles	2.74	12.33	21.92	16.44	1.37	1.37	38.36	5.48
Professional and scientific instruments	1.59	19.05	15.87	22.22	3.17		1.59	36.51

[a] All values are given as percentages. *Source:* Zymelman (1980).

TABLE 6

Three Largest Engineering Specialties Employed in U.S. Manufacturing Industries[a]

Industry	Engineering specialty	Percentage	Engineering specialty	Percentage	Engineering specialty	Percentage
Electrical machinery	Electrical	57	Industrial	17	Mechanical	9.5
Motor vehicles	Specific	38	Mechanical	22	Industrial	16
Professional and scientific instruments	Industrial	22	Electrical	19	Mechanical	16
Petroleum and coal products	Chemical	48	Mechanical	12	Specific	9
Metal products	Mechanical	23	Industrial	19	Electrical	17
Machinery (excl. electrical)	Mechanical	35	Industrial	19	Electrical	9
Chemical and chemical products	Chemical	56	Industrial	14	Mechanical	12
Nonferrous metals	Metallurgical	26	Industrial	26	Mechanical	15
Rubber products and plastics	Industrial	29	Mechanical	17	Chemical	12.5
Iron and steel	Industrial	32	Metallurgical	21	Mechanical	16
Glass, stone, and clay products	Industrial	26	Chemical	10.5	Mechanical	10.5
Paper and paper products	Industrial	25	Mechanical	19	Chemical	12.5
Food and beverages	Industrial	37.5	Mechanical	12.5	Chemical	12.5
Tobacco and tobacco products	Industrial	37.5	Mechanical	25	Chemical	12.5
Textile mill products	Industrial	57	Mechanical	14		
Lumber and wood products	Industrial	33	Mechanical	17		
Leather and its products	Industrial	67				
Printing and publishing	Industrial	50				
Clothing and fabricated textiles	Industrial	100				

[a] *Source:* Zymelman (1980).

(a)   Clothing, leather, and printing and publishing utilize only industrial engineers.

(b)   Textile products and lumber and wood products also employ mechanical engineers in addition to industrial engineers.

(c)   There is a group of "process" industries, that is characterized by the use of chemical engineers. This is the case for food and beverages, tobacco and tobacco products, paper and paper products, rubber and plastics, chemicals and chemical products, petroleum and coal products, and glass, stone, and clay products, which use chemical engineers in a proportion well above the average (6%), ranging from 10.5% for glass, stone, and clay products to 56% for chemicals and chemical products.

(d)   Similarly, mechanical engineers and metallurgical engineers can be used to characterize the "metal-based" group of industries. One part of it, the basic metals subgroup, is characterized by a high proportion of metallurgical engineers, with 21 and 26% for iron and steel and nonferrous metals, respectively. The metal-working or metal-transforming subgroup would include: metal products, with 23% of mechanical engineers; machinery (excluding electrical), with 35% of mechanical engineers; and motor vehicles, with 22%, all above the average for manufacturing.

(e)   The electrical machinery group is characterized by a high proportion of electrical and electronic engineers (57%).

(f)   Industry-specific engineering specialties seem to be important only in motor vehicles (probably automotive engineers), with 38% of the engineering workforce; in petroleum and coal products (probably petroleum engineers or mining engineers), with 9%; and in metal products, with 6%.

IV.   CHARACTERIZATION OF THE LEVEL OF TECHNOLOGICAL DEVELOPMENT BY THE STOCK AND UTILIZATION OF ENGINEERING AND SCIENTIFIC SKILLS

It is not easy to arrive at an overall index of technological competence by using, on a comparative basis, the data available on engineering manpower. The World Bank data on occupational distribution for industries, available for a group of 26 countries, can only be used with some degree of confidence for the total number and proportion of engineers in the manufacturing labor force. Attempts at trying to ascertain whether a pattern exists in the composition of the engineering workforce failed because the data matrix was sparse for important categories such as industrial engineers, chemical engineers, and metallurgical engineers even for some of the most highly industrialized countries. This is probably a reflection of the use of different labor classifications, and it makes the data not directly comparable.

We have also had access to UNESCO data on the stock of engineers and scientists per 10,000 population and on the number of engineers and scientists devoted to R & D per 10,000 population. Although this data goes beyond engineering manpower, because it also includes scientists and covers more sectors than manufacturing, it is useful in providing a numerical indication not only of the quantity of the technically qualified high-level manpower but also of its quality or the nature of its utilization. Put in another way, through this data we learn about the proportion of this manpower engaged in tasks pertaining to the creation of new, or the modification of existing knowledge through basic and applied research and development.

In Table 7, the countries for which the World Bank data are available

TABLE 7

Countries Ranked by the Proportion of Engineers in Their Manufacturing Labor Force[a]

Rank	Country	Year	Proportion (%)
1	United States	1971	3.3
2	United Kingdom	1971	2.7
3	Norway	1970	2.6
4	West Germany	1970	2.2
5	France	1971	1.9
6	Netherlands	1970	1.8
7	Canada	1971	1.7
8	Japan	1970	1.6
9	Israel	1972	1.4
10	Belgium	1970	1.0
11	New Zealand	1971	1.0
12	Singapore	1970	1.0
13	Taiwan	1971	0.8
14	Mexico	1970	0.7
15	Venezuela	1975	0.6
16	Colombia	1971–73	0.4
17	Jamaica	1970	0.4
18	Chile	1971	0.4
19	Tunisia	1975	0.4
20	Costa Rica	1973	0.4
21	Brazil	1970	0.3
22	Panama	1970	0.3
23	Greece	1971	0.3
24	Ireland	1971	0.2
25	Uruguay	1975	0.2

[a] *Source:* Zymelman (1980).

are ranked according to the proportion of engineers in the number of persons engaged in manufacturing. The first 11 countries are clearly highly industrialized countries, with the possible exception of Israel. The unweighted mean of the percentage of engineers in the manufacturing labor force for this group of countries is 1.85, with a standard deviation of 0.74 and a range of 1.0 to 3.3%. For the whole group of 25 countries, the mean is 1.10, with a standard deviation of 0.89 and a range of 0.2 to 3.3%. Most of the countries included in the lower half of the table can be considered as semiindustrialized countries. The descriptive statistics for this subgroup are: mean of 0.46, standard deviation of 0.23, range of 0.2 to 1.0%.

In Tables 8 and 9 we show a group of countries for which comparable data are available, respectively, on the stock of engineers and scientists

TABLE 8

Stock of Engineers and Scientists, Selected Countries[a]

Country	Year	Number of scientists and engineers per 10,000 population
Japan	1975	372.0
Netherlands	1971	335.1
Israel	1974	291.8
Canada	1971	287.8
Switzerland	1970	282.9
Norway	1976	200.5
France	1968	198.8
West Germany	1970	178.6
Austria	1971	158.6
Argentina	1974	155.7
Korea	1975	132.7
Italy	1961	120.9
Australia	1971	115.8
United States	1975	75.8
Ireland	1971	73.4
Belgium	1966–67	73.2
Denmark	1965	72.5
Uruguay	1970	69.4
Mexico	1969	69.1
Brazil	1970	58.5
Spain	1967	57.4
Peru	1974	55.2
Singapore	1975	47.0
Iran	1972	41.8
New Zealand	1973	27.4
India	1971	21.3
Pakistan	1973–74	16.5

[a] *Source:* UNESCO (1978).

TABLE 9

Scientists and Engineers Engaged in Research and Development, for Selected Countries[a]

Country	Year	Scientists and engineers 10,000 population
Japan	1976	35.6
Switzerland	1975	25.3
United States	1975	25.0
Australia	1973–74	19.5
Netherlands	1975	17.4
West Germany	1975	16.8
Norway	1975	15.2
France	1974	12.4
Israel	1974	10.2
New Zealand	1973	10.0
Belgium	1967	9.4
Denmark	1973	9.4
Ireland	1975	8.1
Canada	1975	7.2
Italy	1975	6.8
Uruguay	1971–72	3.9
Argentina	1974	3.2
Singapore	1975	2.8
Austria	1972	2.5
Spain	1974	2.3
Korea	1974	1.9
India	1973	1.7
Iran	1972	1.6
Peru	1975	1.3
Mexico	1969	0.8
Brazil	1974	0.8
Pakistan	1973–74	0.6

[a] *Source:* UNESCO (1978).

per 10,000 population, and for the number of scientists and engineers involved in R & D per 10,000 population. Although accounting for population size may be a way of better ascertaining the *density* of scientific and technical skills in the country, it is necessary to examine further the uses to which such skills are put. As previously indicated, engineers may be employed to carry out a gamut of different activities, such as design, production control, management, trouble-shooting, process improvements, and research and development. In terms of the information handled and generated, it seems legitimate to assume that the latter activity represents the highest level of application of engineering skills. Although this body of data also includes scientists, this does not necessarily mean that we are dealing mostly with basic research, and quite possibly, in a majority of the countries, the bulk of the scientists and engineers are employed instead in applied research and development.[1]

Of course, we should not forget the caveat about the variegated nature of the definitions, methods, etc., applied in compiling the country statistics in this relatively new field of national statistics that accounts for a substantial measure of noncomparability (UNESCO, 1978, p. 1).

The descriptive statistics of the data in Table 8 are: a mean of 132.95 per 10,000, a standard deviation of 102.77 (quite large), and a range of 16.5 to 372.0 per 10,000. We find several relatively highly industrialized countries *below* the average; this group includes Italy, Australia, the United States, Belgium, Denmark, and New Zealand. To this we must add that semiindustrialized countries like Argentina and Korea are above the average, with 155.7 and, close to it, 132.7 per 10,000, respectively, plus the fact that semiindustrialized countries such as Ireland with 73.4, Uruguay with 69.4, and Mexico with 69.1 per 10,000 appear to be quite close to highly industrialized countries such as the United States, Belgium, and Denmark. This points to the limitations of taking the *stock* of scientists and engineers, even when deflated by population size, as an indicator of technical competence.

For Table 9, which indicates the proportion of scientists and engineers engaged in R & D, for the same 27 countries as in Table 8, the descriptive statistics are: a mean of 9.32 per 10,000, a standard deviation of 9.06 (quite high), and a range of 0.6 to 35.6 per 10,000. Examination of the ranking of countries shows no surprises; the first 15 countries are clearly industrialized countries and, furthermore, there is a clear break separating those countries from a group of semiindustrialized and less industrialized countries headed by Uruguay and Argentina. Whereas Italy, the last in the group of industrialized countries, has 6.8 per 10,000 population scientists and engineers engaged in research and development activities, Uruguay, the country that follows, has 3.9 per 10,000. Consequently, we also computed the statistics for each of the subgroups that seem to be quite homogeneous.[2] The group of industrialized countries has a mean of 15.22, a standard deviation of 8.25, and a range of 6.8 to 35.6 per 10,000. The group of semiindustrialized and less industrialized countries has a mean of 1.95, a standard deviation of 1.03, and a range of 0.6 to 3.9 per 10,000 population.

---

[1] In 1972, in the United States, development activities accounted for 64% of total R & D expenditures, applied research for 22%, and basic research for 14%. It is also estimated that industry had about two-thirds of the total scientists and engineers engaged in R & D compared with 13% each for the government and the universities (National Science Foundation, 1973, p. 23).

[2] The presence of Austria in the lower group raises a question.

TABLE 10

Engineering and Scientific Manpower Indicators for Selected Countries, Circa 1970[a]

Country	Engineers in Manufacturing Labor Force		Stock of scientists and engineers per 10,000 population		Scientists and engineers in R & D per 10,000 population		Proportion of scientists and engineers devoted to R & D		Average rank
	%	Rank	0/000	Rank	0/000	Rank	%	Rank	
United States	3.3	1	75.8	8	25.0	2	32.98	2	1
Norway	2.6	2	200.5	5	15.2	5	7.58	7	3
West Germany	2.2	3	178.6	7	16.8	4	9.41	6	4
France	1.9	4	198.8	6	12.4	6	6.24	8	6
Netherlands	1.8	5	335.1	2	17.4	3	5.19	11	5
Canada	1.7	6	287.8	4	7.2	10	2.50	13	9
Japan	1.6	7	372.0	1	35.6	1	9.57	5	2
Israel	1.4	8	291.8	3	10.2	7	3.50	12	7
Belgium	1.0	9	73.2	10	9.4	9	12.84	3	8
New Zealand	1.0	10	27.4	15	10.0	8	36.50	1	10
Singapore	1.0	11	47.0	14	2.8	13	5.96	9	13
Mexico	0.7	12	69.1	12	0.8	14	1.16	15	15
Brazil	0.3	13	58.5	13	0.8	15	1.37	14	14
Ireland	0.2	14	73.4	9	8.1	11	11.04	4	11
Uruguay	0.2	15	69.4	11	3.9	12	5.62	10	12

[a] *Sources:* Zymelman (1980); UNESCO (1978).

Because of the apparent variability of the rankings obtained through the use of the single indicators, we tried to derive an overall indicator of technical competence on the basis of measures of the stock and utilization of highly trained manpower. To the indicators already mentioned, which are proportion of engineers in the manufacturing industry labor force, stock of scientists and engineers per 10,000 population, and number of scientists and engineers employed in R & D per 10,000 population, we added a fourth: the proportion of the number of scientists and engineers devoted to R & D to the total number of scientists and engineers. To be able to use all the indicators, we had to reduce the number of countries to those 15 for which all the data were available. In Table 10, we show the countries ranked by each of the indicators. We also computed an average unweighted overall ranking, which is also shown in the table. The result is quite similar to that obtained by using the proportion of engineers in the manufacturing labor force as an indicator and has no surprises in terms of the ranking of the countries. The Spearman correlation coefficient between the overall ranking and that given by the proportion of engineers is quite high: 0.88, and in fact, if it were not for Japan, which has a surprisingly low rank in the proportion of engineers per 10,000 persons engaged in manufacturing while ranking very high in the stock of scientists and engineers and in the number of scientists and engineers engaged in R & D, the concordance would have been considerably higher.

ACKNOWLEDGMENTS

I am grateful to M. Zymelman, of the World Bank, for providing access to the data on the occupational composition of industries. I also acknowledge with gratitude the comments received from Z. Hirsch, N. Leff, F. Pazos, G. Ranis, and M. Syrquin. The points of view expressed herein are personal and do not purport to represent the official position of the Inter-American Development Bank.

REFERENCES

National Science Foundation (1973). *Science Indicators 1972*. Washington, D.C.: Report of the National Science Board.
UNESCO (1978). *Development in Human and Financial Resources for Science and Technology*. Basic statistical tables showing the earliest and latest years for which data are available, Division of Statistics on Science and Technology, Office of Statistics (April), Paris.
Teitel, S. (1976). "Labor Homogeneity, Skill Integrity and Factor Reversals—An International Comparison." *Journal of Development Economics* **3**, 355–366.
Teitel, S. (1981). "Productivity, Mechanization and Skills: A Test of the Hirschman Hypothesis for Latin American Industry." *World Development* **9** (4), 355–371.
Zymelman, M. (1980). *Occupational Structures of Industries*. Washington, D.C.: Education Department, World Bank.

Economic and Social Development Department
Inter-American Development Bank
Washington, D.C.

Chapter 16

The Capital Goods Sector in LDCs: Economic and Technical Development

Howard Pack

I. INTRODUCTION[1]

Three arguments may be put forth for fostering the production of capital goods in LDCs: the comparative advantage accruing from low labor costs; the generation of capacity to produce machines having appropriate designs; and the prospect of externalities.

Even in advanced countries, the capital goods sector is relatively labor-intensive, more specifically, skilled-labor-intensive. A number of LDCs have a substantial supply of skilled workers available at a fraction of the wage paid to their counterparts in developed countries. If they do not exhibit commensurately lower productivity, their wage levels should confer a cost advantage. The remuneration is relatively low not only for skilled operatives but for engineers and technicians. Because the sector requires substantial services from engineers and technicians—services

---

[1] A much longer version of this chapter, drawing largely on the experience of countries in Asia, appears in Pack (1981).

349

ranging from design to prototype production to plant commissioning—its comparative advantage in LDCs is further enhanced.

The production of capital goods often evokes images of large, highly mechanized plants in which scale economies, particularly in the use of capital, may attenuate any advantage LDCs derive from lower labor costs. But many subsectors of the capital goods industry, even in the United States, have a relatively large number of small firms producing a significant portion of value added. Insofar as the industrial structure of the United States provides a guide, firms of varying size may be efficient. It is necessary, however, to consider the two other principal cost components in any sector: materials and capital. As will be shown, full recognition of these components leads to a more qualified view of the probable degree of static comparative advantage currently enjoyed by LDC producers.

The production of appropriate machinery is the second argument. If LDC firms produce machinery more in keeping with the relative factor endowments of LDCs, that production would have a desirable effect on both income generation and employment opportunities.[2] For example, Mexico or Brazil, with their large supply of unskilled labor, would benefit from the local production and adoption of equipment that, for a given investment level, uses more labor than is required by imported equipment from the advanced countries. Cost minimization by local users of equipment may lead to a demand for more labor-intensive machines, a demand that domestic manufacturers might be more likely to fulfill than would producers in developed countries. Satisfying this demand does not imply that the equipment produced would be expected to be frozen at a primitive level. Instead, 1960 or 1965 models could be produced and gradually updated as changing factor scarcities warrant.

The prospect of externalities is the third argument: the skills generated in the mechanical engineering sector are useful in other sectors. Some workers engaged in the production of equipment may move to the equipment-purchasing sectors. Given the frequent process interruptions attributable to poor maintenance and repair, such a diffusion of skilled workers would permit an increase in the utilization rate of plant and unskilled workers. Moreover, the willingness to use second-hand equipment might be greater if firms had confidence in their own repair skills and their ability to produce spare parts.

Although the potential for obtaining an augmented range of equip-

---

[2] Of course, LDC producers should pursue any design changes that will reduce production costs at local input prices, regardless of factor saving bias. However, it seems plausible that the greatest returns may accrue from attention to labor-using innovations. For a recent rehabilitation of the induced innovation concept, see Binswanger and Ruttan (1978, particularly Chapters 2 and 4).

ment, as well as externalities, increases the attractiveness of the machinery industries, it should be emphasized that, even without this potential, the efficient, labor-intensive earning of foreign exchange may offer an important, largely neglected source of future growth for countries with the requisite supplies of skilled labor. As shall be shown, however, such growth may face obstacles typically neglected by the simple theory of comparative advantage.

The focus of this chapter is on the first two arguments for fostering the production of capital goods in LDCs. The externalities to other sectors are not considered because of the paucity of evidence. By their nature, these externalities require evidence of the benefits the engineering sector confers on those other sectors, including the diffusion of skills by movements of workers among industries and the design of special devices that can improve the local performance of imported equipment. Historical evidence indicates that these benefits have been substantial in the industrial countries, whereas nations with a small, backward engineering sector have suffered.[3] There is no reason LDCs could not derive similar benefits. On the other hand, if the encouragement of the capital goods sector cannot be based on the potential for cost efficiency, on adaptive design behavior, or on both, the invocation of externalities cannot, at this stage of knowledge, serve as a justification. The empirical base is too small to argue the relative magnitude of such benefits to other sectors.

II. EVIDENCE OF COST EFFICIENCY

The survey of production problems in this section is not intended to question the eventual emergence of efficient capital goods manufacturing in the countries examined or even in some smaller producers. Instead, it emphasizes that even advanced producer nations encounter severe production problems, which significantly increase their costs. The amelioration of existing difficulties offers an opportunity for the reduction of costs in the intermediate term, a reduction that can provide a cushion in the transition to a status in which production is efficiently executed and domestic innovation, previously of limited significance, begins to make a contribution to the competitiveness of the industry.

To describe and analyze the costs of production in the mechanical engineering sector, we draw on the recent experience of the principal LDC producers: Argentina, Brazil, India, Korea, Mexico, Pakistan, and Tai-

---

[3] See the survey by Murphy (1967) and many of the chapters contained in Rosenberg (1976).

wan. Despite their higher income levels, the three major Latin American producers exhibit characteristics quite similar to the other countries. Illustrative examples will be based mainly on their experience.[4]

We shall consider both the producers of industrial and agricultural equipment and their suppliers in the metal-products sector, particularly foundries and forges. The analysis thus centers on the later stages of production of engineering (excluding electrical and automotive) products and does not include iron and steel operations or specialty metal products necessary for the sector. Although domestic production of basic metals at high cost behind tariff protection would reduce any cost advantage inherent in the LDC fabricating sector, this competitiveness can be restored by liberalizing the trade regime. Any cost disadvantages on this account should not be viewed as militating against the competitiveness of the mechanical engineering sector. If liberalization were not implemented, the sector would, of course, be penalized.

The potential cost advantage among the enormously varied range of engineering products can be rigorously analyzed only within a fully articulated model of the mechanical engineering industry. The optimum technical organization of even a fairly simple engineering product compared with any process-centered production activity is particularly difficult. In a recent study, Lamyai *et al.* (1978) demonstrate that optimal use of either labor *or* equipment can lead, when compared with a suboptimal solution, to as much as a 90% reduction in average cost. Larger batches of an identical product reduce the setup times of equipment and the skilled labor per unit of output; the manufacture of different products with similar requirements of skill and equipment can increase the rate of use of both inputs. Thus, if plants in developed countries typically exhibit higher utilization rates per hour for skilled labor and equipment than LDC firms do, they are likely to exhibit greater plantwide efficiency. If LDCs are to be competitive in engineering activities, productivity on individual tasks must be sufficiently high or factor prices or material costs must be sufficiently low to offset the probable firmwide productivity difference.

As will be shown, a considerable number of simple production problems exist, even for products in which LDCs may have a comparative advantage if reasonable levels of x-efficiency are realized.[5] Of course, simi-

[4] The studies drawn upon are: Cortes (1978) for Argentina; Bonelli and Facanha (1977), Leff (1968), the World Bank (1979a), and the United Nations (1963) for Brazil; and the World Bank (1979b) for Mexico. Examples from the other countries will be found in Pack (1981).

[5] A number of complex issues analyzed by Lamyai *et al.* (1978) are omitted here because an adequate treatment would take the discussion too far afield. For example, large batches of a single product may warrant changing the entire production process—say, substituting special-purpose equipment for general-purpose equipment and concomitantly decreasing the relative importance of skilled operatives—rather than simply leading to reduced costs for a given production regime.

lar problems of static inefficiency arise in most industrial activities within LDCs. Unless x-efficiency is worse and prospects for improvement are poorer in capital goods than in other sectors, the problems described do not constitute an argument against the sector. Instead, the following analysis is designed to move the discussion from the simple factor-proportions model of capital, unskilled labor, and skilled labor toward a fuller consideration of the following: the productivity of workers on tasks, the low productivity of plants, the weakness of the subcontracting network, the poor record of some supplying sectors, and adverse policies of government. These categories are not mutually exclusive but are adopted here for expositional convenience.

A.   Task-Level Productivity

Although skilled operatives in LDCs receive lower wages than those in developed countries, the obvious question is whether labor productivity is proportionally lower than warranted by the smaller quantity of capital per worker, thus nullifying the wage difference. It is useful to distinguish two aspects of labor productivity. The first is the number of items produced per minute by a worker on a set task, such as cutting a block of metal, if is can be assumed that the metal is available, machines are in good order, and so on. The second is the output per operative day, which depends on the first aspect and on the rate at which metal is made available, the frequency of mechanical breakdowns not attributable to the operative, the time operatives spend moving material among work stations, the number of different tasks assigned to each worker and their respective set-up times, and so on. The second aspect reflects the management ability of a firm and the environment outside the firm, though capable managers may be able to mitigate such deleterious external factors as irregular deliveries of raw materials.

Most observations of the factories operating in the LDCs indicate that the performance of operatives on a given task is high, despite the use of less sophisticated equipment. In many activities, their performance equals that of factory workers in developed countries; rarely is it less than 30% of their level.[6] Productivity on a plantwide basis, however, is often much lower.

Lower productivity at the task level may reflect a movement along a production function in response to the low wage–rental ratio (the use of poor-quality cutting tools and the absence of jigs) or a failure to reach the

[6] Studies discussing task- and firm-level productivity are those of Vidossich (1970) on the Brazilian machine tool sector and the World Bank (1979b) study of the Mexican machinery producing industry, which provides a number of examples of "x-inefficient" practices.

production function (the misestimation of machine potential). It is not always easy to determine the group in which a specific observation is best
placed, but the analytical distinction is important because the first group
leads to a decrease in production costs and the latter to an increase in
them. Moreover, as factor prices change, labor productivity improves if
firms are rationally responding to relative factor prices, whereas a movement toward the production function may not occur without some form of
technical aid.

B.   Plantwide Productivity

In contrast to high task-level productivity, plantwide efficiency measured by unit input requirements of labor, equipment, and materials is
generally reported to be low.

Plant layout and scheduling have a substantial effect on productivity.
In many machine-producing activities, neither the order of operation nor
the placement of machines is inherent in the process. Nor is it physically
difficult simply to stop the process and hold a partly finished piece at a
workstation until it is again convenient to work on it. Although the inefficiencies generated by the wide latitude of choice could be solved by adequate management, the detailed studies of plant operations in LDCs demonstrate that this is not the case. The typical plant exhibits a poor layout,
in which the movement of work in process interferes with operations at
individual workstations, where an accumulation of partly finished pieces
is held until workers return to them. And despite the fact that the diversity
of products requires careful scheduling to increase the use of equipment,
all of the studies report poor scheduling. Thus the productivity of both
labor and equipment are decreased, and the substantial work-in-process
inventory generates interest charges that are higher than necessary.[7]

C.   Subcontracting Networks

A principle requirement of the entire mechanical engineering sector is
the development of a subcontracting network. In the machinery sector of
the advanced countries, subcontracting has proved to be important in reducing costs. Small firms concentrating on a few operations or components common to a large number of producers are able to utilize special-
purpose equipment fully, as well as to obtain the benefits of learning over

[7] See World Bank (1979b) and Vidossich (1970), who states that plantwide productivity
in the Brazilian machine-tool sector in the late sixties was comparable to 1930 developed
country practices.

time as a result of specialization in a narrow area. If the volume were sufficient, such specialization could occur within larger firms, but quantities currently produced are too small to allow this. The adverse effect of import restriction policies on the ability of small firms, such as those typically in subcontracting, to obtain metals of the required quality is often cited in the Latin American context.[8]

There are two requisites for obtaining the potential benefits of subcontracting. First, the parent firm must be able to coordinate multiple sources of supply so that production is not interrupted by the absence of components. Second, the subcontractors must be efficient and reliable. The evidence in the studies surveyed in this chapter suggests that subcontracting, although extant in some countries and in some sectors, is limited.[9] This results partly from the unreliability of existing subcontractors in meeting delivery dates and quality specifications, partly from their relatively high costs. It is unclear whether large firms encounter limits on their ability to organize a subcontracting network, because the typical reason adduced for the absence of such a network is the low quality of subcontractors. Nevertheless, the observations of plant layout and other intraplant production difficulties suggest that some of the problem may reside in the parent firms. That would imply that the organizational costs of subcontracting may currently exceed the cost reductions to be derived from it, that is, from the greater factor utilization and the learning stemming from specialization. This also implies that an improved sectoral division of labor would be contingent upon the accumulation of adequate organizational ability.

Although the sectorwide loss in potential cost reduction is widely recognized, effective solutions are difficult to design. But without availing themselves of subcontracting and the real external economies bestowed upon the industry as a whole, LDC machine-producing sectors are subject to an immediate cost handicap in relation to their competitors in developed countries.[10]

D. Backward Linkages

Castings and forgings are principal inputs used by the mechanical engineering sector. The production of these inputs is intensive in skilled labor,

[8] See, for example, World Bank (1979b).

[9] For example, Vidossich (1970) claims that in the late sixties the extent and quality of subcontracting in the Brazilian machine-tool sector were roughly equivalent to the level that advanced developed country producers had achieved by 1920.

[10] An excellent discussion of conditions that may have fostered the evolution of subcontracting in Japan can be found in Watanabe (1978).

and mechanization is not economical, except at very high volume. They can thus contribute to the competitiveness of the machinery sector if they are efficiently produced, that is, at less than CIF prices.[11] Two sets of questions arise about the performance of most LDCs in this production: first, narrow questions of intraplant efficiency; second, broad questions arising from the complex interventions associated with import substitution.

Foundries and forges in LDCs suffer from technical problems, partly as a result of the absence of earlier incentives to learn. One measure of the technical obstacles facing even an industry with a long history, such as the Indian foundry sector, is the estimate that 65% of foundries would require more than five years, even with substantial technical aid, to produce quality castings at international prices and another 25% would require from one to five years. Even if these periods could be reduced by more competitive pressure, they nevertheless indicate the retardation in learning introduced by previous trade restrictions (World Bank, 1974). The Mexican foundry sector exhibits high cost and low quality, except for those owned by automobile producers; much of the problem has been attributed to the unavailability of critical inputs such as high-quality coke and pig iron, these scarcities reflecting quantitative restrictions on imports. Purely technical production difficulties are also widely noted. (World Bank, 1979b, pp. 142–147). A similar situation exists in Brazil (Vidossich, 1970, Vol. II, p. 30). Cortes (1978) noted that in Argentina a faster technical upgrading has occurred where the purchasers are producers of high-quality consumer goods such as automobiles.

E.   Government Policies

Superimposed on the technical difficulties faced by a young mechanical engineering sector may be the additional difficulties induced by a policy designed to foster that sector's development. For example, in Korea and Mexico, there has been an early emphasis on the encouragement of large-scale firms through the use of a variety of incentives, including low-interest loans, and such favorable tax provisions as accelerated depreciation and investment credits. The outcome has been the purchase of equipment that is severalfold too large for the domestic market: although medium-sized firms may initially possess equipment that will be efficiently used with a doubling of demand, the larger machines may be initially used at a tenth of their capacity. Production is then saddled with high fixed

---

[11] This assumes that low-volume, labor-intensive production can result in prices competitive with high-volume, mechanized processes.

costs, and an attempt is made to diversify the product range. This diversification often competes with the product lines of smaller and medium-scale firms, reducing the size of their production runs. There may thus be a downward filtration of excess capacity and a loss of the benefits of whatever specialization has occurred, increasing production costs for smaller firms.[12] Although this phenomenon is not limited to the mechanical engineering sector, it is more significant than in the process industries, given the much larger range of products that can be manufactured with a given set of equipment and the larger setup costs for each run.

Another policy-induced difficulty affecting the productivity of the machinery-producing sector arises from the appeal of restricting imports of machine tools in the early stages of growth of the typical capital goods sector. One of the main requirements of an efficient capacity to produce capital goods is the use of machine tools of reasonably high quality, that is, cutters and shapers of metal that are used in the production of all equipment. Machine tools are one of the earliest types of capital goods production begun in those LDCs now exhibiting relatively high levels of engineering output. They are a tempting target for import substitution, given the large quantities imported; some types of machine tools, such as simple lathes and presses, are fairly easy to produce and can be used in repair work outside the equipment-producing sector and in the production of other machines. But the locally produced machine tools often are not adequate for the high precision characterizing much of the equipment-producing sector. This inadequacy may not present a problem as long as imported machine tools are available. But, in some countries, the pressure from domestic machine-tool producers or the desire of the government to foster the more rapid growth of heavy industry has led to the licensing of all machine-tool imports.

The import of machine tools is often permitted only when domestic producers certify their inability to produce the imports proposed. Under such a policy, machine-tool purchasers attempt to maintain an ability to import, while producers are likely to argue that they can match the foreign product. In their anxiousness to encourage new production, some governments may lend more weight to the claims of producers, at least until the effects on purchasers become apparent. In the interim, the resulting inability to obtain high-quality equipment may retard growth in sectors outside the machine-tool sector. In such sectors, many items are simpler to

---

[12] Once the large-scale capacity is in place, the private cost of producing a given level of output may be lower as a result of filtration: that is, the reduction in costs by larger firms may exceed the increase imposed on the smaller ones. The critical point is that sectorwide costs are unnecessarily high as a result of the premature introduction of large-scale equipment.

produce than machine tools, and those items enjoy a comparative advantage relative to machine tools.[13] The growth of the entire mechanical engineering sector may thus be slowed by the premature emphasis on machine tools.[14]

F. Conclusions about Comparative Cost Structures

The foregoing discussion of technological difficulties suggests that the low-efficiency wages of LDC equipment producers are likely to be offset, at least partly, by a variety of inefficiencies related to production. It also

TABLE 1

Brazilian-to-Foreign Price Ratios for Selected Machinery[a]

Machinery	Country of origin of foreign product	Ratio
Machine tools		
Bench lathe	Taiwan	1.03
	United States	1.12
Parallel lathe	Czechoslovakia	1.42
	Argentina	0.94
Bench perforator	Rhodesia	1.06
	United States	0.60
Textile machinery		
Spinning machine	Europe	1.02
	Europe	1.04
Loom	South Korea	1.22
	Europe	0.81
Agricultural machinery		
Automated harvester	Europe	1.27
	Europe	1.42
	Europe	1.27
	Europe	1.05
Tractor with wheels	Europe	0.79
	United States	0.92
	Europe	1.22

[a] *Source:* World Bank (1979a, p. 43).

[13] Those items require less fine tolerances and less knowledge of metallurgical properties.

[14] This problem is similar, of course, to that in other industries in which inefficient, protected domestic intermediates reduce the competitiveness of efficient purchasing industries. The difference is that poor equipment leads to long-term handicaps, even if the trade regime is liberalized. In contrast, liberalization, say, of textiles can have an immediate effect on clothing costs.

raises the possibility that the establishment of an integrated equipment sector, rather than a fabrication sector, is likely to be considerably more difficult than envisioned by those calling for the end of dependence on imported equipment and the technology it embodies.

Some recently available (and tentative) evidence indicates that, despite the factors that decrease plantwide productivity per day and the cost increasing effects of a weak supplying sector, a few Brazilian producers have approached international competitiveness in some products. Some comparisons of Brazilian-to-foreign prices are shown in Table 1.[15] Although such data must be treated with caution, given the large number of taxes and subsidies affecting the Brazilian sector, its prices are sufficiently close to world levels in these items to suggest the likelihood that a more competitive atmosphere, combined with technical help to foster the diffusion of appropriate technological knowledge, could yield competitiveness relatively soon. However, in the much smaller Mexican sector, the largely impressionistic evidence is different, with much of the problem arising from the high cost of foundries (World Bank, 1979b).

III. EVIDENCE OF DESIGN ADAPTATION TO DOMESTIC FACTOR PROPORTIONS

Before proceeding to the evidence, some of the issues related to innovation will be briefly discussed. The market wage–rental ratio, however distorted it may be relative to a social optimum, is considerably lower in the principal LDCs producing equipment than in the developed countries. If it is assumed that purchasers of equipment are interested in reducing their production costs, the derived demand for locally produced machinery should lead to equipment and processes that are more labor-intensive. Nevertheless, the rather thin evidence on the existence and extent of adaptation of *designs* by LDC capital goods producers does not verify this expectation. The alternative for responding to local factor prices—production of vintages of equipment no longer produced by more advanced countries—is more widely confirmed. Both mechanisms for adjusting to different relative factor prices will be discussed together, though there are important differences between them.

Reliance solely on equipment of older vintage, though an important option for producers in the short or intermediate term, has important limitations. Continued design improvement by machine producers in the de-

---

[15] The original table (World Bank, 1979a) is unclear about the specific comparisons, including whether they are FOB or CIF at a common destination.

veloped countries, not at least partly offset by similar activity in the LDCs, may lead to a situation of technical dominance in which the equipment produced in developed countries is less expensive to use, regardless of relative factor prices. But reductions that can be achieved in the cost of production by eliminating some of the inefficiences discussed in the preceding section may permit price reductions that allow LDC-produced equipment to continue to be competitive for a longer period.

Design research may be less important for smaller local producers that typically do not rely on licensing. Their evolution may reflect the differences in creative ability as well as their links to the more competitive sectors of the economy. There are a number of instances of companies modifying imported designs, upgrading them, and producing a machine that permits a lower capital–labor ratio in the using sector. For example, Argentine companies are currently producing food-processing equipment that is less mechanized than advanced country equipment designed for the same product (Cortes, 1978), a large Mexican machinery producer has developed its own grain and rice milling equipment. (World Bank, 1979b, p. 138). In these two instances, there unfortunately is no evidence of whether the adapted equipment is economically efficient. Other pieces of evidence indicate that smaller firms in many countries, usually not manufacturing under license, have produced simple equipment that is often used for the production of goods whose quality is too low for international trade.[16]

IV. SOME HYPOTHESES ABOUT THE RESEARCH PROCESS

The absence of adaptive research is one part of a larger picture in which the LDCs appear to carry out limited industrial research of any type. There are some descriptions, but few systematic studies, of the extent or absence of research on design in the capital goods sector. The most general impression conveyed by the existing studies is the absence of product research; but this impression may partly reflect the disproportionate attention analysts have given to publicly funded research insti-

---

[16] See Bell (1978), Child and Kaneda (1971), Cooper and Kaplinsky (1974), Johnston and Kilby (1975), and Timmer (1972). Many of these illustrations, such as the Child–Kaneda documentation of the production of small engines and other equipment in response to demands generated by the green revolution, reflect limited adaptation of design but confirm the existence of considerable small-scale engineering ability. The most thorough study of adaptation by small-scale producers is that of Bell on Thailand's generation of locally adapted cassava-processing equipment.

tutes in contrast with the activities of firms.[17] The limited evidence on firms suggests that if a research staff exists, it is most often devoted to questions not related to design.[18] If this is assumed to be the case, some tentative exploration of the reasons for the pattern may be useful.

The pursuit of import substitution may discourage design efforts but encourage other cost-reducing activities. Because of the restriction on imports, the unpredictability of licensing procedures, and the insistence that firms achieve specified levels of domestic content, it may be profitable to employ research personnel in three activities: identifying local sources of raw and intermediate materials; identifying and upgrading potential local suppliers; and improving technical processes within the firm. In fact, these are reported to be the principal activities of many engineers and technicians employed in research and development.[19] But if a firm has a research budget, the allocation of that budget should equate the marginal return from design with the return obtainable from responding to policies for import substitution. There is little reason to believe that the marginal returns from the latter systematically exceed the former. Other explanations are needed.[20]

In its simplest form, a firm's calculation of whether to allocate some of its research budget to design should weigh the costs of achieving a given objective by carrying out its own research, say, meeting the competition of a new design from the developed countries, against those of acquisition through licensing. The ability to evaluate correctly the wisdom of licensing as opposed to research will depend on some prior experience in research to allow the calculation of the likely costs of internal development. Familiarity with the relevant licensing options and their evaluation will also depend on a strong technical and economic staff, whose skills may be a function of previous research. Thus even the simple choice just cited between licensing and research undoubtedly is too simple: it ignores the investment required to structure the decision correctly.

---

[17] Crane (1977) presents a fairly complete bibliography.

[18] See Cortes (1978) on Argentina, Katz and Ablin (1978) and the World Bank (1979b) on Mexico, and Bonelli and Facanha (1977) as well as Vidossich (1970) on Brazil.

[19] In Mexico, engineers are used to alter the product to allow the use of local suppliers, a fairly widespread practice.

[20] Although it might be argued that an ''export'' orientation is conducive to design research, the principal exporting countries have, until recently, emphasized relatively simple, labor-intensive products not requiring an intensive design effort. Whether the increasing emphasis of the East Asian countries on engineering products will be accompanied by a local design effort or by a reliance on licenses is still unclear. In existing technology-based industries producing mainly for the local market, such as chemicals, the emphasis has been mainly on licensing. For an example, see the study of Korea, by the World Bank (1978, Chapter 7).

In the light of scale economies in research, the relative endowments of research personnel and physical facilities in LDCs and in developed countries, and their probable relative efficiency as a result of previous learning, a one-time objective, say, in response to a major new design innovation, is likely to be achieved most cheaply through licensing. In general, a firm will have to respond to a stream of ongoing innovations. For the optimal strategy, it must not only consider the simple trade-off associated with current costs of acquisition of a license in relation to internal research.[21] It must also consider the effect of current research on the cost and effectiveness of future research.[22] The current paucity of research may be attributable to the myopia of firms, to the capital market imperfections facing even the largest LDC firms, and to risk aversion. Public intervention to foster local technical development can be justified on all of these grounds. There nevertheless is the possibility that LDCs may suffer from a comparative disadvantage in research and development, and the case for public aid should plausibly demonstrate that the appropriately discounted value of benefits from the local effort will exceed the discounted costs. The benefits should be defined to include additional income obtainable from the given investment if the local sector produces more appropriate equipment than suppliers in developed countries. If technical independence is viewed as a good in itself, no such calculation need be made, though I suspect that behind such views lies the intuition that infant-industry arguments about technology development are valid.

If the foregoing sketch of the probable effects of the overhang in developed countries of a large body of innovations and effectiveness in generating further ones is even roughly correct, the relatively small amount of design research in the engineering sectors of LDCs becomes easier to understand. It would also help to explain the paucity of labor-using innovations: a firm successfully undertaking such research, which increase the present discounted value of a given machine in the user industry, may find its competitive edge removed by rivals that purchase licenses that in-

---

[21] The research decision in an export-oriented economy would differ only insofar as the licensing costs would be higher, given the threat to third-country markets. This may force firms in such countries as Taiwan and Korea to pursue a local technical capacity in engineering rather earlier than did such large import-substituting countries as India and Brazil. Until exporting countries enter more sophisticated industries in which competition is based upon design, it may well be optimal for them to delay research and emphasize cheaper labor-intensive products.

[22] Mansfield *et al.* (1977) have recently produced estimates showing that research and development costs per project are negatively related to experience. If this relation were generally confirmed, it would support an infant-industry view of research and development.

crease the present discounted value of their equipment.[23] A labor-using adaptation might be matched by a rival's ability to incorporate material-saving features or higher speeds. The rival need not compete in labor saving. Although a complete analysis would depend on the license fees, the "shelf" of licenses available in developed countries, and the intensity and bias of innovation by the local firm, it is possible that successful local innovators would not realize greater profits from adaptive research.[24]

V. REQUIREMENTS OF COST EFFICIENCY AND DESIGN INNOVATION

The long-term competitiveness of LDC capital goods producers depends on activities related to two capacities: reducing excess production costs attributable to the types of inefficiencies cited earlier and undertaking research and particularly altering designs.

In the longer term, the LDC producer must compete not only in cost but in design. The engineering sector in developed countries engages in a considerable amount of research. This leads to a steady flow of improvements, which reduce operating costs at the input prices in developed countries. Such alterations are relevant to LDC producers, particularly those producing equipment under license. The licensee generally will not be able to obtain complete information on new improvements that the licensor makes to enhance the performance of equipment. Moreover, these improvements frequently are not labor saving in the sense of requiring fewer workers per machine. Instead, the speed of the machine or its efficiency in using materials is increased. Depending on the price of the newer machine, potential buyers may prefer the newer design because a given investment expenditure will result in a larger present discounted value. Thus, even if the LDC firms initially can match or undercut the international price, there is an inexorable attenuation of their initial cost advantage, unless their product is upgraded.

The necessity of newer designs in the longer term is not limited to the requirements of the export market. Domestically produced equipment may initially be available at lower cost than imported equipment. But if foreign companies improve the design of their equipment more rapidly than local ones, a point will be reached at which production costs arising

[23] See Baldwin and Childs (1969) for an explicit model of this type.

[24] The extensive use of licenses and the widespread copying of older imported machines is reported *inter alia* in Vidossich (1970) and Bonelli and Facanha (1977).

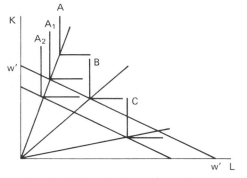

Fig. 1. Choices facing equipment users.

from the use of locally produced equipment will exceed those associated with imported machinery. Unless the domestic engineering sector is protected, purchasers will gravitate toward imports and the sector will exhibit stagnant production and excess capacity, much as the Indian textile-machinery sector has done.[25]

The need for research is likely to be greater if the LDC industry has not adapted the factor proportions of the equipment. The reason is that research in developed countries is localized in the more capital-intensive part of the isoquant. But even if local designs are used, the need to offset the effects of new improvements from abroad will eventually occur. As long as domestically produced equipment is used in the production of commodities whose production is also possible with imported equipment, efficiency will eventually require domestic producers to meet this competition. These considerations are conveniently summarized in Fig. 1.

In Fig. 1, let A denote the initial unit isoquant in the developed country, B the somewhat more labor-intensive isoquant achievable by LDC-produced equipment, and $w'w'$ the initial wage–rental ratio. Initially, minimum costs are achieved by producing with type-B equipment. If B remains unchanged while A moves toward the origin as a result of ongoing research, the two techniques yield equal costs when A_1 is reached.[26] Any further improvement leads to type-A equipment's becoming cheaper, even at LDC costs. It can also be seen that if considerably more labor-intensive processes, such as C, are available, reflecting, say indigenous designs, these will remain competitive for a longer time, until A_2 is achieved.

[25] For a detailed description of the many types of equipment in which the failure to upgrade design has been a deterrent to exports and a cost-raising factor for domestic firms forced to rely on such equipment, see Frankena (1971, pp. 339–407).

[26] Figure 1 assumes no factor-saving bias in technical improvement.

But even *C*, an indigenous technique, will eventually be displaced, unless it can be improved.

Thus although LDC production capable of replicating earlier vintages presents an attractive potential for achieving a desirable rate of technical upgrading, the world is not this benign. Unimproved versions of *B* or *C* may not be competitive for very long, though this is an empirical question about which little is known. The desired goal—obtaining some indigenous control over the rate of introduction of technology—will surely be conditioned by the continuing design progress of equipment producers in developed countries. Without significant abilities to reduce costs and achieve design improvements, the scope for controlling a nation's technical evolution is limited.

The reason for the earlier emphasis on possible sources of cost reduction in LDC equipment production should now be clear. For a time, LDC companies may, in the absence of a design ability, forestall the loss of competitiveness by reducing costs of production through process research. But the efficiency gains from such improvements may be costly to obtain and are exhaustible. Reorganizing the flow of work, improving maintenance, and cleaning the sand from casting-shop floors are once-and-for-all changes, though they may have large, cost-cutting effects.[27] Eventually, more fundamental efforts will be required to increase competitiveness, particularly by design changes. By maintaining short- and intermediate-term competitiveness, however, disembodied efficiency gains can allow the gradual buildup of the requisite research capacity.[28] Building up that capacity is, of course, a major undertaking, which ranges from training technical personnel, to establishing institutions in which they are usefully employed, to developing institutes of weights and measures.[29]

VI. IMPLICATIONS FOR POLICY

Production in the mechanical engineering sector may provide an efficient growth opportunity for some of the more advanced LDCs if a vari-

---

[27] Continuing process innovation resulting from internal research may also occur after the principal flaws are corrected, but there is no reason to believe that these will be greater than those in the developed countries.

[28] Productivity growth may also encourage more research and development insofar as lower marginal costs allow firms to increase their quantity of output. Larger quantities encourage research and development because the benefit of that research and development can be allocated over a greater output at zero marginal cost.

[29] All of the studies on Latin America report deficiencies in standardization and large costs associated with it. See, for example, Vidossich (1970, Vol. II, p. 18).

ety of cost-increasing features do not offset the advantages accruing from lower costs of skilled labor. But the sector's competitiveness in the long run requires, in addition to improvements in static efficiency, greater effort and success in research on new or improved designs.

Specific policy measures to increase static efficiency depend on the source of the inefficiency. It is useful to emphasize the distinction between cost-minimizing responses to existing relative factor prices and those to such x-inefficient practices as unnecessary overcrowding in the placement of machines. Only the latter are of policy interest, but only insofar as increased competition, particularly from imports, is insufficient to reduce x-inefficiency with desired rapidity. In this case, x-inefficiency may warrant establishment of an industrial extension service, efforts to provide technical materials in translation, and encouragement of visits by local personnel to foreign factories or by the representatives of those factories to the local industry.

The financing of these activities depends on the organization of the sector. If there are a large number of small and medium-sized firms, it is likely that some learning will be diffused to firms that are not direct recipients of technical aid. The externalities generated by this diffusion may justify subsidization, if the conventional benefit–cost test can be met. But if the organization of the sector is oligopolistic, as in several of the countries currently active in capital goods production, any externalities will extend to only a small group of firms. It would then seem appropriate for the costs of improving efficiency to be borne by these firms.

If it can be assumed that the evidence accurately conveys the paucity of domestic research activity, it may be desirable for the public sector to act as a catalyst for such activity. The character of the actions required can be arrayed along a spectrum from implicit technology policies—those working indirectly through changes in economic policies—to such explicit policies as the subsidization of training of engineers or the establishment of research institutes. Because the desirable mode of intervention is likely to differ significantly by country, no universal recommendations are applicable.

In countries already possessing significant numbers of research personnel and laboratory facilities, implicit policies may be the only ones required if the existing incentive structure, particularly the tariff regime, leads to suboptimal levels of research. For example, a more competitive environment in the machinery-purchasing sectors may stimulate a demand for local adaptations of imported design or for wholly new designs. Or the removal of import restrictions, whether these be quotas or high tariffs on sectors supplying the machinery industry, would enable qualified personnel to engage in research rather than concentrate on bringing suppliers up to the standards required.[30]

Other policies short of direct intervention may also affect decisions about research and development. Of particular note are the tax treatment of license fees and the limits on the magnitude and duration of such payments. If the ready availability of licenses at relatively low prices is perceived to reduce research and development below socially desirable levels, policies could be designed to raise their net cost or to make them more difficult to obtain, though implementation may be difficult.

Explicit technology policies include those related to the acquisition of hardware, the subsidization of operating expenses, and the subsidization of training for scientists, engineers, and technicians. In addition, a variety of institutional mechanisms can be used to implement the actual research, ranging from government-owned and industrywide institutes to subsidies for research by private firms.

It seems likely that countries such as Mexico with a smaller volume (and history) of machinery production may require a greater emphasis on explicit policies because of their relatively small endowments of research personnel and facilities. Such countries as Argentina, Brazil, and India, on the other hand, are more likely to derive relatively large benefits from changes in economic policies. Just as for measures to increase x-efficiency, it is desirable to avoid public-sector financing of activities that the private sector should find profitable, unless there is strong evidence of significant capital–market imperfections or excessive risk aversion. It is also important to note that the subsidization of research is simply a variant of infant-industry encouragement and should meet the same tests as those for commodity production.

Two other policies are desirable. First, barriers to the import of high-quality machine tools should be removed. Although a relatively low uniform tariff may be used to protect the entire machinery sector, prohibiting the import of machine tools vital for achieving high-quality output is counterproductive. Second, given the complexities of marketing producers' goods, some aid may be justified if lumpy investments prevent individual firms from establishing sufficiently large marketing efforts. Again, it is necessary to avoid financing activities that the private sector should find profitable.

Finally, some observations can be made about the choice of additional products. Argentina and Brazil (less so for Mexico) produce a fairly large

---

[30] Of course, such upgrading is also beneficial, and the forgone benefits must be weighed against the gains from additional research.

range of capital goods. Any expansion of production would best be concentrated in products exhibiting two characteristics: first, current production techniques should not require competence in advanced sciences, such as metallurgy, in particularly difficult production technologies; second, the product should not be undergoing rapid design changes. An activity that conforms to both guidelines is the production of standardized components that producers in other countries can use: bearings, gears, and fasteners are examples. Similarly, structural items, such as beds for machine tools and frame bodies for engines, could be manufactured. All these product lines require an achievable level of upgrading in foundries, forges, and stamping operations but no major improvement in metallurgical or design skills. In addition, expansion of these product lines provides an interim source of export earnings as well as an incentive to achieve greater competence in fundamental skills whose labor-intensive character must provide much of any comparative advantage based on the low wage rates for skilled labor.

ACKNOWLEDGMENTS

The author would like to thank M. Cortes, F. Moore, J. R. Pack, Y. W. Rhee, and F. Stewart for many discussions and comments on earlier versions of this chapter. Many helpful comments were received at the Bar-Ilan University Symposium. Conversations with Larry E. Westphal and his detailed comments on earlier drafts have greatly contributed to this chapter. The responsibility for the final product is mine.

This was written while I was a consultant to the Economics of Industry Division of the World Bank and was financed by RPO 671-51.

REFERENCES

Baldwin, W. L., and Childs, G. L. (1969). "The Fast Second and Rivalry in Research and Development." *Southern Economic Journal* **36** (1) (July), 18–24.
Bell. R. M. (1978). "Cassave Processing in Thailand: A Case Study of Appropriate Technical Change." Brighton: University of Sussex.
Binswanger, H. P., and Ruttan, V. W. (1978). *Induced Innovation Technology, Institutions and Development*. Baltimore, Maryland: Johns Hopkins University Press.
Bonelli, R., and Facanha, L. O. (1977). "The Capital Goods Sector in Brazil: Development, Problems, and Perspectives (October).
Child, F., and Kaneda, H. (1971). "Small-Scale, Agriculturally Related Industry in the Punjab," a working paper. Davis, California: University of California.
Cooper, C. and Kaplinsky, R. (1974). *Second-Hand Equipment in a Developing Country*. Geneva: International Labour Organisation.
Cortes, M. (1978). "Argentina: Technical Development and Technology Exports to Other LDCs." Washington, D.C.: Economics of Industry Division, World Bank (February).
Crane, D. (1977). "Technological Innovation in Developing Countries: A Review of the Literature." *Research Policy* **6** (4) (October), 374–395.
Frankena, M. (1971). "Export of Engineering Goods from India." Ph.D. dissertation. Cam-

bridge, Massachusetts: Department of Economics, Massachusetts Institute of Technology.

Johnston, B. and Kilby, P. (1975). *Agriculture and Structural Transformation*. London and New York: Oxford University Press.

Katz, J. (1977). "Imports of Technology, Domestic Learning and Dependent Industrialization." Buenos Aires: Inter-American Development Bank.

Katz, J., and Ablin, E. (1978). "Technology and Industrial Exports: A Microeconomic Analysis of Argentina's Recent Experience." Buenos Aires: n.p.

Lamyai, T., Rhee, Y., and Westphal, L. (1978). "Factor Substitution, Returns to Scale and the Organization of Production in the Mechanical Engineering Industry." Washington, D.C.: Economics of Industry Division, World Bank.

Leff, N. (1968). *The Brazilian Capital Goods Industry, 1929–1964*. Cambridge, Massachusetts: Harvard University Press.

Mansfield, E. *et al.* (1977). *The Production and Application of New Industrial Technology*. New York: Norton.

Murphy, J. J. (1967). "Transfer of Technology: Retrospect and Prospect." In *The Transfer of Technology to the Developing Countries* (L. Spencer and A. Woroniak, eds.). New York: Praeger.

Pack, H. (1981). "Fostering the Capital Goods sector in LDC's." *World Development* **9** (3) (March), 227–250.

Pack, H., and Todaro, M. (1969). "Technological Change, Labour Absorption and Economic Development." *Oxford Economic Papers* **21** (3) (November), 395–403.

Rosenberg, N. (1976). *Perspectives on Technology*. London and New York: Cambridge University Press.

Stewart, F. (1979). "International Technology Transfer: Issues and Policy Options." Washington, D.C.: Policy Planning and Program Review Department, World Bank.

Timmer, C. P. (1972). "Employment Aspects of Investment in Rice Marketing in Indonesia." *Food Research Institute: Studies In Agricultural Economics, Trade and Development* **10** (1) 59–88.

United Nations (1963). "Economic Commission for Latin America." *The Manufacture of Industrial Machinery and Equipment in Latin America I: Basic Equipment in Brazil*. New York.

Vidossich, F. (1970). "The Transfer of Technical Know-How in the Machine Tool Industry in Brazil." Inter-American Development Bank and Economic Commission for Latin America.

Watanabe, S. (1978). "Technological Linkages between Formal and Informal Sectors of Manufacturing Industries." Geneva: Technology and Employment Programme, International Labour Organisation.

World Bank (1974). "India: Survey of the Foundry Industry." Washington, D.C. (1974).

World Bank (1978). Industrial Development and Finance Department. "Korea: Development of the Machinery Industries." Washington, D.C. (April).

World Bank (1979a). Latin American and Caribbean Region. "Brazil: Protection and Competitiveness of the Capital Goods Producing Industries." Washington, D.C. (April).

World Bank (1979b). "Mexico: Manufacturing Sector: Situation, Prospects and Policies." Washington, D.C. (March).

Department of Economics
Swarthmore College
Swarthmore, Pennsylvania

Part V

Equity

Chapter 17

Basic Needs, Distribution, and Growth: The Beginnings of a Framework

Gustav Ranis

I. INTRODUCTION

The post-World War II era has witnessed significant transitions in many LDCs toward modern economic growth. In terms of rates of growth of per capita income, average performance levels have exceeded expectations. It had been assumed that such growth would more or less automatically bring with it improvements in the quality of life of all people in LDCs. This expectation has unfortunately not been fulfilled: large numbers of people remain poor, with high rates of mortality, low life expectancy, chronic malnutrition, illness, and illiteracy.

The reaction to this disappointment has been a movement in national and international planning circles to include quality-of-life indicators as explicit development goals. Under the name "Basic Needs" (BN), this approach has had strong normative overtones. Too much of the voluminous literature to date on this phenomenon has either been polemical in nature [see ILO (1977)] or failed to relate the concept analytically to the

373

rest of development theory in a general equilibrium context [see, e.g., Streeten and Burki (1978)]. Without an underlying analytical framework, however, a purely normative approach is likely to prove insufficient for well-founded policy proposals. This chapter, therefore, provides a suggested framework for a positive, behavioristic approach to BN. Viewing BN as one part of a general economic system, as we do here, helps establish boundary lines for the BN approach, identifies the relations between BN and familiar national accounting variables, and points out areas for possible policy intervention. Section II states the BN concept within a general economic system from both a production and an organizational point of view. Section III presents the alternative ways in which various types of BN goods are likely to be alloted to families. Section IV deals with the implications for planning, policy, and organizational choices.

II.   BASIC NEEDS WITHIN A GENERAL ECONOMIC SYSTEM

A.   Total Resources and Resource Allocation

Figure 1 is a preliminary attempt to consider BN in the context of an entire economic system. The economy's resource endowment is indicated by level I. Various production sectors are postulated, as shown at level III, including BN sectors and other, non-BN, sectors. During any given year, total productive services are allocated as inputs to the production sectors, such as to education (R_e), health (R_h), food or nutrition (R_f),[1] and others (R_o). This sectoral representation points out that the BN approach is concerned not only with aggregate production but also with the specific commodity mix and indicates the basic, inescapable choice of allocating inputs to BN sectors or to non-BN activities. The output (Q_o) of the other sector is divided into non-BN consumption goods C and investment goods I. The products of the BN sector are education services Q_e, health services Q_h, and food Q_f. More will be said later about the production of these outputs in the context of particular organizational modes.

---

[1] Other BN sectors such as shelter could, of course, be added. At the same time, the BN sectors (R_e, R_h, etc.) refer only to that portion of the total health and education programs of a society related to BN. Such distinctions may not always be easy to draw in practice, but there is no problem conceptually in distinguishing between music education and literacy, for instance.

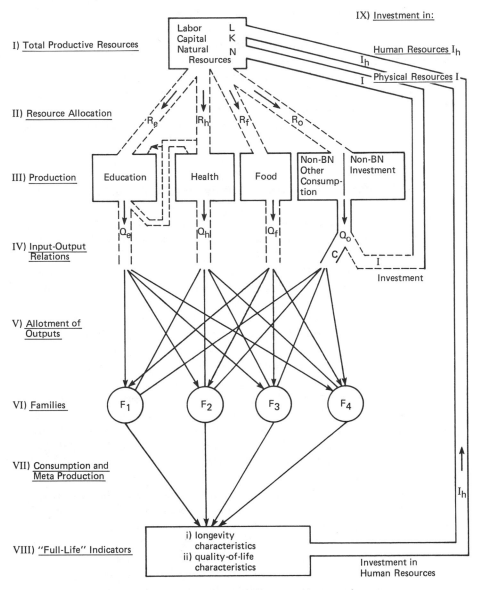

Fig. 1. Framework of basic needs in a general economic system.

B.   Family Structure and the Allotment of Output

A society's families, as represented by F_1, F_2, . . . , F_4 at level VI in Fig. 1, are the basic units or social organization. The composition of these families, including their labor endowment and dependent population, will be taken as given, and for simplicity, all families will be assumed to have the same composition. Beyond the output mix encountered at level III, the BN approach is very concerned with the equality or inequality of the allotment of Q_o, Q_e, Q_h, and Q_f to individual families.

C.   The Meta-Production Function and the "Full-Life" Indicators

By consuming BN and non-BN goods, families derive benefits. These benefits are conventionally treated in "utility" analyses but are viewed in the BN approach in terms of what are called "full-life" indicators. Though there are two views of these indicators, their level and distribution clearly lie at the heart of the BN approach. One type of full-life indicator (see level VIII) emphasizes longevity characteristics, such as life expectancy at birth or infant mortality. Another type stresses quality-of-life characteristics, such as literacy and morbidity. We shall refer to the functional relationship between the allotted pattern of consumption of BN goods and these full-life indicators as the meta-production function (see level VII). Formally, if we let $q_i = q_{ie}$, q_{ih}, q_{if}, q_{io} represent the consumption pattern of BN and non-BN goods for family i and let $J = (J_1, J_2,$ . . . , $J_k)$ be a set of k full-life indicators, the meta-production function represents a mapping $J = F(q_1, q_2, . . . , q_n)$. There exist both substitutability and complementary in the meta-production function such that there may be various alternative combinations of goods that achieve any defined level of the "full life."

The basic implicit assumption of the BN approach might be that this meta-production function is a stable relation that can at least be approximated empirically. Though there exists some hard evidence on some portions of the function and its characteristics, most portions are, however, only hypothesized about and many are seldom even made explicit. The production function for food, mentioned at level III, for example, is being studied by economists, though usually only at an aggregate level. With the exception of economic demographers studying the demographic transition and some education specialists studying functional literacy, economists have paid almost no attention to the meta-production function. Yet we cannot speak of a rational plan for meeting BN requirements without some notion of how the full-life indicators flow from the allocation of resources and the allotment of BN outputs. Indeed, the ultimate feasibility —and respectability—of the BN approach is likely to stand or fall with the progress made in understanding the meta-production function.

D. Full-Life Objectives and Investment in Human Resources

As mentioned, two views exist on the role of full-life indicators in the BN approach. According to one, these indicators represent the ultimate objective of economic activity and therefore require no further defense as planning goals. Other indicators, such as human rights or the enjoyment of music, are occasionally added to the list to provide added richness, a complication that should, we believe, be avoided at this stage in our understanding of the meta-production function.[2] According to the second view, improvements in the full-life indicators are not only ends in themselves but also feed back positively into the economic system. As represented in level VIII, the indicators constitute an investment in human capital in both the quantitative (e.g. life expectancy) and qualitative (e.g., literacy) senses and so augment the system's productive capacity. In the long run, such feedbacks would also reduce the conflict between current BN goals and some current non-BN, but growth-related, consumption. It should be noted that these feedback relations pose a whole new set of planning problems. Because they are so difficult to estimate empirically, they must be considered, along with the meta-production function, as weak links in the practical application of the BN approach.

E. National Income and Full Income

Adherents to the "new household economics" have pointed out that the value of output in the monetized sectors of an economy, measured as national income, seriously understates the "full income" of an economy. By omitting parts of the nonmonetized sector, such as the output of family members engaged in the household, national income may underestimate full income by as much as 40%. Full income is probably the income concept most relevant to the BN approach because of the overwhelming importance of families in BN production. The housewife customarily provides cleaning, cooking, health care, and care for children and the elderly, activities that directly relate to health and nutrition, and is an important agent of education as well. It is, in fact, difficult to name a significant house-

---

[2] It is clearly even more difficult, if not impossible, to establish a functional relationship between the intermediate outputs and, say, the enjoyment of music.

wifely activity whose output does not enter the meta-production function, affecting the full-life indicators of the family.[3] We believe that the BN approach must widen its scope to include important non-market-oriented activities, ameliorating the deficiencies of conventional income measures and bringing into consideration inputs for BN production that can be increased without decreasing non-BN output.

F. Full Income and the Organization of Production

The resources flow framework of Fig. 1 is institution- or organization-neutral in the sense that the same set of functions (allocation, production, allotment, consumption, meta production, investment in physical and human resources) must be performed regardless of the broad institutional arrangement (e.g., capitalism or socialism) and the specific organizational devices (e.g., local government or farmers' associations). Having emphasized the distinction between national and full income, we can now elaborate on Fig. 1 and consider different types of production organizations as indicated in Fig. 2. All productive resources in the economy, whether privately or publicly owned, are allocated to one of four modes of economic activity: activities in the private market P, by families F, by government G, or by community groups U such as farmers' associations or neighborhood associations. Each of these modes contains actual or potential organizations, represented by the boxes at level III, which can produce BN and non-BN goods. Organizations from all four modes may participate in producing the goods shown at level IV. In the health sector, for example, the total output of Q_h of health services may be the sum of the outputs of P^h (representing private hospitals and clinics), F^h (family health care), U^h (communal fly-eradication groups), and G^h (public health and sanitation activities).

G. Output and Organizational Heterogeneity

The variety of organizational forms possible within each BN sector arises in part because the public-good attributes of BN goods often induce government and community responses. The public-good attributes will be discussed later, but it should be noted at this point that whether or not a good is "public" is independent of whether the good is produced by a public organization. The important point to be made here is that certain

---

[3] In contrast, the household's contribution to non-BN production is generally quite small.

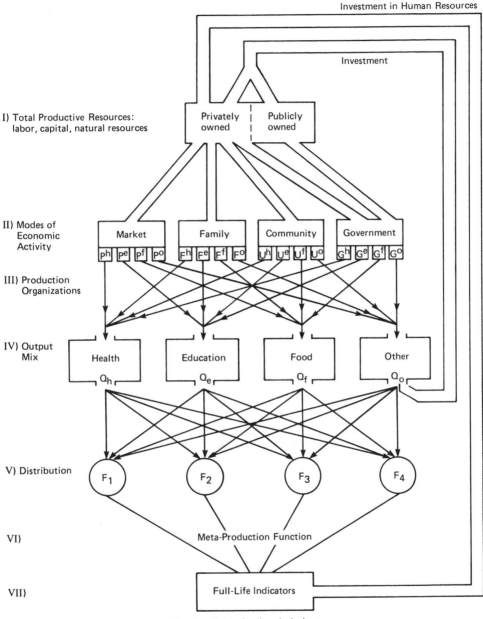

Fig. 2. Organizational choices.

organizational forms may be especially well suited to the production of certain BN goods, so that many policy issues central to the BN approach focus on the selection of appropriate organizations and on promoting their efficiency.

III. INCOMES, ALLOTMENTS, AND BASIC NEEDS

The level and distribution of achievement measured by the full-life indicators depend not only on the allocation of inputs to BN production and the choice of producing organizations, which have been discussed, but also on the distribution among families of the BN goods themselves. Figure 3 presents an accounting framework in which to consider allotment. A family's full income F_i consists of its wages W_i, property income Π_i, imputed household and community income d_i, and income from government revenue, made up of monetary transfers T_i and subsidized or "free" goods and services G_i. The distribution $V = (V_1, V_2, V_3, V_4)$ of full income can be described by the pattern of wages $W = (W_1, W_2, W_3, W_4)$, property income $\Pi = (\Pi_1, \Pi_2, \Pi_3, \Pi_4)$, transfers $T = (T_1, T_2, T_3, T_4)$, publicly provided goods $g = (g_1, g_2, g_3, g_4)$, and household income $d = (d_1, d_2, d_3, d_4)$. The primary family income distribution $Y = (Y_1, Y_2, Y_3, Y_4)$, composed of W and Π, has received most of the attention in the income-distribution literature, but V is the relevant concept for BN analysis.

It is the distribution of BN goods, not V, that directly determines the full-life indicators, but V is closely related. Families decide how to allocate W_i, Π_i, and T_i among BN goods, non-BN goods, and savings. For income from g_i and d_i, however, the production choice and consumption choice are usually identical and are made simultaneously, exogenously in the public sector for g and within the family for d. We can formally represent the disposition of family full income V_i among the seven types of goods as follows:

$C_b = (C_{1b}, C_{2b}, C_{3b}, C_{4b})$, family consumption of BN goods produced by private firms;

$C_n = (C_{1n}, C_{2n}, C_{3n}, C_{4n})$, family consumption of non-BN goods produced by private firms;

$S = (S_{1n}, S_{2n}, S_{3n}, S_{4n})$, family savings pattern[4] for acquiring investment goods;

---

[4] The family acquisition of ownership in new investment goods, of course, may require financial mediation.

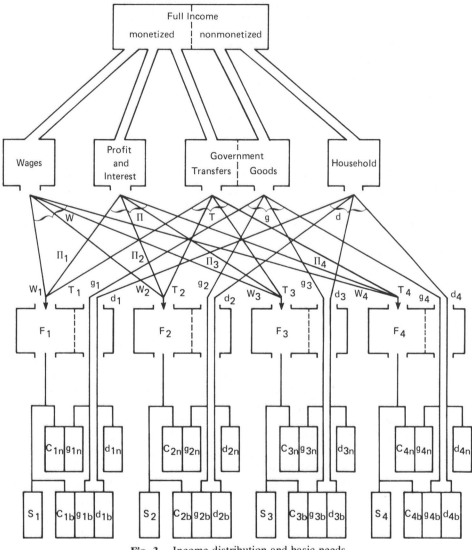

Fig. 3. Income distribution and basic needs.

$$d_b = (d_{1b}, d_{2b}, d_{3b}, d_{4b}),$$ family consumption of BN goods produced by families;

$$d_n = (d_{1n}, d_{2n}, d_{3n}, d_{4n}),$$ family consumption of non-BN goods produced by familes;[5]

[5] The sum of d^b and d^n is d, the imputed household income.

$g_b = (g_{1b}, g_{2b}, g_{3b}, g_{4b})$,   imputed benefits to families of government expenditures on BN goods;

$g_n = (g_{1n}, g_{2n}, g_{3n}, g_{4n})$,   imputed benefits to families of government expenditures on non-BN goods.

We shall refer to these patterns collectively as $b = (C_b, C_n, S, d_b, d_n, g_b, g_n)$.

A. Analysis of Allotments

We shall now consider the factors determining each of the seven allotment patterns. Market-sector goods (C_b, C_n, S), government-sector goods (g_b, g_n), and household-sector goods (d_b, d_n) will be discussed separately. We shall examine first how income is distributed among families and then how it is disposed of with respect to BN and non-BN goods, noting again that these two stages are really independent only with respect to market-sector goods.

1. MARKET-SECTOR GOODS

The determination of family income distribution (FID) has been examined extensively elsewhere [see Chenery *et al.* (1974); Adelman and Robinson (1978); Fei *et al.* (1979)], especially to explain primary income and its constitutent wage and property shares. We shall therefore take the pattern of primary income distribution $Y = (Y_1, Y_2, Y_3, Y_4)$ as given by other determinants. No separate analysis is done here for the distribution of government transfer payments T because we can assume that this income is disposed of in the same way as primary income. Though there are exceptions (most notably Sri Lanka), it appears that, in most LDCs, T is similar to Y. New research is needed on the determinants of T, including political, sociological, and administrative factors. We shall explore here the relationship between Y, as characterized by mean income $\bar{Y}$ and the Gini coefficient G_y, and the allotment of this income to C_b, C_n, and S.[6]

Figure 4 depicts the allotment of family income to the patterns C_b, C_n, and S, observing the accounting identity $Y = C_b + C_n + S$. Assuming that the primary data on these four patterns are available, we can draw a scatter diagram such as Fig. 5. Family incomes and mean income $\bar{Y}$ are

[6] In Figs. 4 and 5, we show four types of goods: C_b, C_n', C_n'', and S, of which two are non-BN consumption goods. The first non-BN consumption good is introduced to show what happens when one of the goods is an inferior good. This is an elaboration that will be ignored in the text.

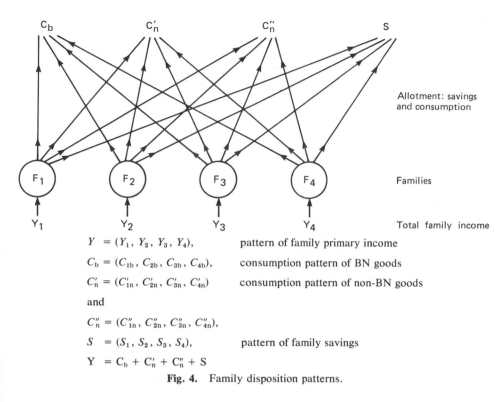

$$Y = (Y_1, Y_2, Y_3, Y_4), \qquad \text{pattern of family primary income}$$

$$C_b = (C_{1b}, C_{2b}, C_{3b}, C_{4b}), \qquad \text{consumption pattern of BN goods}$$

$$C'_n = (C'_{1n}, C'_{2n}, C'_{3n}, C'_{4n}) \qquad \text{consumption pattern of non-BN goods}$$

and

$$C''_n = (C''_{1n}, C''_{2n}, C''_{3n}, C''_{4n}),$$

$$S = (S_1, S_2, S_3, S_4), \qquad \text{pattern of family savings}$$

$$Y = C_b + C'_n + C''_n + S$$

Fig. 4.   Family disposition patterns.

arranged on the horizontal axis. The vertical axis in each section represents the amounts of each good consumed or the savings. To simplify the
exposition, we assumed that the consumption and savings functions are
linear, as shown, with b_1, b_2, and b_3 as intercepts and a_1, a_2, and a_3 as
slopes. Because of the accounting identity previously mentioned,
$b_1 + b_2 + b_3 = 0$ and $a_1 + a_2 + a_3 = 1$.

Some elements important to BN and FID analysis can now be introduced. To analyze the issue of the so-called conflict between growth and
equity, let $\bar{C}_b = (C_{1b} + C_{2b} + C_{3b} + C_{4b})/4$ be the mean value of BN consumption and let the inequality of BN consumption be measured by the
Gini coefficient G_b. Basic needs advocates also speak of a critical minimum level of BN consumption, represented by C_m, corresponding to a
caloric minimum food requirement, for example. Both $\bar{C}_b$ and C_m appear
in the last section of Fig. 5.

In the linear model, a useful linking equation is $G_b = e_b G_y$, where
$e_b = a_1 \bar{Y}/\bar{C}_b > 0$ (when $a_i > 0$) is the elasticity of the BN consumption

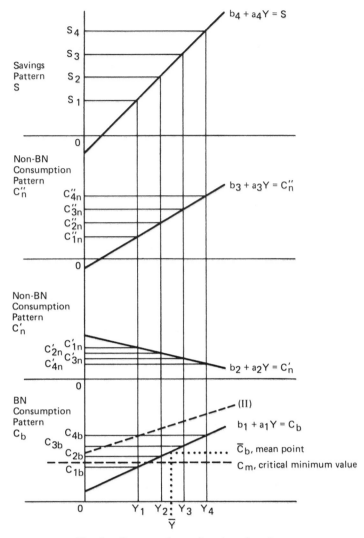

Fig. 5. Consumption and savings functions.

function at the mean point.[7] If $e_b = 0.8$, for example, G_b is 80% of G_y and the inequality of the BN consumption pattern is less than for income.

---

[7] In case the slope is negative, as illustrated by a_2 in Fig. 5 for the first non-BN good, the linking equation must be modified to read $G'_n = e_2 G_y$, where $e_2 = -a_2 \bar{Y}/\bar{c}_2 > 0$ when $a_2 < 0$). Because the Gini coefficients are always positive numbers, the elasticities as defined must be positive numbers.

Whether G_b is greater or less than G_y depends on whether e_b is greater or less than unity, which depends, in turn, on the values of b_1 and a_1. It is empirical information of this type that is needed to strengthen the analytical foundations of the BN approach. Intuitively, we assume that b_1 will be positive because families at all income levels must consume positive amounts of BN goods like food. It is also likely that as incomes rise, families will increase their consumption of the BN goods less than proportionately with income, whereas non-BN consumption and savings will increase more than proportionately. If, as hypothesized, $b_1 > 0$ and $0 < a_1 < 1$, then $G_b < G_y$ and BN consumption is distributed more equally than family income.

Transforming our linking equation, we can explore the impact of an increase in income per family. Substituting $\bar{C}_b = b_1 + a_1 \bar{Y}$ into the expression for e_b, we can write

$$G_b = e_b G_y = \frac{a_1 \bar{Y}}{b_1 + a_1 \bar{Y}} G_y.$$

It is evident that changes in G_b over time will be determined by the course of $\bar{Y}$ and G_y. Suppose that an increase in income per family occurs without any change in G_y. The effect on G_b is then seen by taking the derivative with respect to $\bar{Y}$:

$$\frac{\partial}{\partial \bar{Y}} G_b = \frac{\partial}{\partial \bar{Y}} \frac{a_1 \bar{Y}}{b_1 + a_1 \bar{Y}} G_y = \frac{a_1 b_1}{(b_1 + a_1 \bar{Y})^2} G_y > 0.$$

Inequality of BN consumption increases as income per family increases, even without increasing inequality in income distribution itself. At the same time, however, the number of families falling below a minimum level of BN consumption will decrease. This is evident from the last section of Fig. 5. If each Y_i is increased by some multiple, G_y is unchanged but each C_{ib} increases, putting more or all of the C_{ib}s above the level C_m. Though many BN advocates regard the process of increasing BN consumption through growth as too slow, it may be the most feasible solution for most LDCs. The recent experience of Taiwan seems to indicate that simultaneous rapid and equitable growth *can* solve the BN problem. In other cases, even if there is a conflict between growth and equity, those who focus on the number of families below critical minimum levels of BN consumption may record progress. Which path will produce the most desirable outcome in the full-life indicators is a very complicated subject to which more thought must be given by national as well as international planners.

2. Public-Sector Goods

We are concerned in this section with the imputed value to families of government expenditures on goods. In this area there is no history of research comparable to that in the market sector upon which to draw. As a starting point, we might use a very preliminary and tentative finding that suggests a loose association between the distribution of money income and the distribution and disposition of publicly provided goods. In countries with a more egalitarian distribution of monetized or market income, there is some tendency for a more egalitarian distribution of publicly provided goods and an associated tendency for a higher proportion of publicly provided goods to be BN goods. The positive relation between equality in Y and equality in g_b and g_n might be explained by connections between political power, or administrative machinery, and economic power, related to income. There are also more straightforward economic explanations. The consumption of publicly provided goods may impose costs on the consumer that can be better borne by consumers with higher incomes. Examples in education would be the opportunity cost of attending school and the complementary costs of clothes and transportation. If this relation were established, some of the methods suggested for analysis in the market sector could be applied to the public sector as well; more research on these relations would likely be very fruitful. But this still leaves unexplained the determination of the magnitude of publicly provided goods and their allocation between BN and non-BN goods. For market goods, we use given tastes as the explanatory factor. For publicly provided goods, we have to assume that political factors are the underlying determinants, but we are much less confident about the stability of these factors and their functions. To the extent that planners are bound by these factors, the task of changing the distribution and BN content of publicly provided goods is consequently rendered more difficult.

3. Household-Sector Goods

Recent research and analysis into the distribution of household income have produced the not unexpected result that d_n and d_b are more equally distributed than Y. Although this obviously means that full income is more equally distributed than monetized income, in normative terms this may not mean much because standards of equity have to be adjusted to allow for the inclusion of full income. It may also be incorrect to conclude that moving more economic activities into the household would improve full-life indicators by making V more equal, because activity outside the home, especially for women, may result in learning that increases the efficiency of the meta-production function. Efficiency gains of this type are likely to be quite equally accessible to all families because household activities are generally non-capital-intensive and production scale, related to household size, does not vary much. Efficiency increases would thus probably increase the equity of the d_b and d_n patterns. Here again, clearly, much more work is required.

IV. BASIC NEEDS PLANNING POLICY AND ORGANIZATIONAL CHOICES

A. Basic Needs Planning Models

The methods of the so-called planning school represented by Chenery, Tinbergen and others, have been significant in the policy portion of the BN approach. From this tradition, many BN advocates have adopted the idea of target setting and an emphasis on resource utilization. Specifically, the BN approach is often directed to a target group, such as the number of people below the "poverty line," with time-phased objectives for reducing this number. It is recognized that meeting BN goals requires productive resources and that diverting them may conflict with growth goals, but this conflict is reduced or eliminated by the growth-promoting effects of BN consumption.

The general economic system presented in Fig. 1 may be a useful framework for thinking about the construction of a resources-oriented planning model tailored to the BN approach. We see, for instance, that total resources may be inputs either to the BN sectors (R_e, R_h, or R_f) to the non-BN sector producing consumption goods (C) or investment goods (I). Here there is a clear case of a possible conflict between growth (or some BN consumption tomorrow) and BN consumption today, necessitating consistent resources planning. As suggested by the diagram, the first step would be to estimate the production functions $Q_i = f^i(K_i, L_i)$, where i = education, health, food, and other. In the BN literature, this production function corresponds to the "costs" of certain BN goods. The next step in the planning process would be the allotment of every component of the BN and non-BN output to all the families, $q_i = (q_{ie}, q_{ih}, q_{if}, q_{io})$ for each family i. These patterns must, in turn, be linked to the full-life indicators through the meta-production function $J = F(q_1, q_2, q_3, q_4)$. If maximization of J is taken as the ultimate objective, an optimizing process should be able to determine how a consistent resource allocation and BN allotment plan is to be constructed. If J is specified for a future target date, the solution to the dynamic resources model can conceptually yield the appropriate decisions. If J is also regarded as contributing to the improvement of the human capital stock, the resources planning task is more complicated but is still conceptually feasible.

1. ESTIMATING THE META-PRODUCTION FUNCTION

Though simple enough in theory, such a BN planning effort would be difficult to implement. The hardest problems are encountered in trying to identify and estimate the meta-production function. Some of these problems are indicated here.

(1)   Statistically, a full-life indicator value in one year may be correlated with the level of BN consumption over many previous years. Producing "literacy" or a "long life," for instance, may take the cumulative effects of BN consumption over a considerable stretch of time.

(2)   Both complementary and substitute relations exist between the BN inputs in the meta-production function. Without education, for instance, health services may not be effective in producing a longer life. Food may be a substitute for health services. The economics of such relations and their definition as complementarity and/or substitution elasticities among inputs in a production process are well understood, but both the conceptual and empirical problems are formidable. They are further complicated by dynamic lead and lag considerations. Thus it may well be true that education expenditures must temporally precede health expenditures if maximum resource efficiency is to be realized.

(3)   The multidimensional characteristic of the full-life indicators $J = (J_1, J_2, \ldots, J_k)$ makes simple maximization more difficult than maximizing a single variable (e.g., growth in GNP per capita) in ordinary resources planning. Moreover, the objective function contains not only the level of these indicators but also their distribution across families.

(4)   The meta-production function is sensitive not only to the levels of inputs, the BN goods, but also to their distribution across families. Moreover, this sensitivity to distribution is likely to be different for each J_i. For example, an unequal distribution of food may lead to a shorter life for the undernourished families and a somewhat longer life for the well nourished. The maldistribution of sanitation facilities, on the other hand, may result in illness that reduces health levels for all families.

2. ESTIMATING FEEDBACK RELATIONS

A whole new additional set of challenging and important problems arises once the qualities described by the full-life indicators are also regarded as human resource investments that augment the system's total productive capacity in the future. One of these problems arises because substitutability and complementarity also exist among full-life "inputs" feeding back into the system. An example is the effects of literacy and good health on worker productivity. Aptitude tests, administered by the employment offices of certain industries, may provide some clues to these issues. Others can be gathered from research results in the relevant labor market–human capital literature.

The distribution of the full-life indicators across families will affect feedback relations differently for some relations than for others, causing further estimation difficulties. In health, to cite one specific instance, it is probable (but by no means certain) that when average health is adequate, a more equally distributed increase in health services for the entire population is more productive than an unequally distributed one. On the other hand, in the case of education, this may be inaccurate if a modernizing economy can be expected to require a skill hierarchy or pyramid of workers unequal in education. All such societies, regardless of their preference for equity, will demand a small fraction of professionals (doctors, engineers, etc.), and a larger group of skilled workers, resting on a still larger base of unskilled labor.

It may be instructive to review the attempts to relate one set of full-life indicators to the resource needs of the economic system. When the age structure declines in the course of demographic transition, the fraction of the dependent population increases, the resource requirements to feed the dependent population increase, and the investment fund, *ceteris paribus*, declines. Expert demographers disagree among themselves, however, on what causes the decline in age structure. This difficulty in analyzing even one relatively simple dimension of meta-production relations should give us pause before rushing into a resources-oriented planning approach to BN.

A resources planning model approach to BN has an unmistakable logical appeal—as had the simple growth-oriented planning models of yesteryear—and its political appeal and possible effect on DC aid giving should not be underestimated. Nevertheless, the conceptual difficulties that stand in its way must be clearly admitted. Perhaps the best role for BN planning will be similar to the use now made of conventional planning exercises. Five-year plans are no longer looked on as spelling out actions in quantitative terms, but more as tools in organizing the thinking of decision makers and as pointing out gross inconsistencies in proposed programs. We do not wish to sound negative on the subject of BN-oriented resources planning, but we believe that, at this stage in our understanding, scarce energies should be directed toward more modest and realistic objectives. One of these is the determination of better policies addressed to BN objectives.

B. Basic Needs Policy

Whether BN resources planning is exhaustive or only suggestive, the implementation of any plan is, of course, not automatic. The macro mechanisms must underlie any BN plan, and the micro organizations charged with specific tasks within the plan are, to a greater or lesser degree, the objects of policy choice; meaningful planning cannot take place without reference to the institutional and organizational backdrop. Conversely, policies regarding organizational forms and plan implementation obviously cannot be framed without reference to the intended plan. Though more work evidently is needed on these interrelationships, it may be useful to highlight some of the relevant policy choices here.

1. SPECIFICATION OF THE FULL-LIFE INDICATORS

An important task for policy makers is the specification of the full-life indicators $J = (J_1, J_2, \ldots, J_k)$ to be pursued. It is assumed that a country adopting a BN strategy is giving special weight to the full-life indicators, more weight than would be justified by the human resource aspects alone. But this assumption by no means provides a fuller or sufficiently well specified objective function for decisions about policy. Additional specification is needed in answer to the following questions as well:

(1) How much special weight will be given to J?
(2) What elements will enter the objective function J? These elements must be carefully and specifically defined if J is to become truly operational.
(3) What relative weights will be assigned to the elements of J?
(4) Besides the levels of these elements, how does their distribution across families enter the objective function?
(5) What trade-offs across time are acceptable, e.g., what future increases in J are needed to compensate for present abstinence?

2. IMPLEMENTATION OF THE BN PLAN

Another important policy task is plan implementation. Decisions on resource allocation to BN and non-BN sectors, allocation among BN sectors, and distribution across families, already discussed as part of a BN plan, must be translated into reality. This translation is relatively direct for centrally planned economies where resource flows and production levels are simultaneously assigned by planners. A relatively egalitarian income distribution may result from employment of intensive incomes planning in the mixed economy, whereas in a society of few privately held assets, large public-sector expenditures with egalitarian allotment should ensure that there is widespread consumption of BN goods.

The market mechanism, which may be largely bypassed by planned economy systems, lies at the heart of another policy option in the mixed economy context. In the market-oriented approach, the main emphasis is placed on the growth of primary income through employment and asset redistribution, whereas resource allocation and production decisions are left largely in private hands. High-income growth rates enable families to spend enough on BN goods to achieve what is considered an adequate level of full-life indicators.

For most LDCs, neither full central planning nor total laissez-faire is either likely or acceptable. Central planning requires a pervasive political system and institutional choices far beyond the range of the realistic administrative capacities and political economy options of most LDCs. On the other hand, even the most market-oriented countries will allow for the need for major "corrections" of market solutions. Intervention in various forms will be justified as income redistribution, to offset private information inadequacies or to correct underinvestment in public goods. For one thing, some BN goods, such as food, can be provided more appropriately through the market route, whereas others, such as education, are traditionally public goods. In addition, many countries favoring a market-oriented, growth-centered approach at an early stage will choose more BN intervention in the medium term, once incomes are rising. We shall, finally, consider some of the policy instruments available to us in the majority of typical "mixed economy" LDCs and end with a comment on organizational choices.

a. Direct Income Transfer Policies. This type of policy aims at the transfer of incomes from wealthy to poor families by such means as taxes and subsidies. In the simplest case, relative commodity prices are not affected. An extreme policy would be to transfer incomes until all are equalized, and $(\bar{Y}, \bar{Y}, \bar{Y}, \bar{Y})$ replaces (Y_1, Y_2, Y_3, Y_4). In our model, complete equality of income would lead to the complete equality of BN consumption. If the critical minimum consumption level C_m is less than the mean consumption level $\bar{C}_b$, a less extreme solution would be to transfer incomes until the incomes of the poor are just sufficient to consume C_m. Such transfers will not solve the BN problem if C_b is below C_m but will result in only an equal sharing of poverty. In this case, income growth is needed to raise average consumption above C_b.

There are at least two arguments against heavy reliance on transfer policies, based on considerations of economic efficiency and political realism. It is often alleged that income equalization will hurt economic growth because of disincentive effects. These effects are difficult to assess because at both ends of the income scale they depend on the form of the transfer. It may be possible, particularly for transfer recipients, to devise forms that encourage rather than discourage economic activity. Moreover, any negative effects on the work and productivity of the poor may be offset by positive effects arising from better nutrition and health. In many cases, administrative and political economy factors, however, may be the real limiting factor on the use of transfers to achieve BN objectives. Though more research is once again needed here, most of the empirical evidence suggests that governments rarely succeed in greatly reducing inequality through transfers alone, particularly when primary income inequality is substantial. In fact, transfers usually are slightly unequalizing.

b. Publicly Provided Goods. Increasing the volume of publicly provided BN goods—raising $g_b = (g_{1b}, g_{2b}, g_{3b}, g_{4b})$—is another form of transfer. The disincentive effects of such a policy may be less than with income transfers if families try to earn more income to provide the complementary resources needed for effective consumption of the publicly provided goods. A major problem with the public provision of BN goods is that they may be "hijacked" and diverted from the groups in need. An associated problem is that of "targeting" to reduce the cost of the policies. Where income inequality is very great, a small additional expenditure on fiscal transfers of publicly provided goods can make a major difference to income levels among the poorest groups. In Brazil, for example, where the income share of the bottom 20% is 2% increasing public consumption by one-fifth would double the income level of the bottom quintile. The real problem is ensuring that the middle classes do not manage to take their customary place at the head of the queue.

c. Relative Prices and Consumption Patterns. LDC governments may also attempt to change families' consumption patterns in order to increase the proportion of income spent on BN goods. This may be achieved by controlling the price of a particular BN good or by education and information policies. The aim of the policy is to shift the BN consumption function (as indicated by line II in Fig. 5). Although everyone consumes more BN goods, low-income families (Y_1, Y_2) increase their consumption more than the high-income families (Y_3, Y_4). Thus G_b is reduced, so that BN goods are more equally allotted, and a_1 is reduced. Fewer families remain below the deprivation line C_m because the b_1 intercept is now higher. Income levels need not be affected, although in real terms they normally are if the good forms a large proportion of total consumption of the poor.

When relative prices are manipulated, other measures such as rationing and food coupons are often required to effect a smooth delivery of the BN good. The government may impose a tax on the wealthy and subsidize BN prices for the poor. For these reasons, (Y_1, Y_2, Y_3, Y_4) is probably made more equal by the use of this policy, even if associated with some disincentive effects.

Aside from these partial equilibrium effects on BN consumption, there are also general equilibrium implications. In our model, other consumption patterns must move downward (and the slopes become steeper) in response to the change in BN consumption. For example, as BN consumption increases, non-BN consumption C_n, or savings S, must drop. These other goods must also be consumed more unequally. Not only is there no "free lunch" today, but the manipulation of relative prices may have other, unintended effects on the production side tomorrow.

3. BN Organizational Choices

We noted earlier the variety of organizational forms that may be employed in the production and distribution of BN goods. One reason for this potential variety, of course, is that BN sectors differ in their "natural" relative reliance on public versus private activity. It is typical, for example, to find relatively heavy government participation in education and public health services, somewhat less in primary health care, still less in shelter, and least in food. This ranking by degree of public intervention corresponds roughly to the ranking implied by the degree of market failure likely in the various sectors. Natural monopoly conditions, under which competitive forces are suspended because only one or a few productive units can operative at efficient scale, are commonly given as grounds for public intervention. For example, indivisibilities in production and consumption (as with a school) might justify a relevant geographic area (say, two or three villages) cooperating in building and running a school but do not require central government participation. Similarly, the inappropriability of benefits or a high ratio of inappropriable to appropriable benefits (e.g., most public health services) may often apply to a level higher than the normal consuming unit (the individual family) but lower than the whole economy. Hence the most appropriate organizational form, from the point of view of optimal motivation and efficiency, varies according to the level at which public-goods-type characteristics apply. A natural monopoly exists in providing public health services and, to some extent education as well. Information to households may be inadequate in the health and education sectors, also inviting market correction. The most frequently cited reason for public intervention is the presence of external benefits in the consumption of public health services and education, in particular, and of BN goods, in general, through investment in human capital. The public provision of BN goods and services can, of course, also serve to redistribute income, as noted earlier.

While noting the theoretical desirability of correcting market solutions, we should point out that, at least in theory, several alternative means of correction remain available. Refuse collection, one example of natural monopoly in the health sector, can be carried out by a public agency, a regulated private firm, or by a franchised competitive firm. Distortions owing to imperfect information about nutrition might be corrected by the public provision of certain foods or by public information services. Positive externalities in education might be dealt with through a subsidy program. These possibilities exist "in theory," but it may be difficult to change from one mode of correction to another. In particular, public organizations already in place in LDCs are not likely to atrophy quietly to make way for alternative solutions. Still, some range of alternatives for BN intervention should be considered, especially for the longer run.

After deciding on the desirable "natural" mix of public and private activity in each BN sector from the point of view of the production conditions, scale, externalities, etc., there still remains some choice about what organizational forms will be depended on to carry out the activity. Unfortunately, there is not a great deal of information about the relative performance of various organizational forms or about the circumstances that favor the emergence of one form rather than another.[8] Nor is it always clear whether a public or private organization should be chosen. We therefore limit ourselves here to a few suggestive comments concerning the type of consideration affecting organizational choice as an important part of BN research.

One reason why BN sectors may have been relatively neglected in some areas is the absence of suitable organizational forms, which in many cases fall somewhere between the family and the central government and require an appropriate level of decentralization. Identifying and filling such gaps must be one focus of a realistic BN strategy.

Second, the efficiency of an organization, as ordinarily defined, is not the only criterion for organizational choice. Participation, both moral and

---

[8] Ostrom, (1973, p. 2) wrote that public administration "should be able to indicate the conditions and consequences which derive from the choice of alternative organizational arrangements," but it cannot in its present state of development. Writing about the private sector, Coase (1972, p. 64) points out that "we are, in fact, appallingly ignorant about the forces which determine the organization of industry," including what firm structure is best suited to a particular group of activities and what activities can best be grouped together.

financial, may also be significant. To the extent that a BN approach involves determining people's needs, participation enables the producer and consumer to exercise genuine control and choice. The sense of commitment that can arise from participation may be crucial to the long-run sustainability of the producing units, especially where recurring costs must be met, as in schools and health clinics. It has also been argued that minimal control over one's life is itself part of a "full-life." We did not include it among the full-life indicators, preferring to regard participation formally as a means rather than an end, but we do agree on its importance.

Third, as previously, argued, the family is the primary determinant of the meta-production function. Hence the efficiency of the family becomes critical to the BN approach. In virtually every society, cooking, cleaning, health-care, and child-care habits, etc., are learned within the family. In a traditional society, this learning process is a "closed circuit," which receives relatively little infusion of information from the outside. It is possible and desirable to infuse modern technology into sanitation, nutrition, health care, and education as activities, for example, as wider contacts outside the family system open up in the transition to modern growth.

Last, much more emphasis should be placed, we believe, on how to use publicly provided information and services to increase the efficiency of BN production within families and other communal arrangements like farmers' cooperatives. This type of BN production is also much less likely to represent a real drain on the resources required for the growth of the monetized portion of the full income. In the longer run, this may be the most reliable way to infuse a modernizing outlook as well as more modern technology into an area that can have a very substantial and relatively clear impact on various full-life indicators.

In sum, this chapter has attempted to present a provisional framework that may be useful for the further analysis of the BN approach. It is our view that the ultimate validity and usefulness of the BN approach, beyond that of a political rallying cry, depends critically on our success or failure in clarifying many of the theoretical and empirical issues that lie at its center. Among these issues are the meta-production function, the feedback relations, the production characteristics, and the organizational choices attending various BN goods categories. It is our conviction that, in the absence of such additional "homework," the concept will be remembered a decade hence as a politically motivated passing fad rather than as a potentially useful analytical concept.[9]

[9] For an even more skeptical view on its potential, see Srinivasan, (1977).

ACKNOWLEDGMENTS

This chapter owes much to John Fei and Frances Stewart and to the World Bank for its financial assistance. Thanks are due also to Kent Mikkelsen for his research assistance.

REFERENCES

Adelman, I., and Robinson, S. (1978). *Income Distribution Policy in Developing Countries: A Case Study of Korea,* Stanford, California: World Bank (Stanford Univ. Press).

Chenery, H. B., Ahluwalia, M., Bell, C. L. E., Duley, J. H., and Jolly, R. (1974). *Redistribution with Growth.* London and New York: Oxford Univ. Press.

Coase, R. H. (1972). *Policy Issues and Research Opportunities in Industrial Organization* (V. R. Fuchs, ed.), p. 64. New York: National Bureau of Economic Research (Columbia Univ. Press).

Fei, J. C. H., Ranis, G., and Kuo, S. W. Y. (1979). *Growth with Equity: The Taiwan Case.* London and New York: World Bank (Oxford Univ. Press).

ILO (1977). "Employment, Growth, and Basic Needs: A One World Problem." New York: Praeger.

Ostrom, V. (1973). *The Intellectual Crisis in American Public Administration.* p. 2. University, Alabama: University of Alabama Press.

Srinivasan, T. N. (1977). "Development, Poverty and Basic Human Needs: Some Issues." *Food Research Institute Studies* **16,** 2.

Streeten, P., and Burki, S. J. (1978). "Basic Needs: Some Issues." *World Development* **6** (March).

Economic Growth Center
Yale University
New Haven, Connecticut

Chapter 18

Trying to Appraise a Decade of Development: Latin America in the Sixties

Jacques Silber

I. INTRODUCTION

The need for an authentic development path has been a recurrent theme in the development literature. Prebisch (1976), for example, presents the question in the following way:

> The problem is . . . that of how to use the vast scientific and technological heritage of the centre to advantage by adopting this know-how to the factual conditions of the periphery, to widen the narrow sphere of technological options, and to provide an impulse for our own innovative ability. In other words, to achieve authenticity by going a step farther than mere imitation and making a progressive creative effort.

Such a position naturally raises the central question of how to measure development. Usher (1980), in his introduction to the *Measurement of Ec-*

397

onomic Growth writes, "To economists, journalists, historians, politicians and the general public, the rate of economic growth is a summary measure of all favourable developments in the economy." What may these favorable developments be? Can we think of a synthetic measure summarizing them? And if so, how do the various countries in the world rate?

The purpose of this chapter is to take another look at the development performance of the world in the 1960s and, in particular, at that of various Latin American countries. In order to do so, we propose to use as development standard a summary measure that we have called the Equivalent Length of Life or E.L.L. (see Silber, 1980), whose properties we recall briefly in the first section of this study. Then, in a second section, we compare the achievements of various countries of Latin America in 1960 and in 1970, stressing, in particular, the differences that appear when development is measured by GDP per capita and when one uses life expectancy or the equivalent length of life (E.L.L.) as standard.

II. THE SEARCH FOR A DEVELOPMENT INDICATOR

It is a well known fact that important changes in meaning and approach usually begin with what seem to be or are considered as purely formal or semantic modifications. A case in point is the transition from the concept of growth to that of development where the conceptual difference between them took time to crystallize . . . Let us first of all investigate the origins . . . of the interest shown in this matter . . . In the first place it derives from the growing dissatisfaction with the quality of life and the deterioration of the environment in the industrialized or post-industrialized societies . . . Secondly the same and other arguments are reproduced to a lesser degree but definitely growing degree in the semi-industrialized countries (in Latin America for example) . . . A fact which is less often considered but is of prime importance in the discussion of these concerns is that they and the consequent criticisms and reservations are limited to a fairly restricted, although broadening, social context. That is to say, everywhere the broad masses are excluded from the discussion . . . What is more, if their feelings on these points could be ascertained it seems fairly obvious that the overwhelming majority would be inclined to suffer the ills of the affluent society rather than remain in their present situation.

These statements (Pinto, 1976) clearly indicate that two rather conflicting goals could be assigned to many developing countries: the search for a high quality of life, which would probably be the immediate aim of only the high-income classes, and the quest for a decent standard of living, which is likely to be the main aspiration of the masses. Recent efforts have indeed been made to take these targets into account when measuring the level of development of a country. The attempts to include leisure in the computation of the GNP [e.g., Nordhaus and Tobin (1972) or Usher (1980)] and the proposal for a physical quality of life index (PQLI) (Morris and Liser, 1977) are witnesses of this research for an indicator of life quality. On the other hand, the desire to include income distribution considerations when measuring economic welfare was at the center of the analysis of Chenery *et al.* (1974), who proposed to attach explicit weights to the growth of income of the various income groups, as well as of Atkinson (1970) and Kolm (1976a,b), who proposed, each in his way, to compute the "equally distributed equivalent level of income," that is, the level of income that, if equally distributed, would give the same social welfare as the one actually prevailing with unequal incomes.

In a recent study (Silber, 1980), we proposed to use a development indicator that would take into account both worries, that of not neglecting quality-of-life aspects as well as that of not ignoring income distribution considerations. This measure, called the E.L.L., for equivalent length of life, is an application of Atkinson's and Kolm's ideas to life tables data. The detailed derivation of this index is summarized in the Appendix. The basic idea is that utility depends on the number of years lived, and in this regard, we follow Hicks and Streeten's (1979) conclusion that life expectancy is the most useful social indicator. However, we suggest that the whole life table be taken into account; i.e., to include in our welfare measure the existence of inequality in the number of years lived. Concerning income inequality, two approaches can be used, as emphasized by Kolm (1976) in his analysis. Accordingly, we may require that *proportional increases* in all incomes not change the value of the inequality measure. This is Atkinson's (1970) approach, which has been labeled "rightist" by Kolm. But it is also possible to assume that *equal additions* to all incomes would not change the value of the inequality index, and this is Kolm's "leftist" approach.

The same ideas can be applied to the analysis of life tables. In other words, an Atkinson's-type index would assume the inequality in the number of years lived as invariant to proportional increases in the number of years lived, whereas a Kolm-type index would see inequality as invariant to equal increases (additions) in the number of years lived. Each index depends on a parameter α, which measures, as indicated in the Appendix, the weight to be attached to various age groups. The computation of the E.L.L. requires therefore two choices: one between the "rightist" and "leftist" approaches and a second one concerning the value of the parameter α. An illustration of these computations will be given in the next section where we shall assess Latin America's overall performance in the sixties on the basis of this new indicator, the E.L.L.

III. ANOTHER ATTEMPT AT QUANTIFYING LATIN AMERICA'S DEVELOPMENT BETWEEN 1960 AND 1970

In Table 1, the values are given for several development indicators for Puerto Rico and various Latin American countries for which the data were available either for 1960 or 1970 (or both years). The indicators chosen were per capita gross domestic product, life expectancy, and the equivalent length of life (E.L.L.) computed for three different values of the parameter α. In Table 2, we rank the countries for which we had data

TABLE 1

Development Indicators for Puerto Rico and Various Latin American Countries, 1960 and 1970[a]

| | Gross domestic product per capita ($1970) | | Life expectancy | | Equivalent length of life (E.L.L.)[b] | | | | | |
| | | | | | $\alpha = +1.25$ (Atkinson's approach) | | $\alpha = -1.25$ (Atkinson's approach) | | $\alpha = +0.05$ (Kolm's leftist measure) | |
Country	1960	1970	1960	1970	1960	1970	1960	1970	1960	1970
Argentina	794	—	65.8	—	32.9	—	70.7	—	43.7	—
Barbados	445	—	65.1	—	28.6	—	70.3	—	41.8	—
Chile	359	689	54.6	61.2	14.1	25.1	63.0	67.1	30.6	39.0
Colombia	330	401	54.2	57.8	15.7	21.7	63.2	64.8	30.0	34.8
Costa Rica	500	566	64.4	67.0	28.9	35.1	70.0	71.5	40.5	44.9
Dominican Republic	312	—	58.1	—	17.0	—	66.6	—	31.9	—
El Salvador	310	300	58.5	61.2	21.6	28.4	66.5	67.1	33.9	39.0
Guatemala	359	373	48.2	52.9	13.3	17.7	58.7	61.9	26.0	29.9
Mexico	434	685	56.9	61.0	18.7	25.6	65.1	67.6	32.6	37.5
Panama	514	731	63.2	65.7	29.1	34.9	69.3	71.0	39.5	43.0
Puerto Rico	1032	1898	69.3	71.6	40.7	49.7	73.6	74.8	47.8	53.8
Venezuela	1366	—	61.6	—	25.9	—	67.8	—	38.4	—

[a] *Sources:* Preston *et al.* (1972) and World Bank (1975).

[b] As indicated in the Appendix, a positive value of α implies giving more weight to young age groups if α is greater than -1 when using Atkinson's rightist measure and if α is positive when using Kolm's leftist measure.

TABLE 2

Ranking of Puerto Rico and Selected Latin American Countries According to the Level of Various Development Indicators, 1960 and 1970[a]

| | Gross domestic product per capita | | Life expectancy | | Equivalent length of life (E.L.L.) | | | | | |
| | | | | | $\alpha = +1.25$ | | $\alpha = -1.25$ | | $\alpha = +0.05$ | |
Country	1960	1970	1960	1970	1960	1970	1960	1970	1960	1970
Chile	5	3	6	4	7	6	6	5	6	4
Colombia	7	6	7	8	6	7	7	7	7	7
Costa Rica	3	5	2	2	3	2	2	2	2	2
El Salvador	8	8	4	4	4	4	4	5	4	4
Guatemala	5	7	8	7	8	8	8	8	8	8
Mexico	4	4	5	6	5	5	5	4	5	6
Panama	2	2	3	3	2	3	3	3	3	3
Puerto Rico	1	1	1	1	1	1	1	1	1	1

[a] *Sources:* Preston *et al.* (1972) and World Bank (1975).

in 1960 as well as in 1970, according to the various development indicators used. We notice first that in the sample of Latin American countries chosen there are some significant differences in the rankings obtained when the level of development is measured by GDP per capita and when life expectancy or E.L.L. are used as standard. El Salvador, for example, ranks much better in the latter case than in the former one (cf. Table 2), this being true in 1960 as well as in 1970. We see also that the changes in ranking obtained when comparing 1970 with 1960 are much more important when per capita GDP is used (rather than life expectancy or E.L.L.). We observe also that differences between countries are much more significant in the case of per capita GDP (in 1960, Venezuela's GDP per capita was more than four times as large as El Salvador's) than when life expectancy or E.L.L. is used. (In this case, the biggest difference corresponds to a ratio of 3 to 1, observed when $\alpha = 1.25$, in which case Puerto Rico's E.L.L. is equal to 40.7 and Guatemala's to 13.3. years.)

It appears, therefore, that the use of life expectancy or E.L.L. instead of the more common GDP per capita tends to soften differences, whether one uses cross-sectional or time-series data. In order to illustrate this, we have drawn various graphs of the relation between life expectancy or E.L.L., on the one hand (axis), and per capita GDP on the other.

These overall relations were obtained from regressions in which the dependent variable was the natural logarithm of life expectancy or E.L.L.

TABLE 3

Income Elasticity of the Various Development Indicators[a]

Regression coefficients and data base	Development indicators			
		Equivalent length of life		
	Life expectancy	$\alpha = +1.25$ (Atkinson's approach)	$\alpha = -1.25$ (Atkinson's approach)	$\alpha = -0.05$ (Kolm's leftist approach)
1960 Data (43 observations)				
R^2	0.69	0.79	0.66	0.79
Elasticity[b]	0.16 (9.6)	0.54 (12.3)	0.10 (8.9)	0.29 (12.4)
1970 Data (36 observations)				
R^2	0.66	0.69	0.65	0.72
Elasticity	0.11 (8.1)	0.44 (8.7)	0.07 (8.0)	0.23 (9.4)
Combined 1960 and 1970 Data (79 observations)				
R^2	0.66	0.74	0.64	0.75
Elasticity	0.14 (12.2)	0.49 (14.6)	0.08 (11.6)	0.26 (15.2)

[a] Income is measured by GDP per capita.
[b] t values are given in parentheses.

and the explanatory variable was GDP per capita. The results of these regressions and the corresponding income elasticities of life expectancy and E.L.L. are given in Table 3. On the whole, these elasticities tend to be smaller in 1970 than in 1960. We notice also that for both years the highest elasticities were obtained for E.L.L. when a higher weight was given to young age groups (independently of whether Atkinson's or Kolm's approach was used). This clearly implies that mortality at lower ages is more responsive to income than overall mortality or mortality at older ages. Let us now analyze these results in more details.

A. Cross-Sectional Comparisons

In Fig. 1, we represent the relation between life expectancy and GDP per capita, as obtained from data concerning countries from all over the world in 1960 and 1970; 43 countries were computed for 1960 and 36 for 1970, so that we have 79 observations for the combined 1960–1970 relation. On the same graph, identify Puerto Rico and the Latin American

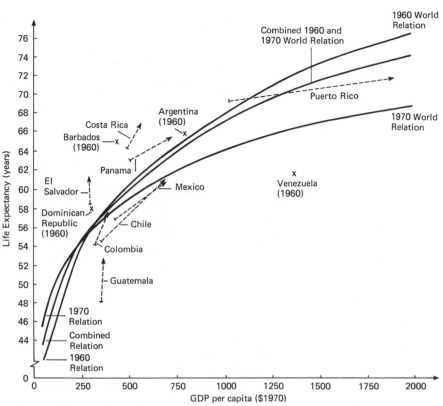

Fig. 1. The relation between life expectancy and GDP per capita in 1960 and 1970.

countries for which we had data on 1960 or 1970 (or both). These countries can be clearly classified into two categories; those that fared better than would have been expected on the basis of their GDP per capita and those that fared worse. Among those who do not rate well, we have Guatemala, Chile, and Mexico in 1960, as well as in 1970, and Venezuela in 1960. In the category of those who had a higher life expectancy than predicted, we have Panama, Costa Rica, and El Salvador for both 1960 and 1970, as well as Barbados, Argentina, and the Dominician Republic in 1960. For Colombia and Puerto Rico, we have mixed results: Colombia fared better in 1970 than in 1960, the opposite being true for Puerto Rico.

This rating is based on life expectancy data, that is (as explained in the Appendix), on the assumption that equal weights are given to the various age groups. However, if one desires to take into account the existence of inequality before death when classifying various countries, one should use, as explained in the previous section, the equivalent length of life. In

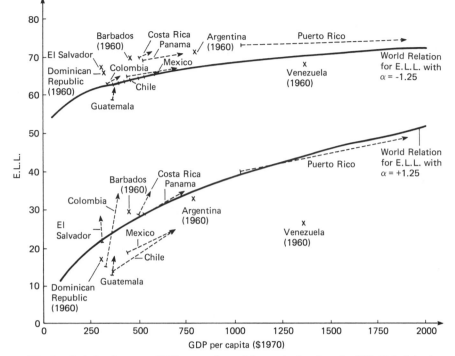

Fig. 2. Relation between GDP per capita and the equivalent length of life (E.L.L.) when $\alpha = + 1.25$ and $\alpha = - 1.25$, using a "rightist" approach.

Figs. 2 and 3, we represented the E.L.L. as a function of GDP per capita, using as a data base the combination of observations we had for 1960 and 1970. For Fig. 2, the E.L.L. was computed using Atkinson's "rightist" approach, whereas for Fig. 3, Kolm's "leftist" option was used.

Let us first take a look at Fig. 2. When $\alpha = 1.25$ (when the relative inequality aversion coefficient ϵ is equal to 2.25), the results are quite similar to those of Fig. 1, the only difference being that now Argentina and the Dominican Republic (in 1960) did worse than expected on the basis of their GDP per capita. On the contrary, when $\alpha = - 1.25$ (when the relative inequality aversion coefficient ϵ is equal to $- 0.25$), most Latin American countries fared better than expected on the basis of their GDP per capita, the only exceptions being Guatemala (in both 1960 and 1970) and Venezuela (in 1960). These results should not be surprising because when α is smaller than $- 1$, the marginal utility of life duration increases with life duration, and because most Latin American countries are character-

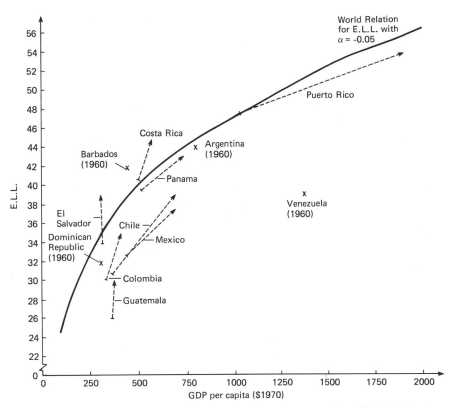

Fig. 3. Relation between GDP per capita and the equivalent lenght of life (E.L.L.) when $\alpha = -0.05$, using a "leftist" approach.

ized by high infant and child mortality rates, they fare better when small weights are given to these young age groups.

The results of Fig. 3 are even more striking. Here we used Kolm's "leftist" approach with a negative α, that is, the marginal utility of life duration decreases with life duration, but now equal absolute additions to life duration imply equal absolute decreases in marginal utility. In other words, young age groups are given more weight; it appears then that only Costa Rica (in 1960 as well as in 1970) and Barbados (1960 data) fared better than expected on the basis of their GDP per capita. Latin America's weakness concerning mortality performance is now well illustrated. Because, on one hand, inequality before death certainly reflects income inequality, whereas on the other hand, the duration of life is a good indicator of the quality of life, we could conclude that, measured accordingly, the level of development of some Latin American countries is lower than the one obtained on the basis of GDP per capita data.

B.   Changes Over Time

A last question that one may want to ask concerns the progress accomplished during this decade. In Table 4, we have growth rates based first on GDP data and then on data relative to life expectancy and E.L.L. It appears that Chile, whatever indicator was used, accomplished most during these 10 years (only eight countries were classified because they were the only ones for which we found life tables for both 1960 and 1970). On the other hand, we notice that Puerto Rico, which ranked second according to the rate of growth of GDP per capita, ranked much worse with respect to the rate of growth of life expectancy or E.L.L. The opposite was true for Guatemala. Both results should not be too surprising because Puerto Rico started with the highest level of life expectancy or E.L.L., hence its slow progress afterward, whereas Guatemala started with the lowest level, hence its relatively fast progress during the decade. These various rates of growth can also be observed in Figs. 1–3 for the eight countries for which data were available in 1960 and 1970. For each of them, we have drawn a vector whose origin corresponds to the situation in 1960 and whose end (arrow) represents the situation in 1970. The more vertical the vectors, the higher the rates of growth of life expectancy (or E.L.L.) relative to those of GDP per capita. The longer the vector, the bigger the absolute changes in GDP per capita, life expectancy, and E.L.L.

C.   What Can Be Concluded from the Previous Analysis?

First, concerning the overall performance of Latin American countries (with respect to the rest of the world), it appears that the conclusion depends very much on which indicator is used, but on the whole, when E.L.L. is used and a bigger weight is given to young age groups, the region did not rate as well as would have been expected on the basis of the level of GDP per capita.

Second, there are very significant differences between these Latin American countries, not only with respect to GDP per capita, but even when life expectancy or E.L.L. is used as an indicator, despite the fact that the potential distribution of the latter indicator is much narrower. For example, Guatemala is "distant" from Argentina, whichever indicator is used.

TABLE 4

Growth Rate of Some Development Indicators for Puerto Rico and Selected Latin American Countries, 1960–1970[a]

Country	Gross domestic product per capita		Life expectancy		Equivalent length of life					
					$\alpha = +1.25$		$\alpha = -1.25$		$\alpha = -0.05$	
	% Change	Ranking	% Change	Ranking	% Change	Ranking	% Change	Ranking	% Change	Ranking
Chile	91.9	1	12.2	1	78.3	1	6.5	1	27.7	1
Colombia	21.5	5	6.6	4	38.4	3	2.6	4	16.3	2
Costa Rica	13.2	6	4.1	6	21.4	7	2.1	6	10.9	7
El Salvador	−3.3	8	4.6	5	31.1	5	0.8	8	15.0	5
Guatemala	3.9	7	9.8	2	32.8	4	5.4	2	15.2	3
Mexico	57.8	3	7.3	3	36.6	2	3.9	3	15.1	4
Panama	42.2	4	3.9	7	19.7	8	2.5	5	8.8	8
Puerto Rico	83.9	2	3.3	8	22.2	6	1.7	7	12.5	6

[a] *Sources:* Preston *et al.* (1972) and World Bank (1975).

Third, some countries fare much better with one indicator than with the other. For example, Venezuela ranked well on the basis of its GDP per capita but badly on the basis of the other indicators, the reverse being true for Costa Rica.

Finally, there were significant differences also in the progress accomplished during this decade. Chile did best, whatever criterion was used. Puerto Rico, on the other hand, had a high growth rate only when the criterion used was GDP per capita, whereas Colombia, Guatemala, and Mexico did quite well when life expectancy or E.L.L. were used as development indicators.

This brings us back to the problem of chosing a single indicator of development. We believe that the E.L.L. combines many properties desirable for a development indicator and that it responds better to modern approaches to development problems, as put forth recently, for example, by Iglesias, (1976):

> The emphasis being placed on the Quality of Life, defense of the environment, protection of natural resources and common assets, greater equity in income distribution, of well being, and other objectives which are beginning to form the new development ideology of the present time, can and must, involve significant changes in the patterns of development and assignment of resources.

APPENDIX

The utility functions and the equivalent length-of-life functions corresponding to the Atkinson and Kolm approaches are herewith derived.

A. The "Rightist" Approach: Constant Relative Inequality Aversion

With an additive social welfare function, we apply the definition of relative risk aversion to the concept of relative inequality aversion. The assumption therefore is that if $U(X)$ is the utility derived by the individual from the number of years lived, by definition of constant relative risk aversion, we have

$$- x \, U''(x)/U'(x) = \epsilon, \qquad (1)$$

from which we derive $U'(X) = bX^{-\epsilon}$ and hence,

$$U(X) = a + \frac{b}{1 - \epsilon} X^{1-\epsilon}. \qquad (2)$$

We compute now the equivalent length of life (E.L.L.), i.e., the length of life x_E, which, if equally distributed, would give the same welfare as the sum of the utility functions $U(x)$. So we must have

$$NU(x_E) = \sum_{i=1}^{n} U(x_i)f(x_i), \tag{3}$$

where $f(x_i)$ is the frequency of x_i and $N = \sum_{i=1}^{n} f(x_i)$. Combining (2) and (3), we obtain

$$\left[a + \frac{b}{1 - \epsilon} x_E^{1-\epsilon} \right] N = Na + \frac{b}{1 - \epsilon} \left[\sum_{i=1}^{n} x_i^{1-\epsilon} f(x_i) \right],$$

$$x_E = \left[\sum_{i=1}^{n} x_i^{1-\epsilon} \frac{f(x_i)}{N} \right]^{\frac{1}{1-\epsilon}} \tag{4}$$

clearly, x_E is a generalized mean defined by

$$g(x_E) = \sum_{i=1}^{n} g(x_i)f(x_i)/N,$$

where

$$g(x_i) = x_i^{1-\epsilon} = \exp\left(-\alpha \ln x_i\right) \tag{5}$$

with $\alpha = \epsilon - 1$.

We notice also that if all life durations x_i are increased by $\lambda\%$, the equivalent length of life x_E will increase by $\lambda\%$.

If we now define inequality as $I_r = (\bar{x} - x_E)/\bar{x} = 1 - (x_E/\bar{x})$, we see that if all x_i increase by $\lambda\%$, x_E and $\bar{x}$ increase by $\lambda\%$, so that the inequality measure I_r keeps the same value. This is the essence of what has been called the "rightist" approach to inequality.

B.   The Leftist Approach: Constant Absolute Inequality Aversion

By the definition of absolute risk aversion and given that the welfare function is additive, we have

$$\frac{-U''(X)}{U'(X)} = \theta, \tag{6}$$

from which we derive $U'(X) = de^{-\theta x}$ and, hence,

$$U(X) = C - (d/\theta)e^{-\theta x} \tag{7}$$

In this case, the equivalent length of life (E.L.L.) x_E' must be such that

$$NU(x'_E) = \sum_{i=1}^{n} U(x_i)f(x_i)$$

$$N[c - d/\theta e^{-\theta x'_E}] = Nc - (d/\theta)\left[\sum_{i=1}^{n} e^{-\theta x_i}f(x_i)\right]$$

$$e^{-\theta x'_E} = \sum_{i=1}^{n} e^{-\theta x_i}f(x_i)/N$$

$$x'_E = -(1/\theta) \ln\left[\sum_{i=1}^{n} e^{-\theta x_i}f(x_i)/N\right]. \tag{8}$$

We see that x'_E is a generalized mean defined by $h(x'_E) \approx \Sigma_{i=1}^{n}f(x_i)h(x_i)/N$, where

$$h(x_i) = e^{-\alpha x_i} \quad \text{(with } \alpha = \theta\text{)}. \tag{9}$$

We notice that if all x_i increase by the *same amount* k, the equivalent length of life x'_E will increase by the same amount k.

If we now define inequality as $I_l = \bar{x} - x'_E$, we see that if all x_i increase by k, $\bar{x}$ and x'_E will also increase by k so that the inequality measure I_l will keep the same value. This is the essence of what we called the ''leftist'' approach to inequality.

REFERENCES

Atkinson, A. B. (1970). "On the Measurement of Inequality." *Journal of Economic Theory* **2**, No. 31, pp 244–263.

Chenery, H. B., Ahluwalia, M., Bell, C. L. E., Duley, J. H., and Jolly, R. (1974). *Redistribution with Growth*. London and New York: Oxford Univ. press.

Hicks, N., and Streeten, P. (1979). "Indicators of Development: The Search for a Basic Needs Yardstick." *World Development* **7**, 567–580.

Iglesias, E. V. (1976). "Situation and Prospects of the Latin American Economy in 1975." *CEPAL Review, U.N. First Semester,* 77–98.

Kolm, S.-C. (1976a). "Unequal Equalities. I." *Journal of Economic Theory* **12**, 416–442.

Kolm, S. C. (1976b). "Unequal Equalities. II." *Journal of Economic Theory* **13**, 82–111.

Morris, M. D., and Liser, F. B. (1977). "The P.Q.L.I.: Measuring Progress in Meeting Human Needs." *Communiqué on Development Issues* (32), Overseas Development Council.

Nordhaus, W., and Tobin, J. (1972). "Is Growth Obsolete?" *Economic Growth*. New York: Columbia University Press.

Pinto, A. (1976). "Styles of Development in Latin America" *CEPAL Review, U.N. First Semester,* 99–130.

Prebisch, R. (1776). "A Critique of Peripheral Capitalism." *CEPAL Review, U.N. First Semester,* 9–76.

Preston, S., Keyfitz, N., and Schoen, R. (1972). *Causes of Death. Life Tables for National Populations*. New York: Seminar Press.

Silber, J. (1980). "E.L.L. (the Equivalent Length of Life) or Another Attempt of Measuring Development," mimco. Bar-Ilan University.

Usher, D. (1973). "An Imputation to the Measure of Economic Growth for Changes in Life Expectancy." In *The Measure of Economic and Social Performance* (M. Moss, ed.). New York: N.B.E.R.

Usher, D. (1980). *The Measurement of Economic Growth.* London and New York: Oxford Univ. Press: (Blackwell).

World Bank, (1975). *World Tables for 1975.*

Department of Economics
Bar-Ilan University
Ramat-Gan, Israel

Chapter 19

Growth, Underemployment, and Income Distribution

Víctor E. Tokman

I. INTRODUCTION

The economic literature has witnessed a revival of the discussion about the relationship between growth and income distribution. Many of the recent contributions on this subject have adopted Kuznets's (1955) analytical framework, which postulates the inevitability of widening inequality in the early phases of transition from preindustrial to industrial economies, and before growth results in increased equity. This behavior is expected as the result of both a greater degree of inequality and a higher income per capita prevailing in those sectors receiving the migrants from the rural areas. According to Kuznets's estimates, inequality should increase until the weight of the nonagricultural sectors reaches 60–70% of the total labor force.

Using cross-country data and different specifications of the regression equations,[1] Ahluwalia (1976) and Lydall (1977) both obtained results consistent with the Kuznets hypothesis; i.e., that inequality is low in poor

413

countries, reaches a maximum at higher levels of income per capita, and then declines. Ahluwalia shows that the income share of the bottom 20% declines until the US$600 of per capita GNP at 1971 prices level is reached, whereas the bottom 40% reaches its minimum at US$468 per capita. Using as measures of concentration both the Gini coefficient and the shares of various percentile groups, Lydall obtains somewhat similar results because the Gini coefficient reaches a maximum at US$243 per capita GNP,[2] whereas the share of the bottom 20% of income units declines until a level of nearly US$500 per capita is reached.[3]

Bacha (1979) examined the changes in income distribution for 30 countries during the sixties, using the same raw data as Ahluwalia and Lydall but including only those countries for which estimates were available for the distribution of income at two points in time spanning about ten years in each case. By fitting a regression equation between changes in the share of the bottom 40% and GNP per capita,[4] he also found support for a behavior similar to that suggested by Kuznets, but the turning point was recorded at US$900 instead of the US$468 found by Ahluwalia.

This outward movement of the curve is also very clear when the scarce trend data available for the distribution of income of several Latin American countries is considered. Although most of them have already surpassed the turning point estimated from cross-country data, there is no evidence that they have left the first phase of the Kuznets curve. Ahluwalia *et al.* (1979) show, for instance, that four out of the five Latin American countries included in their analysis (Brazil, Colombia, Mexico, and Peru),[5] although registering higher levels of GNP per capita than the turning point, still show increasing inequality. The same situation can be seen in Table 1, which contains the data available for the Gini coefficient in two distant years, the changes registered in the share of the bottom 40% dur-

---

[1] Ahluwalia used a quadratic function of the type $S = a_0 - a_1 \ln Y_t + a_2 (\ln Y)^2$, where S is the share of different percentile groups and $\ln Y$ the logarithm of income. Lydall used a function $S = a_0 + a_1 \ln Y + a_2 (Y)^{-1}$, where S is the given measure of inequality and $\ln Y$ the logarithm of income.

[2] His result is also consistent with the one reached by Paukert (1973) because the Gini ratio reaches a maximum of 0.50 for countries between US$201 and US$300 per capita GDP at 1965 prices.

[3] When Lydall used a similar function to that of Ahluwalia, the turning points were reached at higher level of incomes but the coefficients in the equation, where the bottom 20% is the dependent variable, were insignificant.

[4] The function used is $\dot{S} = a_0 \ln Y - a_1$, where $\dot{S}$ represents changes in the share of the bottom 40% divided by the rate of growth of the GNP per capita and Y the GNP per capita in the mid-sixties. This equation is the first derivative of the equation used by Ahluwalia.

[5] The only exception is Costa Rica.

TABLE 1

Concentration and Growth in Some Latin American Countries[a]

Country	Initial year	Terminal year	GNP at midpoint (US$ 1975)	Gini coefficient Initial year	Gini coefficient Terminal year	Change in the share of the bottom 40%
Colombia	1962	1970	354	0.525	0.562	−1.4
Brazil	1960	1970	470	0.590	0.647	−2.2
Peru	1961	1970–71	547	0.612	0.594	−0.8
Costa Rica	1961	1971	556	0.521	0.445	1.6
Mexico	1963	1969	640	0.539	0.583	−2.0
Panama	1960	1970	642	0.500	0.448	0.4

[a] *Source:* Jain (1975); GNP from Bacha (1979).

ing the same period, and the GNP per capita in the middle year. Three of the six countries included register-increased concentration, one is more or less constant, and Panama and Costa Rica show some improvement in their income distribution. All of them had surpassed the estimated turning point by 1973. The improvement in the distribution of income seems to be taking longer than expected and the concentration ratios are reaching higher levels than anticipated.

This chapter intends to explore some of the factors that determine this behavior of the distribution of income in Latin American countries. For such purpose, the functioning of the labor markets and the changes in the employment structure will be analyzed because it will be argued that they are the main determinants of the primary distribution of income.

In Kuznets's analysis, as well as in some of the more recent work, it is assumed that labor mobility occurs in a two-sector framework and that one of the main characteristics of the process of growth of less developed countries is the existence of a significant and nondisappearing urban informal sector. The presence of an important urban informal sector affects the present distribution of income and its evolution.

On the one hand, income distribution within the informal sector is expected to be more egalitarian than that prevailing in modern urban activities. This can be as a result of higher competition between units within the sector as well as the mechanisms of surplus distribution that prevail within the productive units. However, one can expect that these trends would still imply a higher degree of inequality than in the agricultural sector. On the other hand, the evolution of the employment structure in less developed countries is showing that the share of the informal sector in the total labor force is not decreasing during the process of growth. Employment trends are combined with increasing income differentials between the modern and informal sectors. As a result, although inequality during the first phase can be smaller than that anticipated by Kuznets, it could indeed increase during the process of growth and postpone for a long period the expected improvement in income distribution.

In the next section, the methodology used in the chapter will be presented. In Sections III and IV, the behavior of the intra- and intersectoral inequality will be analyzed, on both theoretical and empirical grounds. Given such behaviors, the turning point and the level of concentration will be estimated and compared with those predicted by models that do not take proper account of the functioning of the labor markets.

II. THE METHODOLOGY

As the purpose of this chapter is to analyze the factors that determine the changes in the distribution of income during the process of growth in the Latin American countries and as we postulate that they are closely linked to the functioning of the labor markets, a simple methodology will be followed to observe explicitly the incidence of three crucial variables on income inequality. These three variables, which capture the main dynamic characteristics of the labor market, are: the level of income concentration in each segment of the market, the level and evolution of the intersectoral income differentials, and the level and evolution of the weights of each sector on total employment, in particular, of the urban informal sector.

The first task was to select an indicator of inequality that could be easily decomposed in, within, and between components because the variables mentioned can be allocated to each component. For this purpose, we selected the variance of the logarithms of income, which is the simplest measure possible, because it directly follows the statistical decomposition of the variance formula. The total log variance equals the between-group log variance plus the weighted average of the within-group log variances.

In addition, after considering the attractive decomposition analysis of the Gini coefficient made by Fei *et al.* (1978) and extended to the modern–traditional dichotomy by Fields (1979), we followed the basic methodology presented by Lydall (1977), which has, again, the advantage of simplicity and the possibility of explicitly considering the factors involved through the iteration process of the model. Following Lydall's general methodological approach, we built a three-sector model, allowing for un-

equal degrees of concentration within sector, income differentials between sectors, and changes through time and in the share of each sector in
total employment.

The algebra of the model used is as follows:

$$V = \sum_{g=1}^{G} (n_g/n)[\ln(\bar{Y}_g/\bar{Y})]^2 + \sum_{g=1}^{G} (n_g/n)(1/n_g) \sum_{i=1}^{n_g} \ln(Y_i/\bar{Y}_g)^2, \quad (1a)$$

$$V = V_b + \sum_{g=1}^{G} (n_g/n)V_g, \quad (1b)$$

$$Y_a = a_1 - a_2 \ln \bar{Y} + a_3(\ln \bar{Y})^2, \quad (2)$$

$$Y_i = b_1 - b_2 \ln \bar{Y} + b_3(\ln \bar{Y})^2, \quad (3)$$

$$Y_f = c_1 - c_2 \ln \bar{Y} + c_3(\ln \bar{Y})^2, \quad (4)$$

$$Y_a = X_a Y_i, \quad (5)$$

$$Y_f = X_f Y_i, \quad (6)$$

$$Y = Y_i(n_a X_a + n_f X_f + n_i), \quad (7)$$

$$Y_i' = Y_i \pm \epsilon, \quad (8)$$

$$l = n_a + n_i + n_f, \quad (9)$$

$$n_a = k, \quad (10)$$

$$n_i = d_1 - d_2 \ln \bar{Y} + d_3(\ln \bar{Y})^2, \quad (11)$$

$$n_i' = n_i/(n_i + n_f), \quad (12)$$

$$n_f = 1 - n_i - n_a \quad (13)$$

$$V_{ga} \le V_{gi} \le V_{gf}, \quad (14)$$

where V is the variance of the logs of income; V_b the between-group component; V_g the within-group log variance; n_g the weight of each sector on
economically active population (EAP); n the total EAP; $\bar{Y}_g$ the mean income of the gth sector; ϵ the estimation error; $\bar{Y}$ the total mean income; Y_a
the agricultural income per sectoral EAP; Y_i the informal sector income
per sectoral EAP; Y_f the formal sector income per sectoral EAP; X_a the
ratio between agricultural and informal incomes; X_f the ratio between formal and informal incomes; Y_i' the observed informal income; n_a the weight
of the agricultural sector in total EAP; n_i the weight of the informal sector
in total EAP; n_i' the weight of the informal sector in nonagricultural EAP;
n_f the weight of the formal sector in total EAP; k exogenous; and V_{ga}, V_{gi},
V_{gf} the within-group variance of agriculture, informal and formal sectors,
respectively.

TABLE 2

Kuznets's Hypothesis: Inequality and Population Shifts[a]

Share of agricultural labor force n_a	Log variance V	Between-group component V_b	Within-group component V_g
1.0	0.500	0.0	0.50
0.9	0.564	0.044	0.52
0.8	0.619	0.079	0.54
0.7	0.664	0.104	0.56
0.6	0.699	0.119	0.58
0.5	0.724	0.124	0.60
0.4	0.738	0.118	0.62
0.3	0.743	0.103	0.64
0.2	0.738	0.078	0.66
0.1	0.712	0.044	0.68
0.0	0.700	0.0	0.70

[a] For assumptions and methodology, see text.

The functions were fitted on the basis of time-series data for as many Latin American countries as available. Detailed sources and definitions will be given in the next three sections. Inequality (14) will be justified in the next section, but as information was only partially available for two countries, it was assumed that $V_{ga} = 0.40$, $V_{gi} = 0.50$, and $V_{gf} = 0.60$.

In order to translate the Kuznets hypothesis in terms of the model used, a first run was made assuming that there are only two sectors, that the relative inequality of the receiving sector is higher than in the sector of origin (0.70 versus 0.50 for the log variance[6]), and that the mean income in the former sector is twice as large as the mean income of the latter. Table 2 shows the effects on the log variance and its components when the proportion of the population in the nonagricultural sector increases. Inequality increases until the proportion of the population outside the agricultural sector reaches around 70% and then starts to decrease. However, before that point, at around 50% of the labor force in each sector, the log variance reaches a level close to the maximum, which is maintained without significant variations until the agricultural labor weight is less than 20%. The turning point then roughly coincides with that calculated by Kuznets (1955) under more or less similar assumptions. It can also be seen that the within component always increases because of the assumed greater concentration of the receiving sector, but the between component reaches a

[6] These are larger than those used by Lydall (0.42) but are more representative of Latin American concentration levels.

maximum at the 50% share of agriculture in the total economically active population and immediately afterward more than compensates for the effect of the within component. If the simulation is calculated using increasing incomes per economically active population as Lydall does, the maximum inequality is reached at US$2500, which, according to his conversion, corresponds to about US$937 per capita at 1971 U.S. prices.

III. INFORMAL SECTOR: UNDEREMPLOYMENT AND EQUITY AT LOW INCOME LEVELS

The model outlined in the previous section postulates that intrasectoral inequality increases from agriculture to the urban formal sector, the degree of inequality of the informal sector being between both. The higher concentration of income in the nonagricultural sector is an assumption made in most of the models related to this subject starting with Kuznets's own contribution. For this reason, we shall not devote much time to justifying it but rather concentrate on the determination of the expected levels of concentration in the informal vis-à-vis the formal sector. Lydall (1977) clearly shows, on the basis of worldwide cross-country data, that income distributions in rural areas (or among the agricultural population) are more equal than income distributions in urban areas (or among the nonagricultural population).[7] The scarce and weak data available for some Latin American countries also support the previous assumption, in spite of the high land ownership concentration prevailing in the region. As can be seen in Table 3, all the countries included register around 1970 higher Gini coefficients in urban than in rural areas.

Previous analyses assumed that the urban areas were homogeneous or, in those cases where a distinction was made between modern and traditional sectors (presumably reflecting different technologies used), arbitrary assumptions were introduced of equality in the concentration of income in both sectors (as Lydall, 1977) or of higher inequality in the modern sector (as Fields, 1979). We have argued elsewhere (Tokman, 1979) that there are theoretical explanations why inequality in the modern sector should be higher than in the informal sector.

Although the informal sector can be seen as composed of three heterogeneous subgroups, all of them share a common feature, i.e., long-run equilibrium is reached at a point, at which no supernormal profits exist

[7] Lydall determined this by adding two dummy variables to the equation mentioned in footnote 1. The first dummy variable takes a value of 1 for the rural or agricultural sector and 0 otherwise, and the second takes a value of 1 for the urban or nonagricultural sector and 0 otherwise.

TABLE 3

Rural and Urban Concentration of Income in Some Latin American Countries, circa 1970[a]

Country	Year	Income unit[b]	Gini coefficient	
			Urban	Rural
Brazil	1970	EAP	0.556	0.448
Chile	1968	H	0.455	0.428
Colombia	1970	I	0.552	0.476
Costa Rica[c]	1971	H	0.443	0.367
Mexico	1963	H	0.524	0.482
Honduras	1967–68	H	0.501	0.486

[a] *Source:* Jain (1975).

[b] EAP is the economically active population, H the household, and I the individual.

[c] Reference is to metropolitan versus rural areas. A comparison of the rest of the urban areas and the rural areas shows the same direction but smaller differences (0.393 versus 0.367).

and only those profits that are just sufficient to induce the entrepreneur to stay in the industry can be generated. This is the case for (i) those informal activities operating at the base of concentrated markets, (ii) under monopolistic competition when product differentiation and location are important, and (iii) for those inserted in a perfectly competitive market.

In the first case, the adjustment of the market in the long run will be reached at a price level that exceeds the minimum average cost of the oligopolistic firm, ensuring supernormal profits for it and, in general, will not exceed the minimum average cost of competitive (informal) firms. The same happens in the case of the second group because, although it confronts a negatively sloped demand curve for its distinct product and its decisions do not affect its competitors because of its small share of the total market, simultaneous movements on the part of all sellers cause shifts in demand. The short-run equilibrium for the individual seller will be reached when costs equate revenues, but the competitive pressure given by the large number of firms restricts the possibilities of obtaining supernormal profits and reduces them in the long run to a normal level. In the third and last case, equilibrium at zero profit is ensured by the characteristics of the perfectly competitive market.

The long-run equilibrium condition is linked to the main characteristic of urban informal activities, that is, ease of entry (ILO, 1972; Tokman, 1980). Competition is ensured by the existence of a certain number of persons who fulfill the conditions of entry or by the possibility of expansion of the established firms. The number of new entrants required to eliminate supernormal profits will be associated with the size of the market, which, given the subordinated position of the informal sector, is not likely to expand (Tokman, 1978).

Barriers to entry into the informal sector should be assessed in relation to modern-sector activities. There is no doubt that entrance to the informal sector is easier than to the rest of the urban activities because the only barriers to entry will be product differentiation related to the offering of auxiliary services to buyers and to location. The barrier generated by this factor can be explained by differences in access to complementary resources and by the lack of transparence in the market, especially for repair and personal services. Given the imperfection in market information, informal networks of insertion tend to operate based on personal contacts and recommendations of relatives and friends, which, although not homogeneously distributed, are of easy access for everybody. Additional services surrounding the product's sale that are particularly important in retail activities for low purchasing power consumers, such as longer business hours, product divisibility, credit, personal seller–customer relationship, closer location to residence, can be met by any new firm entering into that particular market. However, income differentials can be generated by the monopolistic factors that operate between neighborhoods of different acquisition power. But such differences will, in general, be owing to rents, interests, and/or costs of products from quality differentials, and the barriers will be the amount of capital required rather than product differentiation.

Different possibilities of entry are restricted to heterogeneous access to complementary factors, mostly skill and capital. However, several studies have shown that skill requirements to perform informal activities are generally low, that the time required for on-the-job training is short, and that formal training and experience are substitutes in skill upgrading. Similarly, other studies show that the average capital needed for informal units is substantially lower than for the same activities in the modern sector and that most informal activities can be started with little capital and then can accumulate it during the operation of the firm until a ceiling is reached, which constitutes a barrier for the informal firm to become a modern unit (Tokman, 1980).

Zero-profit equilibrium and relatively easier access to the low complementary factors required ensure that the distribution of income between informal units will be more homogeneously distributed than in the formal sector. Because parts of these units are small firms organized on a quasi-capitalistic or family basis, surplus distribution within the unit could still generate inequality among persons working in the informal sector. The entrepreneur in such firms usually offers an indivisible package composed by his own labor, that of his family, and some capital. Return on capital is low because mobility is restricted, owing to its dual role as productive and household asset, and because the minimum requirements for outside investment exceed the average return available (Tokman, 1978, 1980).

This leads us to analyze the distribution of labor incomes. However, the alternative return to family labor is also limited by part-time availability and job scarcity in the modern sector. The alternative income is the salary that the head of the family could earn by working in that sector. The situation is similar for the quasi-capitalistic entrepreneur whose actual alternative will be to become a dependent in a modern establishment of the same kind of activity, where his entrepreneurial capacity would be mostly unused and not remunerated. This implies that the surplus created within the unit will be small, limiting the range of concentration and that, in addition, family participation ensures its equitable distribution within firms organized on a family basis.

The scarce evidence available for the Dominican Republic, El Salvador, Paraguay, and Colombia supports this hypothesis. In the first three cases, the data collected by PREALC around 1974 on the basis of household surveys in Santo Domingo, San Salvador, and Asuncion were adjusted for three common biases: (1) the underreporting of nonlabor income, which was estimated by comparing its share according to the national accounts and that declared in the survey. The underreporting was around 30% of the total income in San Salvador and around 40% in the other two cases. As nonlabor incomes declared were a higher percentage in the upper incomes of the informal sector, the correction was allocated to the top decile. (2) An income was imputed to those who declared being unpaid family members. Because this part of the labor force usually helps the head of the household without receiving an established wage, the total income of the household was divided by the working members of such households and the resulting figure was allocated to unpaid family members. (3) The domestic servants' income was adjusted because of the underreporting of wages received in kind, mostly food and shelter. In the case of Colombia, the data discussed by Bourguignon (1979) were used, adjusting for only the first type of bias, which was the one recognized by the author as important. Underreporting was arbitrarily assumed by him to be 30% of total income and it was allocated to the top decile of the formal sector.

In Table 4, it can be seen that in the four cases the estimated Gini coefficients within the informal sector are smaller than those calculated within the formal sector. In those cases for which data were available, the estimate of the Gini coefficients by sex within each sector shows that the smaller inequality in the informal sector is entirely explained by the males

TABLE 4

Gini Coefficients within Sectors in Four Latin American Countries, circa 1974[a]

Countries	Informal sector	Formal sector
Colombia		
Total	0.48	0.53
Adjusted	—	0.62
Dominican Republic		
Total	0.47	0.50
Males	0.44	0.50
Females	0.45	0.37
El Salvador		
Total	0.61	0.67
Males	0.61	0.70
Females	0.53	0.47
Paraguay		
Total	0.59	0.65
Males	0.54	0.66
Females	0.58	0.54

[a] See text discussion for details.

coefficients because informal females register an index of inequality larger than females in the formal sector in all cases.

IV. INTERSECTORAL INCOME DIFFERENTIALS AND NONDECREASING GAPS

Although Kuznets (1955) correctly assumed that the average income of the recipient sector was higher than the one prevailing in the sector of origin, he did not allow for changes in the intersectoral income gap during the process of growth. Variations in the size of the income gaps are, however, a normal factor in the course of development because population shifts from one sector to another tend to affect the income levels in both of them. Increasing intersectoral income differentials will widen inequality, whereas the opposite would occur if the intersectoral gaps were diminishing.

The main issue is to explain and anticipate the expected behavior of such gaps. Nelson *et al.* (1971), in their analysis of Colombia, postulate that, during the early stages of development, an increased dispersion of incomes within the urban sector associated with the phenomenon of dualism will contribute to the widening of inequality. Lydall (1977), after clearly illustrating empirically, in the context of a two-sector model, the effects of both increase and reduction of intersectoral income differences on inequality, concludes that the gap between the modern and traditional sector will tend to diminish because growth of the former must tend to pull up productivity in the latter. Thus, he suggests, "the hard-and-fast division between the traditional and the modern sectors begins to melt away."

If the presence of a significant urban informal sector is recognized, there are two intersectoral income gaps that should be analyzed. The first refers to agricultural–informal-sector differences and the second to those prevailing between the informal and formal sectors. It seems clear that, as the process of growth takes place within a framework of rapid population mobility from rural to urban areas, diminishing returns to natural factors, and supply inelasticity of agricultural products, the agricultural–urban informal income gap will tend to diminish during the first stage of growth until constant differential is reached, which is explained mostly by differences in cost of living.

The previous hypothesis is supported by the evidence available for 13 Latin American countries during the 1965–1977 period. If agricultural wages are taken as a proxy for agricultural incomes, urban minimum wages as a proxy for informal incomes, and both are related to changes in the gross national product (GNP) per economically active population, we observe, first, that a quadratic form adequately describes the relationship between both variables. Results of the regressions are shown in Table 5. We note first that all the regression coefficients are significant at very low levels; second, that the minimum agricultural wage is reached at US\$1437 GNP per person at 1970 prices, and the minimum informal income is reached at US\$1677 GNP per person; and third, that the income differential between both tends to decrease from 37% of the minimum wage at US\$200 GNP per person to 14% at US\$2500 GNP per person and then remains almost constant (see Fig. 1).

The reduction in the gap between agricultural and urban minimum incomes would suggest a trend toward income equalization. The urban areas, however, show symptoms of nondecreasing dualism,[8] evidenced mostly by the persistent existence of an important informal sector in spite of the high rate of economic growth registered in most Latin American countries. Theories explaining such behavior have been advanced in the

---

[8] "Dualism" is used here only in the sense of productivity and income differentials, not in the usual meaning of isolated subsectors, because, as we argue elsewhere, we think that the opposite is true (Tokman, 1978).

TABLE 5

Regression of Sectoral Wages with Income Per Capita in Selected Latin American Countries, 1964–1977[a]

Equation	n	Constant	$\ln Y$[b]	$(\ln Y)^2$ [b]	R^2	F
A. Agricultural wages	140	0.2419	−0.06514 (4.000)	0.04480 (4.178)	0.579	34.55
B. Urban minimum wages	153	0.3642	−0.09637 (6.860)	0.06490 (7.018)	0.603	42.91
C. Manufacturing industry wages	149	0.3856	−0.10628 (3.911)	0.07567 (4.215)	0.720	78.47

[a] The data include information on wages in Argentina, Brazil, Colombia, Costa Rica, Chile, Ecuador, El Salvador, Guatemala, Mexico, Nicaragua, Paraguay, and Peru. The number of observations varies because some countries did not have information for some years. *Sources:* Data from PREALC (1980) in national currencies at current prices are then expressed in local 1970 prices using the cost of living of each country and in U.S. dollars of 1970 using the parity exchange rate calculated by the Economic Commission for Latin America. GNP in US$ at 1970 prices is also from ECLA, and the EAP was calculated by PREALC on the basis of population censuses.

[b] Y is the GNP per economically active population. The figures in parentheses are the t coefficients.

literature (Pinto, 1965; Prebisch, 1976; PREALC, 1978), and the subject falls beyond the scope of this chapter. It will suffice, however, to remark that it is associated with the type of growth followed by these countries, which, among other characteristics, shows a restricted internal technological diffusion. This process of restricted technological diffusion caused by the concentration in the distribution of income prevailing in most of the countries and by factors associated with the importation of technology generates a concentration of modern, highly capital-intensive technology in certain subsectors, and even in establishments (mostly large) within sectors, whereas the rest of the economy continues to operate with traditional technologies. This process is also associated with higher returns to factors of production in the modern sector derived, in part, from productivity differentials but also as a result of imperfections in factor markets. The outcome is that the initial concentration of income tends to widen.

The process occurs in a context in which modern establishments do not face strong competition, either from the outside, because of high tariff protection, or from the rest of the firms, because of great market concentration. They then do not pass on the gains in productivity through price reductions, but rather, factor incomes become higher. In addition, and

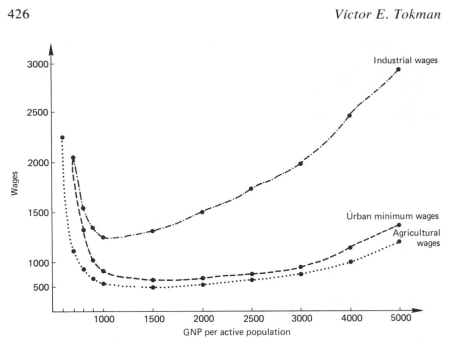

Fig. 1. Agricultural, urban minimum, and industrial wages in relation to income per capita in Latin America (1965–1977).

not totally independent from the increase in factor incomes, capital intensity tends to increase and employment creation in the modern sector becomes insufficient to absorb the rapidly growing labor supply.[9]

The data available on the evolution of the employment structure in most Latin American countries between 1950 and 1970 clearly show that the informal sector has been absorbing labor, practically *pari passu*, with the total increase of the labor force. This can be seen in Table 6, Eq. A, where the share of urban self-employed and unpaid family workers in the total labor force remains around 9% as the GNP per economically active population expands. On the other hand, the share of the informal sector in the urban labor force follows an asymptotic path. It starts at 35% or more at the early stages of growth, decreases until around 20% when a GNP of US$2750 per economically active population is reached, and remains close to that share at higher levels of income. (Again see Table 6, Eq. B, and also Fig. 2).

Data on income differentials between informal and formal sectors and their changes can be obtained from two sources: (i) case studies and (ii)

---

[9] Nelson *et al.* (1971) have developed a formal model of restricted technological diffusion.

TABLE 6

Changes in the Employment Structure in Latin American Countries, as a Function of Changes in Income per Capita, 1950–1970[a]

Equation	n	Constant	$\ln Y$	$(\ln Y)^2$	R^2	F
A. Informal sector in total labor force (n_i)[b]	45	9.018759	0.001353 (2.73614)	—	0.385	7.47
B. Informal sector in urban labor force (n'_i)[c]	45	35.8713	−0.01150 (4.69259)	0.0001 (4.18342)	0.786	34.67

[a] *Source:* Population censuses of 1950, 1960, and 1970 computed for Argentina, Bolivia, Brazil, Colombia, Costa Rica, Chile, Ecuador, El Salvador, Guatemala, Haiti, Honduras, Mexico, Nicaragua, Panama, Peru, Dominican Republic, Uruguay, and Venezuela. Some countries did not have information for the three years considered (Tokman, 1979). GNP from the same source as in Table 5.

[b] n_i is the share of urban self-employed and unpaid family members in the total economically active population and Y the GNP per economically active population. The figures in parentheses are the t coefficients.

[c] n'_i is as in Eq. A, but refers to the urban economically active population, and Y the nonagricultural GNP per active population in those sectors. The figures in parentheses are the t coefficients.

wage statistics, where manufacturing industry wages are taken as a proxy for the formal sector and urban minimum wages are taken, as before, as a proxy for informal incomes. Table 7, built on the basis of the first sources, shows that informal incomes were, on average, one-third of those of the formal sector around 1970 in the eight countries included, ranging from a gap of more than four (formal over informal income) in Peru and Mexico to less than two in Panama and Dominican Republic. The time-series data are scarcer and less reliable, but the three countries for which they are available suggest that the intersectoral income gap has been increasing during the sixties. The situation is less clear for the seventies because income differentials in Panama tend to diminish, whereas data available for Colombia, although not strictly comparable, also indicate the same behavior.

The data on industrial wages and the comparison with minimum wages also seem to suggest a widening of the intersectoral gap during the first period and then a reduction after a certain level of output is reached. As can be seen again in Table 5 and Fig. 1, a quadratic form gives a significant fit to the relationship between industrial wages and changes in GNP per economically active person, as in the case of agricultural and urban

TABLE 7

Urban Intersectoral Income Gap in Several Latin American Countries[a]

Countries[b]	Year	Formal sector income / Informal sector income
Chile	1970	2.7
Mexico	1970	4.4
Paraguay[c]	1973	2.8
El Salvador[d]	1974	2.6
Dominican Republic[e]	1973	1.9
Colombia	1951	1.5
Colombia	1964	2.7
Colombia[f]	1974	1.9
Peru	1950	3.6
Peru	1970	4.4
Panama	1960	1.7
Panama	1970	1.7
Panama	1975	1.2

[a] *Source:* Chile and Mexico (Tokman, 1980); Paraguay, El Salvador, and Dominican Republic (Souza and Tokman, 1978); Colombia 1951 and 1964 (Nelson *et al.* 1971), 1974 (Bourguignon, 1979); Peru (Webb, 1974); Panama (PREALC, 1979).
[b] Data are for all urban areas unless noted otherwise.
[c] Asuncion.
[d] San Salvador.
[e] Santo Domingo.
[f] Seven cities.

minimum wages. Such a function reaches its minimum before the other two at a US$1124 GNP per active person, and afterward, during a second period, it grows more rapidly, generating an increasing gap, which passes from almost zero at a US$200 GNP level to 129% of the minimum wage at the US$2500 GNP level. For larger GNP the gap tends to decrease, reaching 106% of the minimum wage at US$5000.

To sum, the evidence concerning the evolution of intersectoral income differentials indicates a two-direction effect on total inequality. On the one hand, the diminishing agricultural–informal income gap tends to reduce inequality, and on the other, the widening of the within-urban-sector gap up to a certain level of GNP produces the opposite result. The net effect depends on the magnitudes of such changes as well as on the extent of labor absorption in each sector. To this latter aspect, we shall turn next.

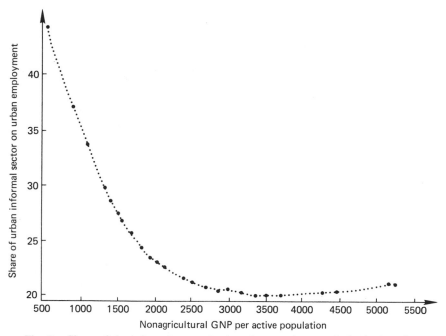

Fig. 2. Share of the informal sector in the urban employment in Latin America as a function of income per capita (1950–1970).

V. EMPLOYMENT PATTERN AND INCOME INEQUALITY

Changes in the employment structure affect the degree of inequality by influencing both the between and within components. This can be seen very clearly in the case of the decomposition of the logarithm of the variance, which is used as a measure of inequality in this chapter, because the variance of the logs of between-group income is weighted by the contribution of each sector to total employment and the same weight is used to determine the contribution of the within-group log variances to overall inequality.

In the previous section, the employment pattern observed in the last two decades was analyzed, showing that the informal sector absorbed an important share of the growth of the urban labor supply. Its share in the total labor force has remained constant, and its contribution to urban employment has decreased to a level of around 20%.

The decreasing weight of the component, which reduces inequality via a smaller agricultural–informal incomes gap, is more than compensated for by the increased weight of the widening formal–informal differential. The result is an increase in the between-group inequality. On the other hand, the differences in the components of the within-group variance is also reinforced by the evolution of the weights resulting in increasing inequality. The labor absorption of the informal sector plays a buffer role, however, because its nondecreasing share on total employment is accompanied by a smaller within-sector inequality. The Kuznets-type two-sector scenario would imply a greater effect on inequality than is actually the case, owing to the presence of the informal sector.

VI. GROWTH, LABOR MARKET, AND INEQUALITY

The model outlined in Section II was worked out on the basis of the characteristics of the labor markets discussed in the three previous sections. To sum, they refer to three main aspects: (i) that the within inequality is larger in the formal than informal sector, and that, in the latter, the inequality exceeds that in the agricultural sector; (ii) that the agricultural–informal income gap decreases during a first phase and then remains constant, whereas the informal–formal income gap increases during a period and then starts to reduce; and (iii) that the share of the informal sector in urban employment decreases and then remains constant during the pro-

TABLE 8

Growth, Employment, and Inequality: A Latin American Profile[a]

Share of agricultural labor force n_a	GNP per active population Y_n	Log variance V	Between-group component V_b	Within-group component V_g
1.0	200	0.500	—	0.500
0.9	400	0.537	0.021	0.516
0.8	600	0.583	0.049	0.534
0.7	800	0.636	0.085	0.551
0.6	1000	0.693	0.125	0.568
0.5	1500	0.786	0.200	0.586
0.4	2000	0.832	0.229	0.603
0.3	2500	0.845	0.225	0.620
0.2	3000	0.842	0.205	0.637
0.1	4000	0.746	0.159	0.653
0.0	5000	0.783	0.113	0.670

[a] For assumptions and methodology, see text.

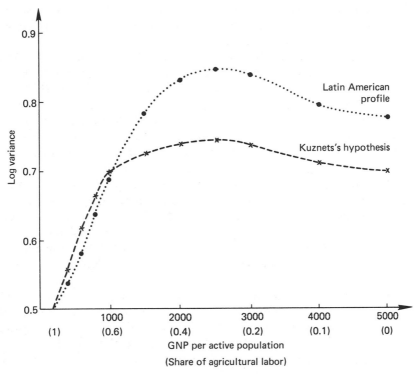

Fig. 3. Growth, employment, and inequality.

cess of growth. These characteristics adequately reflect what has been the observed behavior in Latin American countries. Let us see what the implications are on the changes of the distribution of income.

Table 8 and Fig. 3 show that, given the assumptions mentioned, inequality increases until 70% of the labor force is in nonagricultural sectors and at around US$937 GNP per capita at 1971 U.S. prices.[10] The turning point is reached immediately after the between-group component reaches its maximum because the within-group log variance grows monotonically from 0.5 to 0.67.

Comparison with the results given by the model when the Kuznets hypothesis was introduced (see Table 2 and Fig. 3) shows that the turning point is reached at similar levels of income and distribution of population but at 0.105 points of higher log variance. This greater inequality is en-

[10] The maximum is reached at US$2500 GNP per active person, which, according to Lydall's conversion, is equivalent to US$937 per capita.

tirely explained by the larger between-group component, because the within-group component at that point is 0.02 lower, owing to the influence of the more equitable informal sector.

A comparison of both patterns denotes two additional points. The first is that the Latin American profile shows increasing inequality at slower rates than that anticipated by the Kuznets hypothesis until more than 40% of the labor force is in nonagricultural sectors. This can be attributed partly to the influence of the informal sector on the within-group component and partly to the decrease in the income gap between the agricultural and informal sectors, which affects positively the between-group component at the early stages of the process. The second is that, given the ''plateau'' form that the Kuznets curve takes in this model, the actual turning point of the Latin American profile seems to occur at a later stage. As was discussed in Section II, the turning point in the Kuznets alternative practically starts at the 50% level of population in each sector, which is equivalent to around US$560 GNP per capita. This outward shift of the curve is explained by the growing income differential between the formal and informal sectors.

The effects of the main factors on inequality can also be examined by changing some of the assumptions introduced in the model. Results of these simulations are shown in Table 9. If the informal sector shows a higher rate of decrease in its share of urban employment (following, for instance, Eq. A in Table 6), the turning point would be anticipated but the

TABLE 9

Simulations on Latin American Profile[a]

	Simulation I[b]			Simulation II[c]			Simulation III[d]		
n_a	V	V_b	V_g	V	V_b	V_g	V	V_b	V_g
1.0	0.500	0.0	0.500	0.500	0.0	0.500	0.500	0.0	0.500
0.9	0.603	0.092	0.511	0.535	0.024	0.511	0.603	0.092	0.511
0.8	0.662	0.131	0.531	0.617	0.086	0.531	0.665	0.131	0.534
0.7	0.731	0.180	0.551	0.678	0.127	0.551	0.740	0.180	0.560
0.6	0.806	0.235	0.571	0.716	0.145	0.571	0.824	0.235	0.589
0.5	0.925	0.334	0.591	0.694	0.103	0.591	0.941	0.334	0.607
0.4	0.959	0.348	0.611	0.693	0.082	0.611	0.970	0.348	0.622
0.3	0.941	0.310	0.631	0.698	0.067	0.631	0.943	0.310	0.633
0.2	0.903	0.252	0.651	0.707	0.056	0.651	0.893	0.252	0.641
0.1	0.838	0.167	0.671	0.709	0.038	0.671	0.812	0.167	0.645
0.0	0.773	0.082	0.691	0.705	0.014	0.691	0.727	0.082	0.645

[a] *Source:* See text.
[b] Same assumptions as Table 8, except using Eq. A instead of Eq. B of Table 6.
[c] Same as simulation I but replacing Eq. (6) with $X_f = 1.5$.
[d] Same as simulation I but replacing assumption $V_f = 0.7$ with $0.8 \leq V_f \leq 0.65$.

level of inequality would be higher (0.114 points of log variance) because it would negatively affect both the within- and between-group components. If to the previous assumption a constant, instead of an increasing, income gap were added between the formal and informal sector, the turning point would be further anticipated and the level of inequality would be 0.129 points lower, owing to the reduction in the between-group component. Finally, if, as suggested by the observed increased dispersion of wages in the modern sector (see Tokman, 1979), the concentration within that sector were not constant but increased during a period and then started to decrease, the turning point would be reached at the same income level but concentration would be higher.

VII. CONCLUSIONS

We may now draw some tentative conclusions about the incidence of labor-market behavior on inequality during the process of growth. The main characteristics of such market behavior are the continuous existence of a significant urban informal sector with a more equitable distribution of income within it and a decreasing income gap between agriculture and the informal sector, together with increasing income differentials between the latter and the formal sector.

Although the Kuznets hypothesis is still valid, the behavior of the labor market affects it in three ways. First, the turning point is reached at a later stage of growth than anticipated. Second, the turning point is reached at higher levels of inequality, owing to the increased between-group component, which is somewhat compensated for by the influence of the informal sector on the within-group component. Finally, the transition from agricultural to urban activities costs less in terms of inequality than anticipated during the early stages of growth because of the migrants' entrance to the urban economy through the informal sector. Indeed, the simulations made suggest that inequality would be higher if the informal sector were not there, unless intersectoral income differentials remained constant.

ACKNOWLEDGMENTS

This chapter was written for the *International Symposium on Latin America: Trade, Development and Equity,* organized by the Research Center for Latin American Development Studies of Bar-Ilan University, Ramat-Gan, Israel, May 5–8, 1980. It is the result of extensive discussions held with PREALC colleagues, especially with N. García and A. Uthoff. The econometric assistance of E. Dupré was invaluable. The statistical collaboration of H. Szretter and V. Contreras is also acknowledged. Of course, the responsibility for the content is entirely the author's.

REFERENCES

Ahluwalia, M. S. (1976). "Inequality, Poverty and Development." *Journal of Development Economics* **3**(4), 307–342.

Ahluwalia, M. S., Carter, N., and Chenery, H. B. (1979). "Growth and Poverty in Developing Countries." *Journal of Development Economics* **6**, No. 3, pp 299–341.

Bacha, E. (1979). "Más allá de la curva de Kuznets: Crecimiento y cambio en las desigualdades." In *Distribución del ingreso en América Latina* (O. Muñoz, ed.). Buenos Aires: El Cid.

Bourguignon, F. (1979). "Pobreza y dualismo en el sector urbano de las economías en desarrolo: El caso de Colombia." *Desarrollo y Sociedad* (1), 37–72.

Fei, J., Ranis, G., and Kuo, S. (1978). "Growth and the Family Distribution of Income by Factor Components."*The Quarterly Journal of Economics* **92**(1), 17–53.

Fields, G. (1979). "Desigualdad y desarrollo económico." In *Distribución del ingreso en América Latina* (O. Muñoz, ed.). Buenos Aires: El Cid.

ILO (1972). *Employment, Incomes and Equality. A Strategy for Increasing Productive Employment in Kenya*. Geneva: ILO.

Jain, S. (1975). *Size Distribution of Income. A Compilation of Data*. Washington, D.C.: IBRD.

Kuznets, S. (1955). "Economic Growth and Income Inequality." *American Economic Review* **45** (1).

Lydall, H. (1977). *Income Distribution During the Process of Development*. Geneva: ILO, Income Distribution and Employment Programme, Working Paper 52.

Nelson, R., Schultz, T. P., and Slighton, R. (1971). *Structural Change in a Developing Economy: Columbia's Problems and Prospects*. Princeton, New Jersey: Princeton University Press.

Paukert, F. (1973). "Income Distribution at Different Levels of Development: A Survey of Evidence." *International Labour Review* (108).

Pinto, A. (1965). "Concentración del progreso técnico y de sus frutos en el desarrollo latinoamericano." *El Trimestre Económico* **32** (125).

PREALC (1978). *Sector informal: Funcionamiento y politicas*. Santiago: PREALC.

PREALC (1979). *Panamá: Estrategia de necesidades básicas y empleo*. Santiago: PREALC (borrador para discusión).

PREALC (1980). *Asalariados de bajos ingresos y salarios mínimos en América Latina*. Santiago: PREALC.

Prebisch, R. (1976). "Crítica al capitalismo periférico". *Revista de la CEPAL*, primer semestre.

Souza, P. R., and Tokman, V. E. (1978). "Distribución del ingreso, pobreza y empleo en áreas urbanas." *El Trimestre Económico* **45** (179) (July–September).

Tokman, V. E. (1978). "An Exploration into the Nature of Informal–Formal Sector Relationships." *World Development* **6** (9–10) (September–October).

Tokman, V. E. (1979). *Dinámica de los mercados de trabajo y distribución del ingreso en América Latina*. Santiago: PREALC.

Tokman, V. E. (1980). *The Influence of the Urban Informal Sector on Economic Inequality*. Santiago: PREALC. Also as *Discussion Paper 337*. Economic Growth Center, Yale University, New Haven, Connecticut.

Webb, R. (1974). *Income and Employment in the Urban Modern and Traditional Sectors of Peru*. Princeton, New Jersey: Princeton University Press.

PREALC
Santiago, Chile

Chapter 20

Labor, Education, and Development: Whither Latin America?

*Manuel Zymelman**

As Latin America approaches the last decades of the twentieth century, it has the protean task of catching up with the affluent nations of the world. This task will require a basic transformation of its economic structure, a change in the occupational mix of its labor force, and an improvement in quality of the skills and in the educational requirements of occupations. How should Latin America respond to this challenge? To provide an answer to this question, we start by comparing data on the distribution of employment and productivity of economic sectors, the occupational distribution of the labor force, and the educational attainments of the labor force of Latin American and OECD countries in the 1970s.

---

* The views and interpretations in this chapter are those of the author and should not be attributed to the World Bank, to its affilliated organizations, or to any individual acting in their behalf.

435

I. SECTORAL EMPLOYMENT

Economic development can be viewed as a process of continuous change in the allocation of resources. Historically, the shift has been from agriculture into industry and thence into the teritary sector. So consistent has the direction of the shift been that the sectoral distribution of employment has been widely used as an indicator of economic development. For example, the proportion of the labor force in agriculture is highly correlated with many economic development indexes, such as literacy, death rates, and school enrollments.

Of course, within these broad sectoral groups, there are constant shifts that produce changes in the relative proportions of employment in the different industries comprising these sectors. For example, as manufacturing as a whole develops, there is a tendency for the relative share of employment in the textile and food-processing industries to drop vis-à-vis employment in the chemical or electrical machinery industries.

There are two main reasons for these shifts: changes in the consumption patterns of the population related to income increases and technologi-

TABLE 1

Employment Distribution by Sector, circa 1970[a]

Sector	Latin America[b]	OECD[c]
Agriculture, forestry, and fishing	33.7	12.5
Mining and quarrying	1.1	0.9
Construction	6.4	8.7
Manufacturing	13.9	26.7
Transport and warehousing	4.2	5.3
Communications	0.5	2.2
Utilities	0.9	1.1
Trade	13.0	15.3
Finance, insurance, and real estate	1.6	3.3
Services	24.6	24.2
Total	100.0	100.0

[a] *Source:* Zymelman (1980b).

[b] Data on "Latin America" are averages of data from Brazil, Chile, Colombia, Costa Rica, Jamaica, Mexico, Panama, Uruguay, and Venezuela.

[c] Data on "OECD" are averages of Belgium, Canada, France, German Federal Republic, Greece, Ireland, Japan, Netherlands, New Zealand, Norway, Sweden, United Kingdom, and the United States.

TABLE 2

Employment Distribution of Industries in Manufacturing, circa 1970[a]

Industry	Latin America	OECD
Total manufacturing	100.0	100.0
Food and beverages	22.75	12.23
Textiles	12.58	6.98
Clothing	14.00	6.24
Leather and footwear	5.27	1.93
Lumber, wood, and furniture	9.08	7.13
Paper and paper products	2.29	3.73
Printing and publishing	3.68	5.70
Rubber and plastics	2.29	2.77
Chemicals	4.47	5.27
Glass, stone, and glass products	5.43	4.51
Metal and metal products	10.69	13.37
Fabricated metals[b]	(3.68)	(7.76)
Machinery (excl. electrical)	1.57	8.46
Electrical machinery	1.95	8.38
Transportation equipment	2.11	9.01
Others (incl. scientific instruments)	1.84	4.29

[a] *Source:* Zymelman (1980b).

[b] Fabricated metal is part of metal and metal products.

cal progress. As income goes up, the proportion spent on food and necessities goes down (income elasticity of necessities is less than 1) and the proportion spend on durable goods and services goes up (income elasticity for these goods is higher than 1).

At the same time, technological progress demands the introduction of new methods of production to produce increases in productivity. These, in turn, are based on the development of industries that provide some of the inputs required to increase productivity in other sectors, such as machinery and equipment for processing industries, chemicals and fertilizers for agriculture, and better transportation and communications. These two effects, the change in consumption patterns and technological progress, are mutually reinforcing because some of the industries propelling modernization also produce durable consumption goods whose proportion in the consumption budget increases as income rises. The end result is a further accelerated shift among industries and sectors. The data in Tables 1 and 2, showing the employment structure of sectors and industries for a group of countries in Latin America and OECD, confirm this conclusion.

II. OCCUPATIONAL DISTRIBUTION OF THE LABOR FORCE

The relative shift of employment from one sector to another affects the occupational distribution of the labor force because each industry has its particular occupational requirements. For example, most of the labor in agriculture consists of unskilled and semiskilled laborers, whereas in industry, we find a larger variety of skills, e.g., professional, technical, clerical, and blue-collar workers. If there is a relative shift of employment from agriculture to industry, the proportion of farmers and unskilled laborers will go down and the proportion of white-collar occupations will go up. The process of change in the occupational distribution of the labor force is also reinforced by the ongoing technological change in each industry considered separately.[1] The combined impact of increased productivity in each industry and the changes in the distribution of employment among sectors and industries on the occupational structure of an economy is to effect a shift toward more and better skilled workers and to decrease the demand for the unskilled and uneducated (see Tables 3 and 4.)

Because the labor productivity of an economy is determined by the sectoral distribution of employment and the occupational distribution of each sector, we should ask ourselves which variables has the greatest impact on total productivity. Table 5 presents the productivity levels and the occupational distribution of the labor force assuming, for one case, a hypothetical economy with a sectoral employment distribution of an "average" OECD country and an occupational distribution by sector of an "average" Latin American country and, for another, a hypothetical country with the sectoral distribution of an "average" Latin American country and the occupational distribution by sectors of an "average" OECD country. From this table, it is possible to infer that the occupational structure and, hence, labor productivity in each sector have the greatest influence on the labor productivity of the economy as a whole.

III. EDUCATIONAL REQUIREMENTS OF OCCUPATIONS

Technological development has an effect on the content of occupations. As productivity increases, the required level of theoretical knowledge necessary to perform a job successfully becomes higher, and less

---

[1] Analysis of detailed data from 26 countries for the year 1970 on productivity and occupational distribution in different industries confirms that there is a relationship between the occupational profile of a particular industry and labor productivity in the same industry. See Zymelman (1980a).

physical effort and slower reaction time are required. Precision is supplanted by instruments. Whereas, before, a high degree of skill was synonymous with manual dexterity, the introduction of modern methods of production demands a better understanding of the principles involved in the production and distribution processes, the skill to control and repair machines, and the ability to combine manual and mental work. The complexity of the equipment and its high cost impose a higher responsibility, coupled with the ability to communicate by means of the written word to assure continuity of operations and to be able to evaluate results. Finally, the advance of technology requires workers to take on additional tasks; first, the ones relating to their immediate occupation and later branching out into quite different ones. This broadening of occupational profiles necessitates more knowledge on the part of employees in each occupation.

All these new requirements for new occupations or modified traditional ones demand increased education and training. This greater demand for better training and greater knowledge finds its expression in the ever-increasing formal educational attainments of workers in different occupations all over the world. As an illustration, Table 6 compares years of schooling by major occupational groups in Japan and Argentina in 1960. The differences between the educational distributions, especially at the upper secondary school levels (9–12), are quite significant. Similar differences are assumed to exist between the average OECD and latin American countries.

IV. WHITHER LATIN AMERICA?

Without implying that, in order to achieve a level of income per capita equivalent to that of the OECD countries, Latin America must have an employment and occupational distribution similar to that of the OECD or attain a similar level of education for its labor force (because different employment distributions could be balanced by different occupational distributions of sectors and years of education could be substituted by years of off-school training and experience), the tables previously presented point toward a strategy of growth through increases in productivity in each sector rather than through the reallocation of resources among sectors. Of course, increases in productivity in agriculture will imply a need for shifting labor out of agriculture, preferably into industry if we wish to keep unemployment rates low, but without the growth in productivity of the sectors to which labor is going to be shifted, the results will be disappointing. Similarly, an increase in labor productivity in manufacturing, unless coupled or followed by an increase in productivity in agriculture and

TABLE 3

Percentages of Occupational Distributions by Economic Sector for Latin America and OECD Countries, circa 1970[a]

Industry	Professional and technical workers	Administrators and managers	Clerical workers	Sales workers	Manual workers	Productivity (1970 US$)
Latin America						
Agriculture, forestry, and fishing	0.4	2.1	0.3	0.1	97.1	1060
Mining and quarrying	4.8	2.7	6.1	0.4	86.2	18,190
Construction	3.6	2.0	2.4	0.2	91.7	2530
Manufacturing	3.2	4.2	7.2	1.4	82.5	5060
Transport and warehousing	2.6	3.3	12.2	1.2	81.1	3520
Communications	5.5	5.1	50.5	0.5	38.5	—
Utilities	8.2	3.7	19.1	1.0	68.3	5520[b]
Trades	2.2	6.1	9.5	61.0	21.2	3620
Finance, insurance, and real estate	11.3	9.0	53.3	10.0	7.1	16,350
Services	22.9	2.2	11.3	1.0	62.8	1880
Total	7.17	3.13	7.13	8.64	73.93	2830

OECD

Agriculture, forestry and fishing	0.7	0.9	2.5	97.4	4100
Mining and quarrying	6.5	7.2	0.6	83.0	11,690
Construction	4.5	4.7	0.5	87.2	6890
Manufacturing	5.6	10.4	3.2	76.6	8440
Transport and warehousing	7.1	17.3	1.2	70.6	7420
Communications	5.8	48.6	0.7	37.3	—
Utilities	11.0	4.1	1.2	62.6	19,040[b]
Trades	2.9	15.8	49.0	26.3	4950
Finance, insurance, and real estate	5.0	62.9	14.7	11.4	18,330
Services	35.7	16.7	1.3	40.0	5800
Total	11.91	13.91	9.60	60.00	7000

[a] *Source:* Zymelman (1980).
[b] Figures on productivity are those of Utilities and Communications.

441

TABLE 4

Percentages of Occupational Structures of Industries for Latin America and OECD Countries, circa 1970[a]

Industry	Professional and technical workers	Engineers and technicians	Administrators and managers	Clerical workers	Sales workers	Manual workers	Laborers	Service workers	Productivity (1970 US$)
Latin America									
Manufacturing	3.2	1.1	4.2	7.2	1.4	82.5	7.7	3.5	5060
Food and beverages[b]	3.4	1.3	5.5	7.9	6.8	76.7	13.7	5.1	5000
Textiles[b]	1.6	0.6	3.0	4.8	1.0	89.7	4.7	2.0	3090
Clothing[c]	0.6	0.1	2.1	2.2	1.9	92.3	2.1	5.7	2280
Leather and footwear[d]	0.9	0.3	3.7	4.4	2.0	78.2	3.9	1.4	2480
Lumber, wood, and furniture[e]	0.9	0.3	3.4	3.5	1.3	91.1	3.2	1.7	2630
Paper and paper products[f]	5.8	1.8	4.8	11.1	3.8	75.1	11.9	4.0	5670
Printing and publishing[g]	8.4	1.1	6.0	13.7	5.6	66.2	4.4	2.6	3680
Rubber and plastics[g]	3.5	1.5	7.2	9.5	4.3	75.2	10.1	3.3	6860
Chemicals[b]	12.1	2.5	7.6	16.6	9.6	55.0	16.3	4.9	7640
Glass, stone, and glass products[a]	3.3	1.2	4.7	5.7	1.4	85.5	8.6	3.4	5190
Metal and metal products[h]	2.7	1.4	4.3	7.0	1.2	85.2	6.2	2.3	4290
Fabricated metal[i]	1.9	0.8	4.8	6.2	1.2	85.9	6.9	2.1	3680

Machinery (excl. electrical)[j]	4.7	2.9	5.4	11.1	2.9	76.0	6.7	2.7	4650
Electrical machinery[j]	6.8	4.7	5.7	15.7	2.9	69.0	8.1	3.0	5160
Transportation equipment[k]	3.9	2.3	5.2	10.2	1.1	79.6	5.8	3.5	5390
OECD Manufacturing	5.6	3.7	3.6	10.4	3.2	76.6	4.8	2.2	8440
Food and beverages[b]	2.8	0.9	3.9	10.2	7.4	75.6	8.2	3.6	9770
Textiles[b]	2.5	1.3	3.2	8.2	2.0	84.2	3.9	2.1	6000
Clothing[c]	1.1	0.4	3.0	5.8	2.5	87.6	1.4	3.1	4040
Leather and footwear[d]	1.5	0.7	2.9	7.1	2.2	86.3	2.4	1.5	5610
Lumber, wood, and furniture[e]	1.9	1.1	3.4	6.4	1.9	86.5	4.9	1.3	6570
Paper and paper products[f]	4.6	2.3	3.4	10.9	2.4	78.8	6.3	2.7	9000
Printing and publishing[g]	10.2	0.9	5.0	17.1	5.8	61.8	2.8	2.4	7780
Rubber and plastics[g]	4.8	2.6	4.3	11.3	2.8	76.8	6.1	2.0	9060
Chemicals[b]	13.3	5.5	4.8	16.8	6.7	58.4	7.8	3.4	13,210
Glass, stone, and glass products[a]	4.3	2.5	3.9	8.8	1.9	81.2	7.3	1.7	8530
Metal and metal products[h]	5.5	3.7	3.0	9.3	1.5	80.7	6.2	2.2	10,410

TABLE 4 (*Cont.*)

Industry	Professional and technical workers	Engineers and technicians	Administrators and managers	Clerical workers	Sales workers	Manual workers	Laborers	Service workers	Productivity (1970 US$)
Fabricated metal[i]	4.7	3.5	4.2	9.3	2.0	79.8	4.8	1.6	7760
Machinery (excl. electrical)[j]	8.8	7.1	4.4	11.8	2.8	72.3	3.5	1.7	8000
Electrical machinery[j]	12.2	9.7	3.6	13.3	2.4	68.5	3.8	1.9	7910
Transportation equipment[k]	7.3	5.7	2.5	8.9	1.1	80.2	4.3	2.0	8240

[a] *Source:* Zymelman (1980b).
[b] Chile not included.
[c] Chile, Jamaica, and Sweden not included.
[d] Chile, Belgium, New Zealand, Norway, and Sweden not included.
[e] Chile and New Zealand not included.
[f] Chile and Belgium not included.
[g] Chile and Jamaica not included.
[h] Chile, Panama, Netherlands, and New Zealand not included.
[i] Brazil and Jamaica not included.
[j] Jamaica and Panama not included.
[k] Jamaica not included.

TABLE 5

Comparison of Weighted Occupational Structures and Productivities[a]

Occupational group	(LA occ.) × (LA emp.)	(LA occ.) × (OECD emp.)[b]	(OECD occ.) × (OECD emp.)	(OECD occ.) × (LA emp.)[c]
Professional and technical workers	7.17	7.86	11.91	11.04
Administrators and managers	3.13	3.66	4.58	3.72
Clerical workers	7.13	10.14	13.91	10.30
Sales workers	8.64	10.40	9.60	8.32
Manual workers	73.93	67.94	60.00	67.12
Productivity (1970 US$)	2830	3740	7000	6010

[a] Occupational distribution and productivities have been computed by using employment structures as weights. *Source:* Zymelman (1980b).

[b] Assumption of a hypothetical economy with a sectoral employment distribution of an "average" OECD country and an occupational distribution by sector of an "average" Latin American country.

[c] Assumption of a hypothetical country with the sectoral distribution of an "average" Latin American country and the occupational distribution by sectors of an "average" OECD country.

TABLE 6

Percent Distribution of Education by Occupational Groups for Argentina and Japan, 1960[a]

	Years of schooling					
	Argentina			Japan		
Occupational group	0–8	9–12	13+	0–8	9–12	13+
Professional and technical workers	27.9	39.4	32.6	9.9	40.3	49.8
Administrators and managers	80.8	17.0	2.1	22.8	46.0	31.2
Clerical workers	62.2	31.3	6.5	19.7	59.5	20.8
Sales workers	79.5	17.9	2.5	43.7	50.3	6.0
Manual workers	94.8	4.8	.3	60.5	38.4	1.1
Total work force[b]	85.9	10.8	3.3	45.5	43.0	11.5

[a] *Source:* Horowitz *et al.* (1966).

[b] The vector distribution of education of the total work force is obtained by multiplying the vector occupational distribution by the matrix of occupation by education.

TABLE 7

*Percentage Relationships between Expenditures in
Education by Levels and GNP, circa 1973[a]*

Level	OECD	Latin America
Expenditure		
Primary	1.68	1.63
Secondary	1.79	0.84
High	0.71	0.55
Total	4.40	3.14
Distribution of educational budget		
Primary	38.1	51.9
Secondary	40.7	26.7
Higher	16.2	17.5

[a] *Source:* Zymelman (1976).

services, will not have a great effect on the total rates of economic growth over the long run.

Increased labor productivity requires capital investments and the complementary human resources. The task is enormous, not only in terms of large amounts of investments in physical capital but also in terms of resources for education and training. Recent figures on the distribution of expenditures on education by level, its share in the budget, enrollment rates, and unit costs in terms of income per capita, and demographic burdens of Latin America and OCED countries are as given in Tables 7 and 8.

From these tables it is possible to advance the proposition that in order to achieve enrollment rates equivalent to those prevailing in the OECD countries, thus leading to a similar stock of education in the labor force, Latin America will have to increase its educational expenditures in relation to GNP per capita beyond those levels spent by OECD countries. As long as the number of children of primary school age in the population is almost twice as high as in the OECD countries, instead of having to dedicate 4.4% of GNP as OECD countries do, Latin America will have to dedicate 5.8% of GNP to education; almost doubling the existing efforts for many years.

A correlation analysis of data from 22 Latin American countries relating enrollment rates in primary and secondary levels to income per capita shows that in order to achieve enrollment rates equivalent to those of OECD (97.5 in primary and 70 in secondary levels) income per capita

TABLE 8

Factors Influencing Educational Costs[a]

Level	Unit cost per GNP per Capita (%)[b]	Enrollment rate (%)	Demographic burden (%)[c]
Primary			
OECD	16	97.5	10
Latin America	11	67.8	22
Secondary			
OECD	21	70	12
Latin America	22	24.2	15
Higher			
OECD	55	11.8	11
Latin America	121	5.34	8

[a] *Source:* Zymelman (1976).

[b] Unit costs are the total of recurrent costs divided by the number of students.

[c] Demographic burden is the share of the school age group in the population.

would have to reach 1973 US$3400, which is similar to the average OECD income per capita in 1973.[2] With an average income per capita of around 1973 US$900, it will take almost 45 years to reach this level of income per capita if income per capita grows at 3% per year.

How can this process be accelerated? A necessary but not sufficient policy should be the reduction of the rate of growth of population. The present high rate militates against increases in labor productivity and, hence, income per capita and against freeing resources from primary to secondary education to change the character of the work force. Ways have to be found to lower the costs of education and training. For that purpose, perhaps new forms will have to evolve combining the advantages of classroom teaching and experience acquired in the work place. At the same time, to accelerate the transformation of the labor force, there should be reliance on not only an improved flow into the labor force;

[2] The equations are:

$$\log E_p = 1.4642 + 0.1453 \log Y/c, \quad R^2 = 0.406, \quad N = 22,$$
$$(2.52)$$

$$\log E_s = -0.1868 + 0.5670 \log Y/C \quad R^2 = 0.444, \quad N = 22,$$
$$(3.99)$$

where E_p is the enrollment rate on primary education (number of students enrolled as a proportion of this age group), E_s the enrollment rate in secondary education, (number of students enrolled as a proportion of their age group), and Y/c the income per capita in 1973 US$.

rather, a strong effort should be aimed at upgrading those already in the labor force through programs ranging from basic education for illiterate farmers to refresher courses for graduate engineers.

The road to high income per capita is not an easy one. Policies affecting investments, savings, sectorial distribution of production, exchange rates, etc., will have to be coordinated with policies affecting the development of human resources, perhaps the most sensitive element in the whole process of economic growth.

REFERENCES

Horowitz, M., Zymelman, M., and Herrnstadt, L. (1966). *Manpower Requirements for Planning*. Boston, Massachusetts: University of Boston.

Zymelman, M. (1976). *Patterns of Educational Expenditures*. Washington, D.C.: World Bank Staff Working Paper No. 246.

Zymelman, M. (1980a). *Forecasting Manpower Demand*. Washington, D.C.: Education Department, The World Bank.

Zylmelman, M. (1980b). *Occupational Structures of Industries*. Washington, D.S.: Education Department, The World Bank.

The World Bank
Washington, D.C.

Chapter 21

Economic Growth, Rural and Urban Wages: The Case of Brazil

Edmar L. Bacha

I. INTRODUCTION

The wage for unskilled labor is the single most important indicator of the standard of living of the Brazilian population. Surprisingly enough, the literature on income distribution in this country is devoid of analyses of the long-term behavior of rural and urban wages. This chapter is a first attempt at closing this gap in empirical knowledge.

Lewis's (1954) growth model predicts that, during the surplus labor stage, industrialization will proceed, with the unskilled urban wage fixed in terms of agricultural produce. Two assumptions underlie this hypothesis. The first is that agricultural workers' earnings do not change, which implies that labor productivity is assumed stagnant in traditional agricultural pursuits. The second is that there is free entry in urban markets, with rural–urban migration being sufficiently price responsive to guarantee the maintenance of a constant urban–rural unskilled wage differential.

At first sight, Brazil's post-World War II industrialization process seems to confirm the dual growth model prediction about the constancy of

449

wage behavior. However, a closer scrutiny of the available data shows that Lewis's concept of surplus labor is a straitjacket that does not come near to explaining the complexities of the evolution of urban and rural wages in southern Brazil. This chapter suggests that the behavior of wages can be understood only in a frame of analysis that takes into account the agrarian structure, the agricultural terms of trade, the government labor policy, and the strength of labor unions.

We first analyze the evolution of rural wages in São Paulo, then study the behavior of median wages in Rio de Janeiro's manufacturing. A discussion of the interactions among the political–institutional framework, the agriculture terms of trade, and the urban–rural wage differential closes the chapter.

II. RURAL WAGES

Figure 1 shows the behavior of the wages of the resident daily worker in São Paulo agriculture from 1948 through 1978.[1] Two wage concepts are displayed: the product wage results from the division of the money wage by the producers' price index of agricultural products in São Paulo; the deflated wage is the quotient between the money wage and an overall price index.[2] The product wage is a cost concept, which is related to the labor-demand decision of capitalist farmers. When compared with physical labor productivity in the rural sector, it shows the share of agricultural produce that accrues to workers. The deflated wage is a purchasing power concept. It indicates the command that the rural wage enables workers to exert over the basket of goods entering Brazil's GDP.

Until 1963, the rural wage was a free market rate and reflected closely the alternative value of labor time in family farming at least in São Paulo. In 1963, the federal government introduced the Estatuto do Trabalhador Rural and started enforcing the minimum wage legislation in the rural sector. This might have created a cleavage between the minimum wage paid in the capitalist rural sector and the value of labor time in petty agriculture, but, no definite judgments are possible.

Consider the product-wage series: short-term fluctuations aside, the 30-year span can be divided into two periods, 1948–1966 and 1967–1978. Within each of these periods, the rural wage is reasonably constant in

---

[1] See the Appendix for details on the construction of this and the other statistical series in the chapter.

[2] The overall price index is equal to the Vargas Foundation general price index (column 2 of *Conjuntura Econômica*) for 1948 to 1964 and 1978 and to the GDP price deflator for 1965 to 1977. For details, see the Appendix, Table 3.

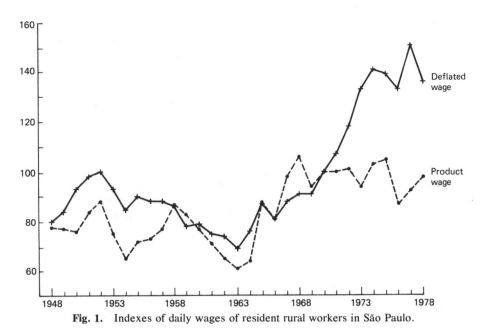

Fig. 1.   Indexes of daily wages of resident rural workers in São Paulo.

terms of agricultural produce, but in the later period, it is nearly 30% higher than in the former.[3] Figure 1 suggests the hypothesis that the rise in the product wage between 1963–1964 and 1967–1968 was linked to the change in labor legislation rather than to the interplay of market forces in the rural labor sector.

The constancy of the product wage since 1967 is particular telling, as other analysts (e.g., the annual, *Prognósticos,* of the São Paulo Instituto de Economia Agrícola) have called attention only to the behavior of the deflated-wage series, which increased by more than 50% during the last decade. Notice in Fig. 1 that the general trend of the deflated wage is downward until 1963, when a trough is reached from which the wage rises dramatically through 1977. The behavior of this series after 1963 can be

---

[3] The relevant regression equation is

$$u = 76.0 + 22.2 \, \text{DUM}, \qquad R^2 = 0.70, \quad d = 1.33, \quad Se = 7.38,$$
$$(1.7) \quad (2.7)$$

where u is the product-wage index and DUM a dummy variable equal to zero in 1948 to 1966 and equal to 1 in 1967 to 1978. The numbers in parentheses are the standard errors of estimate of the regression coefficients. The Durbin–Watson statistic is on the low side, indicating that there are variables missing from the equation, but otherwise the statistical test supports the description in the text.

explained in two parts. From 1963 to 1967, the wage increase seems to be due to the accommodation of São Paulo agriculture to the new minimum wage legislation. After 1967, it is the spectactular increase in the agriculture terms of trade that causes the explosion of rural wages. The terms-of-trade shift is displayed in Tables 3 and 4 and in Fig. 4. The rise in relative agriculture prices since 1968 is commanded from abroad, but indexes of food costs in Rio and São Paulo also indicate a considerable improvement in the relative position of domestic agriculture during this period.

It is important to stress that the rise in deflated agricultural wages since the mid-sixties resulted from the terms-of-trade shift. It did not imply an increase in the purchasing power of the rural wage earner over his own product. The wage increase thus may be temporary, unless world market conditions remain such as to establish a permanently higher plateau for agricultural prices in Brazil.

The observed long-term increase in rural wages does not seem to be closely linked to the upward trend to labor productivity in São Paulo agriculture. Yearly series are not available, but the IBGE (Instituto Brasileiro de Geografia e Estatistica) agricultural census estimates the São Paulo agricultural labor force to have been 1.5, 1.7, 1.4, and 1.5 million people, respectively, in 1950, 1960, 1970, and 1975.[4] An index of the real value of rural output for São Paulo is also available from the Instituto de Economia Agrícola.[5] Assuming that the labor input per man employed is constant, an index of rural labor productivity in São Paulo can be calculated for the census years. Table 1 displays this index together with the product-wage index for the relevant years.

The rural wage increased by only 2.5% between 1950 and 1960, although labor productivity expanded by 26% in the same period. Between 1960 and 1970, wages went up by nearly as much as productivity, but previously we have seen that the wage rise was a one-shot phenomenon, associated with the introduction of the urban labor legislation in the rural sector. By contrast, labor productivity must have risen much more uniformly through the period. Between 1970 and 1975, the wage increased by 5%, whereas productivity either remained constant (according to the

---

[4] The São Paulo Institute de Economia Agrícola (IEA) diverges from this last estimate and, in an unpublished document, proposes the figure of 1.3 million people for the rural labor force in 1975: this figure includes both resident and daily workers.

[5] The IEA output series in current prices includes 21 products, the same that enter the price series in Table 3. The index of real output results from the division of the value of production series by the price index series.

TABLE 1

*Agricultural Labor Productivity and Rural Wages for São Paulo,
Selected Years, 1950–1975[a]*

Year	Labor productivity index[b]	Product-wage index
1950	58.2	75.5
1960	73.4	77.4
1970	100	100
1975	101 (115)	105

[a] 1970 = 100. *Sources:* IBGE, São Paulo Instituto de Economia Agrícola (unpublished data), and Table 2.

[b] The labor productivity index is according to the IBGE estimates of agricultural labor force (agricultural census). The number in parentheses uses the Instituto de Economia Agrícola labor force estimate for 1975.

IBGE labor force estimate) or went up by 15% (according to the IEA estimate).[6] It is very uncertain whether any definite conclusions will be possible for this last period.

In summary, it is an institutional phenomenon, the statute of rural laborers, that seems to explain the one-term jump in the product-wage series. Were it not for this legislation, the hypothesis might be advanced that rural wages would have remained constant at the productivity level of family farming in the country.

One puzzle remains: how can the wage go up when agricultural prices increase and at the same time remain constant when the productivity changes? Were labor in fixed supply, this indeed would be in contradiction to the labor-demand theory. However, the prevalence in Brazil of precapitalist modes of employment guarantees an unlimited supply of labor for capitalist farming. In this context, an improvement in agricultural prices raises the rural wage because it increases the value of labor time in petty agriculture as well. But labor-augmenting technical change in capitalist agriculture leaves the rural wage constant if it does not affect the productivity level of family farming. Exogenous technical progress also might not raise capitalist rural employment if the later is limited by a sales constraint or agricultural output, as some Brazilian economists

[6] Notice that 1975 is the year when the product-wage reached it maximum value. A three-year average centered in 1975 yields an average wage slightly lower than that prevailing in 1970.

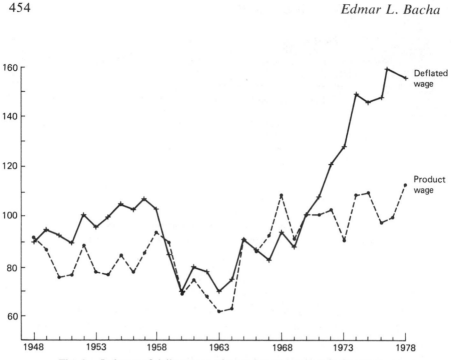

Fig. 2.   Indexes of daily wages of casual rural workers in São Paulo.

believe is the case (Paiva, 1971, 1975). Hence, the conclusion follows that market forces may not operate to transfer the benefits of agriculture modernization to rural workers unless they equally favor the small agricultural producer.

   These findings are broadly supported by the long-term behavior of the wage series for casual rural laborers in São Paulo (see Fig. 2). The main difference is that casual laborers, being more mobile, gained relatively more than permanent workers did from the rise in agricultural prices since 1968. A wage pattern similar to that of the permanent worker is revealed by the wage behavior of the tractor driver in São Paulo agriculture (Table 2).

III.   URBAN WAGES

   Whereas rural wages in product terms followed a simple step function pattern, the urban wage of unskilled labor behaved in a much more complex way in the period under analysis. Figure 3 displays the trends of me-

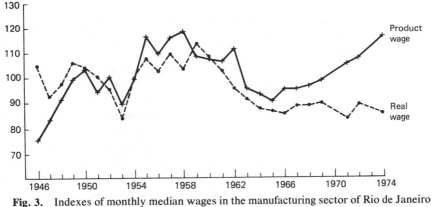

Fig. 3. Indexes of monthly median wages in the manufacturing sector of Rio de Janeiro City.

dian wages in Rio de Janeiro's manufacturing sector from 1952 to 1973.[7] Two wage concepts are shown. Product wages result from the division of money wages by the Vargas Foundation's wholesale price index for industrial products. Real wages are equal to the quotient between money wages and an index of food costs in Rio.[8]

In spite of certain statistical pitfalls, which are discussed in the Appendix, the median-wage series seems to be a more adequate index of unskilled urban wages than either the minimum wage or the average wage in manufacturing.

Elsewhere, we have argued that the behavior of the median wage in Rio de Janeiro's manufacturing could be explained by the trends of the legal minimum wage, the GDP per capita, and the Vargas Foundation's cost-of-living index in Rio (Bacha and Taylor, 1978). The elasticity of the median wage with respect to the minimum wage was estimated as 0.5, and the elasticities with respect to the price level and the productivity proxies were estimated, respectively, as 0.3 and 0.2. These results indicate that the minimum wage mattered for the determination of the unskilled urban wage and also that a "wage drift" was present in the period under consid-

[7] Three different sources were put together to construct this wage series for the 22-year period. For statistical details, see Appendix. For lack of data, use could not be made of either the modal wage or the unskilled wage in São Paulo manufacturing. Median wages for the Rio manufacturing sector are not available after 1973. The wages in Fig. 3 do not include the 13th salary prevailing since 1962.

[8] For the 1952–1966 period, food costs are taken from the Vargas Foundation's cost-of-living index for Rio. The values for 1967 to 1973 are our own estimates, which are presented in Bacha (1979).

eration, preventing observed wages from falling as steeply as the minimum wage did during the 1960s. Hence, the minimum wage overestimated somewhat the effects of the post-1964 wage crunch on the earnings of unskilled urban laborers.

In two other papers, we argued that average urban wages are a poor index of the wage level of unskilled labor (da Mata and Bacha, 1973; Bacha, 1974). In da Mata and Bacha, average manufacturing wages were shown to increase by 95.7% in product terms between 1949 and 1969, while average blue-collar wages went up by two-thirds of this value, or 66.3% in the same period. In Bacha (1974), analysis of a sample of large manufacturing firms in southcentral Brazil revealed that the real wage of unskilled laborers decreased by 8% between 1966 and 1972, while in the same period the wages of skilled laborers went up by 20% and the salaries of managers grew by 52%.

The continuing trend toward the concentration of the distribution of earnings in Brazil's urban sector, which is apparent from these and other data [for references, see Bacha and Taylor (1978)], prevents the use of average wages as an approximation to the wage level of unskilled urban laborers in Brazil in the post-WW II period.

The long-run urban wage picture that emerges is roughly consistent with the predictions of Lewis's model, when use is made of the median wage in Rio de Janeiro's manufacturing as an index of unskilled urban labor earnings in southern Brazil. Over the 1946–1973 period, the real wage fluctuated cyclically, although shifting downward between the fifties and the sixties. When account is taken of the 13th salary introduced in December 1962, the average difference in wage levels between the 1950s and the 1960s lessens, and in the long run, the urban wage in terms of food prices appears relatively constant.[9]

This result was conditioned by the interplay of urban political struggle with the evolution of the agriculture terms of trade. With the introduction

---

[9] The relevant regression results are as follows. When real wages are measured, excluding the post-1962 13th salary, we have

$$v = 101.2 - 10.2 \text{ SHIFT}, \qquad R^2 = 0.38, \quad d = 1.35, \quad Se = 6.65,$$
$$\quad (17.2) \quad (2.7)$$

where v is the index of real median wages (with 1969–1971 = 100) and SHIFT a dummy variable equal to zero in 1946 to 1961 and equal to 1 in 1962 to 1973. The coefficient of the shift variable decreases in value and becomes statistically nonsignificant when the 13th salary is added to the wage:

$$v^* = 101.2 - 2.55 \text{ SHIFT}, \qquad R^2 = 0.04, \quad d = 1.34, \quad Se = 6.78,$$
$$\quad (17.5) \quad (2.78)$$

where v^* is the index of real median wages including the 13th salary since 1962.

of minimum wage legislation in January 1952, populist politics, helped by a decline in relative agricultural prices, managed to raise both the product-wage and the real-wage through 1958 and 1959. There followed a period of accelerated inflation and increased agriculture terms of trade. In product terms, wages peaked in 1962 (when account is taken of the 13th salary started being paid in December of that year), but in real terms, the wage followed a continuous downward course starting in 1959.

Stopping the accelerating price-wage spiral required a military coup and the institution of an authoritarian government in 1964, under which labor unions were pushed away from the political scene and the minimum wage legislation was made inoperant. Inflation was then put under control with the real wage continuing to decline until 1966, after which it was kept constant to the end of the period.[10]

The furthering of the decline of the real wage and the maintenance of its value at a relatively low level were done in a politically authoritarian context. The conclusion seems to be that the long-term constancy of the real urban wage was the result of a political cycle, not the consequence of labor-market adjustments of the type contemplated in the dual growth model literature. The next section will dwell further on these themes, looking first at the evolution of the urban–rural wage differential.

IV. URBAN–RURAL WAGE RATIO

Figure 4 pictures an approximate estimate of the evolution of the urban–rural wage differential in southern Brazil during the post-WW II period. The rural wage is the 30-day equivalent of the resident daily worker wage in Fig. 1, with the urban wage composed of two pieces. For the period 1948–1973, the data are derived from the median wage in Rio de Janeiro's manufacturing, in Table 5 (with a geometric interpolation procedure applied to center the observations for 1965 to 1973 on June of each year). The average hourly wage of bricklayers in Brazil's construction industry (which is presented in Bacha, 1979) is then linked to this median wage-series to complete the information for the 1974–1977 period.

If 30% is the equilibrium urban–rural wage differential, as suggested by Lewis (1954), according to Fig. 4, normality started prevailing in post-WW II Brazil only very recently. At the beginning of the period, in the

---

[10] The behavior of the urban unskilled wage after 1973 can be gauged from a wage series for the construction industry published by IBGE. According to this series, the real wage rose slowly since 1973 but without reaching, until 1977, the value observed in 1969. For details, see Bacha (1979). Adding this evidence to Fig. 3, one is entitled to say that the basic urban wage has remaining roughly constant in real terms since 1966.

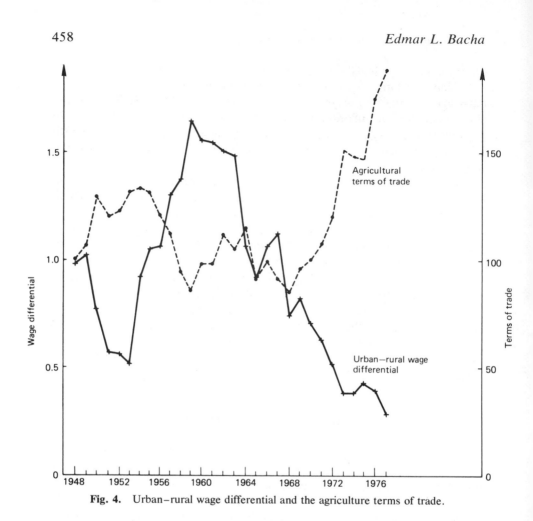

Fig. 4.   Urban–rural wage differential and the agriculture terms of trade.

late forties, the urban–rural wage differential was about 100%. It declined
to 50% in the early fifties and then grew to 150% in the late fifties and early
sixties. Henceforth, it went down steadily through the sixties and seventies, until it reached the value of 28% in 1977.

Figure 4 also indicates that the agriculture terms of trade are closely
associated to the wage differential. The relationship between these two
variables is more clearly depicted in scatter form in Fig. 5. Three periods
are identified as: 1948–1962, 1963–1968, and 1969–1977. The sensitivity
of the wage ratio to the terms of trade is stronger during the first period.
The relationship is nonexistent between 1963 and 1968, but it reappears in
the 1969–1977 period, with the wage ratio being much less sensitive to the
terms of trade than before.

There is little doubt that institutional phenomena were responsible for

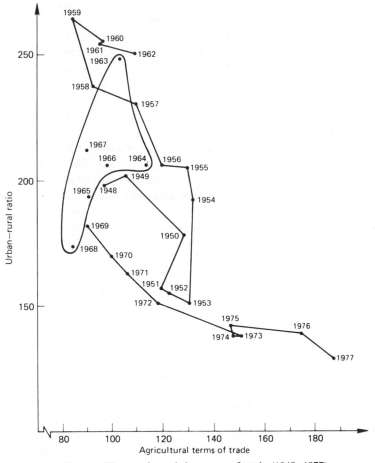

Fig. 5.   Wage ratio and the terms of trade (1948–1977).

the observed decline in the urban–rural wage differential between 1963 and 1968, a period during which the agricultural terms of trade followed a downward trend. On one side, the labor policy adopted by the post-1964 military regime squeezed the urban minimum wage. On the other side, the rural wage was raised by the 1963 extension of the labor legislation to the rural sector. The combined effect of these policies led to a substantial reduction of the urban–rural wage differential.

The negative relationship between the agriculture terms of trade and the urban–rural wage ratio for the two other periods in the figure can be explained if we accept that the wage share in the urban sector is fixed institutionally by the prevailing conditions of social bargain between urban workers and capitalists, under the aegis of the state. The money wage in the rural sector, on the other hand, is determined by the value of the average productivity of labor in petty agriculture. An increase in the price ratio of rural to urban products should then lead to a decline in the urban–rural wage ratio. But if this is correct, what is the explanation for the marked decline between the periods 1948 to 1962 and 1969 to 1977 of the sensitivity of the wage ratio with the respect to the sectorial terms of trade? Three hypothesis may be contemplated.

The first would emphasize institutional phenomena, denying causal validity to the relationship depicted in Fig. 5. According to this view, the wage differential increased in the fifties because the government was populist and the urban labor unions were relatively strong. And it decreased in the sixties and seventies because the government was authoritarian and the labor unions weak. The terms-of-trade changes were incidental to these political modifications, and their relationship to the wage differential accidental.

This hypothesis asserts that the level and rate of change of the urban–rural wage ratio are functions of political factors. If the later can be represented by dummy variables, a possible econometric test of the hypothesis is given by

$$\ln w = 4.11 + 0.639t + 2.85D - 0.183\,DT,$$
$$\quad\;\;(0.13)\;\;(0.0142)\;\;(0.81)\;\;\;\;(0.0340)$$
$$R^2 = 0.82,\quad d = 0.73,\; Se = 0.24,$$

where $\ln w$ is the natural log of the urban–rural wage ratio index, t time, and D a dummy variable equal to zero in 1948 to 1962 and equal to 1 in 1969 to 1977. (The observations for 1963 to 1968 are excluded from the equation.) The numbers in parentheses are the standard errors of estimate of the regression coefficients.

The rate of change of the wage ratio behaves as predicted by the institutional hypothesis: it goes up in the first period and down in the second. But the level of the ratio is higher in the second period. Worse still is the size of the Durbin–Watson statistics, which denote the existence of serial correlation in the residuals, hence the lack of additional explanatory variables in the regression equation. Politics may explain some but not all of the observed wage movements.

A second hypothesis, although accepting the terms-of-trade effect on the wage ratio, would argue that there is a missing variable in the figure, namely the growth rate of labor productivity in the urban sector. In the first period (1948–1962), the productivity factor tended to broaden the wage difference and the terms of trade worked in the same direction. As a consequence, the effect of the latter is magnified by the exclusion of the productivity variable. By contrast, in the seventies, the agriculture terms of trade were tending to reduce the wage differential, whereas the productivity factor operated in the opposite direction. Thus, the exclusion of the productivity variable makes for an underestimation of the effects of the terms of trade on the wage differential during the 1970s.

On the assumption that urban labor productivity is an exponential function of time, the second hypothesis may be represented econometrically by the equation

$$\ln w = 13.1 - 1.80 \ln P - 0.0147t, \qquad R^2 = 0.70,$$
$$ (1.6) \quad (0.35) \qquad (0.0072)$$
$$d = 0.81, \quad Se = 0.302,$$

where P is the agriculture terms of trade and the other symbols are as before.

Contrary to the hypothesis, the coefficient of the productivity proxy is negative: as time goes by, the urban–rural wage ratio goes down rather than up as predicted.

The sign of the time coefficient plus the fact that the urban wage was higher than the rural wage in the beginning of the period indicate the existence of an adjustment mechanism tending to reduce the wage differential.

A third hypothesis takes into account the existence of this adjustment mechanism and attempts to explain the reduction in the sensitivity of the wage ratio to the terms of trade in terms of faster rates of intersectoral labor mobility. An indicator of this phenomenon would be the expansion of daily nonresident laborers in agriculture, i.e., people who work casually in the rural or urban sectors, depending on alternative job opportunities. This would be a consequence of the penetration of purely capitalistic relations of production in the rural sector, producing a tendency toward the homogenization of the wage rate independently of the sector of economic activity.

The econometric implications of this hypothesis are that the urban–rural wage ratio at time t depends negatively on the agriculture terms of trade, positively on the growth of (relative) urban labor productivity, and negatively on the wage ratio at time $t - 1$.[11] Labor will migrate faster

---

[11] We write the wage ratio as a negative function of the terms of trade and a positive function of relative labor productivities:

$$w = AP^aQ^bL^{-b}, \qquad a < 0, \quad b > 0,$$

where Q is the ratio of urban-to-rural output and L the ratio of urban-to-rural employment. We measure migration as the ratio of L to L_{-1} and assume this to be a function of the differential between the wage ratio at time $t - 1$ and the equilibrium wage ratio w^*:

$$L/L_{-1} = B(w_{-1}/w^*)^c, \quad c > 0.$$

from rural to urban pursuits, the higher the wage ratio at time $t - 1$, and this will tend to reduce the wage ratio at time t. If the hypothesis is correct, the coefficient of the lagged wage ratio should increase in absolute terms between 1948 to 1962 and 1969 to 1977 (the same should happen to the constant term, as shown in the previous footnote).

The estimated equation is

$$\ln w = 9.62 + 0.11D - 0.388 \ln P + 0.0271t - 0.502 \ln w_{-1}$$
$$(2.00) \quad (2.29) \quad (0.253) \quad\quad (0.0059) \quad (0.518)$$
$$- 0.151D \ln w_{-1}, \quad R^2 = 0.92, \quad d = 1.14, \quad Se = 0.077,$$
$$(0.437)$$

where w_{-1} is the lagged value of the wage ratio.

All signs are as predicted although standard errors are quite large.[12] Moreover, Durbin's test for autocorrelation of the residuals in the presence of the lagged value of the dependent variable among the regressors indicates the existence of serial correlation in the residuals.

Thus, our preliminary econometric tests are not sufficient to discriminate among the alternative hypotheses that were put forward. However, they do lend some credence to the third hypothesis, according to which increased intersectoral labor mobility tends to erode the effect of the terms of trade on the urban–rural wage ratio.

V. CONCLUSIONS

Our tentative findings lead to one sobering conclusion: in spite of the spectacular increase in Brazil's GDP per capita since World War II, in terms of food, median urban wages today are not higher, and are probably

---

Let

$$K = AB^{-b}w^{*bc}$$

and assume (for lack of data on Q and L_{-1}) that

$$(Q/L_{-1})^b = e^{ht}, \quad h > 0.$$

Then, substituting the equation for L in the formula for w and simplifying, we obtain an expression that can be estimated

$$w = KP^a e^{ht} w_{-1}^{-bc}.$$

A higher labor mobility can be specified as an increase in the value of c, hence increasing both K and the absolute value of the coefficient of w_{-1}.

[12] In a comparison with the previous equation, particularly interesting is the reversal of the sign of the coefficient of the time variable. This shift vindicates the theoretical expectation on the sign of this coefficient.

lower, than 30 years ago. As a functional group, in terms of the most basic of needs, unskilled urban workers do not seem to have benefited at all from the more than threefold increase in the country's per capita income since the war.

The agricultural wage earner in the south gained with the extension of the labor legislation to the rural sector starting in 1963. Except for this one-time improvement, in spite of significant productivity gains in the agricultural sector, the rural wage in terms of agricultural produce remained relatively constant during a 30-year span.

The question may be asked if this was not the necessary consequence of the surplus labor condition prevailing at the beginning of the post-WW II period. The answer seems to be in the negative for two independent reasons.

First, an agrarian reform program allowing for agricultural modernization under a family farm system would have forced an increase of the unskilled labor wage, both in capitalist farming and in urban pursuits. Second, apparently, for most of the period under observation, intersectoral labor mobility was not sufficiently strong to anchor the urban wage to rural earnings. Terms-of-trade movements aside, the value of the urban wage seems to have depended more than anything else on the political muscle of the urban proletariat.

Our results suggest that a fatalist attitude toward the surplus labor situation is uncalled for. Government policy, particularly the minimum wage legislation, is an important determinant of the wage gains of unskilled laborers. The effectiveness of this legislation would be enhanced if it were accompanied by policy measures designed to raise the productivity of small farming, as could be accomplished by a forward-looking agrarian reform program.

APPENDIX[13]

This appendix consists of five tables to explain the data discussed in the chapter.

Table 2 presents the series for rural wages in São Paulo. The data for 1948 to 1970 are from Sendin (1972), who, in 1968 and 1969, applied a questionnaire to about 20 farms in the state of São Paulo that had kept books since 1948. In this fashion, he obtained monthly wage information from 1948 through 1968. Starting in 1962, Sendin added to this information data from the annual crop forecasts of the São Paulo Instituto de

---

[13] Explanatory notes to the Appendix are available from the author upon request.

TABLE 2

Rural Wages, São Paulo, 1948–1978[a]

Year	Resident daily worker			Casual labor			Resident tractor driver		
	Money wages[b]	Deflated wages[c]	Product wages[d]	Money wages[b]	Deflated wages[c]	Product wages[d]	Money wages[b]	Deflated wages[c]	Product wages[d]
1948	0.016	80.2	77.9	0.020	88.7	91.2	0.020	84.3	82.0
1949	0.018	84.3	77.3	0.022	93.7	85.9	0.022	86.7	79.5
1950	0.022	92.8	75.5	0.024	92.2	75.0	0.025	88.7	72.1
1951	0.027	97.6	83.5	0.027	88.8	76.0	0.029	88.3	75.5
1952	0.031	100.0	87.9	0.034	100.0	87.8	0.035	95.3	83.5
1953	0.033	93.0	75.3	0.037	94.9	76.8	0.038	90.1	72.9
1954	0.039	84.4	64.8	0.049	99.0	76.1	0.042	78.4	60.3
1955	0.047	89.6	72.0	0.060	104.0	83.5	0.052	83.4	67.0
1956	0.055	87.7	73.3	0.063	91.8	76.7	0.063	84.4	70.5
1957	0.063	87.9	77.8	0.076	86.4	85.4	0.071	82.9	73.4
1958	0.070	86.1	87.2	0.082	91.8	92.9	0.078	81.0	82.1
1959	0.087	77.5	82.8	0.103	83.5	89.2	0.100	75.2	80.4
1960	0.114	79.0	77.4	0.110	69.4	67.9	0.138	80.4	78.7
1961	0.148	74.8	70.7	0.171	78.7	74.4	0.174	74.0	70.0

1962	0.223	74.3	64.5	0.254	77.1	66.9	0.261	73.1	63.4
1963	0.362	69.0	60.7	0.398	69.0	60.7	0.427	68.5	60.3
1964	0.764	76.4	63.9	0.814	73.8	61.8	0.904	75.9	63.5
1965	1.37	87.3	88.1	1.55	89.5	90.4	2.08	111.0	112.0
1966	1.78	81.0	80.7	2.07	85.7	85.3	2.45	93.9	93.5
1967	2.49	88.0	98.0	2.54	81.8	91.1	2.89	86.0	95.7
1968	3.29	91.0	106.0	3.70	93.2	108.0	3.63	84.5	98.3
1969	3.97	91.3	94.1	4.16	87.0	89.8	4.76	92.1	95.0
1970	5.14	100.0	100.0	5.65	100.0	100.0	6.11	100.0	100.0
1971	6.45	107.0	100.0	7.04	107.0	100.0	7.80	109.0	102.0
1972	8.38	118.0	101.0	9.36	120.0	102.0	9.16	109.0	92.6
1973	11.35	135.0	93.6	11.90	127.0	89.4	12.55	123.0	86.9
1974	15.85	141.0	103.0	18.25	148.0	108.0	16.77	126.0	91.9
1975	20.65	139.0	105.0	23.75	145.0	109.0	22.97	130.0	97.9
1976	27.85	133.0	86.7	34.05	147.0	96.5	30.89	124.0	81.0
1977	45.20	151.0	93.4	52.50	159.0	98.7	47.73	134.0	83.0
1978 (April)	52.40	136.0	97.6	66.10	156.0	112.1	59.78	130.0	93.7

[a] Sources: Sendin (1972) and São Paulo Instituto de Economia Agrícola, Prognóstico, 1978–1979.

[b] In Cr$ per day.
[c] Money wages per implicit price deflator, with 1970 = 100.
[d] Money wages per prices received by São Paulo agriculture, with 1970 = 100.

Economia Agrícola. Since 1968, the annual wage data were obtained by averaging out the wage information for March and November of each year collected by the local branches of the I.E.A. and published in its annual, *Prognósticos*. Clearly, the information for the latter period is the most trustworthy.

Deflation of the wage data is done by use of the two price series in Table 3. The series of prices received by São Paulo agriculture is an index published in *Conjuntura Econômica* but collected by the I.E.A. It is a Laspeyres index for the 21 most important products in São Paulo agriculture. At least for the more recent period, the weights for this index are derived from the average quantities produced in 1962 to 1966. The overall price index is a mixture of the Vargas Foundation's general price index (column 2 of the *Conjuntura Econômica*) for the 1948–1974 period and for April 1978, with the GDP price deflator for the 1965–1977 period. Use of the Vargas Foundation's general price index during the seventies was avoided because its construction involved the computation of the cost of living in Rio, the wholesale price index, and the index for construction costs in Rio, all of which are suspected of not having reflected the true evolution of prices in this period. (For a discussion of this problem, see the October 1978 issue of the *Boletim do Instituto dos Economistas do Rio de Janeiro*.)

Table 4 presents the estimates for the agriculture terms of trade. In the numerator is the series of prices received by São Paulo agriculture from Table 3. In the denominator is the Vargas Foundation's wholesale price index for the industrial sector, colum 18 of *Conjuntura Econômica*. The latter index probably also underestimates the evolution of industrial prices in the country, as pointed out by Bonelli (1978), but unfortunately no other series were available.

Table 5 contains estimates for the monthly median wages in the manufacturing sector of Rio de Janeiro. The annual averages for 1949 to 1956 are taken from *Conjuntura Econômica 12*(1), January 1958. It is a wage index calculated by the former Centro de Estudos Socials of the Vargas Foundation, based on a sample of 177 industrial establishments. The estimates for April 1957 through April 1963 are presented in IBGE, *Anuário Estatístico do Brasil,* and refer to the median wage in establishments with five or more employees in Rio de Janeiro. Bacha *et al.* (1972, p. 97) present an argument showing that these series are reasonably compatible with each other. The estimates for April 1965 through April 1973 are obtained by linear interpolation from wage distributions for the industrial sector of Rio. The information is from the law of two-thirds, which used to be published annually by the Servico de Estatística da Previdência do

TABLE 3

Selected Price Indexes, Brazil and São Paulo, 1948–1978[a]

Year	General price index linked to GDP price deflator	Prices received by São Paulo agriculture	Agriculture price ratio index[b]
1948	0.388	0.399	103.0
1949	0.415	0.453	109.0
1950	0.461	0.567	123.0
1951	0.538	0.629	117.0
1952	0.601	0.686	114.0
1953	0.690	0.853	124.0
1954	0.876	1.14	130.0
1955	1.02	1.27	125.0
1956	1.22	1.46	120.0
1957	1.40	1.58	113.0
1958	1.58	1.56	98.7
1959	2.18	2.04	93.6
1960	2.81	2.87	102.1
1961	3.85	4.07	105.7
1962	5.84	6.73	115.2
1963	10.2	11.6	113.7
1964	19.5	23.3	119.5
1965	30.6	30.3	99.0
1966	42.7	42.9	100.0
1967	55.0	49.4	89.8
1968	70.3	60.4	85.9
1969	84.6	82.0	96.9
1970	100.0	100.0	100.0
1971	117.0	125.0	107.0
1972	138.0	162.0	117.0
1973	166.0	236.0	142.0
1974	218.0	298.0	137.0
1975	290.0	384.0	132.0
1976	409.0	625.0	153.0
1977	584.0	941.0	161.0
1978 (April)	750.0	1044.0	139.0

[a] 1970 = 100. *Sources:* Vargas Foundation, *Conjuntura Econômica;* Sendin (1972); and São Paulo Instituto de Economia Agrícola, *Prognóstico,* 1978–1979.

[b] Computed as 100 times column three value divided by column two value.

Trabalho of the Ministério do Trabalho. The law of two-thirds' data are not based on a fixed sample of firms, hence intertemporal comparability is problematic. Moreover, there is no way to check the degree of compatibilization between this series and the two previous ones.

The wholesale price index for the industrial sector is the index in col-

TABLE 4

Agriculture Terms of Trade, South Central Brazil, 1948–1978[a]

Year	Wholesale prices, industrial sector	Agriculture terms of trade = prices received by São Paulo agriculture/wholesale prices, industrial sector
1948	0.406	98.3
1949	0.425	100.0
1950	0.441	129.0
1951	0.524	120.0
1952	0.563	122.0
1953	0.651	131.0
1954	0.856	133.0
1955	0.969	131.0
1956	1.21	121.0
1957	1.41	112.0
1958	1.66	94.0
1959	2.38	85.7
1960	2.93	98.0
1961	4.17	97.6
1962	6.07	111.0
1963	11.1	105.0
1964	20.3	115.0
1965	32.8	92.4
1966	43.4	98.8
1967	54.6	90.5
1968	71.2	84.8
1969	85.6	95.8
1970	100.0	100.0
1971	117.0	107.0
1972	136.0	119.0
1973	156.0	151.0
1974	202.0	148.0
1975	262.0	147.0
1976	357.0	175.0
1977	407.0	189.0
1978 (April)	626.0	167.0

[a] 1970 = 100. *Source:* Vargas Foundation, *Conjuntura Econômica.*

umn 18 of *Conjuntura Econômica.* Food costs for the 1949 to 1966 period are taken from the Vargas Foundation's cost-of-living index for Rio, published in *Conjuntura Econômica.* The estimates for 1967 to 1973 are the author's. They were derived from food prices at the retail level, collected in Rio de Janeiro on a monthly basis since 1967 by the IBGE. Twenty-three food products were taken into account, with weights derived from

TABLE 5

Monthly Median Wages of Employees in the Manufacturing Sector, Rio de Janeiro City, 1946–1972[a]

Year[b]	Median wages		Wholesale prices, industrial sector (1970 = 100)	Food costs in Rio (1970 = 100)	Product wages[c]	Real wages[d]
	Cr$ per month	Index with (1969–1971 = 100)				
1946	0.789	0.305	0.409	0.290	74.6	105.0
1947	0.865	0.335	0.405	0.363	82.7	92.3
1948	0.950	0.368	0.406	0.381	90.6	96.6
1949	1.09	0.422	0.425	0.400	99.3	106.0
1950	1.17	0.453	0.441	0.435	103.0	104.0
1951	1.27	0.491	0.524	0.491	93.7	100.0
1952	1.45	0.561	0.563	0.592	99.6	94.8
1953	1.49	0.576	0.661	0.697	88.5	82.6
1954	2.19	0.847	0.856	0.844	98.9	100.0
1955	2.89	1.12	0.969	1.05	116.0	107.0
1956	3.40	1.32	1.21	1.30	109.0	102.0
1957	4.27	1.65	1.42	1.51	116.0	109.0
1958	4.69	1.81	1.53	1.76	118.0	103.0
1959	6.63	2.56	2.36	2.27	108.0	113.0
1961	10.60	4.10	3.87	4.03	106.0	102.0
1962	15.49	5.99	5.41	6.30	111.0	95.1
1963	24.59	9.51	10.0	10.4	95.1	91.4
1965	75.05	29.0	32.4	33.3	89.5	87.1
1966	102.70	39.7	41.9	46.8	94.7	84.8
1967	131.00	50.6	53.3	57.4	94.9	88.2
1968	169.50	65.6	68.1	67.2	96.3	97.6
1969	208.80	80.8	82.5	81.3	97.9	99.4
1971	308.20	119.0	113.0	128.0	105.0	93.0
1972	365.80	141.0	132.0	158.0	107.0	89.2
1973	453.40	175.0	151.0	207.0	116.0	84.5

[a] *Sources:* Median wages: 1946–1956, Vargas Foundation, *Conjuntura Econômica,* January, 1958; 1957–1963, IBGE, *Anuário Estatístico;* 1965–1973; Ministério do Trabalho, Serviço de Estatística da Previdência do Trabalho (law of two-thirds). Wholesale prices: Vargas Foundation *Conjuntura Econômica.* Food Costs: 1946–1966, Vargas Foundation, *Conjuntura Econômica;* 1967–1973, author's estimates.

[b] Values were computed for the month of April for 1957 to 1973.

[c] Computed by dividing column three by column four.

[d] Computed by dividing column three by column five.

the most palatable minimum cost diet described in Fundação Getúlio Vargas, *Dietas de Custo Mínimo* (Rio de Janeiro, 1978). Although the wage observation is for April of each year, the food-price estimates were computed as an annual average. Interpolation of the two food-price series was done by use of the ratio between the annual averages of the two

TABLE 6

Approximate Urban–Rural Wage Differentials, South Central Brazil, 1948–1977[a]

Year	Median monthly urban wage[b]	30-Day wages of resident rural daily worker in São Paulo[b]	Urban–rural wage differential[c]
1948	0.950	0.480	97.9
1949	1.09	0.540	102.0
1950	1.17	0.660	77.3
1951	1.27	0.810	56.8
1952	1.45	0.930	55.9
1953	1.49	0.990	50.5
1954	2.19	1.14	92.1
1955	2.89	1.41	105.0
1956	3.40	1.65	106.0
1957	4.84	1.89	130.0
1958	4.97	2.10	137.0
1959	6.89	2.61	164.0
1960	8.72	3.42	155.0
1961	11.30	4.44	154.0
1962	16.70	6.69	150.0
1963	27.00	10.9	148.0
1964	47.20	22.9	106.0
1965	79.10	41.1	92.5
1966	110.0	53.4	106.0
1967	158.0	74.7	112.0
1968	172.0	98.7	74.3
1969	216.0	119.0	81.5
1970	262.0	154.0	70.1
1971	317.0	194.0	63.4
1972	379.0	251.0	51.0
1973	469.0	341.0	97.5
1974	657.0	476.0	58.6
1975	879.0	620.0	41.8
1976	1163.0	836.0	39.1
1977	1736.0	1356.0	28.0

[a] *Sources:* See text.

[b] In Cr$ per month

[c] Computed by subtracting column three from column two and dividing the result by column two.

indexes in 1967. In Bacha (1979), we show that the Vargas foundation's food-price index for the seventies is way out of line with alternative credible indicators of the evolution of food costs in the country.

Table 6 presents the evolution of the urban–rural wage differential. The median monthly urban wage is partially taken from Table 5. The observations for April 1957 to April 1972 were recentered on June of each year, through a geometric interpolation procedure. These are our proxy estimates for the annual means of the monthly median wages. The observations for 1973 to 1977 are estimated from the annual averages of the hourly wages of bricklayers in Brazilian construction industry. This index is presented in Bacha (1979) and was constructed from information published in IBGE, *Indústria de Construção*. Interpolation between the two series was done in the following way. First, the median monthly wage in April 1973 was extrapolated to June 1973 by use of the growth factor observed in this series between April 1972 and April 1973. Then, the ratio to the median manufacturing wage in June 1973 of the average hourly wage of bricklayers in 1973 was used as a constant multiplier to link the two series.

The rural wage in Table 6 is the same series presented in Table 2 but multiplied by 30 to convert the daily wage into a monthly wage.

ACKNOWLEDGMENTS

Research support was provided by PREALC/ILO (Santiago, Chile). The author is indebted for comments to Regis Bonelli, Jose-Marcio Camargo, Eliana Cardoso, Rodolfo Hoffmann and Victor Tokman. A previous version of this chapter appeared in Bacha (1979).

REFERENCES

Bacha, E. (1974). "Hierarquia e remuneração gerencial." *Estudos Econômicos* **4** (1), 142–175. Reproduced in (1976). *Os Mitos de uma Década*, pp. 107–134. Rio de Janeiro: Paz e Terra.

Bacha, E. (1979). "Crescimento econômico, salários urbanos e rurais: o caso do Brasil" *Pesquisa e Planejamento Econômico* **9**(3) (December), 585–628.

Bacha, E., da Mata, M., and Modenesi, R. (1972). *Encargos Trabalhistas e Absorção de Mão-de-Obra*. Rio de Janeiro: INPES/IPEA.

Bacha, E., and Taylor, L. (1978). "Brazilian Income Distribution in the 1960s: 'facts,' model results and the controversy." *The Journal of Development Studies* **14**(3) (April), 271–297.

Bonelli, R. (1978). "Mais dificuldades na interpretação dos dados da indústria." *Pesquisa e Planejamento Econômico* **8**(2) (August), 505–523.

da Mata, M., and Bacha, E. (1973). "Emprego e salários na indústria de transformação, 1949/1969." *Pesquisa e Planejamento Econômico* **3**(2) (Julho), 303–39. Reproduced in (1976). *Os Mitos de uma Década*, pp. 67–73. Rio de Janeiro: Paz e Terra.

Lewis, W. A. (1954). "Economic Development with Unlimited Supplies of Labor." The Manchester School (May). Reproduced in (1958). *The Economics of Underdevelopment* (A. Agarwala and S. Singh, eds.). London and New York: Oxford University Press.

Paiva, R. M. (1971). "Modernização e dualismo tecnológico na agricultura." *Pesquisa e Planejamento* **1**(2) (December), 1971–2234.

Paiva, R. M. (1975). Modernização e dualismo tecnológico na agricultura: uma reformulação.'' *Pesquisa e Planejamento Econômico* **5**(1) (June).

Sendin, P. (1972). ''Elaboração de um índice de salários rurais para o Estado de São Paulo.'' *Agricultura em São Paulo* **19**(2), 167–189.

Catholic University of Rio de Janeiro
Rio de Janeiro, Brazil

Index

The index includes the names of authors mentioned in the text; authors cited only parenthetically are not included.